Introduction to Econometrics

Brief Edition

James H. Stock
HARVARD UNIVERSITY

Mark W. Watson
PRINCETON UNIVERSITY

PEARSON

Addison
Wesley

Boston   San Francisco   New York
London   Toronto   Sydney   Tokyo   Singapore   Madrid
Mexico City   Munich   Paris   Cape Town   Hong Kong   Montreal

Publisher: Greg Tobin
Editor-in-Chief: Denise Clinton
Director of Development: Kay Ueno
Senior Acquisitions Editor: Adrienne D'Ambrosio
Development Editor: Mike Elia
Managing Editor: Nancy Fenton
Design Manager: Charles Spaulding
Supplements Editor: Heather McNally
Associate Media Producer: Bridget Page
Senior Marketing Manager: Roxanne Hoch
Manufacturing Buyer: Carol Melville
Project Management, Art Studio, and Electronic Composition: Thompson Steele, Inc.

Library of Congress Cataloging-in-Publication Data
Stock, James H.
  Introduction to econometrics: brief edition / James H. Stock, Mark W. Watson.
     p. cm.
  Includes bibliographical references and index.
  ISBN 0-321-43251-7 (alk. paper)
  1. Econometrics. I. Watson, Mark W. II. Title.
  HB139.S765 2007b
  330.01'5195--dc22

                                   2006039352

ISBN 978-0-321-43251-3
ISBN 0-321-43251-7

10 9 8 7 6 5 4 3 2 1—CRW—10 09 08 07 06

Brief Contents

Contents

Key Concepts

General Interest Boxes

Preface

Econometrics can be a fun course for both teacher and student. The real world of economics, business, and government is a complicated and messy place, full of competing ideas and questions that demand answers. Is it more effective to tackle drunk driving by passing tough laws or by increasing the tax on alcohol? Can you make money in the stock market by buying when prices are historically low, relative to earnings, or should you just sit tight as the random walk theory of stock prices suggests? Can we improve elementary education by reducing class sizes, or should we simply have our children listen to Mozart for ten minutes a day? Econometrics helps us to sort out sound ideas from crazy ones and to find quantitative answers to important quantitative questions. Econometrics opens a window on our complicated world that lets us see the relationships on which people, businesses, and governments base their decisions.

This textbook is designed for a first course in undergraduate econometrics which includes a substantial amount of statistics review. It is our experience that to make econometrics relevant in an introductory course, interesting applications must motivate the theory and the theory must match the applications. This simple principle represents a significant departure from the older generation of econometrics books, in which theoretical models and assumptions do not match the applications. It is no wonder that some students question the relevance of econometrics after they spend much of their time learning assumptions that they subsequently realize are unrealistic, so that they must then learn "solutions" to "problems" that arise when the applications do not match the assumptions. We believe that it is far better to motivate the need for tools with a concrete application, and then to provide a few simple assumptions that match the application. Because the theory is immediately relevant to the applications, this approach can make econometrics come alive.

This Brief Edition

This brief edition consists of the first nine chapters of the second edition of Stock and Watson (2007), *Introduction to Econometrics*, plus a new chapter (Chapter 10) on conducting an empirical analysis using economic data. Part I (the first three chapters) provides a review of probability and statistics. Part II (the remaining chapters) covers the core material of regression with cross-sectional data: regression with a single regressor, multiple regression, nonlinear regression functions, and assessing studies that use regression analysis. This brief edition was developed in response to requests from instructors who do not have enough time to cover more advanced material, such as regression with time series data or instrumental variables regression, which are covered in the full edition of Stock and Watson. This brief edition should prove especially useful for courses in which a considerable amount of class time is spent reviewing statistics and probability. The final chapter on conducting an empirical analysis will support the instructor who wants to round out his or her econometrics course with a substantial empirical project.

Like the full edition of Stock and Watson, this textbook differs from others in three main ways. First, we integrate real-world questions and data into the development of the theory, and we take seriously the substantive findings of the resulting empirical analysis. Second, our choice of topics reflects modern theory and practice. Third, we provide theory and assumptions that match the applications. Our aim is to teach students to become sophisticated consumers of econometrics and to do so at a level of mathematics appropriate for an introductory course.

Real-World Questions and Data

We organize the discussion of methods and theory around important real-world questions that demand specific numerical answers. We teach single-variable regression, multiple regression, and functional form analysis in the context of estimating the effect of school inputs on school outputs. (Do smaller elementary school class sizes produce higher test scores?) We also illustrate statistical and regression methods by estimating the returns to education, an application that is revisited throughout the book. These and other applications in special-interest boxes can all be understood with only a single introductory course in economics. Thus the instructor can focus on teaching econometrics, not microeconomics or macroeconomics.

Through each application, we teach students to explore alternative specifications and thereby to assess whether their substantive findings are robust. The questions asked in the empirical applications are important, and we provide serious and, we think, credible answers. We encourage students and instructors to disagree, however, and invite them to reanalyze the data, which are provided on the textbook's Companion Website (**www.aw-bc.com/stock_watson**).

Contemporary Choice of Topics

Econometrics has come a long way in the past two decades. The topics we cover reflect the best of contemporary applied regression analysis of cross-sectional data.

For many students in the class, this will be their only course in econometrics. With this in mind, what is the most important material for them to learn? What should the students take away from this course for use in a subsequent course in applied economics and thereafter?

This book is shaped around our answers to these questions. From our perspective, the key lasting lessons from a single introductory econometric course concern omitted variable bias, how multiple regression can address omitted variable bias by estimating a partial effect, an understanding of sampling variability and the methods of statistical and econometric inference (estimation, testing, confidence intervals), an understanding of how regression analysis is done in practice, the ability to read and to critique papers in economics that use regression analysis, and an understanding of the conditions under which regression analysis can (and cannot) provide credible estimates of causal effects.

This book reflects this perspective, both in the development in the text and in the multiple general interest boxes. The review of probability and statistics emphasizes sampling variability, sampling distributions, and how sampling uncertainty is handled using the methods of statistical inference. This treatment is continued in parallel in the subsequent chapters on regression methods. The treatment of multiple regression focuses not only on mechanics and tools (a necessary part of any introductory course), but also on how those tools are useful because they address omitted variable bias. This is accompanied by an ongoing treatment of two empirical examples: the effect on test scores of class size reductions and the returns to education. These examples are used as a platform to motivate and to illustrate regression methods, omitted variable bias, the use of control variables in multiple regression, different ways to handle nonlinearities, the presentation of regression results, and, crucially, how systematically to assess the internal and external validity of a regression study.

The decision to focus on these large "take-away" ideas means that some topics found in older books receive less emphasis in this text. For example, while perfect multicollinearity is treated thoroughly, imperfect multicollinearity is treated as a feature of the data that implies that certain questions will not be well answered by a given data set, and we do not go into technical (and rarely used) devices to mitigate imperfect multicollinearity. In modern econometrics, the dummy variable trap is important; ridge regression is not.

Similarly, our least squares assumptions do not include homoskedasticity, so the first standard error formula for the ordinary least squares (OLS) estimator is what econometricians will recognize as the heteroskedasticity-robust formula, even though the terms heteroskedasticity and homoskedasticity have not yet been introduced. This constitutes a substantial departure from other treatments, which introduce homoskedasticity as an assumption, give the homoskedasticity-only variance and standard error formulas, state that homoskedasticity often does not hold, then "solve" the "problem" of falsely assuming homoskedasticity by using either heteroskedasticity-robust standard errors or weighted least squares. In the approach of this book, there is no problem to begin with, and our experience is that students have no difficulty with this method. After all, the standard formula for the differences-in-means t-statistic is heteroskedasticity-robust—typically the pooled variance formula is presented as the homoskedasticity-only special case— and neither instructors nor students balk at this treatment. In addition to reducing student frustration, a payoff of our approach is that instructors can devote the week that is usually spent "solving the problem" of heteroskedasticity to other more important topics, such as interaction effects, critiquing regression studies, having the students do an empirical study, and so forth. This said, some instructors find it useful to teach the formulas for the variance of the OLS estimator under homoskedasticity, the Gauss-Markov theorem, and the t- and F-distributions arising from the homoskedastic normal regression model. For this reason, the additional assumption of homoskedasticity (and, for the t- and F-distributions, normality of the errors) is introduced toward the end of the basic treatment of regression, prior to the optional sections on the Gauss-Markov theorem and the classical normal regression model (including the t- and F-distribution).

Theory That Matches Applications

Although econometric tools are best motivated by empirical applications, students need to learn enough econometric theory to understand the strengths and limitations of those tools. We provide a modern treatment in which the fit between theory and applications is as tight as possible, while keeping the mathematics at a level that requires only algebra.

Modern empirical applications share some common characteristics: the data sets typically are large (hundreds of observations, often more); regressors are not fixed over repeated samples but rather are collected by random sampling (or some other mechanism that makes them random); the data are not normally distributed; and there is no *a priori* reason to think that the errors are homoskedastic (although often there are reasons to think that they are heteroskedastic).

These observations lead to important differences between the theoretical development in this textbook and other textbooks.

- *Large-sample approach.* Because data sets are large, from the outset we use large-sample normal approximations to sampling distributions for hypothesis testing and confidence intervals. Our experience is that it takes less time to teach the rudiments of large-sample approximations than to teach the Student t and exact F distributions, degrees-of-freedom corrections, and so forth. This large-sample approach also saves students the frustration of discovering that, because of nonnormal errors, the exact distribution theory they just mastered is irrelevant. Once taught in the context of the sample mean, the large-sample approach to hypothesis testing and confidence intervals carries directly through differences of means and regression with a single or multiple regressors.

- **Random sampling.** Because regressors are rarely fixed in econometric applications, from the outset we treat data on all variables (dependent and independent) as the result of random sampling. This assumption matches our applications to cross-sectional data; it extends readily to panel and time series data; and because of our large-sample approach, it poses no additional conceptual or mathematical difficulties.

- **Heteroskedasticity.** Applied econometricians routinely use heteroskedasticity-robust standard errors to eliminate worries about whether heteroskedasticity is present or not. In this book, we allow for heteroskedasticity from the outset and simply use heteroskedasticity-robust standard errors.

Skilled Producers, Sophisticated Consumers

We hope that students using this book will become sophisticated consumers of empirical analysis. To do so, they must learn not only how to use the tools of regression analysis, but also how to assess the validity of empirical analyses presented to them.

Our approach to teaching how to assess an empirical study is threefold. First, after introducing the main tools of regression analysis, we devote Chapter 9 to the threats to internal and external validity of an empirical study. This chapter discusses data problems and issues of generalizing findings to other settings. It also examines the main threats to regression analysis, including omitted variables, functional form misspecification, errors-in-variables, selection, and simultaneity—and ways to recognize these threats in practice.

Second, we apply these methods for assessing empirical studies to the ongoing examples in the book. We do so by considering alternative specifications and by systematically addressing the various threats to the validity of the analyses.

Third, to become sophisticated consumers, students need firsthand experience as producers. Active learning beats passive learning, and econometrics is an ideal course for active learning. For this reason, the textbook Web site features data sets, software, and suggestions for empirical exercises of differing scopes.

Mathematical Prerequisites and Level of Rigor

The mathematical prerequisites for this book are Algebra II and an introductory course in statistics at the high school AP Statistics level. Part I of this book provides a thorough review of probability and statistics, and if the statistical background of students coming into the course is sketchy the instructor using this book might choose to spend several weeks going through Part I; however the material in Part I is not intended to be a student's first introduction to probability and statistics.

This book has fewer equations, and more applications, than many introductory econometrics books. But more equations do not imply a more sophisticated treatment, and a more mathematical treatment does not lead to a deeper understanding for most students. On the contrary, it is our experience that a deeper understanding is achieved through repeated treatment of serious empirical applications, both in class and in homework exercises. For this reason, this book (supported by the student resources on the book's Web site) includes many empirical exercises. Like the empirical analysis in the text, the data sets in the empirical exercises are revisited in multiple chapters, in each case using the methods introduced in the chapter to take a closer look at the empirical issue under study. The key formulas and derivations of regression analysis are provided in chapter appendices, so that this material is available to students with a stronger mathematical background but does not get in the way of learning for students who are less prepared mathematically.

Contents and Organization

There are two parts to the textbook. Part I reviews probability and statistics, and Part II covers the core material of regression analysis.

Part I

Chapter 1 introduces econometrics and stresses the importance of providing quantitative answers to quantitative questions. It discusses the concept of causality in statistical studies and surveys the different types of data encountered in econometrics. Material from probability and statistics is reviewed in Chapters 2 and 3, respectively.

Part II

Chapter 4 introduces regression with a single regressor and OLS estimation, and Chapter 5 discusses hypothesis tests and confidence intervals in the regression model with a single regressor. In Chapter 6, students learn how they can address omitted variable bias using multiple regression, thereby estimating the effect of one independent variable while holding other independent variables constant. Chapter 7 covers hypothesis tests, including *F*-tests, and confidence intervals in multiple regression. In Chapter 8, the linear regression model is extended to models with nonlinear population regression functions, with a focus on regression functions that are linear in the parameters (so that the parameters can be estimated by OLS). In Chapter 9, students step back and learn how to identify the strengths and limitations of regression studies, seeing in the process how to apply the concepts of internal and external validity.

This brief edition concludes with Chapter 10, which is new and does not appear in the full edition, on conducting a regression study using economic data. Many of the steps involved in doing a regression study have been illustrated in the previous chapters via the ongoing treatment of the empirical examples. This final chapter summarizes these steps and includes additional suggestions for identifying a topic, finding a data set, and writing up the results.

Pedagogical Features

The textbook has a variety of pedagogical features aimed at helping students to understand, to retain, and to apply the essential ideas. *Chapter introductions* provide a real-world grounding and motivation, as well as a brief road map highlighting the sequence of the discussion. *Key terms* are boldfaced and defined in context throughout each chapter, and *Key Concept boxes* at regular intervals recap the central ideas. *General interest boxes* provide interesting excursions into related topics and highlight real-world studies that use the methods or concepts being discussed in the text. A numbered *Summary* concluding each chapter serves as a helpful framework for reviewing the main points of coverage. The questions in the *Review the Concepts* section check students' understanding of the core content, *Exercises* give more intensive practice working with the concepts and techniques introduced in the chapter, and *Empirical Exercises* allow the students to apply what they have learned to answer real-world empirical questions. At the end of the textbook, the *References* section lists sources for further reading, the *Appendix* provides statistical tables, and a *Glossary* conveniently defines all the key terms in the book.

Supplements to Accompany the Textbook

The online supplements accompanying *Introduction to Econometrics, Brief Edition* include the Solutions Manual, Test Bank (by Manfred W. Keil of Claremont McKenna College), and Lecture Notes (in both Microsoft Word and PowerPoint formats) with text figures, tables, and Key Concepts. The Solutions Manual includes solutions to all the end-of-chapter exercises, while the Test Bank, offered in Test Generator Software (TestGen with QuizMaster), provides a rich supply of easily edited test problems and questions of various types to meet specific course needs. These resources are available for download from the Instructor's Resource Center at **www.aw-bc.com/irc.** If instructors prefer their supplements on a CD-ROM, our Instructor's Resource Disk, compatible with both Windows and Macintosh, contains the Lecture Notes, the Test Bank, and the Solutions Manual.

In addition, the Companion Website, found at **www.aw-bc.com/stock_watson,** provides a wide range of additional resources for students. These include data sets for all the text examples, replication files for empirical results reported in the text, data sets for the end-of-chapter *Empirical Exercises*, and EViews and STATA tutorials for students.

Acknowledgments

A great many people contributed to the full edition of this book, and their advice, efforts, and support are detailed in the preface to the second edition of Stock and Watson, *Introduction to Econometrics*. Here, we would like to thank those who specifically helped to make this brief edition a reality. We are grateful to the many instructors who appreciated the treatment in the full edition but pushed us to consider a shorter book that would be more suitable for their course. We are particularly grateful to the panel of reviewers who provided specific advice about what to include in the brief edition:

James Cardon, Brigham Young University

Scott England, California State University, Fresno

Barry Falk, Iowa State University

Gerry Ferrier, University of Arkansas

Shelby Gerking, University of Central Florida

Carolyn J. Heinrich, University of Wisconsin-Madison

Christiana Hilmer, Virginia Polytechnic Institute

Luojia Hu, Northwestern University

Elena Pesavento, Emory University

Brian Peterson, Central College

Susan Porter-Hudak, Northern Illinois University

John Spitzer, SUNY at Brockport

Justin Tobias, Iowa State University

Rob Wassmer, California State University, Sacramento

William Wood, James Madison University

Finally, we thank Addison-Wesley, and Adrienne D'Ambrosio in particular, for helping us bring out this version of Stock and Watson that will, we hope, meet the needs of many instructors whose courses do not use the more advanced material appearing in the full edition.

PART ONE

Introduction and Review

Economic Questions and Data

Ask a half dozen econometricians what econometrics is and you could get a half dozen different answers. One might tell you that econometrics is the science of testing economic theories. A second might tell you that econometrics is the set of tools used for forecasting future values of economic variables, such as a firm's sales, the overall growth of the economy, or stock prices. Another might say that econometrics is the process of fitting mathematical economic models to real-world data. A fourth might tell you that it is the science and art of using historical data to make numerical, or quantitative, policy recommendations in government and business.

In fact, all these answers are right. At a broad level, econometrics is the science and art of using economic theory and statistical techniques to analyze economic data. Econometric methods are used in many branches of economics, including finance, labor economics, macroeconomics, microeconomics, marketing, and economic policy. Econometric methods are also commonly used in other social sciences, including political science and sociology.

This book introduces you to the core set of methods used by econometricians. We will use these methods to answer a variety of specific, quantitative questions taken from the world of business and government policy. This chapter poses two of those questions and discusses, in general terms, the econometric approach to answering them. The chapter concludes with a survey of the main types of data available to econometricians for answering these and other quantitative economic questions.

1.1   Economic Questions We Examine

Many decisions in economics, business, and government hinge on understanding relationships among variables in the world around us. These decisions require quantitative answers to quantitative questions.

This book examines several quantitative questions taken from current issues in economics. Two of these questions concern education policy, and the economic value, or returns, to education.

Question #1: Does Reducing Class Size Improve Elementary School Education?

Proposals for reform of the U.S. public education system generate heated debate. Many of the proposals concern the youngest students, those in elementary schools. Elementary school education has various objectives, such as developing social skills, but for many parents and educators the most important objective is basic academic learning: reading, writing, and basic mathematics. One prominent proposal for improving basic learning is to reduce class sizes at elementary schools. With fewer students in the classroom, the argument goes, each student gets more of the teacher's attention, there are fewer class disruptions, learning is enhanced, and grades improve.

But what, precisely, is the effect on elementary school education of reducing class size? Reducing class size costs money: It requires hiring more teachers and, if the school is already at capacity, building more classrooms. A decision maker contemplating hiring more teachers must weigh these costs against the benefits. To weigh costs and benefits, however, the decision maker must have a precise quantitative understanding of the likely benefits. Is the beneficial effect on basic learning of smaller classes large or small? Is it possible that smaller class size actually has no effect on basic learning?

Although common sense and everyday experience may suggest that more learning occurs when there are fewer students, common sense cannot provide a quantitative answer to the question of what exactly is the effect on basic learning of reducing class size. To provide such an answer, we must examine empirical evidence—that is, evidence based on data—relating class size to basic learning in elementary schools.

In this book, we examine the relationship between class size and basic learning using data gathered from 420 California school districts in 1998. In the California data, students in districts with small class sizes tend to perform better on standardized tests than students in districts with larger classes. While this fact is consistent with the idea that smaller classes produce better test scores, it might simply reflect many other advantages that students in districts with small classes have over their counterparts in districts with large classes. For example, districts with small class sizes tend to have wealthier residents than districts with large classes, so students in small-class districts could have more opportunities for learning outside the classroom. It could be these extra learning opportunities that lead to higher test scores, not smaller class sizes. In Part II, we use multiple regression analysis to isolate the effect of changes in class size from changes in other factors, such as the economic background of the students.

Question #2: What Are the Economic Returns to Education?

From the perspective of an economist, one of the most important of the many virtues of formal education is that education prepares students for future jobs and careers. Formally, labor economists think of education as an investment in human capital: the greater a worker's human capital, the more productive the worker will be, the more choices he or she will have in the labor market, and the more the worker will earn. Informally, we know that college graduates have more choices than individuals with only a high school diploma, and high school graduates have more job opportunities than high school dropouts. But what, specifically, is the economic value of an education, as measured by the increase in earnings resulting from additional schooling?

Initially, one might imagine estimating the economic value of a college degree, relative to a high school diploma, by comparing the earnings of college graduates to those of high school graduates. But if there are systematic differences between the two groups, then this comparison will confound the effect of additional education with the effect of those other systematic differences. For example, if more men than women graduate from college, then the differences in earnings between high school and college graduates will reflect differences in both education and gender between the two groups. In Part II, we examine data on earnings, education, and other characteristics of individuals, taken from the Current Population Survey conducted by the U.S. Bureau of Labor Statistics. Using multiple regression analysis, we use these data to estimate the economic returns to education, holding constant other characteristics of the worker, such as gender.

Quantitative Questions, Quantitative Answers

Both of these questions require a numerical answer. Economic theory and everyday experience provide clues about that answer—another year of education should make a worker more productive, and thus better paid—but the actual value of the number must be learned empirically, that is, by analyzing data. Because we use data to answer quantitative questions, our answers always have some uncertainty: A different set of data would produce a different numerical answer. Therefore, the conceptual framework for the analysis needs to provide both a numerical answer to the question and a measure of how precise the answer is.

The conceptual framework used in this book is the multiple regression model, the mainstay of econometrics. This model, introduced in Part II, provides a mathematical way to quantify how a change in one variable affects another variable, holding other things constant. For example, what effect does a change in class size have on test scores, *holding constant* student characteristics (such as family income) that a school district administrator cannot control? What effect does another year of education have on a worker's earnings, *holding constant* other worker characteristics such as gender? The multiple regression model and its extensions provide a framework for answering these questions using data and for quantifying the uncertainty associated with those answers.

1.2 Causal Effects and Idealized Experiments

Like many questions encountered in econometrics, the questions in Section 1.1 concern causal relationships among variables. In common usage, an action is said to cause an outcome if the outcome is the direct result, or consequence, of that action. Touching a hot stove causes you to get burned; drinking water causes you to be less thirsty; putting air in your tires causes them to inflate; putting fertilizer on your tomato plants causes them to produce more tomatoes. Causality means that a specific action (applying fertilizer) leads to a specific, measurable consequence (more tomatoes).

Estimation of Causal Effects

How best might we measure the causal effect on tomato yield (measured in kilograms) of applying a certain amount of fertilizer, say 100 grams of fertilizer per square meter?

One way to measure this causal effect is to conduct an experiment. In that experiment, a horticultural researcher plants many plots of tomatoes. Each plot is tended identically, with one exception: Some plots get 100 grams of fertilizer per square meter, while the rest get none. Moreover, whether a plot is fertilized or not is determined randomly by a computer, ensuring that any other differences between the plots are unrelated to whether they receive fertilizer. At the end of the growing season, the horticulturalist weighs the harvest from each plot. The difference between the average yield per square meter of the treated and untreated plots is the effect on tomato production of the fertilizer treatment.

This is an example of a **randomized controlled experiment**. It is controlled in the sense that there are both a **control group** that receives no treatment (no fertilizer) and a **treatment group** that receives the treatment (100 g/m^2 of fertilizer). It is randomized in the sense that the treatment is assigned randomly. This random assignment eliminates the possibility of a systematic relationship between, for example, how sunny the plot is and whether it receives fertilizer, so that the only systematic difference between the treatment and control groups is the treatment. If this experiment is properly implemented on a large enough scale, then it will yield an estimate of the causal effect on the outcome of interest (tomato production) of the treatment (applying 100 g/m^2 of fertilizer).

In this book, the **causal effect** is defined to be the effect on an outcome of a given action or treatment, as measured in an ideal randomized controlled experiment. In such an experiment, the only systematic reason for differences in outcomes between the treatment and control groups is the treatment itself.

It is possible to imagine an ideal randomized controlled experiment to answer the questions in Section 1.1. For example, to study class size one can imagine randomly assigning "treatments" of different class sizes to different groups of students. If the experiment is designed and executed so that the only systematic difference between the groups of students is their class size, then in theory this experiment would estimate the effect on test scores of reducing class size, holding all else constant.

The concept of an ideal randomized controlled experiment is useful because it gives a definition of a causal effect. In practice, however, it is not possible to perform ideal experiments. In fact, experiments are rare in econometrics because often they are unethical, impossible to execute satisfactorily, or prohibitively expensive. The concept of the ideal randomized controlled experiment does, however, provide a theoretical benchmark for an econometric analysis of causal effects using actual data.

Forecasting and Causality

Although the questions in Section 1.1 concern causal effects, one empirical problem of importance to economists—forecasting—does not. You do not need to know a causal relationship to make a good forecast. A good way to "forecast" if it is raining is to observe whether pedestrians are using umbrellas, but the act of using an umbrella does not cause it to rain.

Even though forecasting need not involve causal relationships, economic theory suggests patterns and relationships that might be useful for forecasting. Multiple regression analysis allows us to quantify historical relationships suggested by economic theory, to check whether those relationships have been stable over time, to make quantitative forecasts about the future, and to assess the accuracy of those forecasts.

1.3   Data: Sources and Types

In econometrics, data come from one of two sources: experiments or nonexperimental observations of the world.

Experimental versus Observational Data

Experimental data come from experiments designed to evaluate a treatment or policy or to investigate a causal effect. For example, the state of Tennessee financed a large randomized controlled experiment examining class size in the 1980s. In that experiment, thousands of students were randomly assigned to classes of different sizes for several years and were given annual standardized tests.

The Tennessee class size experiment cost millions of dollars and required the ongoing cooperation of many administrators, parents, and teachers over several years. Because real-world experiments with human subjects are difficult to administer and to control, they have flaws relative to ideal randomized controlled experiments. Moreover, in some circumstances experiments are not only expensive and difficult to administer but also unethical. (Would it be ethical to offer randomly selected teenagers inexpensive cigarettes to see how many they buy?) Because of these financial, practical, and ethical problems, experiments in economics are rare. Instead, most economic data are obtained by observing real-world behavior.

Data obtained by observing actual behavior outside an experimental setting are called **observational data**. Observational data are collected using surveys, such as a telephone survey of consumers, and administrative records, such as historical records on mortgage applications maintained by lending institutions.

Observational data pose major challenges to econometric attempts to estimate causal effects, and the tools of econometrics to tackle these challenges. In the real world, levels of "treatment" (the amount of fertilizer in the tomato example, the student–teacher ratio in the class size example) are not assigned at random, so it is difficult to sort out the effect of the "treatment" from other relevant factors. Much of econometrics, and much of this book, is devoted to methods for meeting the challenges encountered when real-world data are used to estimate causal effects.

Whether the data are experimental or observational, data sets come in three main types: cross-sectional data, time series data, and panel data.

Cross-Sectional Data

Data on different entities—workers, consumers, firms, governmental units, and so forth—for a single time period are called **cross-sectional data**. For example, the data on test scores in California school districts are cross sectional. Those data are for 420 entities (school districts) for a single time period (1998). In general, the number of entities on which we have observations is denoted by n; so for example, in the California data set $n = 420$.

The California test score data set contains measurements of several different variables for each district. Some of these data are tabulated in Table 1.1. Each row lists data for a different district. For example, the average test score for the first district ("district #1") is 690.8; this is the average of the math and science test scores for all fifth graders in that district in 1998 on a standardized test (the Stanford Achievement Test). The average student–teacher ratio in that district is 17.89, that is, the number of students in district #1, divided by the number of classroom teachers in district #1, is 17.89. Average expenditure per pupil in district #1 is $6,385. The percentage of students in that district still learning English—that is, the percentage of students for whom English is a second language and who are not yet proficient in English—is 0%.

The remaining rows present data for other districts. The order of the rows is arbitrary, and the number of the district, which is called the **observation number**, is an arbitrarily assigned number that organizes the data. As you can see in the table, all the variables listed vary considerably.

With cross-sectional data, we can learn about relationships among variables by studying differences across people, firms, or other economic entities during a single time period.

TABLE 1.1   **Selected Observations on Test Scores
and Other Variables for California School Districts in 1998**

Observation (District) Number	District Average Test Score (Fifth Grade)	Student–Teacher Ratio	Expenditure per Pupil ($)	Percentage of Students Learning English
1	690.8	17.89	$6385	0.0%
2	661.2	21.52	5099	4.6
3	643.6	18.70	5502	30.0
4	647.7	17.36	7102	0.0
5	640.8	18.67	5236	13.9
. . .	. . .	. . .	. . .	. . .
418	645.0	21.89	4403	24.3
419	672.2	20.20	4776	3.0
420	655.8	19.04	5993	5.0

Note: The California test score data set is described in Appendix 4.1.

Time Series Data

Time series data are data for a single entity (person, firm, country) collected at multiple time periods. A data set on the rates of inflation and unemployment in the United States from the second quarter of 1959 through the fourth quarter of 2004 is an example of a time series data set. That data set contains observations on two variables (the rates of inflation and unemployment) for a single entity (the United States) for 183 time periods. Each time period in this data set is a quarter of a year (the first quarter is January, February, and March; the second quarter is April, May, and June; and so forth). The observations in this data set begin in the second quarter of 1959, which is denoted 1959:II, and end in the fourth quarter of 2004 (2004:IV). The number of observations (that is, time periods) in a time series data set is denoted by T. Because there are 183 quarters from 1959:II to 2004:IV, this data set contains $T = 183$ observations.

Some observations in this data set are listed in Table 1.2. The data in each row correspond to a different time period (year and quarter). In the second quarter of 1959, for example, the rate of price inflation was 0.7% per year at an annual rate.

TABLE 1.2 Selected Observations on the Rates of Consumer Price Index (CPI) Inflation and Unemployment in the United States: Quarterly Data, 1959–2000

Obervation Number	Date (Year:quarter)	CPI Inflation Rate (% per year at an annual rate)	Unemployment Rate (%)
1	1959:II	0.7%	5.1%
2	1959:III	2.1	5.3
3	1959:IV	2.4	5.6
4	1960:I	0.4	5.1
5	1960:II	2.4	5.2
.	.	.	.
.	.	.	.
.	.	.	.
181	2004:II	4.3	5.6
182	2004:III	1.6	5.4
183	2004:IV	3.5	5.4

In other words, if inflation had continued for 12 months at its rate during the second quarter of 1959, the overall price level (as measured by the Consumer Price Index, CPI) would have increased by 0.7%. In the second quarter of 1959, the rate of unemployment was 5.1%; that is, 5.1% of the labor force reported that they did not have a job but were looking for work. In the third quarter of 1959, the rate of CPI inflation was 2.1%, and the rate of unemployment was 5.3%.

By tracking a single entity over time, time series data can be used to study the evolution of variables over time and to forecast future values of those variables.

Panel Data

Panel data, also called **longitudinal data**, are data for multiple entities in which each entity is observed at two or more time periods. The number of entities in a panel data set is denoted by n, and the number of time periods is denoted by T. For example, Table 1.3 lists some observations from a data set on cigarette prices, consumption, and taxes for $n = 48$ continental U.S. states (entities) for total of $T = 11$ years (time periods), from 1985 to 1995.

In this cigarette consumption panel data set, there is a total of $n \times T = 48 \times 11 = 528$ observations. As Table 1.3 illustrates, the first block of 48 observations

TABLE 1.3   Selected Observations on Cigarette Sales, Prices, and Taxes, by State and Year for U.S. States, 1985–1995

Observation Number	State	Year	Cigarette Sales (packs per capita)	Average Price per Pack (including taxes)	Total Taxes (cigarette excise tax + sales tax)
1	Alabama	1985	116.5	$1.022	$0.333
2	Arkansas	1985	128.5	1.015	0.370
3	Arizona	1985	104.5	1.086	0.362
. . .	. . .	. . .	. . .	. . .	. . .
47	West Virginia	1985	112.8	1.089	0.382
48	Wyoming	1985	129.4	0.935	0.240
49	Alabama	1986	117.2	1.080	0.334
. . .	. . .	. . .	. . .	. . .	. . .
96	Wyoming	1986	127.8	1.007	0.240
97	Alabama	1987	115.8	1.135	0.335
. . .	. . .	. . .	. . .	. . .	. . .
528	Wyoming	1995	112.2	1.585	0.360

lists the data for each state in 1985, organized alphabetically from Alabama to Wyoming. The next block of 48 observations lists the data for 1986, and so forth, through 1995. For example, in 1985, cigarette sales in Arkansas were 128.5 packs per capita (the total number of packs of cigarettes sold in Arkansas in 1985 divided by the total population of Arkansas in 1985 equals 128.5). The average price of a pack of cigarettes in Arkansas in 1985, including tax, was $1.015, of which 37¢ went to federal, state, and local taxes.

Panel data can be used to learn about economic relationships from the experiences of the many different entities in the data set and from the evolution over time of the variables for each entity.

The definitions of cross-sectional data, time series data, and panel data are summarized in Key Concept 1.1.

CROSS-SECTIONAL, TIME SERIES, AND PANEL DATA

- Cross-sectional data consist of multiple entities observed at a single time period.
- Time series data consist of a single entity observed at multiple time periods.
- Panel data (also known as longitudinal data) consist of multiple entities, where each entity is observed at two or more time periods.

Summary

1. Many decisions in business and economics require quantitative estimates of how a change in one variable affects another variable.
2. Conceptually, the way to estimate a causal effect is in an ideal randomized controlled experiment, but performing such experiments in economic applications is usually unethical, impractical, or too expensive.
3. Econometrics provides tools for estimating causal effects using either observational (nonexperimental) data or data from real-world, imperfect experiments.
4. Cross-sectional data are gathered by observing multiple entities at a single point in time; time series data are gathered by observing a single entity at multiple points in time; and panel data are gathered by observing multiple entities, each of which is observed at multiple points in time.

Key Terms

randomized controlled experiment (7)
control group (7)
treatment group (7)
causal effect (7)
experimental data (8)
observational data (8)

cross-sectional data (9)
observation number (9)
time series data (10)
panel data (11)
longitudinal data (11)

Review the Concepts

1.1   Describe a hypothetical ideal randomized controlled experiment to study the effect of hours spent studying on performance on microeconomics exams. Suggest some impediments to implementing this experiment in practice.

1.2   Describe a hypothetical ideal randomized controlled experiment to study the effect on highway traffic deaths of wearing seat belts. Suggest some impediments to implementing this experiment in practice.

1.3   You are asked to study the relationship between hours spent on employee training (measured in hours per worker per week) in a manufacturing plant and the productivity of its workers (output per worker per hour). Describe:

   a. an ideal randomized controlled experiment to measure this causal effect;

   b. an observational cross-sectional data set with which you could study this effect;

   c. an observational time series data set for studying this effect; and

   d. an observational panel data set for studying this effect.

CHAPTER 2

Review of Probability

This chapter reviews the core ideas of the theory of probability that are needed to understand regression analysis and econometrics. We assume that you have taken an introductory course in probability and statistics. If your knowledge of probability is stale, you should refresh it by reading this chapter. If you feel confident with the material, you still should skim the chapter and the terms and concepts at the end to make sure you are familiar with the ideas and notation.

Most aspects of the world around us have an element of randomness. The theory of probability provides mathematical tools for quantifying and describing this randomness. Section 2.1 reviews probability distributions for a single random variable, and Section 2.2 covers the mathematical expectation, mean, and variance of a single random variable. Most of the interesting problems in economics involve more than one variable, and Section 2.3 introduces the basic elements of probability theory for two random variables. Section 2.4 discusses three special probability distributions that play a central role in statistics and econometrics: the normal, chi-squared, and F distributions.

The final two sections of this chapter focus on a specific source of randomness of central importance in econometrics: the randomness that arises by randomly drawing a sample of data from a larger population. For example, suppose you survey ten recent college graduates selected at random, record (or "observe") their earnings, and compute the average earnings using these ten data points (or "observations"). Because you chose the sample at random, you could have chosen ten different graduates by pure random chance; had you done so, you would have observed ten different earnings and you would have computed a different sample average. Because the average earnings vary from one randomly chosen sample to the next, the sample average is itself a random variable. Therefore, the sample average has a probability distribution, referred to as its sampling distribution because this distribution describes the different possible values of the sample average that might have occurred had a different sample been drawn.

Section 2.5 discusses random sampling and the sampling distribution of the sample average. This sampling distribution is, in general, complicated. When the sample size is sufficiently large, however, the sampling distribution of the sample average is approximately normal, a result known as the central limit theorem, which is discussed in Section 2.6.

2.1 Random Variables and Probability Distributions

Probabilities, the Sample Space, and Random Variables

Probabilities and outcomes.   The gender of the next new person you meet, your grade on an exam, and the number of times your computer will crash while you are writing a term paper all have an element of chance or randomness. In each of these examples, there is something not yet known that is eventually revealed.

The mutually exclusive potential results of a random process are called the **outcomes**. For example, your computer might never crash, it might crash once, it might crash twice, and so on. Only one of these outcomes will actually occur (the outcomes are mutually exclusive), and the outcomes need not be equally likely.

The **probability** of an outcome is the proportion of the time that the outcome occurs in the long run. If the probability of your computer not crashing while you are writing a term paper is 80%, then over the course of writing many term papers, you will complete 80% without a crash.

The sample space and events.   The set of all possible outcomes is called the **sample space**. An **event** is a subset of the sample space, that is, an event is a set of one or more outcomes. The event "my computer will crash no more than once" is the set consisting of two outcomes: "no crashes" and "one crash."

Random variables.   A random variable is a numerical summary of a random outcome. The number of times your computer crashes while you are writing a term paper is random and takes on a numerical value, so it is a random variable.

Some random variables are discrete and some are continuous. As their names suggest, a **discrete random variable** takes on only a discrete set of values, like $0, 1, 2, \ldots$, whereas a **continuous random variable** takes on a continuum of possible values.

Probability Distribution of a Discrete Random Variable

Probability distribution.   The **probability distribution** of a discrete random variable is the list of all possible values of the variable and the probability that each value will occur. These probabilities sum to 1.

For example, let M be the number of times your computer crashes while you are writing a term paper. The probability distribution of the random variable M is the list of probabilities of each possible outcome: the probability that $M = 0$, denoted $\Pr(M = 0)$, is the probability of no computer crashes; $\Pr(M = 1)$ is the probability of a single computer crash; and so forth. An example of a probability distribution for M is given in the second row of Table 2.1; in this distribution, if your computer crashes four times, you will quit and write the paper by hand. According to this distribution, the probability of no crashes is 80%; the probability of one crash is 10%; and the probability of two, three, or four crashes is, respectively, 6%, 3%, and 1%. These probabilities sum to 100%. This probability distribution is plotted in Figure 2.1.

Probabilities of events.   The probability of an event can be computed from the probability distribution. For example, the probability of the event of one or two crashes is the sum of the probabilities of the constituent outcomes. That is, $\Pr(M = 1 \text{ or } M = 2) = \Pr(M = 1) + \Pr(M = 2) = 0.10 + 0.06 = 0.16$, or 16%.

Cumulative probability distribution.   The **cumulative probability distribution** is the probability that the random variable is less than or equal to a particular value. The last row of Table 2.1 gives the cumulative probability distribution of the random

TABLE 2.1   Probability of Your Computer Crashing M Times

	Outcome (number of crashes)				
	0	1	2	3	4
Probability distribution	0.80	0.10	0.06	0.03	0.01
Cumulative probability distribution	0.80	0.90	0.96	0.99	1.00

variable *M*. For example, the probability of at most one crash, $\Pr(M \leq 1)$, is 90%, which is the sum of the probabilities of no crashes (80%) and of one crash (10%).

A cumulative probability distribution is also referred to as a **cumulative distribution function**, a **c.d.f.**, or a **cumulative distribution**.

The Bernoulli distribution.   An important special case of a discrete random variable is when the random variable is binary, that is, the outcomes are 0 or 1. A binary random variable is called a **Bernoulli random variable** (in honor of the seventeenth-century Swiss mathematician and scientist Jacob Bernoulli), and its probability distribution is called the **Bernoulli distribution**.

FIGURE 2.1   Probability Distribution of the Number of Computer Crashes

The height of each bar is the probability that the computer crashes the indicated number of times. The height of the first bar is 0.8, so the probability of 0 computer crashes is 80%. The height of the second bar is 0.1, so the probability of 1 computer crash is 10%, and so forth for the other bars.

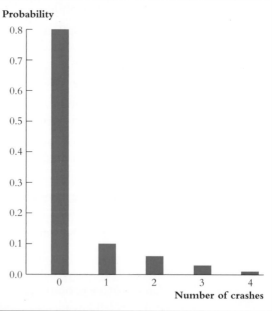

For example, let G be the gender of the next new person you meet, where $G = 0$ indicates that the person is male and $G = 1$ indicates that she is female. The outcomes of G and their probabilities thus are

$$G = \begin{cases} 1 \text{ with probability } p \\ 0 \text{ with probability } 1 - p, \end{cases} \tag{2.1}$$

where p is the probability of the next new person you meet being a woman. The probability distribution in Equation (2.1) is the Bernoulli distribution.

Probability Distribution of a Continuous Random Variable

Cumulative probability distribution.   The cumulative probability distribution for a continuous variable is defined just as it is for a discrete random variable. That is, the cumulative probability distribution of a continuous random variable is the probability that the random variable is less than or equal to a particular value.

For example, consider a student who drives from home to school. This student's commuting time can take on a continuum of values and, because it depends on random factors such as the weather and traffic conditions, it is natural to treat it as a continuous random variable. Figure 2.2a plots a hypothetical cumulative distribution of commuting times. For example, the probability that the commute takes less than 15 minutes is 20% and the probability that it takes less than 20 minutes is 78%.

Probability density function.   Because a continuous random variable can take on a continuum of possible values, the probability distribution used for discrete variables, which lists the probability of each possible value of the random variable, is not suitable for continuous variables. Instead, the probability is summarized by the **probability density function**. The area under the probability density function between any two points is the probability that the random variable falls between those two points. A probability density function is also called a **p.d.f.**, a **density function**, or simply a **density**.

Figure 2.2b plots the probability density function of commuting times corresponding to the cumulative distribution in Figure 2.2a. The probability that the commute takes between 15 and 20 minutes is given by the area under the p.d.f. between 15 minutes and 20 minutes, which is 0.58, or 58%. Equivalently, this probability can be seen on the cumulative distribution in Figure 2.2a as the difference

---

FIGURE 2.2   Cumulative Distribution and Probability Density Functions of Commuting Time

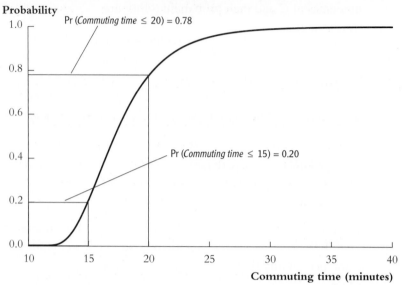

(a) Cumulative distribution function of commuting time

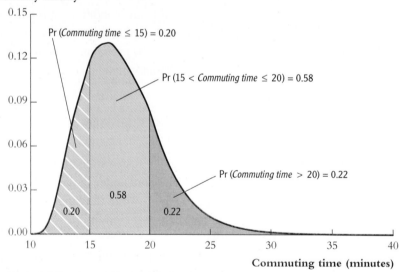

(b) Probability density function of commuting time

Figure 2.2a shows the cumulative probability distribution (or c.d.f.) of commuting times. The probability that a commuting time is less than 15 minutes is 0.20 (or 20%), and the probability that it is less than 20 minutes is 0.78 (78%). Figure 2.2b shows the probability density function (or p.d.f.) of commuting times. Probabilities are given by areas under the p.d.f. The probability that a commuting time is between 15 and 20 minutes is 0.58 (58%), and is given by the area under the curve between 15 and 20 minutes.

between the probability that the commute is less than 20 minutes (78%) and the probability that it is less than 15 minutes (20%). Thus, the probability density function and the cumulative probability distribution show the same information in different formats.

2.2   Expected Values, Mean, and Variance

The Expected Value of a Random Variable

Expected value.   The **expected value** of a random variable Y, denoted $E(Y)$, is the long-run average value of the random variable over many repeated trials or occurrences. The expected value of a discrete random variable is computed as a weighted average of the possible outcomes of that random variable, where the weights are the probabilities of that outcome. The expected value of Y is also called the **expectation** of Y or the **mean** of Y and is denoted by μ_Y.

For example, suppose you loan a friend $100 at 10% interest. If the loan is repaid you get $110 (the principal of $100 plus interest of $10), but there is a risk of 1% that your friend will default and you will get nothing at all. Thus, the amount you are repaid is a random variable that equals $110 with probability 0.99 and equals $0 with probability 0.01. Over many such loans, 99% of the time you would be paid back $110, but 1% of the time you would get nothing, so on average you would be repaid $110 \times 0.99 + $0 \times 0.01 = $108.90. Thus the expected value of your repayment (or the "mean repayment") is $108.90.

As a second example, consider the number of computer crashes M with the probability distribution given in Table 2.1. The expected value of M is the average number of crashes over many term papers, weighted by the frequency with which a crash of a given size occurs. Accordingly,

$$E(M) = 0 \times 0.80 + 1 \times 0.10 + 2 \times 0.06 + 3 \times 0.03 + 4 \times 0.01 = 0.35. \qquad (2.2)$$

That is, the expected number of computer crashes while writing a term paper is 0.35. Of course, the actual number of crashes must always be an integer; it makes no sense to say that the computer crashed 0.35 times while writing a particular term paper! Rather, the calculation in Equation (2.2) means that the average number of crashes over many such term papers is 0.35.

The formula for the expected value of a discrete random variable Y that can take on k different values is given as Key Concept 2.1.

Expected value of a Bernoulli random variable.   An important special case of the general formula in Key Concept 2.1 is the mean of a Bernoulli random

KEY CONCEPT

2.1

EXPECTED VALUE AND THE MEAN

Suppose the random variable Y takes on k possible values, $y_1, \ldots, y_k$, where y_1 denotes the first value, y_2 denotes the second value, and so forth, and that the probability that Y takes on y_1 is p_1, the probability that Y takes on y_2 is p_2, and so forth. The expected value of Y, denoted $E(Y)$, is

$$E(Y) = y_1 p_1 + y_2 p_2 + \cdots + y_k p_k = \sum_{i=1}^{k} y_i p_i, \tag{2.3}$$

where the notation "$\sum_{i=1}^{k} y_i p_i$" means "the sum of $y_i p_i$ for i running from 1 to k." The expected value of Y is also called the mean of Y or the expectation of Y and is denoted μ_Y.

variable. Let G be the Bernoulli random variable with the probability distribution in Equation (2.1). The expected value of G is

$$E(G) = 1 \times p + 0 \times (1 - p) = p. \tag{2.4}$$

Thus the expected value of a Bernoulli random variable is p, the probability that it takes on the value "1."

Expected value of a continuous random variable. The expected value of a continuous random variable is also the probability-weighted average of the possible outcomes of the random variable. Because a continuous random variable can take on a continuum of possible values, the formal mathematical definition of its expectation involves calculus and its definition is omitted.

The Standard Deviation and Variance

The variance and standard deviation measure the dispersion or the "spread" of a probability distribution. The **variance** of a random variable Y, denoted var(Y), is the expected value of the square of the deviation of Y from its mean: var(Y) = $E[(Y - \mu_Y)^2]$.

Because the variance involves the square of Y, the units of the variance are the units of the square of Y, which makes the variance awkward to interpret. It is therefore common to measure the spread by the **standard deviation**, which is the square root of the variance and is denoted σ_Y. The standard deviation has the same units as Y. These definitions are summarized in Key Concept 2.2.

VARIANCE AND STANDARD DEVIATION

The variance of the discrete random variable Y, denoted σ_Y^2, is

$$\sigma_Y^2 = \text{var}(Y) = E[(Y - \mu_Y)^2] = \sum_{i=1}^{k} (y_i - \mu_Y)^2 p_i. \qquad (2.5)$$

The standard deviation of Y is σ_Y, the square root of the variance. The units of the standard deviation are the same as the units of Y.

For example, the variance of the number of computer crashes M is the probability-weighted average of the squared difference between M and its mean, 0.35:

$$\text{var}(M) = (0 - 0.35)^2 \times 0.80 + (1 - 0.35)^2 \times 0.10 + (2 - 0.35)^2 \times 0.06$$
$$+ (3 - 0.35)^2 \times 0.03 + (4 - 0.35)^2 \times 0.01 = 0.6475. \qquad (2.6)$$

The standard deviation of M is the square root of the variance, so $\sigma_M = \sqrt{0.6475} \cong 0.80$.

Variance of a Bernoulli random variable. The mean of the Bernoulli random variable G with probability distribution in Equation (2.1) is $\mu_G = p$ [Equation (2.4)] so its variance is

$$\text{var}(G) = \sigma_G^2 = (0 - p)^2 \times (1 - p) + (1 - p)^2 \times p = p(1 - p). \qquad (2.7)$$

Thus the standard deviation of a Bernoulli random variable is $\sigma_G = \sqrt{p(1 - p)}$.

Mean and Variance of a Linear Function of a Random Variable

This section discusses random variables (say, X and Y) that are related by a linear function. For example, consider an income tax scheme under which a worker is taxed at a rate of 20% on his or her earnings and then given a (tax-free) grant of $2000. Under this tax scheme, after-tax earnings Y are related to pre-tax earnings X by the equation

$$Y = 2000 + 0.8X. \qquad (2.8)$$

That is, after-tax earnings Y is 80% of pre-tax earnings X, plus $2000.

Suppose an individual's pre-tax earnings next year are a random variable with mean μ_X and variance σ_X^2. Because pre-tax earnings are random, so are after-tax earnings. What are the mean and standard deviations of her after-tax earnings under this tax? After taxes, her earnings are 80% of the original pre-tax earnings, plus $2,000. Thus the expected value of her after-tax earnings is

$$E(Y) = \mu_Y = 2000 + 0.8\mu_X. \tag{2.9}$$

The variance of after-tax earnings is the expected value of $(Y - \mu_Y)^2$. Because $Y = 2000 + 0.8X$, $Y - \mu_Y = 2000 + 0.8X - (2000 + 0.8\mu_X) = 0.8(X - \mu_X)$. Thus, $E[(Y - \mu_Y)^2] = E\{[0.8(X - \mu_X)]^2\} = 0.64E[(X - \mu_X)^2]$. It follows that var$(Y) = 0.64var(X)$, so, taking the square root of the variance, the standard deviation of Y is

$$\sigma_Y = 0.8\sigma_X. \tag{2.10}$$

That is, the standard deviation of the distribution of her after-tax earnings is 80% of the standard deviation of the distribution of pre-tax earnings.

This analysis can be generalized so that Y depends on X with an intercept a (instead of $2000) and a slope b (instead of 0.8), so that

$$Y = a + bX. \tag{2.11}$$

Then the mean and variance of Y are

$$\mu_Y = a + b\mu_X \text{ and} \tag{2.12}$$

$$\sigma_Y^2 = b^2\sigma_X^2, \tag{2.13}$$

and the standard deviation of Y is $\sigma_Y = b\sigma_X$. The expressions in Equations (2.9) and (2.10) are applications of the more general formulas in Equations (2.12) and (2.13) with $a = 2000$ and $b = 0.8$.

Other Measures of the Shape of a Distribution

The mean and standard deviation measure two important features of a distribution: its center (the mean) and its spread (the standard deviation). This section discusses measures of two other features of a distribution: the skewness, which measures the lack of symmetry of a distribution, and the kurtosis, which measures how thick, or "heavy," are its tails. The mean, variance, skewness, and kurtosis are all based on what are called the **moments of a distribution**.

Skewness.   Figure 2.3 plots four distributions, two which are symmetric and two which are not. Visually, the distribution in Figure 2.3d appears to deviate more from symmetry than does the distribution in Figure 2.3c. The skewness of a distribution provides a mathematical way to describe how much a distribution deviates from symmetry.

The **skewness** of the distribution of a random variable Y is

$$\text{Skewness} = \frac{E[(Y - \mu_Y)^3]}{\sigma_Y^3}, \tag{2.14}$$

where σ_Y is the standard deviation of Y. For a symmetric distribution, a value of Y a given amount above its mean is just as likely as a value of Y the same amount below its mean. If so, then positive values of $(Y - \mu_Y)^3$ will be offset on average (in expectation) by equally likely negative values. Thus, for a symmetric distribution, $E[(Y - \mu_Y)^3] = 0$; the skewness of a symmetric distribution is zero. If a distribution is not symmetric, then a positive value of $(Y - \mu_Y)^3$ generally is not offset on average by an equally likely negative value, so the skewness is nonzero for a distribution that is not symmetric. Dividing by σ_Y^3 in the denominator of Equation (2.14) cancels the units of Y^3 in the numerator, so the skewness is unit free; in other words, changing the units of Y does not change its skewness.

Below each of the four distributions in Figure 2.3 is its skewness. If a distribution has a long right tail, positive values of $(Y - \mu_Y)^3$ are not fully offset by negative values, and the skewness is positive. If a distribution has a long left tail, its skewness is negative.

Kurtosis.   The **kurtosis** of a distribution is a measure of how much mass is in its tails and, therefore, is a measure of how much of the variance of Y arises from extreme values. An extreme value of Y is called an **outlier**. The greater the kurtosis of a distribution, the more likely are outliers.

The kurtosis of the distribution of Y is

$$\text{Kurtosis} = \frac{E[(Y - \mu_Y)^4]}{\sigma_Y^4}. \tag{2.15}$$

If a distribution has a large amount of mass in its tails, then some extreme departures of Y from its mean are likely, and these very large values will lead to large values, on average (in expectation), of $(Y - \mu_Y)^4$. Thus, for a distribution with a large amount of mass in its tails, the kurtosis will be large. Because $(Y - \mu_Y)^4$ cannot be negative, the kurtosis cannot be negative.

FIGURE 2.3   Four Distributions with Different Skewness and Kurtosis

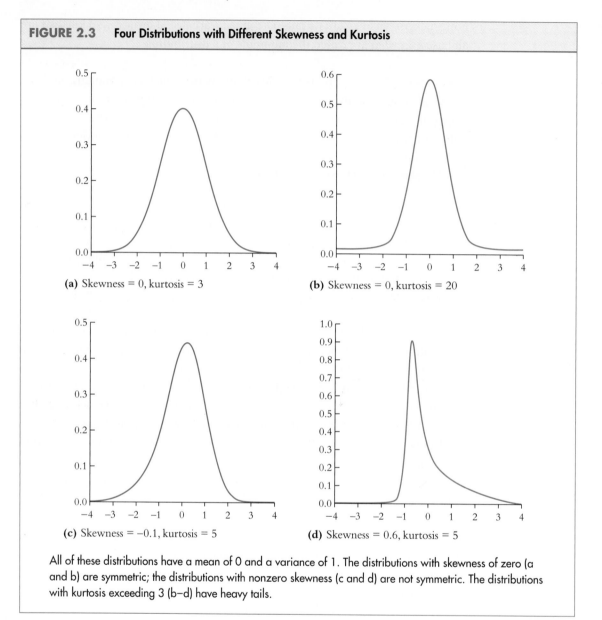

(a) Skewness = 0, kurtosis = 3

(b) Skewness = 0, kurtosis = 20

(c) Skewness = −0.1, kurtosis = 5

(d) Skewness = 0.6, kurtosis = 5

All of these distributions have a mean of 0 and a variance of 1. The distributions with skewness of zero (a and b) are symmetric; the distributions with nonzero skewness (c and d) are not symmetric. The distributions with kurtosis exceeding 3 (b–d) have heavy tails.

The kurtosis of a normally distributed random variable is 3, so a random variable with kurtosis exceeding 3 has more mass in its tails than a normal random variable. A distribution with kurtosis exceeding 3 is called **leptokurtic** or, more simply, heavy-tailed. Like skewness, the kurtosis is unit free, so changing the units of Y does not change its kurtosis.

Below each of the four distributions in Figure 2.3 is its kurtosis. The distributions in Figures 2.3b–d are heavy-tailed.

Moments.   The mean of Y, $E(Y)$, is also called the first moment of Y, and the expected value of the square of Y, $E(Y^2)$, is called the second moment of Y. In general, the expected value of Y^r is called the **r^{th} moment** of the random variable Y. That is, the rth moment of Y is $E(Y^r)$. The skewness is a function of the first, second, and third moments of Y, and the kurtosis is a function of the first through fourth moments of Y.

2.3   Two Random Variables

Most of the interesting questions in economics involve two or more variables. Are college graduates more likely to have a job than nongraduates? How does the distribution of income for women compare to that for men? These questions concern the distribution of two random variables, considered together (education and employment status in the first example, income and gender in the second). Answering such questions requires an understanding of the concepts of joint, marginal, and conditional probability distributions.

Joint and Marginal Distributions

Joint distribution.   The **joint probability distribution of** two discrete random variables, say X and Y, is the probability that the random variables simultaneously take on certain values, say x and y. The probabilities of all possible (x,y) combinations sum to 1. The joint probability distribution can be written as the function $\Pr(X = x, Y = y)$.

For example, weather conditions—whether or not it is raining—affect the commuting time of the student commuter in Section 2.1. Let Y be a binary random variable that equals 1 if the commute is short (less than 20 minutes) and equals 0 otherwise, and let X be a binary random variable that equals 0 if it is raining and 1 if not. Between these two random variables, there are four possible outcomes: it rains and the commute is long ($X = 0$, $Y = 0$); rain and short commute ($X = 0$, $Y = 1$); no rain and long commute ($X = 1$, $Y = 0$); and no rain and short commute ($X = 1$, $Y = 1$). The joint probability distribution is the frequency with which each of these four outcomes occurs over many repeated commutes.

An example of a joint distribution of these two variables is given in Table 2.2. According to this distribution, over many commutes, 15% of the days have rain and a long commute ($X = 0$, $Y = 0$); that is, the probability of a long, rainy commute is 15%, or $\Pr(X = 0$, $Y = 0) = 0.15$. Also, $\Pr(X = 0$, $Y = 1) = 0.15$, $\Pr(X = 1$, $Y = 0) = 0.07$, and $\Pr(X = 1$, $Y = 1) = 0.63$. These four possible outcomes are mutually exclusive and constitute the sample space so the four probabilities sum to 1.

TABLE 2.2 Joint Distribution of Weather Conditions and Commuting Times			
	Rain ($X = 0$)	No Rain ($X = 1$)	Total
Long Commute ($Y = 0$)	0.15	0.07	0.22
Short Commute ($Y = 1$)	0.15	0.63	0.78
Total	0.30	0.70	1.00

Marginal probability distribution.   The **marginal probability distribution** of a random variable Y is just another name for its probability distribution. This term is used to distinguish the distribution of Y alone (the marginal distribution) from the joint distribution of Y and another random variable.

The marginal distribution of Y can be computed from the joint distribution of X and Y by adding up the probabilities of all possible outcomes for which Y takes on a specified value. If X can take on l different values $x_1, \ldots, x_l$, then the marginal probability that Y takes on the value y is

$$\Pr(Y = y) = \sum_{i=1}^{l} \Pr(X = x_i, Y = y). \tag{2.16}$$

For example, in Table 2.2, the probability of a long rainy commute is 15% and the probability of a long commute with no rain is 7%, so the probability of a long commute (rainy or not) is 22%. The marginal distribution of commuting times is given in the final column of Table 2.2. Similarly, the marginal probability that it will rain is 30%, as shown in the final row of Table 2.2.

Conditional Distributions

Conditional distribution.   The distribution of a random variable Y conditional on another random variable X taking on a specific value is called the **conditional distribution of Y given X**. The conditional probability that Y takes on the value y when X takes on the value x is written $\Pr(Y = y | X = x)$.

For example, what is the probability of a long commute ($Y = 0$) if you know it is raining ($X = 0$)? From Table 2.2, the joint probability of a rainy short commute is 15% and the joint probability of a rainy long commute is 15%, so if it is raining a long commute and a short commute are equally likely. Thus, the probability of a long commute ($Y = 0$), conditional on it being rainy ($X = 0$), is 50%, or $\Pr(Y = 0 | X = 0) = 0.50$. Equivalently, the marginal probability of rain is 30%; that is, over many commutes it rains 30% of the time. Of this 30% of commutes, 50% of the time the commute is long (0.15/0.30).

TABLE 2.3	Joint and Conditional Distributions of Computer Crashes (M) and Computer Age (A)

A. Joint Distribution

	M = 0	M = 1	M = 2	M = 3	M = 4	Total
Old computer ($A = 0$)	0.35	0.065	0.05	0.025	0.01	0.50
New computer ($A = 1$)	0.45	0.035	0.01	0.005	0.00	0.50
Total	0.8	0.1	0.06	0.03	0.01	1.00

B. Conditional Distributions of M given A

	M = 0	M = 1	M = 2	M = 3	M = 4	Total
$\Pr(M|A = 0)$	0.70	0.13	0.10	0.05	0.02	1.00
$\Pr(M|A = 1)$	0.90	0.07	0.02	0.01	0.00	1.00

In general, the conditional distribution of Y given $X = x$ is

$$\Pr(Y = y | X = x) = \frac{\Pr(X = x, Y = y)}{\Pr(X = x)}. \tag{2.17}$$

For example, the conditional probability of a long commute given that it is rainy is $\Pr(Y = 0 | X = 0) = \Pr(X = 0, Y = 0)/\Pr(X = 0) = 0.15/0.30 = 0.50$.

As a second example, consider a modification of the crashing computer example. Suppose you use a computer in the library to type your term paper and the librarian randomly assigns you a computer from those available, half of which are new and half of which are old. Because you are randomly assigned to a computer, the age of the computer you use, A ($= 1$ if the computer is new, $= 0$ if it is old), is a random variable. Suppose the joint distribution of the random variables M and A is given in Part A of Table 2.3. Then the conditional distribution of computer crashes, given the age of the computer, is given in Part B of the table. For example, the joint probability $M = 0$ and $A = 0$ is 0.35; because half the computers are old, the conditional probability of no crashes, given that you are using an old computer, is $\Pr(M = 0 | A = 0) = \Pr(M = 0, A = 0)/\Pr(A = 0) = 0.35/0.50 = 0.70$, or 70%. In contrast, the conditional probability of no crashes given that you are assigned a new computer is 90%. According to the conditional distributions in Part B of Table 2.3, the newer computers are less likely to crash than the old ones; for example, the probability of three crashes is 5% with an old computer but 1% with a new computer.

Conditional expectation. The **conditional expectation of Y given X**, also called the **conditional mean of Y given X**, is the mean of the conditional distribution of Y given X. That is, the conditional expectation is the expected value of Y, computed using the conditional distribution of Y given X. If Y takes on k values $y_1, \ldots, y_k$, then the conditional mean of Y given $X = x$ is

$$E(Y|X = x) = \sum_{i=1}^{k} y_i \Pr(Y = y_i | X = x). \tag{2.18}$$

For example, based on the conditional distributions in Table 2.3, the expected number of computer crashes, given that the computer is old, is $E(M|A = 0) = 0 \times 0.70 + 1 \times 0.13 + 2 \times 0.10 + 3 \times 0.05 + 4 \times 0.02 = 0.56$. The expected number of computer crashes, given that the computer is new, is $E(M|A = 1) = 0.14$, less than for the old computers.

The conditional expectation of Y given $X = x$ is just the mean value of Y when $X = x$. In the example of Table 2.3, the mean number of crashes is 0.56 for old computers, so the conditional expectation of Y given that the computer is old is 0.56. Similarly, among new computers, the mean number of crashes is 0.14, that is, the conditional expectation of Y given that the computer is new is 0.14.

The law of iterated expectations. The mean of Y is the weighted average of the conditional expectation of Y given X, weighted by the probability distribution of X. For example, the mean height of adults is the weighted average of the mean height of men and the mean height of women, weighted by the proportions of men and women. Stated mathematically, if X takes on the l values $x_1, \ldots, x_l$, then

$$E(Y) = \sum_{i=1}^{l} E(Y|X = x_i)\Pr(X = x_i). \tag{2.19}$$

Equation (2.19) follows from Equations (2.18) and (2.17) (see Exercise 2.19).

Stated differently, the expectation of Y is the expectation of the conditional expectation of Y given X,

$$E(Y) = E[E(Y|X)], \tag{2.20}$$

where the inner expectation on the right-hand side of Equation (2.20) is computed using the conditional distribution of Y given X and the outer expectation is computed using the marginal distribution of X. Equation (2.20) is known as the **law of iterated expectations**.

For example, the mean number of crashes M is the weighted average of the conditional expectation of M given that it is old and the conditional expectation of M given that it is new, so $E(M) = E(M|A = 0) \times \Pr(A = 0) + E(M|A = 1) \times \Pr(A = 1) = 0.56 \times 0.50 + 0.14 \times 0.50 = 0.35$. This is the mean of the marginal distribution of M, as calculated in Equation (2.2).

The law of iterated expectations implies that if the conditional mean of Y given X is zero, then the mean of Y is zero. This is an immediate consequence of Equation (2.20): if $E(Y|X) = 0$, then $E(Y) = E[E(Y|X)] = E[0] = 0$. Said differently, if the mean of Y given X is zero, then it must be that the probability-weighted average of these conditional means is zero, that is, the mean of Y must be zero.

The law of iterated expectations also applies to expectations that are conditional on multiple random variables. For example, let X, Y, and Z be random variables that are jointly distributed. Then the law of iterated expectations says that $E(Y) = E[E(Y|X, Z)]$, where $E(Y|X, Z)$ is the conditional expectation of Y given both X and Z. For example, in the computer crash illustration of Table 2.3, let P denote the number of programs installed on the computer; then $E(M|A, P)$ is the expected number of crashes for a computer with age A that has P programs installed. The expected number of crashes overall, $E(M)$, is the weighted average of the expected number of crashes for a computer with age A and number of programs P, weighted by the proportion of computers with that value of both A and P.

Exercise 2.20 provides some additional properties of conditional expectations with multiple variables.

Conditional variance.   The **variance of Y conditional on X** is the variance of the conditional distribution of Y given X. Stated mathematically, the conditional variance of Y given X is

$$\text{var}(Y|X = x) = \sum_{i=1}^{k} [y_i - E(Y|X = x)]^2 \Pr(Y = y_i|X = x). \qquad (2.21)$$

For example, the conditional variance of the number of crashes given that the computer is old is $\text{var}(M|A = 0) = (0 - 0.56)^2 \times 0.70 + (1 - 0.56)^2 \times 0.13 + (2 - 0.56)^2 \times 0.10 + (3 - 0.56)^2 \times 0.05 + (4 - 0.56)^2 \times 0.02 \cong 0.99$. The standard deviation of the conditional distribution of M given that $A = 0$ is thus $\sqrt{0.99} = 0.99$. The conditional variance of M given that $A = 1$ is the variance of the distribution in the second row of Panel B of Table 2.3, which is 0.22, so the standard deviation of M for new computers is $\sqrt{0.22} = 0.47$. For the conditional distributions in Table 2.3, the expected number of crashes for new computers (0.14) is less than that for old computers (0.56), and the spread of the distribution of the number of crashes, as measured by the conditional standard deviation, is smaller for new computers (0.47) than for old (0.99).

Independence

Two random variables X and Y are **independently distributed**, or **independent**, if knowing the value of one of the variables provides no information about the other. Specifically, X and Y are independent if the conditional distribution of Y given X equals the marginal distribution of Y. That is, X and Y are independently distributed if, for all values of x and y,

$$\Pr(Y = y \mid X = x) = \Pr(Y = y) \quad \text{(independence of } X \text{ and } Y\text{)}. \qquad (2.22)$$

Substituting Equation (2.22) into Equation (2.17) gives an alternative expression for independent random variables in terms of their joint distribution. If X and Y are independent, then

$$\Pr(X = x, Y = y) = \Pr(X = x)\Pr(Y = y). \qquad (2.23)$$

That is, the joint distribution of two independent random variables is the product of their marginal distributions.

Covariance and Correlation

Covariance.   One measure of the extent to which two random variables move together is their covariance. The **covariance** between X and Y is the expected value $E[(X - \mu_X)(Y - \mu_Y)]$, where μ_X is the mean of X and μ_Y is the mean of Y. The covariance is denoted by $\text{cov}(X,Y)$ or by σ_{XY}. If X can take on l values and Y can take on k values, then the covariance is given by the formula

$$\begin{aligned}
\text{cov}(X,Y) = \sigma_{XY} &= E[(X - \mu_X)(Y - \mu_Y)] \\
&= \sum_{i=1}^{k}\sum_{j=1}^{l}(x_j - \mu_X)(y_i - \mu_Y)\Pr(X = x_j, Y = y_i).
\end{aligned} \qquad (2.24)$$

To interpret this formula, suppose that when X is greater than its mean (so that $X - \mu_X$ is positive), then Y tends be greater than its mean (so that $Y - \mu_Y$ is positive), and when X is less than its mean (so that $X - \mu_X < 0$), then Y tends to be less than its mean (so that $Y - \mu_Y < 0$). In both cases, the product $(X - \mu_X) \times (Y - \mu_Y)$ tends to be positive, so the covariance is positive. In contrast, if X and Y tend to move in opposite directions (so that X is large when Y is small, and vice versa), then the covariance is negative. Finally, if X and Y are independent, then the covariance is zero (see Exercise 2.19).

Correlation.   Because the covariance is the product of X and Y, deviated from their means, its units are, awkwardly, the units of X times the units of Y. This "units" problem can make numerical values of the covariance difficult to interpret.

The correlation is an alternative measure of dependence between X and Y that solves the "units" problem of the covariance. Specifically, the **correlation** between X and Y is the covariance between X and Y, divided by their standard deviations:

$$\operatorname{corr}(X,Y) = \frac{\operatorname{cov}(X,Y)}{\sqrt{\operatorname{var}(X)\,\operatorname{var}(Y)}} = \frac{\sigma_{XY}}{\sigma_X \sigma_Y}. \tag{2.25}$$

Because the units of the numerator in Equation (2.25) are the same as those of the denominator, the units cancel and the correlation is unitless. The random variables X and Y are said to be **uncorrelated** if $\operatorname{corr}(X,Y) = 0$.

The correlation always is between -1 and 1; that is, as proven in Appendix 2.1,

$$-1 \le \operatorname{corr}(X,Y) \le 1 \quad \text{(correlation inequality)}. \tag{2.26}$$

Correlation and conditional mean.   If the conditional mean of Y does not depend on X, then Y and X are uncorrelated. That is,

$$\text{if } E(Y\,|\,X) = \mu_Y, \text{then } \operatorname{cov}(Y,X) = 0 \text{ and } \operatorname{corr}(Y,X) = 0. \tag{2.27}$$

We now show this result. First suppose that Y and X have mean zero, so that $\operatorname{cov}(Y,X) = E[(Y - \mu_Y)(X - \mu_X)] = E(YX)$. By the law of iterated expectations [Equation (2.20)], $E(YX) = E[E(Y|X)X] = 0$ because $E(Y|X) = 0$, so $\operatorname{cov}(Y,X) = 0$. Equation (2.27) follows by substituting $\operatorname{cov}(Y,X) = 0$ into the definition of correlation in Equation (2.25). If Y and X do not have mean zero, first subtract off their means, then the preceding proof applies.

It is *not* necessarily true, however, that if X and Y are uncorrelated, then the conditional mean of Y given X does not depend on X. Said differently, it is possible for the conditional mean of Y to be a function of X but for Y and X nonetheless to be uncorrelated. An example is given in Exercise 2.23.

The Mean and Variance of Sums of Random Variables

The mean of the sum of two random variables, X and Y, is the sum of their means:

$$E(X + Y) = E(X) + E(Y) = \mu_X + \mu_Y. \tag{2.28}$$

The Distribution of Earnings in the United States in 2004

Some parents tell their children that they will be able to get a better, higher-paying job if they get a college degree than if they skip higher education. Are these parents right? Does the distribution of earnings differ between workers who are college graduates and workers who have only a high school diploma, and, if so, how? Among workers with a similar education, does the distribution of earnings for men and women differ? For example, are the best-paid college-educated women paid as well as the best-paid college-educated men?

One way to answer these questions is to examine the distribution of earnings, conditional on the highest educational degree achieved (high school diploma or bachelors' degree) and on gender. These four conditional distributions are shown in Figure 2.4, and the mean, standard deviation, and some percentiles of the conditional distributions are presented in Table 2.4.[1] For example, the conditional mean of earnings for women whose highest degree is a high school diploma—that is, $E(Earnings \mid Highest\ degree = high\ school\ diploma,\ Gender = female)$—is \$13.25 per hour.

The distribution of average hourly earnings for female college graduates (Figure 2.4b) is shifted to the right of the distribution for women with only a high school degree (Figure 2.4a); the same shift can be seen for the two groups of men (Figure 2.4d and Figure 2.4c). For both men and women, mean earnings are higher for those with a college degree (Table 2.4, first numeric column). Interestingly, the spread of the distribution of earnings, as measured

continued on next page

TABLE 2.4	Summaries of the Conditional Distribution of Average Hourly Earnings of U.S. Full-Time Workers in 2004 Given Education Level and Gender						
				Percentile			
	Mean	Standard Deviation	25%	50% (median)	75%	90%
(a) Women with high school diploma	\$13.25	\$ 7.04	\$ 8.79	\$12.02	\$16.06	\$20.75
(b) Women with four-year college degree	21.12	10.85	13.74	19.23	26.04	35.26
(c) Men with high school diploma	17.63	9.26	11.54	15.87	21.63	28.85
(d) Men with four-year college degree	27.83	14.87	17.31	24.23	35.71	48.08

Average hourly earnings are the sum of annual pretax wages, salaries, tips, and bonuses, divided by the number of hours worked annually. The distributions were computed from the March 2005 Current Population Survey, which is described in Appendix 3.1.

by the standard deviation, is greater for those with a college degree than for those with a high school diploma. In addition, for both men and women, the 90th percentile of earnings is much higher for workers with a college degree than for workers with only a high school diploma. This final comparison is consistent with the parental admonition that a college degree opens doors that remain closed to individuals with only a high school diploma.

Another feature of these distributions is that the distribution of earnings for men is shifted to the right of the distribution of earnings for women. This "gender gap" in earnings is an important—and to many, troubling—aspect of the distribution of earnings. We return to this topic in later chapters.

---

[1] The distributions were estimated using data from the March 2005 Current Population Survey, which is discussed in more detail in Appendix 3.1.

FIGURE 2.4   **Conditional Distribution of Average Hourly Earnings of U.S. Full-Time Workers in 2004, Given Education Level and Gender**

The four distributions of earnings are for women and men, for those with only a high school diploma (a and c) and those whose highest degree is from a four-year college (b and d).

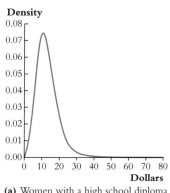

(a) Women with a high school diploma

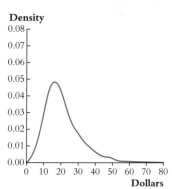

(b) Women with a college degree

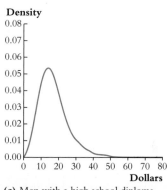

(c) Men with a high school diploma

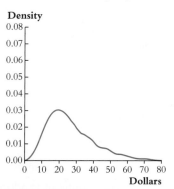

(d) Men with a college degree

MEANS, VARIANCES, AND COVARIANCES OF SUMS OF RANDOM VARIABLES

Let X, Y, and V be random variables, let μ_X and σ_X^2 be the mean and variance of X, let σ_{XY} be the covariance between X and Y (and so forth for the other variables), and let a, b, and c be constants. The following facts follow from the definitions of the mean, variance, and covariance:

$$E(a + bX + cY) = a + b\mu_X + c\mu_Y, \tag{2.29}$$

$$\text{var}(a + bY) = b^2\sigma_Y^2, \tag{2.30}$$

$$\text{var}(aX + bY) = a^2\sigma_X^2 + 2ab\sigma_{XY} + b^2\sigma_Y^2, \tag{2.31}$$

$$E(Y^2) = \sigma_Y^2 + \mu_Y^2, \tag{2.32}$$

$$\text{cov}(a + bX + cV, Y) = b\sigma_{XY} + c\sigma_{VY}, \tag{2.33}$$

$$E(XY) = \sigma_{XY} + \mu_X\mu_Y, \text{ and} \tag{2.34}$$

$$|\text{corr}(X,Y)| \leq 1 \text{ and } |\sigma_{XY}| \leq \sqrt{\sigma_X^2\sigma_Y^2} \text{ (correlation inequality).} \tag{2.35}$$

The variance of the sum of X and Y is the sum of their variances, plus twice their covariance:

$$\text{var}(X + Y) = \text{var}(X) + \text{var}(Y) + 2\text{cov}(X,Y) = \sigma_X^2 + \sigma_Y^2 + 2\sigma_{XY}. \tag{2.36}$$

If X and Y are independent, then the covariance is zero and the variance of their sum is the sum of their variances:

$$\text{var}(X + Y) = \text{var}(X) + \text{var}(Y) = \sigma_X^2 + \sigma_Y^2 \tag{2.37}$$
$$\text{(if } X \text{ and } Y \text{ are independent).}$$

Useful expressions for means, variances, and covariances involving weighted sums of random variables are collected in Key Concept 2.3. The results in Key Concept 2.3 are derived in Appendix 2.1.

FIGURE 2.5   The Normal Probability Density

The normal probability density function with mean μ and variance σ^2 is a bell-shaped curve, centered at μ. The area under the normal p.d.f. between $\mu - 1.96\sigma$ and $\mu + 1.96\sigma$ is 0.95. The normal distribution is denoted $N(\mu, \sigma^2)$. The normal probability density function is

$$f_Y(y) = \frac{1}{\sigma\sqrt{2\pi}} \exp\left[-\frac{1}{2}\left(\frac{y-\mu}{\sigma}\right)^2\right].$$

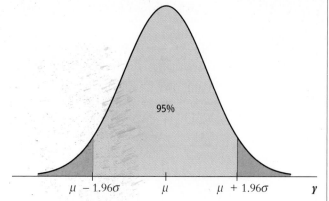

95%

$\mu - 1.96\sigma$ μ $\mu + 1.96\sigma$ y

2.4   The Normal, Chi-Squared, Student *t*, and *F* Distributions

The probability distributions most often encountered in econometrics are the normal, chi-squared, Student *t*, and *F* distributions.

The Normal Distribution

A continuous random variable with a **normal distribution** has the familiar bell-shaped probability density shown in Figure 2.5. As Figure 2.5 shows, the normal density with mean μ and variance σ^2 is symmetric around its mean and has 95% of its probability between $\mu - 1.96\sigma$ and $\mu + 1.96\sigma$.

Some special notation and terminology have been developed for the normal distribution. The normal distribution with mean μ and variance σ^2 is expressed concisely as "$N(\mu, \sigma^2)$." The **standard normal distribution** is the normal distribution with mean $\mu = 0$ and variance $\sigma^2 = 1$ and is denoted $N(0, 1)$. Random variables that have a $N(0,1)$ distribution are often denoted by Z, and the standard normal cumulative distribution function is denoted by the Greek letter Φ; accordingly, $\Pr(Z \leq c) = \Phi(c)$, where c is a constant. Values of the standard normal cumulative distribution function are tabulated in Appendix Table 1.

To compute probabilities for a normal variable with a general mean and variance, it must be **standardized** by first subtracting the mean, then dividing the result

COMPUTING PROBABILITIES INVOLVING NORMAL RANDOM VARIABLES

Suppose Y is normally distributed with mean μ and variance σ^2; in other words, Y is distributed $N(\mu, \sigma^2)$. Then Y is standardized by subtracting its mean and dividing by its standard deviation, that is, by computing $Z = (Y - \mu)/\sigma$.

Let c_1 and c_2 denote two numbers with $c_1 < c_2$, and let $d_1 = (c_1 - \mu)/\sigma$ and $d_2 = (c_2 - \mu)/\sigma$. Then,

$$\Pr(Y \leq c_2) = \Pr(Z \leq d_2) = \Phi(d_2), \tag{2.38}$$

$$\Pr(Y \geq c_1) = \Pr(Z \geq d_1) = 1 - \Phi(d_1), \text{ and} \tag{2.39}$$

$$\Pr(c_1 \leq Y \leq c_2) = \Pr(d_1 \leq Z \leq d_2) = \Phi(d_2) - \Phi(d_1). \tag{2.40}$$

The normal cumulative distribution function Φ is tabulated in Appendix Table 1.

by the standard deviation. For example, suppose Y is distributed $N(1, 4)$, that is, Y is normally distributed with a mean of 1 and a variance of 4. What is the probability that $Y \leq 2$—that is, what is the shaded area in Figure 2.6a? The standardized version of Y is Y minus its mean, divided by its standard deviation, that is, $(Y - 1)/\sqrt{4} = \frac{1}{2}(Y - 1)$. Accordingly, the random variable $\frac{1}{2}(Y - 1)$ is normally distributed with mean zero and variance one (see Exercise 2.8); it has the standard normal distribution shown in Figure 2.6b. Now $Y \leq 2$ is equivalent to $\frac{1}{2}(Y - 1) \leq \frac{1}{2}(2 - 1)$, that is, $\frac{1}{2}(Y - 1) \leq \frac{1}{2}$. Thus,

$$\Pr(Y \leq 2) = \Pr[\tfrac{1}{2}(Y - 1) \leq \tfrac{1}{2}] = \Pr(Z \leq \tfrac{1}{2}) = \Phi(0.5) = 0.691, \tag{2.41}$$

where the value 0.691 is taken from Appendix Table 1.

The same approach can be applied to compute the probability that a normally distributed random variable exceeds some value or that it falls in a certain range. These steps are summarized in Key Concept 2.4. The box, "A Bad Day on Wall Street," presents an unusual application of the cumulative normal distribution.

The normal distribution is symmetric, so its skewness is zero. The kurtosis of the normal distribution is 3.

The multivariate normal distribution. The normal distribution can be generalized to describe the joint distribution of a set of random variables. In this case,

---

FIGURE 2.6   **Calculating the Probability that $Y \le 2$ When Y is Distributed $N(1, 4)$**

To calculate $\Pr(Y \le 2)$, standardize Y, then use the standard normal distribution table. Y is standardized by subtracting its mean ($\mu = 1$) and dividing by its standard deviation ($\sigma = 2$). The probability that $Y \le 2$ is shown in Figure 2.6a, and the corresponding probability after standardizing Y is shown in Figure 2.6b. Because the standardized random variable, $\frac{Y-1}{2}$, is a standard normal (Z) random variable, $\Pr(Y \le 2) = \Pr\left(\frac{Y-1}{2} \le \frac{2-1}{2}\right)$ $= \Pr(Z \le 0.5)$. From Appendix Table 1, $\Pr(Z \le 0.5) = 0.691$.

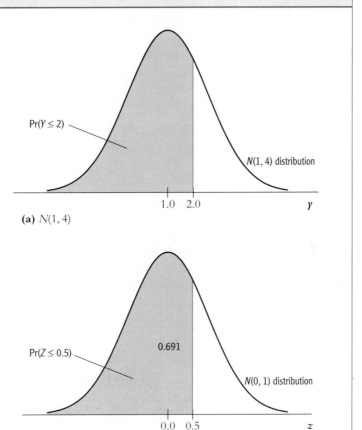

(a) $N(1, 4)$

(b) $N(0, 1)$

the distribution is called the **multivariate normal distribution**, or, if only two variables are being considered, the **bivariate normal distribution**.

The multivariate normal distribution has three important properties. If X and Y have a bivariate normal distribution with covariance σ_{XY}, and if a and b are two constants, then $aX + bY$ has the normal distribution,

$$aX + bY \text{ is distributed } N(a\mu_X + b\mu_Y, a^2\sigma_X^2 + b^2\sigma_Y^2 + 2ab\sigma_{XY}) \tag{2.42}$$
$$(X,Y \text{ bivariate normal})$$

More generally, if n random variables have a multivariate normal distribution, then any linear combination of these variables (such as their sum) is normally distributed.

A Bad Day on Wall Street

On a typical day the overall value of stocks traded on the U.S. stock market can rise or fall by 1% or even more. This is a lot—but nothing compared to what happened on Monday, October 19, 1987. On "Black Monday," the Dow Jones Industrial Average (an average of 30 large industrial stocks) fell by 25.6%! From January 1, 1980, to October 16, 1987, the standard deviation of daily percentage price changes on the Dow was 1.16%, so the drop of 25.6% was a negative return of 22(= 25.6/1.16) stan-

dard deviations. The enormity of this drop can be seen in Figure 2.7, a plot of the daily returns on the Dow during the 1980s.

If daily percentage price changes are normally distributed, then the probability of a drop of at least 22 standard deviations is $\Pr(Z \leq -22) = \Phi(-22)$. You will not find this value in Appendix Table 1, but you can calculate it using a computer (try it!). This probability is 1.4×10^{-107}, that is, $0.000 \ldots .00014$, where there are a total of 106 zeros!

continued

FIGURE 2.7   **Daily Percentage Changes in the Dow Jones Industrial Average in the 1980s**

During the 1980s, the average percentage daily change of "the Dow" index was 0.05% and its standard deviation was 1.16%. On October 19, 1987—"Black Monday"—the index fell 25.6%, or more than 22 standard deviations.

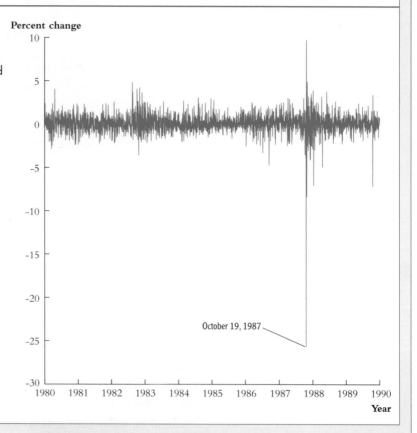

How small is 1.4×10^{-107}? Consider the following:

- The world population is about 6 billion, so the probability of winning a random lottery among all living people is about one in 6 billion, or 2×10^{-10}.

- The universe is believed to have existed for 15 billion years, or about 5×10^{17} seconds, so the probability of choosing a particular second at random from all the seconds since the beginning of time is 2×10^{-18}.

- There are approximately 10^{43} molecules of gas in the first kilometer above the earth's surface. The probability of choosing one at random is 10^{-43}.

Although Wall Street *did* have a bad day, the fact that it happened at all suggests that its probability was more than 1.4×10^{-107}. In fact, stock price percentage changes have a distribution with heavier tails than the normal distribution; in other words, there are more days with large positive or large negative changes than the normal distribution would suggest. For this reason, finance professionals use econometric models in which the variance of the percentage change in stock prices can evolve over time, so some periods have higher volatility than others. These models with changing variances are more consistent with the very bad—and very good—days we actually see on Wall Street.

Second, if a set of variables has a multivariate normal distribution, then the marginal distribution of each of the variables is normal [this follows from Equation (2.42) by setting $a = 1$ and $b = 0$].

Third, if variables with a multivariate normal distribution have covariances that equal zero, then the variables are independent. Thus, if X and Y have a bivariate normal distribution and $\sigma_{XY} = 0$, then X and Y are independent. In Section 2.3 it was stated that if X and Y are independent then, regardless of their joint distribution, $\sigma_{XY} = 0$. If X and Y are jointly normally distributed, then the converse is also true. This result—that zero covariance implies independence—is a special property of the multivariate normal distribution that is not true in general.

The Chi-Squared Distribution

The chi-squared distribution is used when testing certain types of hypotheses in statistics and econometrics.

The **chi-squared distribution** is the distribution of the sum of m squared independent standard normal random variables. This distribution depends on m, which is called the degrees of freedom of the chi-squared distribution. For example, let Z_1, Z_2, and Z_3 be independent standard normal random variables. Then $Z_1^2 + Z_2^2 + Z_3^2$ has a chi-squared distribution with 3 degrees of freedom. The name for this distribution derives from the Greek letter used to denote it: a chi-squared distribution with m degrees of freedom is denoted χ^2_m.

Selected percentiles of the χ^2_m distribution are given in Appendix Table 3. For example, Appendix Table 3 shows that the 95th percentile of the χ^2_3 distribution is 7.81, so $\Pr(Z^2_1 + Z^2_2 + Z^2_3 \leq 7.81) = 0.95$.

The Student t Distribution

The **Student t distribution** with m degrees of freedom is defined to be the distribution of the ratio of a standard normal random variable, divided by the square root of an independently distributed chi-squared random variable with m degrees of freedom divided by m. That is, let Z be a standard normal random variable, let W be a random variable with a chi-squared distribution with m degrees of freedom, and let Z and W be independently distributed. Then the random variable $Z/\sqrt{W/m}$ has a Student t distribution (also called the **t distribution**) with m degrees of freedom. This distribution is denoted t_m. Selected percentiles of the Student t distribution are given in Appendix Table 2.

The Student t distribution depends on the degrees of freedom m. Thus the 95th percentile of the t_m distribution depends on the degrees of freedom m. The Student t distribution has a bell shape similar to that of the normal distribution, but when m is small (20 or less) it has more mass in the tails—that is, it is a "fatter" bell shape than the normal. When m is 30 or more, the Student t distribution is well approximated by the standard normal distribution, and the t_∞ distribution equals the standard normal distribution.

The F Distribution

The **F distribution** with m and n degrees of freedom, denoted $F_{m,n}$, is defined to be the distribution of the ratio of a chi-squared random variable with degrees of freedom m, divided by m, to an independently distributed chi-squared random variable with degrees of freedom n, divided by n. To state this mathematically, let W be a chi-squared random variable with m degrees of freedom and let V be a chi-squared random variable with n degrees of freedom, where W and V are independently distributed. Then $\frac{W/m}{V/n}$ has an $F_{m,n}$ distribution—that is, an F distribution with numerator degrees of freedom m and denominator degrees of freedom n.

In statistics and econometrics, an important special case of the F distribution arises when the denominator degrees of freedom is large enough that the $F_{m,n}$ distribution can be approximated by the $F_{m,\infty}$ distribution. In this limiting case, the denominator random variable V is the mean of infinitely many chi-squared random variables, and that mean is 1 because the mean of a squared standard normal random variable is 1 (see Exercise 2.24). Thus the $F_{m,\infty}$ distribution is the distribution of a chi-squared random variable with m degrees of freedom, divided by m: W/m is distributed $F_{m,\infty}$. For example, from Appendix Table 4, the 95th percentile of the $F_{3,\infty}$ distribution is 2.60, which is the same as the 95th percentile of the χ_3^2 distribution, 7.81 (from Appendix Table 2), divided by the degrees of freedom, which is 3 (7.81/3 = 2.60).

The 90th, 95th, and 99th percentiles of the $F_{m,n}$ distribution are given in Appendix Table 5 for selected values of m and n. For example, the 95th percentile of the $F_{3,30}$ distribution is 2.92, and the 95th percentile of the $F_{3,90}$ distribution is 2.71. As the denominator degrees of freedom n increases, the 95th percentile of the $F_{3,n}$ distribution tends to the $F_{3,\infty}$ limit of 2.60.

2.5 Random Sampling and the Distribution of the Sample Average

Almost all the statistical and econometric procedures used in this book involve averages or weighted averages of a sample of data. Characterizing the distributions of sample averages therefore is an essential step toward understanding the performance of econometric procedures.

This section introduces some basic concepts about random sampling and the distributions of averages that are used throughout the book. We begin by discussing random sampling. The act of random sampling—that is, randomly drawing a sample from a larger population—has the effect of making the sample average itself a random variable. Because the sample average is a random variable, it has a probability distribution, which is called its sampling distribution. This section concludes with some properties of the sampling distribution of the sample average.

Random Sampling

Simple random sampling.　　Suppose our commuting student from Section 2.1 aspires to be a statistician and decides to record her commuting times on various days. She selects these days at random from the school year, and her daily commuting time has the cumulative distribution function in Figure 2.2a. Because these days were selected at random, knowing the value of the commuting time on one of these randomly selected days provides no information about the commuting time on another of the days; that is, because the days were selected at random, the values of the commuting time on each of the different days are independently distributed random variables.

The situation described in the previous paragraph is an example of the simplest sampling scheme used in statistics, called **simple random sampling**, in which n objects are selected at random from a **population** (the population of commuting days) and each member of the population (each day) is equally likely to be included in the sample.

The n observations in the sample are denoted $Y_1, \ldots, Y_n$, where Y_1 is the first observation, Y_2 is the second observation, and so forth. In the commuting example, Y_1 is the commuting time on the first of her n randomly selected days and Y_i is the commuting time on the ith of her randomly selected days.

Because the members of the population included in the sample are selected at random, the values of the observations $Y_1, \ldots, Y_n$ are themselves random. If different members of the population are chosen, their values of Y will differ. Thus, the act of random sampling means that $Y_1, \ldots, Y_n$ can be treated as random variables. Before they are sampled, $Y_1, \ldots, Y_n$ can take on many possible values; after they are sampled, a specific value is recorded for each observation.

i.i.d. draws.   Because $Y_1, \ldots, Y_n$ are randomly drawn from the same population, the marginal distribution of Y_i is the same for each $i = 1, \ldots, n$; this marginal distribution is the distribution of Y in the population being sampled. When Y_i has the same marginal distribution for $i = 1, \ldots, n$, then $Y_1, \ldots, Y_n$ are said to be **identically distributed**.

Under simple random sampling, knowing the value of Y_1 provides no information about Y_2, so the conditional distribution of Y_2 given Y_1 is the same as the marginal distribution of Y_2. In other words, under simple random sampling, Y_1 is distributed independently of $Y_2, \ldots, Y_n$.

When $Y_1, \ldots, Y_n$ are drawn from the same distribution and are independently distributed, they are said to be **independently and identically distributed**, or **i.i.d.**

Simple random sampling and i.i.d. draws are summarized in Key Concept 2.5.

The Sampling Distribution of the Sample Average

The sample average, $\overline{Y}$, of the n observations $Y_1, \ldots, Y_n$ is

$$\overline{Y} = \frac{1}{n}(Y_1 + Y_2 + \cdots + Y_n) = \frac{1}{n}\sum_{i=1}^{n} Y_i. \tag{2.43}$$

An essential concept is that the act of drawing a random sample has the effect of making the sample average $\overline{Y}$ a random variable. Because the sample was drawn at random, the value of each Y_i is random. Because $Y_1, \ldots, Y_n$ are random, their average is random. Had a different sample been drawn, then the observations and their sample average would have been different: the value of $\overline{Y}$ differs from one randomly drawn sample to the next.

For example, suppose our student commuter selected five days at random to record her commute times, then computed the average of those five times. Had she chosen five different days, she would have recorded five different times—and thus would have computed a different value of the sample average.

Because $\overline{Y}$ is random, it has a probability distribution. The distribution of $\overline{Y}$ is called the **sampling distribution** of $\overline{Y}$, because it is the probability distribution associated with possible values of $\overline{Y}$ that could be computed for different possible samples $Y_1, \ldots, Y_n$.

The sampling distribution of averages and weighted averages plays a central role in statistics and econometrics. We start our discussion of the sampling distribution of $\overline{Y}$ by computing its mean and variance under general conditions on the population distribution of Y.

Mean and variance of $\overline{Y}$. Suppose that the observations $Y_1, \ldots, Y_n$ are i.i.d., and let μ_Y and σ_Y^2 denote the mean and variance of Y_i (because the observations are i.i.d. the mean and variance is the same for all $i = 1, \ldots, n$). When $n = 2$, the mean of the sum $Y_1 + Y_2$ is given by applying Equation (2.28): $E(Y_1 + Y_2) = \mu_Y + \mu_Y = 2\mu_Y$. Thus the mean of the sample average is $E[\frac{1}{2}(Y_1 + Y_2)] = \frac{1}{2} \times 2\mu_Y = \mu_Y$. In general,

$$E(\overline{Y}) = \frac{1}{n} \sum_{i=1}^{n} E(Y_i) = \mu_Y. \qquad (2.44)$$

The variance of $\overline{Y}$ is found by applying Equation (2.37). For example, for $n = 2$, $\text{var}(Y_1 + Y_2) = 2\sigma_Y^2$, so [by applying Equation (2.31) with $a = b = \frac{1}{2}$ and $\text{cov}(Y_1, Y_2) = 0$], $\text{var}(\overline{Y}) = \frac{1}{2}\sigma_Y^2$. For general n, because $Y_1, \ldots, Y_n$ are i.i.d., Y_i and Y_j are independently distributed for $i \neq j$, so $\text{cov}(Y_i, Y_j) = 0$. Thus,

$$\text{var}(\overline{Y}) = \text{var}\left(\frac{1}{n}\sum_{i=1}^{n} Y_i\right)$$

$$= \frac{1}{n^2}\sum_{i=1}^{n}\text{var}(Y_i) + \frac{1}{n^2}\sum_{i=1}^{n}\sum_{j=1, j\neq i}^{n}\text{cov}(Y_i, Y_j) \qquad (2.45)$$

$$= \frac{\sigma_Y^2}{n}.$$

The standard deviation of $\overline{Y}$ is the square root of the variance, $\sigma_Y/\sqrt{n}$.

In summary, the mean, the variance, and the standard deviation of $\overline{Y}$ are

$$E(\overline{Y}) = \mu_Y, \qquad (2.46)$$

$$\text{var}(\overline{Y}) = \sigma_{\overline{Y}}^2 = \frac{\sigma_Y^2}{n}, \text{ and} \qquad (2.47)$$

$$\text{std.dev}(\overline{Y}) = \sigma_{\overline{Y}} = \frac{\sigma_Y}{\sqrt{n}}. \qquad (2.48)$$

These results hold whatever the distribution of Y_i is; that is, the distribution of Y_i does not need to take on a specific form, such as the normal distribution, for Equations (2.46), (2.47), and (2.48) to hold.

The notation $\sigma_{\overline{Y}}^2$ denotes the variance of the sampling distribution of the sample average $\overline{Y}$. In contrast, σ_Y^2 is the variance of each individual Y_i, that is, the variance of the population distribution from which the observation is drawn. Similarly, $\sigma_{\overline{Y}}$ denotes the standard deviation of the sampling distribution of $\overline{Y}$.

Sampling distribution of $\overline{Y}$ when Y is normally distributed.   Suppose that $Y_1, \ldots, Y_n$ are i.i.d. draws from the $N(\mu_Y, \sigma_Y^2)$ distribution. As stated following Equation (2.42), the sum of n normally distributed random variables is itself normally distributed. Because the mean of $\overline{Y}$ is μ_Y and the variance of $\overline{Y}$ is σ_Y^2/n, this means that, if $Y_1, \ldots, Y_n$ are i.i.d. draws from the $N(\mu_Y, \sigma_Y^2)$, then $\overline{Y}$ is distributed $N(\mu_Y, \sigma_Y^2/n)$.

2.6   Large-Sample Approximations to Sampling Distributions

Sampling distributions play a central role in the development of statistical and econometric procedures, so it is important to know, in a mathematical sense, what the sampling distribution of $\overline{Y}$ is. There are two approaches to characterizing sampling distributions: an "exact" approach and an "approximate" approach.

The "exact" approach entails deriving a formula for the sampling distribution that holds exactly for any value of n. The sampling distribution that exactly describes the distribution of $\overline{Y}$ for any n is called the **exact distribution** or **finite-sample distribution** of $\overline{Y}$. For example, if Y is normally distributed, and $Y_1, \ldots, Y_n$ are i.i.d., then (as discussed in Section 2.5) the exact distribution of $\overline{Y}$ is normal with mean μ_Y and variance σ_Y^2/n. Unfortunately, if the distribution of Y is not normal, then in general the exact sampling distribution of $\overline{Y}$ is very complicated and depends on the distribution of Y.

The "approximate" approach uses approximations to the sampling distribution that rely on the sample size being large. The large sample approximation to the sampling distribution is often called the **asymptotic distribution**—"asymptotic" because the approximations become exact in the limit that $n \longrightarrow \infty$. As we see in this section, these approximations can be very accurate even if the sample size is only $n = 30$ observations. Because sample sizes used in practice in econometrics typically number in the hundreds or thousands, these asymptotic distributions can be counted on to provide very good approximations to the exact sampling distribution.

This section presents the two key tools used to approximate sampling distributions when the sample size is large, the law of large numbers and the central limit theorem. The law of large numbers says that, when the sample size is large, $\overline{Y}$ will be close to μ_Y with very high probability. The central limit theorem says that, when the sample size is large, the sampling distribution of the standardized sample average, $(\overline{Y} - \mu_Y)/\sigma_{\overline{Y}}$, is approximately normal.

Although exact sampling distributions are complicated and depend on the distribution of Y, the asymptotic distributions are simple. Moreover—remarkably—the asymptotic normal distribution of $(\overline{Y} - \mu_Y)/\sigma_{\overline{Y}}$ does *not* depend on the distribution of Y. This normal approximate distribution provides enormous simplifications and underlies the theory of regression used throughout this book.

The Law of Large Numbers and Consistency

The **law of large numbers** states that, under general conditions, $\overline{Y}$ will be near μ_Y with very high probability when n is large. This is sometimes called the "law of averages." When a large number of random variables with the same mean are averaged together, the large values balance the small values and their sample average is close to their common mean.

For example, consider a simplified version of our student commuter's experiment, in which she simply records whether her commute was short (less than 20 minutes) or long. Let Y_i equal 1 if her commute was short on the ith randomly

KEY CONCEPT **2.6**	**CONVERGENCE IN PROBABILITY, CONSISTENCY, AND THE LAW OF LARGE NUMBERS**

The sample average $\overline{Y}$ converges in probability to μ_Y (or, equivalently, $\overline{Y}$ is consistent for μ_Y) if the probability that $\overline{Y}$ is in the range $\mu_Y - c$ to $\mu_Y + c$ becomes arbitrarily close to one as n increases for any constant $c > 0$. This is written as $\overline{Y} \xrightarrow{p} \mu_Y$.

The law of large numbers says that if $Y_i, i = 1, \ldots, n$ are independently and identically distributed with $E(Y_i) = \mu_Y$ and if large outliers are unlikely (technically if $\mathrm{var}(Y_i) = \sigma_Y^2 < \infty$), then $\overline{Y} \xrightarrow{p} \mu_Y$.

selected day and equal 0 if it was long. Because she used simple random sampling, $Y_1, \ldots, Y_n$ are i.i.d. Thus, $Y_i, i = 1, \ldots, n$ are i.i.d. draws of a Bernoulli random variable, where (from Table 2.2) the probability that $Y_i = 1$ is 0.78. Because the expectation of a Bernoulli random variable is its success probability, $E(Y_i) = \mu_Y = 0.78$. The sample average $\overline{Y}$ is the fraction of days in her sample in which her commute was short.

Figure 2.8 shows the sampling distribution of $\overline{Y}$ for various sample sizes n. When $n = 2$ (Figure 2.8a), $\overline{Y}$ can take on only three values: $0, \frac{1}{2}$, and 1 (neither commute was short, one was short, and both were short), none of which is particularly close to the true proportion in the population, 0.78. As n increases, however (Figures 2.8b–d), $\overline{Y}$ takes on more values and the sampling distribution becomes tightly centered on μ_Y.

The property that $\overline{Y}$ is near μ_Y with increasing probability as n increases is called **convergence in probability** or, more concisely, **consistency** (see Key Concept 2.6). The law of large numbers states that, under certain conditions, $\overline{Y}$ converges in probability to μ_Y or, equivalently, that $\overline{Y}$ is consistent for μ_Y.

The conditions for the law of large numbers that we will use in this book are that $Y_i, i = 1, \ldots, n$ are i.i.d. and that the variance of Y_i, σ_Y^2, is finite. If the data are collected by simple random sampling, then the i.i.d. assumption holds. The assumption that the variance is finite says that extremely large values of Y_i—that is, outliers—are unlikely and observed infrequently; otherwise, these large values could dominate $\overline{Y}$ and the sample average would be unreliable. This assumption is plausible for the applications in this book. For example, because there is an upper limit to our student's commuting time (she could park and walk if the traffic is dreadful), the variance of the distribution of commuting times is finite.

FIGURE 2.8   **Sampling Distribution of the Sample Average of *n* Bernoulli Random Variables**

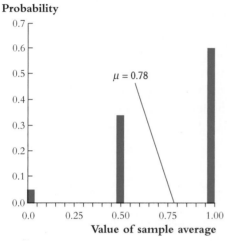

(a) *n* = 2

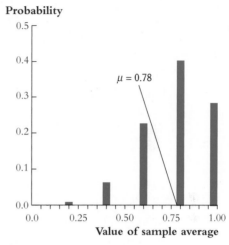

(b) *n* = 5

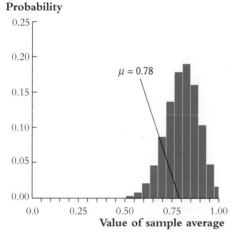

(c) *n* = 25

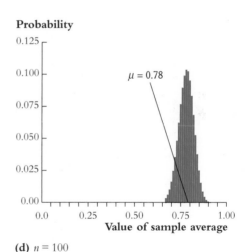

(d) *n* = 100

The distributions are the sampling distributions of $\overline{Y}$, the sample average of *n* independent Bernoulli random variables with $p = \Pr(Y_i = 1) = 0.78$ (the probability of a short commute is 78%). The variance of the sampling distribution of $\overline{Y}$ decreases as *n* gets larger, so the sampling distribution becomes more tightly concentrated around its mean $\mu = 0.78$ as the sample size *n* increases.

The Central Limit Theorem

The **central limit theorem** says that, under general conditions, the distribution of $\overline{Y}$ is well approximated by a normal distribution when n is large. Recall that the mean of $\overline{Y}$ is μ_Y and its variance is $\sigma_{\overline{Y}}^2 = \sigma_Y^2/n$. According to the central limit theorem, when n is large the distribution of $\overline{Y}$ is approximately $N(\mu_Y, \sigma_{\overline{Y}}^2)$. As discussed at the end of Section 2.5, the distribution of $\overline{Y}$ is *exactly* $N(\mu_Y, \sigma_{\overline{Y}}^2)$ when the sample is drawn from a population with the normal distribution $N(\mu_Y, \sigma_Y^2)$. The central limit theorem says that this same result is *approximately* true when n is large even if $Y_1, \ldots, Y_n$ are not themselves normally distributed.

The convergence of the distribution of $\overline{Y}$ to the bell-shaped, normal approximation can be seen (a bit) in Figure 2.8. However, because the distribution gets quite tight for large n, this requires some squinting. It would be easier to see the shape of the distribution of $\overline{Y}$ if you used a magnifying glass or had some other way to zoom in or to expand the horizontal axis of the figure.

One way to do this is to standardize $\overline{Y}$ by subtracting its mean and dividing by its standard deviation, so that it has a mean of 0 and a variance of 1. This leads to examining the distribution of the standardized version of $\overline{Y}$, $(\overline{Y} - \mu_Y)/\sigma_{\overline{Y}}$. According to the central limit theorem, this distribution should be well approximated by a $N(0, 1)$ distribution when n is large.

The distribution of the standardized average $(\overline{Y} - \mu_Y)/\sigma_{\overline{Y}}$ is plotted in Figure 2.9 for the distributions in Figure 2.8; the distributions in Figure 2.9 are exactly the same as in Figure 2.8, except that the scale of the horizontal axis is changed so that the standardized variable has a mean of 0 and a variance of 1. After this change of scale, it is easy to see that, if n is large enough, the distribution of $\overline{Y}$ is well approximated by a normal distribution.

One might ask, how large is "large enough"? That is, how large must n be for the distribution of $\overline{Y}$ to be approximately normal? The answer is "it depends." The quality of the normal approximation depends on the distribution of the underlying Y_i that make up the average. At one extreme, if the Y_i are themselves normally distributed, then $\overline{Y}$ is exactly normally distributed for all n. In contrast, when the underlying Y_i themselves have a distribution that is far from normal, then this approximation can require $n = 30$ or even more.

This point is illustrated in Figure 2.10 for a population distribution, shown in Figure 2.10a, that is quite different from the Bernoulli distribution. This distribution has a long right tail (it is "skewed" to the right). The sampling distribution of $\overline{Y}$, after centering and scaling, is shown in Figures 2.10b, c, and d for $n = 5, 25$, and 100, respectively. Although the sampling distribution is approaching the bell shape for $n = 25$, the normal approximation still has noticeable imperfections.

FIGURE 2.9   **Distribution of the Standardized Sample Average of n Bernoulli Random Variables with $p = 0.78$**

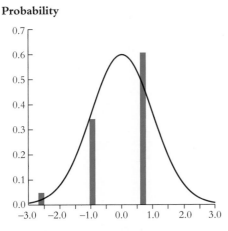

(a) $n = 2$

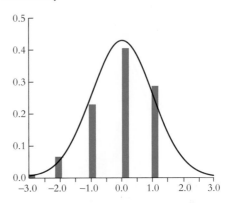

(b) $n = 5$

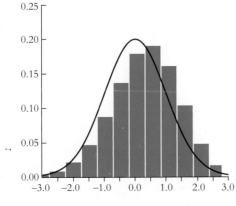

(c) $n = 25$

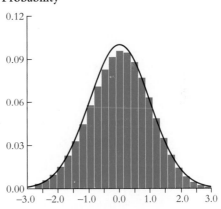

(d) $n = 100$

The sampling distribution of $\overline{Y}$ in Figure 2.8 is plotted here after standardizing $\overline{Y}$. This centers the distributions in Figure 2.8 and magnifies the scale on the horizontal axis by a factor of $\sqrt{n}$. When the sample size is large, the sampling distributions are increasingly well approximated by the normal distribution (the solid line), as predicted by the central limit theorem. The normal distribution is scaled so that the height of the distributions is approximately the same in all figures.

FIGURE 2.10 Distribution of the Standardized Sample Average of *n* Draws from a Skewed Distribution

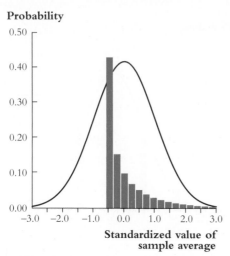

(a) $n = 1$

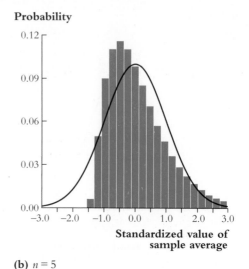

(b) $n = 5$

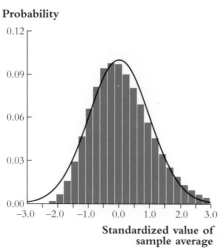

(c) $n = 25$

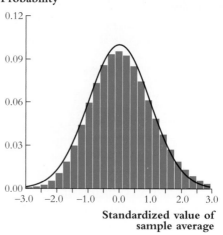

(d) $n = 100$

The figures show the sampling distribution of the standardized sample average of *n* draws from the skewed (asymmetric) population distribution shown in Figure 2.10a. When *n* is small (*n* = 5), the sampling distribution, like the population distribution, is skewed. But when *n* is large (*n* = 100), the sampling distribution is well approximated by a standard normal distribution (solid line), as predicted by the central limit theorem. The normal distribution is scaled so that the height of the distributions is approximately the same in all figures.

THE CENTRAL LIMIT THEOREM   KEY CONCEPT

2.7

Suppose that $Y_1, \ldots, Y_n$ are i.i.d. with $E(Y_i) = \mu_Y$ and $\text{var}(Y_i) = \sigma_Y^2$, where $0 < \sigma_Y^2 < \infty$. As $n \longrightarrow \infty$, the distribution of $(\overline{Y} - \mu_Y)/\sigma_{\overline{Y}}$ (where $\sigma_{\overline{Y}}^2 = \sigma_Y^2/n$) becomes arbitrarily well approximated by the standard normal distribution.

By $n = 100$, however, the normal approximation is quite good. In fact, for $n \geq 100$ the normal approximation to the distribution of $\overline{Y}$ typically is very good for a wide variety of population distributions.

The central limit theorem is a remarkable result. While the "small n" distributions of $\overline{Y}$ in parts b and c of Figures 2.9 and 2.10 are complicated and quite different from each other, the "large n" distributions in Figures 2.9d and 2.10d are simple and, amazingly, have a similar shape. Because the distribution of $\overline{Y}$ approaches the normal as n grows large, $\overline{Y}$ is said to be **asymptotically normally distributed**.

The convenience of the normal approximation, combined with its wide applicability because of the central limit theorem, makes it a key underpinning of modern applied econometrics. The central limit theorem is summarized in Key Concept 2.7.

Summary

1. The probabilities with which a random variable takes on different values are summarized by the cumulative distribution function, the probability distribution function (for discrete random variables), and the probability density function (for continuous random variables).
2. The expected value of a random variable Y (also called its mean, μ_Y), denoted $E(Y)$, is its probability-weighted average value. The variance of Y is $\sigma_Y^2 = E[(Y - \mu_Y)^2]$, and the standard deviation of Y is the square root of its variance.
3. The joint probabilities for two random variables X and Y are summarized by their joint probability distribution. The conditional probability distribution of Y given $X = x$ is the probability distribution of Y, conditional on X taking on the value x.
4. A normally distributed random variable has the bell-shaped probability density in Figure 2.5. To calculate a probability associated with a normal random variable,

first standardize the variable, then use the standard normal cumulative distribution tabulated in Appendix Table 1.

5. Simple random sampling produces n random observations $Y_1, \ldots, Y_n$ that are independently and identically distributed (i.i.d.).

6. The sample average, $\overline{Y}$, varies from one randomly chosen sample to the next and thus is a random variable with a sampling distribution. If $Y_1, \ldots, Y_n$, are i.i.d., then:

a. the sampling distribution of $\overline{Y}$ has mean μ_Y and variance $\sigma_{\overline{Y}}^2 = \sigma_Y^2/n$;

b. the law of large numbers says that $\overline{Y}$ converges in probability to μ_Y; and

c. the central limit theorem says that the standardized version of $\overline{Y}$, $(\overline{Y} - \mu_Y)/\sigma_{\overline{Y}}$, has a standard normal distribution [$N(0, 1)$ distribution] when n is large.

Key Terms

outcomes (16)
probability (16)
sample space (17)
event (17)
discrete random variable (17)
continuous random variable (17)
probability distribution (17)
cumulative probability distribution (17)
cumulative distribution function
   (c.d.f.) (18)
Bernoulli random variable (18)
Bernoulli distribution (18)
probability density function (p.d.f.) (19)
density function (19)
density (19)
expected value (21)
expectation (21)
mean (21)
variance (22)
standard deviation (22)
moments of a distribution (25)
skewness (25)

kurtosis (25)
outlier (25)
leptokurtic (26)
r^{th} moment (27)
joint probability distribution (27)
marginal probability distribution (28)
conditional distribution (28)
conditional expectation (30)
conditional mean (30)
law of iterated expectations (30)
conditional variance (31)
independence (32)
covariance (32)
correlation (33)
uncorrelated (33)
normal distribution (37)
standard normal distribution (37)
standardize a variable (37)
multivariate normal distribution (39)
bivariate normal distribution (39)
chi-squared distribution (41)
Student t distribution (42)

Review the Concepts

2.1 Examples of random variables used in this chapter included: (a) the gender of the next person you meet, (b) the number of times a computer crashes, (c) the time it takes to commute to school, (d) whether the computer you are assigned in the library is new or old, and (e) whether it is raining or not. Explain why each can be thought of as random.

2.2 Suppose that the random variables X and Y are independent and you know their distributions. Explain why knowing the value of X tells you nothing about the value of Y.

2.3 Suppose that X denotes the amount of rainfall in your hometown during a given month and Y denotes the number of children born in Los Angeles during the same month. Are X and Y independent? Explain.

2.4 An econometrics class has 80 students, and the mean student weight is 145 lbs. A random sample of 4 students is selected from the class and their average weight is calculated. Will the average weight of the students in the sample equal 145 lbs.? Why or why not? Use this example to explain why the sample average, $\overline{Y}$, is a random variable.

2.5 Suppose that $Y_1, \ldots, Y_n$ are i.i.d. random variables with a $N(1, 4)$ distribution. Sketch the probability density of $\overline{Y}$ when $n = 2$. Repeat this for $n = 10$ and $n = 100$. In words, describe how the densities differ. What is the relationship between your answer and the law of large numbers?

2.6 Suppose that $Y_1, \ldots, Y_n$ are i.i.d. random variables with the probability distribution given in Figure 2.10a. You want to calculate $\Pr(\overline{Y} \leq 0.1)$. Would it be reasonable to use the normal approximation if $n = 5$? What about $n = 25$ or $n = 100$? Explain.

2.7 Y is a random variable with $\mu_Y = 0$, $\sigma_Y = 1$, skewness $= 0$, and kurtosis $= 100$. Sketch a hypothetical probability distribution of Y. Explain why n random variables drawn from this distribution might have some large outliers.

Exercises

2.1 Let Y denote the number of "heads" that occur when two coins are tossed.

    a. Derive the probability distribution of Y.

    b. Derive the cumulative probability distribution of Y.

    c. Derive the mean and variance of Y.

2.2 Use the probability distribution given in Table 2.2 to compute (a) $E(Y)$ and $E(X)$; (b) σ_X^2 and σ_Y^2; and (c) σ_{XY} and corr(X,Y).

2.3 Using the random variables X and Y from Table 2.2, consider two new random variables $W = 3 + 6X$ and $V = 20 - 7Y$. Compute (a) $E(W)$ and $E(V)$; (b) σ_W^2 and σ_V^2; and (c) σ_{WV} and corr(W,V).

2.4 Suppose X is a Bernoulli random variable with $P(X = 1) = p$.

    a. Show $E(X^3) = p$.

    b. Show $E(X^k) = p$ for $k > 0$.

    c. Suppose that $p = 0.3$. Compute the mean, variance, skewness, and kurtosis of X. (*Hint:* You might find it helpful to use the formulas given in Exercise 2.21.)

2.5 In September, Seattle's daily high temperature has a mean of 70°F and a standard deviation of 7°F. What is the mean, standard deviation, and variance in °C?

2.6 The following table gives the joint probability distribution between employment status and college graduation among those either employed or looking for work (unemployed) in the working age U.S. population, based on the 1990 U.S. Census.

Joint Distribution of Employment Status and College Graduation in the U.S. Population Aged 25–64, 1990			
	Unemployed ($Y = 0$)	Employed ($Y = 1$)	Total
Non-college grads ($X = 0$)	0.045	0.709	0.754
College grads ($X = 1$)	0.005	0.241	0.246
Total	0.050	0.950	1.000

a. Compute $E(Y)$.

b. The unemployment rate is the fraction of the labor force that is unemployed. Show that the unemployment rate is given by $1 - E(Y)$.

c. Calculate $E(Y|X = 1)$ and $E(Y|X = 0)$.

d. Calculate the unemployment rate for (i) college graduates and (ii)non-college graduates.

e. A randomly selected member of this population reports being unemployed. What is the probability that this worker is a college graduate? A non-college graduate?

f. Are educational achievement and employment status independent? Explain.

2.7 In a given population of two-earner male/female couples, male earnings have a mean of $40,000 per year and a standard deviation of $12,000. Female earnings have a mean of $45,000 per year and a standard deviation of $18,000. The correlation between male and female earnings for a couple is 0.80. Let C denote the combined earnings for a randomly selected couple.

a. What is the mean of C?

b. What is the covariance between male and female earnings?

c. What is the standard deviation of C?

d. Convert the answers to (a)–(c) from $ (dollars) to € (euros).

2.8 The random variable Y has a mean of 1 and a variance of 4. Let $Z = \frac{1}{2}(Y - 1)$. Show that $\mu_Z = 0$ and $\sigma_Z^2 = 1$.

2.9 X and Y are discrete random variables with the following joint distribution:

		Value of Y				
		14	22	30	40	65
	1	0.02	0.05	0.10	0.03	0.01
Value of X	**5**	0.17	0.15	0.05	0.02	0.01
	8	0.02	0.03	0.15	0.10	0.09

That is, $\Pr(X = 1, Y = 14) = 0.02$, and so forth.

a. Calculate the probability distribution, mean, and variance of Y.

b. Calculate the probability distribution, mean, and variance of Y given $X = 8$.

c. Calculate the covariance and correlation between X and Y.

2.10 Compute the following probabilities:

   a. If Y is distributed $N(1, 4)$, find $\Pr(Y \leq 3)$.

   b. If Y is distributed $N(3, 9)$, find $\Pr(Y > 0)$.

   c. If Y is distributed $N(50, 25)$, find $\Pr(40 \leq Y \leq 52)$.

   d. If Y is distributed $N(5, 2)$, find $\Pr(6 \leq Y \leq 8)$.

2.11 Compute the following probabilities:

   a. If Y is distributed χ_4^2, find $\Pr(Y \leq 7.78)$.

   b. If Y is distributed χ_{10}^2, find $\Pr(Y > 18.31)$.

   c. If Y is distributed $F_{10,\infty}$, find $\Pr(Y > 1.83)$.

   d. Why are the answers to (b) and (c) the same?

   e. If Y is distributed χ_1^2, find $\Pr(Y \leq 1.0)$. (*Hint:* Use the definition of the χ_1^2 distribution.)

2.12 Compute the following probabilities:

   a. If Y is distributed t_{15}, find $\Pr(Y > 1.75)$.

   b. If Y is distributed t_{90}, find $\Pr(-1.99 \leq Y \leq 1.99)$.

   c. If Y is distributed $N(0, 1)$, find $\Pr(-1.99 \leq Y \leq 1.99)$.

   d. Why are the answers to (b) and (c) approximately the same?

   e. If Y is distributed $F_{7,4}$, find $\Pr(Y > 4.12)$.

   f. If Y is distributed $F_{7,120}$, find $\Pr(Y > 2.79)$.

2.13 X is a Bernoulli random variable with $\Pr(X = 1) = 0.99$, Y is distributed $N(0, 1)$, and W is distributed $N(0, 100)$. Let $S = XY + (1 - X)W$. (That is, $S = Y$ when $X = 1$, and $S = W$ when $X = 0$.)

   a. Show that $E(Y^2) = 1$ and $E(W^2) = 100$.

   b. Show that $E(Y^3) = 0$ and $E(W^3) = 0$. (*Hint:* What is the skewness for a symmetric distribution?)

   c. Show that $E(Y^4) = 3$ and $E(W^4) = 3 \times 100^2$. (*Hint:* Use the fact that the kurtosis is 3 for a normal distribution.)

   d. Derive $E(S)$, $E(S^2)$, $E(S^3)$ and $E(S^4)$. (*Hint:* Use the law of iterated expectations conditioning on $X = 0$ and $X = 1$.)

   e. Derive the skewness and kurtosis for S.

2.14 In a population $\mu_Y = 100$ and $\sigma_Y^2 = 43$. Use the central limit theorem to answer the following questions:

a. In a random sample of size $n = 100$, find $\Pr(\overline{Y} \leq 101)$.

b. In a random sample of size $n = 165$, find $\Pr(\overline{Y} > 98)$.

c. In a random sample of size $n = 64$, find $\Pr(101 \leq \overline{Y} \leq 103)$.

2.15 Suppose Y_i, $i = 1, 2, \ldots, n$ are i.i.d. random variables, each distributed $N(10, 4)$.

a. Compute $\Pr(9.6 \leq \overline{Y} \leq 10.4)$ when (i) $n = 20$, (ii) $n = 100$, and (iii) $n = 1{,}000$.

b. Suppose c is a positive number. Show that $\Pr(10 - c \leq \overline{Y} \leq 10 + c)$ becomes close to 1.0 as n grows large.

c. Use your answer in (b) to argue that $\overline{Y}$ converges in probability to 10.

2.16 Y is distributed $N(5, 100)$ and you want to calculate $\Pr(Y < 3.6)$. Unfortunately, you do not have your textbook and do not have access to a normal probability table like Appendix Table 1. However, you do have your computer and a computer program that can generate i.i.d. draws from the $N(5, 100)$ distribution. Explain how you can use your computer to compute an accurate approximation for $\Pr(Y < 3.6)$.

2.17 Y_i, $i = 1, \ldots, n$, are i.i.d. Bernoulli random variables with $p = 0.4$. Let $\overline{Y}$ denote the sample mean.

a. Use the central limit to compute approximations for

i. $\Pr(\overline{Y} \geq 0.43)$ when $n = 100$.

ii. $\Pr(\overline{Y} \leq 0.37)$ when $n = 400$.

b. How large would n need to be to ensure that $\Pr(0.39 \leq \overline{Y} \leq 0.41) \geq 0.95$? (Use the central limit theorem to compute an approximate answer.)

2.18 In any year, the weather can inflict storm damage to a home. From year to year, the damage is random. Let Y denote the dollar value of damage in any given year. Suppose that in 95% of the years $Y = \$0$, but in 5% of the years $Y = \$20{,}000$.

a. What is the mean and standard deviation of the damage in any year?

b. Consider an "insurance pool" of 100 people whose homes are sufficiently dispersed so that, in any year, the damage to different homes can be viewed as independently distributed random variables. Let $\overline{Y}$ denote the average damage to these 100 homes in a year. (i) What is the expected value of the average damage $\overline{Y}$? (ii) What is the probability that $\overline{Y}$ exceeds \$2000?

2.19 Consider two random variables X and Y. Suppose that Y takes on k values $y_1, \ldots, y_k$, and that X takes on l values $x_1, \ldots, x_l$.

    a. Show that $\Pr(Y = y_j) = \sum_{i=1}^{l} \Pr(Y = y_j | X = x_i)\Pr(X = x_i)$. [*Hint:* Use the definition of $\Pr(Y = y_j | X = x_i)$.]

    b. Use your answer to (a) to verify Equation (2.19).

    c. Suppose that X and Y are independent. Show that $\sigma_{XY} = 0$ and $\text{corr}(X,Y) = 0$.

2.20 Consider three random variables X, Y, and Z. Suppose that Y takes on k values $y_1, \ldots, y_k$, that X takes on l values $x_1, \ldots, x_l$, and that Z takes on m values $z_1, \ldots, z_m$. The joint probability distribution of X, Y, Z is $\Pr(X = x, Y = y, Z = z)$, and the conditional probability distribution of Y given X and Z is $\Pr(Y = y | X = x, Z = z) = \frac{\Pr(Y = y, X = x, Z = z)}{\Pr(X = x, Z = z)}$.

    a. Explain how the marginal probability that $Y = y$ can be calculated from the joint probability distribution. [*Hint:* This is a generalization of Equation (2.16).]

    b. Show that $E(Y) = E[E(Y|X,Z)]$. [*Hint:* This is a generalization of Equations (2.19) and (2.20).]

2.21 X is a random variable with moments $E(X)$, $E(X^2)$, $E(X^3)$, and so forth.

    a. Show $E(X - \mu)^3 = E(X^3) - 3[E(X^2)][E(X)] + 2[E(X)]^3$.

    b. Show $E(X - \mu)^4 = E(X^4) - 4[E(X)][E(X^3)] + 6[E(X)]^2[E(X^2)] - 3[E(X)]^4$.

2.22 Suppose you have some money to invest—for simplicity, \$1—and you are planning to put a fraction w into a stock market mutual fund and the rest, $1 - w$, into a bond mutual fund. Suppose that \$1 invested in a stock fund yields R_s after one year and that \$1 invested in a bond fund yields R_b, that R_s is random with mean 0.08 (8%) and standard deviation 0.07, and that R_b is random with mean 0.05 (5%) and standard deviation 0.04. The correlation between R_s and R_b is 0.25. If you place a fraction w of your money in the stock fund and the rest, $1 - w$, in the bond fund, then the return on your investment is $R = wR_s + (1 - w)R_b$.

    a. Suppose that $w = 0.5$. Compute the mean and standard deviation of R.

    b. Suppose that $w = 0.75$. Compute the mean and standard deviation of R.

    c. What value of w makes the mean of R as large as possible? What is the standard deviation of R for this value of w?

d. (Harder) What is the value of w that minimizes the standard deviation of R? (You can show this using a graph, algebra, or calculus.)

2.23 This exercise provides an example of a pair of random variables X and Y for which the conditional mean of Y given X depends on X but $\text{corr}(X,Y) = 0$. Let X and Z be two independently distributed standard normal random variables, and let $Y = X^2 + Z$.

    a. Show that $E(Y|X) = X^2$.

    b. Show that $\mu_Y = 1$.

    c. Show that $E(XY) = 0$. (*Hint:* Use the fact that the odd moments of a standard normal random variable are all zero.)

    d. Show that $\text{cov}(X, Y) = 0$ and thus $\text{corr}(X, Y) = 0$.

2.24 Suppose Y_i is distributed i.i.d. $N(0, \sigma^2)$ for $i = 1, 2, \ldots, n$.

    a Show that $E(Y_i^2/\sigma^2) = 1$.

    b. Show that $W = \frac{1}{\sigma^2}\sum_{i=1}^{n}Y_i^2$ is distributed χ_n^2.

    c. Show that $E(W) = n$. [*Hint:* Use your answer to (a).]

    d. Show that $V = \dfrac{Y_1}{\sqrt{\dfrac{\sum_{i=2}^{n}Y_i^2}{n-1}}}$ is distributed t_{n-1}.

APPENDIX
2.1 | Derivation of Results in Key Concept 2.3

This appendix derives the equations in Key Concept 2.3.

    Equation (2.29) follows from the definition of the expectation.

    To derive Equation (2.30), use the definition of the variance to write, $\text{var}(a + bY) = E\{[a + bY - E(a + bY)]^2\} = E\{[b(Y - \mu_Y)]^2\} = b^2 E[(Y - \mu_Y)^2] = b^2\sigma_Y^2$.

    To derive Equation (2.31), use the definition of the variance to write

$$
\begin{aligned}
\text{var}(aX + bY) &= E\{[(aX + bY) - (a\mu_X + b\mu_Y)]^2\} \\
&= E\{[a(X - \mu_X) + b(Y - \mu_Y)]^2\} \\
&= E[a^2(X - \mu_X)^2] + 2E[ab(X - \mu_X)(Y - \mu_Y)] \\
&\quad + E[b^2(Y - \mu_Y)^2] \\
&= a^2\text{var}(X) + 2ab\,\text{cov}(X,Y) + b^2\text{var}(Y) \\
&= a^2\sigma_X^2 + 2ab\sigma_{XY} + b^2\sigma_Y^2, \tag{2.49}
\end{aligned}
$$

where the second equality follows by collecting terms, the third equality follows by expanding the quadratic, and the fourth equality follows by the definition of the variance and covariance.

To derive Equation (2.32), write $E(Y^2) = E\{[(Y - \mu_Y) + \mu_Y]^2\} = E[(Y - \mu_Y)^2] + 2\mu_Y E(Y - \mu_Y) + \mu_Y^2 = \sigma_Y^2 + \mu_Y^2$ because $E(Y - \mu_Y) = 0$.

To derive Equation (2.33), use the definition of the covariance to write

$$
\begin{aligned}
\text{cov}(a + bX + cV, Y) &= E\{[a + bX + cV - E(a + bX + cV)][Y - \mu_Y]\} \\
&= E\{[b(X - \mu_X) + c(V - \mu_V)][Y - \mu_Y]\} \\
&= E\{[b(X - \mu_X)][Y - \mu_Y]\} + E\{[c(V - \mu_V)][Y - \mu_Y]\} \\
&= b\sigma_{XY} + c\sigma_{VY},
\end{aligned}
\tag{2.50}
$$

which is Equation (2.33).

To derive Equation (2.34), write $E(XY) = E\{[(X - \mu_X) + \mu_X][(Y - \mu_Y) + \mu_Y]\} = E[(X - \mu_X)(Y - \mu_Y)] + \mu_X E(Y - \mu_Y) + \mu_Y E(X - \mu_X) + \mu_X \mu_Y = \sigma_{XY} + \mu_X \mu_Y$.

We now prove the correlation inequality in Equation (2.35); that is, $|\text{corr}(X, Y)| \leq 1$. Let $a = -\sigma_{XY}/\sigma_X^2$ and $b = 1$. Applying Equation (2.31), we have that

$$
\begin{aligned}
\text{var}(aX + Y) &= a^2 \sigma_X^2 + \sigma_Y^2 + 2a\sigma_{XY} \\
&= (-\sigma_{XY}/\sigma_X^2)^2 \sigma_X^2 + \sigma_Y^2 + 2(-\sigma_{XY}/\sigma_X^2)\sigma_{XY} \\
&= \sigma_Y^2 - \sigma_{XY}^2/\sigma_X^2.
\end{aligned}
\tag{2.51}
$$

Because $\text{var}(aX + Y)$ is a variance, it cannot be negative, so from the final line of Equation (2.51) it must be that $\sigma_Y^2 - \sigma_{XY}^2/\sigma_X^2 \geq 0$. Rearranging this inequality yields

$$
\sigma_{XY}^2 \leq \sigma_X^2 \sigma_Y^2 \quad \text{(covariance inequality)}.
\tag{2.52}
$$

The covariance inequality implies that $\sigma_{XY}^2/(\sigma_X^2 \sigma_Y^2) \leq 1$ or, equivalently, $|\sigma_{XY}/(\sigma_X \sigma_Y)| \leq 1$, which (using the definition of the correlation) proves the correlation inequality, $|\text{corr}(X,Y)| \leq 1$.

| # Review of Statistics

Statistics is the science of using data to learn about the world around us. Statistical tools help to answer questions about unknown characteristics of distributions in populations of interest. For example, what is the mean of the distribution of earnings of recent college graduates? Do mean earnings differ for men and women and, if so, by how much?

These questions relate to the distribution of earnings in the population of workers. One way to answer these questions would be to perform an exhaustive survey of the population of workers, measuring the earnings of each worker and thus finding the population distribution of earnings. In practice, however, such a comprehensive survey would be extremely expensive. The only comprehensive survey of the U.S. population is the decennial census. The 2000 U.S. Census cost $10 billion, and the process of designing the census forms, managing and conducting the surveys, and compiling and analyzing the data takes ten years. Despite this extraordinary commitment, many members of the population slip through the cracks and are not surveyed. Thus a different, more practical approach is needed.

The key insight of statistics is that one can learn about a population distribution by selecting a random sample from that population. Rather than survey the entire U.S. population, we might survey, say, 1000 members of the population, selected at random by simple random sampling. Using statistical methods, we can use this sample to reach tentative conclusions—to draw statistical inferences—about characteristics of the full population.

Three types of statistical methods are used throughout econometrics: estimation, hypothesis testing, and confidence intervals. Estimation entails computing a "best guess" numerical value for an unknown characteristic of a population distribution, such as its mean, from a sample of data. Hypothesis testing entails formulating a specific hypothesis about the population, then using sample evidence to decide whether it is true. Confidence intervals use a set of data to estimate an interval or range for an unknown population characteristic. Sections 3.1, 3.2, and 3.3 review estimation, hypothesis testing, and confidence intervals in the context of statistical inference about an unknown population mean.

Most of the interesting questions in economics involve relationships between two or more variables or comparisons between different populations. For example, is there a gap between the mean earnings for male and female recent college graduates? In Section 3.4, the methods for learning about the mean of a single population in Sections 3.1–3.3 are extended to compare means in two different populations. Section 3.5 discusses how the methods for comparing the means of two populations can be used to estimate causal effects in experiments. Sections 3.2–3.5 focus on the use of the normal distribution for performing hypothesis tests and for constructing confidence intervals when the sample size is large. In some special circumstances, hypothesis tests and confidence intervals can be based on the Student t distribution instead of the normal distribution; these special circumstances are discussed in Section 3.6. The chapter concludes with a discussion of the sample correlation and scatterplots in Section 3.7.

3.1 Estimation of the Population Mean

Suppose you want to know the mean value of Y (μ_Y) in a population, such as the mean earnings of women recently graduated from college. A natural way to estimate this mean is to compute the sample average $\overline{Y}$ from a sample of n independently and identically distributed (i.i.d.) observations, $Y_1, \ldots, Y_n$ (recall that $Y_1, \ldots, Y_n$ are i.i.d. if they are collected by simple random sampling). This section discusses estimation of μ_Y and the properties of $\overline{Y}$ as an estimator of μ_Y.

ESTIMATORS AND ESTIMATES	KEY CONCEPT
An **estimator** is a function of a sample of data to be drawn randomly from a population. An **estimate** is the numerical value of the estimator when it is actually computed using data from a specific sample. An estimator is a random variable because of randomness in selecting the sample, while an estimate is a nonrandom number.	3.1

Estimators and Their Properties

Estimators.   The sample average $\overline{Y}$ is a natural way to estimate μ_Y, but it is not the only way. For example, another way to estimate μ_Y is simply to use the first observation, Y_1. Both $\overline{Y}$ and Y_1 are functions of the data that are designed to estimate μ_Y; using the terminology in Key Concept 3.1, both are estimators of μ_Y. When evaluated in repeated samples, $\overline{Y}$ and Y_1 take on different values (they produce different estimates) from one sample to the next. Thus, the estimators $\overline{Y}$ and Y_1 both have sampling distributions. There are, in fact, many estimators of μ_Y, of which $\overline{Y}$ and Y_1 are two examples.

There are many possible estimators, so what makes one estimator "better" than another? Because estimators are random variables, this question can be phrased more precisely: What are desirable characteristics of the sampling distribution of an estimator? In general, we would like an estimator that gets as close as possible to the unknown true value, at least in some average sense; in other words, we would like the sampling distribution of an estimator to be as tightly centered on the unknown value as possible. This observation leads to three specific desirable characteristics of an estimator: unbiasedness (a lack of bias), consistency, and efficiency.

Unbiasedness.   Suppose you evaluate an estimator many times over repeated randomly drawn samples. It is reasonable to hope that, on average, you would get the right answer. Thus a desirable property of an estimator is that the mean of its sampling distribution equals μ_Y; if so, the estimator is said to be unbiased.

To state this mathematically, let $\hat{\mu}_Y$ denote some estimator of μ_Y, such as $\overline{Y}$ or Y_1. The estimator $\hat{\mu}_Y$ is unbiased if $E(\hat{\mu}_Y) = \mu_Y$, where $E(\hat{\mu}_Y)$ is the mean of the sampling distribution of $\hat{\mu}_Y$; otherwise, $\hat{\mu}_Y$ is biased.

KEY CONCEPT

3.2

BIAS, CONSISTENCY, AND EFFICIENCY

Let $\hat{\mu}_Y$ be an estimator of μ_Y. Then:

- The **bias** of $\hat{\mu}_Y$ is $E(\hat{\mu}_Y) - \mu_Y$.

- $\hat{\mu}_Y$ is an **unbiased estimator** of μ_Y if $E(\hat{\mu}_Y) = \mu_Y$.

- $\hat{\mu}_Y$ is a **consistent estimator** of μ_Y if $\hat{\mu}_Y \xrightarrow{p} \mu_Y$.

- Let $\tilde{\mu}_Y$ be another estimator of μ_Y, and suppose that both $\hat{\mu}_Y$ and $\tilde{\mu}_Y$ are unbiased. Then $\hat{\mu}_Y$ is said to be more **efficient** than $\tilde{\mu}_Y$ if $\text{var}(\hat{\mu}_Y) < \text{var}(\tilde{\mu}_Y)$.

Consistency.   Another desirable property of an estimator $\hat{\mu}_Y$ is that, when the sample size is large, the uncertainty about the value of μ_Y arising from random variations in the sample is very small. Stated more precisely, a desirable property of $\hat{\mu}_Y$ is that the probability that it is within a small interval of the true value μ_Y approaches 1 as the sample size increases, that is, $\hat{\mu}_Y$ is consistent for μ_Y (Key Concept 2.6).

Variance and efficiency   Suppose you have two candidate estimators, $\hat{\mu}_Y$ and $\tilde{\mu}_Y$, both of which are unbiased. How might you choose between them? One way to do so is to choose the estimator with the tightest sampling distribution. This suggests choosing between $\hat{\mu}_Y$ and $\tilde{\mu}_Y$ by picking the estimator with the smallest variance. If $\hat{\mu}_Y$ has a smaller variance than $\tilde{\mu}_Y$, then $\hat{\mu}_Y$ is said to be more efficient than $\tilde{\mu}_Y$. The terminology "efficiency" stems from the notion that, if $\hat{\mu}_Y$ has a smaller variance than $\tilde{\mu}_Y$, then it uses the information in the data more efficiently than does $\tilde{\mu}_Y$.

Bias, consistency, and efficiency are summarized in Key Concept 3.2.

Properties of $\overline{Y}$

How does $\overline{Y}$ fare as an estimator of μ_Y when judged by the three criteria of bias, consistency, and efficiency?

Bias and consistency.   The sampling distribution of $\overline{Y}$ has already been examined in Sections 2.5 and 2.6. As shown in Section 2.5, $E(\overline{Y}) = \mu_Y$, so $\overline{Y}$ is an unbiased estimator of μ_Y. Similarly, the law of large numbers (Key Concept 2.6) states that $\overline{Y} \xrightarrow{p} \mu_Y$, that is, $\overline{Y}$ is consistent.

Efficiency. What can be said about the efficiency of $\overline{Y}$? Because efficiency entails a comparison of estimators, we need to specify the estimator or estimators to which $\overline{Y}$ is to be compared.

We start by comparing the efficiency of $\overline{Y}$ to the estimator Y_1. Because $Y_1, \ldots, Y_n$ are i.i.d., the mean of the sampling distribution of Y_1 is $E(Y_1) = \mu_Y$; thus Y_1 is an unbiased estimator of μ_Y. Its variance is $\text{var}(Y_1) = \sigma_Y^2$. From Section 2.5, the variance of $\overline{Y}$ is σ_Y^2/n. Thus, for $n \geq 2$, the variance of $\overline{Y}$ is less than the variance of Y_1; that is, $\overline{Y}$ is a more efficient estimator than Y_1 so, according to the criterion of efficiency, $\overline{Y}$ should be used instead of Y_1. The estimator Y_1 might strike you as an obviously poor estimator—why would you go to the trouble of collecting a sample of n observations only to throw away all but the first?—and the concept of efficiency provides a formal way to show that $\overline{Y}$ is a more desirable estimator than Y_1.

What about a less obviously poor estimator? Consider the weighted average in which the observations are alternately weighted by $\frac{1}{2}$ and $\frac{3}{2}$:

$$\tilde{Y} = \frac{1}{n}\left(\frac{1}{2}Y_1 + \frac{3}{2}Y_2 + \frac{1}{2}Y_3 + \frac{3}{2}Y_4 + \cdots + \frac{1}{2}Y_{n-1} + \frac{3}{2}Y_n\right), \tag{3.1}$$

where the number of observations n is assumed to be even for convenience. The mean of $\tilde{Y}$ is μ_Y and its variance is $\text{var}(\tilde{Y}) = 1.25\sigma_Y^2/n$ (Exercise 3.11). Thus $\tilde{Y}$ is unbiased and, because $\text{var}(\tilde{Y}) \longrightarrow 0$ as $n \longrightarrow \infty$, $\tilde{Y}$ is consistent. However, $\tilde{Y}$ has a larger variance than $\overline{Y}$. Thus $\overline{Y}$ is more efficient than $\tilde{Y}$.

The estimators $\overline{Y}, Y_1$, and $\tilde{Y}$ have a common mathematical structure: They are weighted averages of $Y_1, \ldots, Y_n$. The comparisons in the previous two paragraphs show that the weighted averages Y_1 and $\tilde{Y}$ have larger variances than $\overline{Y}$. In fact, these conclusions reflect a more general result: $\overline{Y}$ is the most efficient estimator of *all* unbiased estimators that are weighted averages of $Y_1, \ldots, Y_n$. Said differently, $\overline{Y}$ is the **B**est **L**inear **U**nbiased **E**stimator (**BLUE**); that is, it is the most efficient (best) estimator among all estimators that are unbiased and are linear functions of $Y_1, \ldots, Y_n$. This result is stated in Key Concept 3.3 and is proven in Chapter 5.

$\overline{Y}$ is the least squares estimator of μ_Y. The sample average $\overline{Y}$ provides the best fit to the data in the sense that the average squared differences between the observations and $\overline{Y}$ are the smallest of all possible estimators.

KEY CONCEPT

3.3

EFFICIENCY OF $\overline{Y}$: $\overline{Y}$ IS BLUE

Let $\hat{\mu}_Y$ be an estimator of μ_Y that is a weighted average of $Y_1, \ldots, Y_n$, that is, $\hat{\mu}_Y = \frac{1}{n}\sum_{i=1}^{n}a_iY_i$, where $a_1, \ldots, a_n$ are nonrandom constants. If $\hat{\mu}_Y$ is unbiased, then $\text{var}(\overline{Y}) < \text{var}(\hat{\mu}_Y)$ unless $\hat{\mu}_Y = \overline{Y}$. Thus $\overline{Y}$ is the Best Linear Unbiased Estimator (BLUE); that is, $\overline{Y}$ is the most efficient estimator of μ_Y among all unbiased estimators that are weighted averages of $Y_1, \ldots, Y_n$.

Consider the problem of finding the estimator m that minimizes

$$\sum_{i=1}^{n}(Y_i - m)^2, \tag{3.2}$$

which is a measure of the total squared gap or distance between the estimator m and the sample points. Because m is an estimator of $E(Y)$, you can think of it as a prediction of the value of Y_i, so that the gap $Y_i - m$ can be thought of as a prediction mistake. The sum of squared gaps in expression (3.2) can be thought of as the sum of squared prediction mistakes.

The estimator m that minimizes the sum of squared gaps $Y_i - m$ in expression (3.2) is called the **least squares estimator**. One can imagine using trial and error to solve the least squares problem: Try many values of m until you are satisfied that you have the value that makes expression (3.2) as small as possible. Alternatively, as is done in Appendix 3.2, you can use algebra or calculus to show that choosing $m = \overline{Y}$ minimizes the sum of squared gaps in expression (3.2), so that $\overline{Y}$ is the least squares estimator of μ_Y.

The Importance of Random Sampling

We have assumed that $Y_1, \ldots, Y_n$ are i.i.d. draws, such as those that would be obtained from simple random sampling. This assumption is important because nonrandom sampling can result in $\overline{Y}$ being biased. Suppose that, to estimate the monthly national unemployment rate, a statistical agency adopts a sampling scheme in which interviewers survey working-age adults sitting in city parks at 10:00 A.M. on the second Wednesday of the month. Because most employed people are at work at that hour (not sitting in the park!), the unemployed are overly

Landon Wins!

Shortly before the 1936 Presidential election, the *Literary Gazette* published a poll indicating that Alf M. Landon would defeat the incumbent, Franklin D. Roosevelt, by a landslide—57% to 43%. The *Gazette* was right that the election was a landslide, but it was wrong about the winner: Roosevelt won by 59% to 41%!

How could the *Gazette* have made such a big mistake? The *Gazette*'s sample was chosen from telephone records and automobile registration files. But in 1936 many households did not have cars or telephones, and those that did tended to be richer—and were also more likely to be Republican. Because the telephone survey did not sample randomly from the population but instead undersampled Democrats, the estimator was biased and the *Gazette* made an embarrassing mistake.

Do you think surveys conducted over the Internet might have a similar problem with bias?

represented in the sample, and an estimate of the unemployment rate based on this sampling plan would be biased. This bias arises because this sampling scheme overrepresents, or oversamples, the unemployed members of the population. This example is fictitious, but the "Landon Wins!" box gives a real-world example of biases introduced by sampling that is not entirely random.

It is important to design sample selection schemes in a way that minimizes bias. Appendix 3.1 includes a discussion of what the Bureau of Labor Statistics actually does when it conducts the U.S. Current Population Survey (CPS), the survey it uses to estimate the monthly U.S. unemployment rate.

3.2 Hypothesis Tests Concerning the Population Mean

Many hypotheses about the world around us can be phrased as yes/no questions. Do the mean hourly earnings of recent U.S. college graduates equal $20/hour? Are mean earnings the same for male and female college graduates? Both these questions embody specific hypotheses about the population distribution of earnings. The statistical challenge is to answer these questions based on a sample of evidence. This section describes **testing hypotheses** concerning the population mean (Does the population mean of hourly earnings equal $20?). Hypothesis tests involving two populations (Are mean earnings the same for men and women?) are taken up in Section 3.4.

Null and Alternative Hypotheses

The starting point of statistical hypotheses testing is specifying the hypothesis to be tested, called the **null hypothesis**. Hypothesis testing entails using data to compare the null hypothesis to a second hypothesis, called the **alternative hypothesis**, that holds if the null does not.

The null hypothesis is that the population mean, $E(Y)$, takes on a specific value, denoted by $\mu_{Y,0}$. The null hypothesis is denoted H_0 and thus is

$$H_0: E(Y) = \mu_{Y,0}. \tag{3.3}$$

For example, the conjecture that, on average in the population, college graduates earn \$20/hour constitutes a null hypothesis about the population distribution of hourly earnings. Stated mathematically, if Y is the hourly earning of a randomly selected recent college graduate, then the null hypothesis is that $E(Y) = 20$, that is, $\mu_{Y,0} = 20$ in Equation (3.3).

The alternative hypothesis specifies what is true if the null hypothesis is not. The most general alternative hypothesis is that $E(Y) \neq \mu_{Y,0}$; this is called a **two-sided alternative hypothesis**, because it allows $E(Y)$ to be either less than or greater than $\mu_{Y,0}$. The two-sided alternative is written as

$$H_1: E(Y) \neq \mu_{Y,0} \quad \text{(two-sided alternative)}. \tag{3.4}$$

One-sided alternatives are also possible, and these are discussed later in this section.

The problem facing the statistician is to use the evidence in a randomly selected sample of data to decide whether to accept the null hypothesis H_0 or to reject it in favor of the alternative hypothesis H_1. If the null hypothesis is "accepted," this does not mean that the statistician declares it to be true; rather, it is accepted tentatively with the recognition that it might be rejected later based on additional evidence. For this reason, statistical hypothesis testing can be posed as either rejecting the null hypothesis or failing to do so.

The p-Value

In any given sample, the sample average $\overline{Y}$ will rarely be exactly equal to the hypothesized value $\mu_{Y,0}$. Differences between $\overline{Y}$ and $\mu_{Y,0}$ can arise because the true mean in fact does not equal $\mu_{Y,0}$ (the null hypothesis is false), or because the true mean equals $\mu_{Y,0}$ (the null hypothesis is true) but $\overline{Y}$ differs from $\mu_{Y,0}$ because of random sampling. It is impossible to distinguish between these two possibilities with certainty. Although a sample of data cannot provide conclusive evidence about the null hypothesis, it is possible to do a probabilistic calculation that permits testing the null hypothesis in a way that accounts for sampling uncertainty. This calculation involves using the data to compute the *p*-value of the null hypothesis.

The ***p*-value**, also called the **significance probability**, is the probability of drawing a statistic at least as adverse to the null hypothesis as the one you actually computed in your sample, assuming the null hypothesis is correct. In the case at hand, the *p*-value is the probability of drawing $\overline{Y}$ at least as far in the tails of its distribution under the null hypothesis as the sample average you actually computed.

For example, suppose that, in your sample of recent college graduates, the average wage is $22.24. The *p*-value is the probability of observing a value of $\overline{Y}$ at least as different from $20 (the population mean under the null) as the observed value of $22.24 by pure random sampling variation, assuming that the null hypothesis is true. If this *p*-value is small, say 0.5%, then it is very unlikely that this sample would have been drawn if the null hypothesis is true; thus it is reasonable to conclude that the null hypothesis is not true. By contrast, if this *p*-value is large, say 40%, then it is quite likely that the observed sample average of $22.24 could have arisen just by random sampling variation if the null hypothesis is true; accordingly, the evidence against the null hypothesis is weak in this probabilistic sense, and it is reasonable not to reject the null hypothesis.

To state the definition of the *p*-value mathematically, let $\overline{Y}^{act}$ denote the value of the sample average actually computed in the data set at hand and let Pr_{H_0} denote the probability computed under the null hypothesis (that is, computed assuming that $E(Y_i) = \mu_{Y,0}$). The *p*-value is

$$p\text{-value} = \mathrm{Pr}_{H_0}[|\overline{Y} - \mu_{Y,0}| > |\overline{Y}^{act} - \mu_{Y,0}|]. \tag{3.5}$$

That is, the *p*-value is the area in the tails of the distribution of $\overline{Y}$ under the null hypothesis beyond $|\overline{Y}^{act} - \mu_{Y,0}|$. If the *p*-value is large, then the observed value $\overline{Y}^{act}$ is consistent with the null hypothesis, but if the *p*-value is small, it is not.

To compute the *p*-value it is necessary to know the sampling distribution of $\overline{Y}$ under the null hypothesis. As discussed in Section 2.6, when the sample size is small this distribution is complicated. However, according to the central limit theorem, when the sample size is large the sampling distribution of $\overline{Y}$ is well approximated by a normal distribution. Under the null hypothesis, the mean of this normal distribution is $\mu_{Y,0}$, so under the null hypothesis $\overline{Y}$ is distributed $N(\mu_{Y,0}, \sigma_{\overline{Y}}^2)$,

---

FIGURE 3.1   Calculating a p-value

The p-value is the probability of drawing a value of $\overline{Y}$ that differs from $\mu_{Y,0}$ by at least as much as $\overline{Y}^{act}$. In large samples, $\overline{Y}$ is distributed $N(\mu_{Y,0}, \sigma_{\overline{Y}}^2)$ under the null hypothesis, so $(\overline{Y} - \mu_{Y,0})/\sigma_{\overline{Y}}$ is distributed $N(0, 1)$. Thus the p-value is the shaded standard normal tail probability outside $\pm|(\overline{Y}^{act} - \mu_{Y,0})/\sigma_{\overline{Y}}|$.

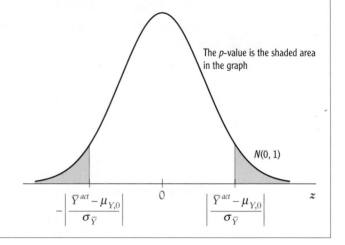

The p-value is the shaded area in the graph

$N(0, 1)$

$$-\left|\frac{\overline{Y}^{act} - \mu_{Y,0}}{\sigma_{\overline{Y}}}\right| \qquad 0 \qquad \left|\frac{\overline{Y}^{act} - \mu_{Y,0}}{\sigma_{\overline{Y}}}\right| \qquad z$$

---

where $\sigma_{\overline{Y}}^2 = \sigma_Y^2/n$. This large-sample normal approximation makes it possible to compute the p-value without needing to know the population distribution of Y, as long as the sample size is large. The details of the calculation, however, depend on whether σ_Y^2 is known.

Calculating the p-Value When σ_Y Is Known

The calculation of the p-value when σ_Y is known is summarized in Figure 3.1. If the sample size is large, then under the null hypothesis the sampling distribution of $\overline{Y}$ is $N(\mu_{Y,0}, \sigma_{\overline{Y}}^2)$, where $\sigma_{\overline{Y}}^2 = \sigma_Y^2/n$. Thus, under the null hypothesis, the standardized version of $\overline{Y}$, $(\overline{Y} - \mu_{Y,0})/\sigma_{\overline{Y}}$, has a standard normal distribution. The p-value is the probability of obtaining a value of $\overline{Y}$ farther from $\mu_{Y,0}$ than $\overline{Y}^{act}$ under the null hypothesis or, equivalently, is the probability of obtaining $(\overline{Y} - \mu_{Y,0})/\sigma_{\overline{Y}}$ greater than $(\overline{Y}^{act} - \mu_{Y,0})/\sigma_{\overline{Y}}$ in absolute value. This probability is the shaded area shown in Figure 3.1. Written mathematically, the shaded tail probability in Figure 3.1 (that is, the p-value) is

$$p\text{-value} = \Pr_{H_0}\left(\left|\frac{\overline{Y} - \mu_{Y,0}}{\sigma_{\overline{Y}}}\right| > \left|\frac{\overline{Y}^{act} - \mu_{Y,0}}{\sigma_{\overline{Y}}}\right|\right) = 2\Phi\left(-\left|\frac{\overline{Y}^{act} - \mu_{Y,0}}{\sigma_{\overline{Y}}}\right|\right), \quad (3.6)$$

where Φ is the standard normal cumulative distribution function. That is, the p-value is the area in the tails of a standard normal distribution outside $\pm (\overline{Y}^{act} - \mu_{Y,0})/\sigma_{\overline{Y}}$.

The formula for the p-value in Equation (3.6) depends on the variance of the population distribution, σ_Y^2. In practice, this variance is typically unknown. [An exception is when Y_i is binary so its distribution is Bernoulli, in which case the variance is determined by the null hypothesis; see Equation (2.7).] Because in general σ_Y^2 must be estimated before the p-value can be computed, we now turn to the problem of estimating σ_Y^2.

The Sample Variance, Sample Standard Deviation, and Standard Error

The sample variance s_Y^2 is an estimator of the population variance σ_Y^2; the sample standard deviation s_Y is an estimator of the population standard deviation σ_Y; and the standard error of the sample average $\overline{Y}$ is an estimator of the standard deviation of the sampling distribution of $\overline{Y}$.

The sample variance and standard deviation.   The **sample variance**, s_Y^2, is

$$s_Y^2 = \frac{1}{n-1} \sum_{i=1}^{n} (Y_i - \overline{Y})^2. \tag{3.7}$$

The **sample standard deviation**, s_Y, is the square root of the sample variance.

The formula for the sample variance is much like the formula for the population variance. The population variance, $E(Y - \mu_Y)^2$, is the average value of $(Y - \mu_Y)^2$ in the population distribution. Similarly, the sample variance is the sample average of $(Y_i - \mu_Y)^2$, $i = 1, \ldots, n$, with two modifications: First, μ_Y is replaced by $\overline{Y}$, and second, the average uses the divisor $n - 1$ instead of n.

The reason for the first modification—replacing μ_Y by $\overline{Y}$—is that μ_Y is unknown and thus must be estimated; the natural estimator of μ_Y is $\overline{Y}$. The reason for the second modification—dividing by $n - 1$ instead of by n—is that estimating μ_Y by $\overline{Y}$ introduces a small downward bias in $(Y_i - \overline{Y})^2$. Specifically, as is shown in Exercise 3.18, $E[(Y_i - \overline{Y})^2] = [(n-1)/n]\sigma_Y^2$. Thus, $E\sum_{i=1}^{n}(Y_i - \overline{Y})^2 = n E[(Y_i - \overline{Y})^2] = (n-1)\sigma_Y^2$. Dividing by $n - 1$ in Equation (3.7) instead of n corrects for this small downward bias, and as a result s_Y^2 is unbiased.

Dividing by $n - 1$ in Equation (3.7) instead of n is called a **degrees of freedom** correction: Estimating the mean uses up some of the information—that is, uses up one "degree of freedom"—in the data, so that only $n - 1$ degrees of freedom remain.

KEY CONCEPT	THE STANDARD ERROR OF $\overline{Y}$
3.4	The standard error of $\overline{Y}$ is an estimator of the standard deviation of $\overline{Y}$. The standard error of $\overline{Y}$ is denoted by $SE(\overline{Y})$ or by $\hat{\sigma}_{\overline{Y}}$. When $Y_1, \ldots, Y_n$ are i.i.d.,

$$SE(\overline{Y}) = \hat{\sigma}_{\overline{Y}} = s_Y/\sqrt{n}. \tag{3.8}$$

Consistency of the sample variance. The sample variance is a consistent estimator of the population variance:

$$s_Y^2 \xrightarrow{p} \sigma_Y^2. \tag{3.9}$$

In other words, the sample variance is close to the population variance with high probability when n is large.

The result in Equation (3.9) is proven in Appendix 3.3 under the assumptions that $Y_1, \ldots, Y_n$ are i.i.d. and Y_i has a finite fourth moment; that is, $E(Y_i^4) < \infty$. Intuitively, the reason that s_Y^2 is consistent is that it is a sample average, so s_Y^2 obeys the law of large numbers. But for s_Y^2 to obey the law of large numbers in Key Concept 2.6, $(Y_i - \mu_Y)^2$ must have finite variance, which in turn means that $E(Y_i^4)$ must be finite; in other words, Y_i must have a finite fourth moment.

The standard error of $\overline{Y}$. Because the standard deviation of the sampling distribution of $\overline{Y}$ is $\sigma_{\overline{Y}} = \sigma_Y/\sqrt{n}$, Equation (3.9) justifies using $s_Y/\sqrt{n}$ as an estimator of $\sigma_{\overline{Y}}$. The estimator of $\sigma_{\overline{Y}}$, $s_Y/\sqrt{n}$, is called the **standard error** of $\overline{Y}$ and is denoted by $SE(\overline{Y})$ or by $\hat{\sigma}_{\overline{Y}}$ (the "^" over the symbol means that this is an estimator of $\sigma_{\overline{Y}}$). The standard error of $\overline{Y}$ is summarized as Key Concept 3.4.

When $Y_1, \ldots, Y_n$ are i.i.d. draws from a Bernoulli distribution with success probability p, the formula for the variance of $\overline{Y}$ simplifies to $p(1-p)/n$ [see Equation (2.7)]. The formula for the standard error also takes on a simple form that depends only on $\overline{Y}$ and n: $SE(\overline{Y}) = \sqrt{\overline{Y}(1-\overline{Y})/n}$.

Calculating the p-Value When σ_Y Is Unknown

Because s_Y^2 is a consistent estimator of σ_Y^2, the p-value can be computed by replacing $\sigma_{\overline{Y}}$ in Equation (3.6) by the standard error, $SE(\overline{Y}) = \hat{\sigma}_{\overline{Y}}$. That is, when σ_Y is unknown and $Y_1, \ldots, Y_n$ are i.i.d., the p-value is calculated using the formula

$$p\text{-value} = 2\Phi\left(-\left|\frac{\overline{Y}^{act} - \mu_{Y,0}}{SE(\overline{Y})}\right|\right). \tag{3.10}$$

The t-Statistic

The standardized sample average $(\overline{Y} - \mu_{Y,0})/SE(\overline{Y})$ plays a central role in testing statistical hypotheses and has a special name, the *t-statistic* or *t-ratio*:

$$t = \frac{\overline{Y} - \mu_{Y,0}}{SE(\overline{Y})}. \tag{3.11}$$

In general, a **test statistic** is a statistic used to perform a hypothesis test. The t-statistic is an important example of a test statistic.

Large-sample distribution of the t-statistic. When n is large, s_Y^2 is close to σ_Y^2 with high probability. Thus the distribution of the t-statistic is approximately the same as the distribution of $(\overline{Y} - \mu_{Y,0})/\sigma_{\overline{Y}}$, which in turn is well approximated by the standard normal distribution when n is large because of the central limit theorem (Key Concept 2.7). Accordingly, under the null hypothesis,

$$t \text{ is approximately distributed } N(0,1) \text{ for large } n. \tag{3.12}$$

The formula for the p-value in Equation (3.10) can be rewritten in terms of the t-statistic. Let t^{act} denote the value of the t-statistic actually computed:

$$t^{act} = \frac{\overline{Y}^{act} - \mu_{Y,0}}{SE(\overline{Y})}. \tag{3.13}$$

Accordingly, when n is large, the p-value can be calculated using

$$p\text{-value} = 2\Phi(-|t^{act}|). \tag{3.14}$$

As a hypothetical example, suppose that a sample of $n = 200$ recent college graduates is used to test the null hypothesis that the mean wage, $E(Y)$, is \$20/hour. The sample average wage is $\overline{Y}^{act} = \$22.64$ and the sample standard deviation is $s_Y = \$18.14$. Then the standard error of $\overline{Y}$ is $s_Y/\sqrt{n} = 18.14/\sqrt{200} = 1.28$. The value of the t-statistic is $t^{act} = (22.64 - 20)/1.28 = 2.06$. From Appendix Table 1, the p-value is $2\Phi(-2.06) = 0.039$, or 3.9%. That is, assuming the null hypothesis to be true, the probability of obtaining a sample average at least as different from the null as the one actually computed is 3.9%.

Hypothesis Testing with a Prespecified Significance Level

When you undertake a statistical hypothesis test, you can make two types of mistakes: You can incorrectly reject the null hypothesis when it is true, or you can fail to reject the null hypothesis when it is false. Hypothesis tests can be performed without computing the *p*-value if you are willing to specify in advance the probability you are willing to tolerate of making the first kind of mistake—that is, of incorrectly rejecting the null hypothesis when it is true. If you choose a prespecified probability of rejecting the null hypothesis when it is true (for example, 5%), then you will reject the null hypothesis if and only if the *p*-value is less than 0.05. This approach gives preferential treatment to the null hypothesis, but in many practical situations this preferential treatment is appropriate.

Hypothesis tests using a fixed significance level. Suppose it has been decided that the hypothesis will be rejected if the *p*-value is less than 5%. Because the area under the tails of the normal distribution outside ±1.96 is 5%, this gives a simple rule:

$$\text{Reject } H_0 \text{ if } |t^{act}| > 1.96. \tag{3.15}$$

That is, reject if the absolute value of the *t*-statistic computed from the sample is greater than 1.96. If *n* is large enough, then under the null hypothesis the *t*-statistic has a $N(0, 1)$ distribution. Thus, the probability of erroneously rejecting the null hypothesis (rejecting the null hypothesis when it is in fact true) is 5%.

This framework for testing statistical hypotheses has some specialized terminology, summarized in Key Concept 3.5. The significance level of the test in Equation (3.15) is 5%, the critical value of this two-sided test is 1.96, and the rejection region is the values of the *t*-statistic outside ±1.96. If the test rejects at the 5% significance level, the population mean μ_Y is said to be statistically significantly different from $\mu_{Y,0}$ at the 5% significance level.

Testing hypotheses using a prespecified significance level does not require computing *p*-values. In the previous example of testing the hypothesis that the mean earning of recent college graduates is $20, the *t*-statistic was 2.06. This exceeds 1.96, so the hypothesis is rejected at the 5% level. Although performing the test with a 5% significance level is easy, reporting only whether the null

---

THE TERMINOLOGY OF HYPOTHESIS TESTING   KEY CONCEPT

3.5

A statistical hypothesis test can make two types of mistakes: a **type I error**, in which the null hypothesis is rejected when in fact it is true, and a **type II error**, in which the null hypothesis is not rejected when in fact it is false. The prespecified rejection probability of a statistical hypothesis test when the null hypothesis is true—that is, the prespecified probability of a type I error—is the **significance level** of the test. The **critical value** of the test statistic is the value of the statistic for which the test just rejects the null hypothesis at the given significance level. The set of values of the test statistic for which the test rejects the null hypothesis is the **rejection region**, and the values of the test statistic for which it does not reject the null hypothesis is the **acceptance region**. The probability that the test actually incorrectly rejects the null hypothesis when it is true is the **size** of the test, and the probability that the test correctly rejects the null hypothesis when the alternative is true is the **power** of the test.

The *p*-value is the probability of obtaining a test statistic, by random sampling variation, at least as adverse to the null hypothesis value as is the statistic actually observed, assuming that the null hypothesis is correct. Equivalently, the *p*-value is the smallest significance level at which you can reject the null hypothesis.

---

hypothesis is rejected at a prespecified significance level conveys less information than reporting the *p*-value.

What significance level should you use in practice?   In many cases, statisticians and econometricians use a 5% significance level. If you were to test many statistical hypotheses at the 5% level, you would incorrectly reject the null on average once in 20 cases. Sometimes a more conservative significance level might be in order. For example, legal cases sometimes involve statistical evidence, and the null hypothesis could be that the defendant is not guilty; then one would want to be quite sure that a rejection of the null (conclusion of guilt) is not just a result of random sample variation. In some legal settings the significance level used is 1% or even 0.1%, to avoid this sort of mistake. Similarly, if a government agency is considering permitting the sale of a new drug, a very conservative standard might be in order so that consumers can be sure that the drugs available in the market actually work.

Being conservative, in the sense of using a very low significance level, has a cost: The smaller the significance level, the larger the critical value, and the more difficult it becomes to reject the null when the null is false. In fact, the most conservative thing to do is never to reject the null hypothesis—but if that is your view, then you never need to look at any statistical evidence, for you will never change your mind! The lower the significance level, the lower the power of the test. Many economic and policy applications can call for less conservatism than a legal case, so a 5% significance level is often considered to be a reasonable compromise.

Key Concept 3.6 summarizes hypothesis tests for the population mean against the two-sided alternative.

One-Sided Alternatives

In some circumstances, the alternative hypothesis might be that the mean exceeds $\mu_{Y,0}$. For example, one hopes that education helps in the labor market, so the relevant alternative to the null hypothesis that earnings are the same for college graduates and nongraduates is not just that their earnings differ, but rather that graduates earn more than nongraduates. This is called a **one-sided alternative hypothesis** and can be written

$$H_1: E(Y) > \mu_{Y,0} \quad \text{(one-sided alternative).} \tag{3.16}$$

The general approach to computing p-values and to hypothesis testing is the same for one-sided alternatives as it is for two-sided alternatives, with the modification that only large positive values of the t-statistic reject the null hypothesis, rather than values that are large in absolute value. Specifically, to test the one-sided hypothesis in Equation (3.16), construct the t-statistic in Equation (3.13). The p-value is the area under the standard normal distribution to the right of the calculated t-statistic. That is, the p-value, based on the $N(0, 1)$ approximation to the distribution of the t-statistic, is

$$p\text{-value} = \text{Pr}_{H_0}(Z > t^{act}) = 1 - \Phi(t^{act}). \qquad (3.17)$$

The $N(0, 1)$ critical value for a one-sided test with a 5% significance level is 1.645. The rejection region for this test is all values of the t-statistic exceeding 1.645.

The one-sided hypothesis in Equation (3.16) concerns values of μ_Y exceeding $\mu_{Y,0}$. If instead the alternative hypothesis is that $\text{E}(Y) < \mu_{Y,0}$, then the discussion of the previous paragraph applies except that the signs are switched; for example, the 5% rejection region consists of values of the t-statistic less than -1.645.

3.3 Confidence Intervals for the Population Mean

Because of random sampling error, it is impossible to learn the exact value of the population mean of Y using only the information in a sample. However, it is possible to use data from a random sample to construct a set of values that contains the true population mean μ_Y with a certain prespecified probability. Such a set is called a **confidence set**, and the prespecified probability that μ_Y is contained in this set is called the **confidence level**. The confidence set for μ_Y turns out to be all the possible values of the mean between a lower and an upper limit, so that the confidence set is an interval, called a **confidence interval**.

Here is one way to construct a 95% confidence set for the population mean. Begin by picking some arbitrary value for the mean; call this $\mu_{Y,0}$. Test the null hypothesis that $\mu_Y = \mu_{Y,0}$ against the alternative that $\mu_Y \neq \mu_{Y,0}$ by computing the t-statistic; if it is less than 1.96, this hypothesized value $\mu_{Y,0}$ is not rejected at the 5% level, and write down this nonrejected value $\mu_{Y,0}$. Now pick another arbitrary value of $\mu_{Y,0}$ and test it; if you cannot reject it, write this value down on your list. Do this again and again; indeed, keep doing this for all possible values of the population mean. Continuing this process yields the set of all values of the population mean that cannot be rejected at the 5% level by a two-sided hypothesis test.

This list is useful because it summarizes the set of hypotheses you can and cannot reject (at the 5% level) based on your data: If someone walks up to you with a specific number in mind, you can tell him whether his hypothesis is rejected or not simply by looking up his number on your handy list. A bit of clever reasoning shows that this set of values has a remarkable property: The probability that it contains the true value of the population mean is 95%.

CONFIDENCE INTERVALS FOR THE POPULATION MEAN

A 95% two-sided confidence interval for μ_Y is an interval constructed so that it contains the true value of μ_Y in 95% of all possible random samples. When the sample size n is large, 95%, 90%, and 99% confidence intervals for μ_Y are

95% confidence interval for $\mu_Y = \{\overline{Y} \pm 1.96 SE(\overline{Y})\}$.

90% confidence interval for $\mu_Y = \{\overline{Y} \pm 1.64 SE(\overline{Y})\}$.

99% confidence interval for $\mu_Y = \{\overline{Y} \pm 2.58 SE(\overline{Y})\}$.

The clever reasoning goes like this. Suppose the true value of μ_Y is 21.5 (although we do not know this). Then $\overline{Y}$ has a normal distribution centered on 21.5, and the t-statistic testing the null hypothesis $\mu_Y = 21.5$ has a $N(0, 1)$ distribution. Thus, if n is large, the probability of rejecting the null hypothesis $\mu_Y = 21.5$ at the 5% level is 5%. But because you tested all possible values of the population mean in constructing your set, in particular you tested the true value, $\mu_Y = 21.5$. In 95% of all samples, you will correctly accept 21.5; this means that in 95% of all samples, your list will contain the true value of μ_Y. Thus, the values on your list constitute a 95% confidence set for μ_Y.

This method of constructing a confidence set is impractical, for it requires you to test all possible values of μ_Y as null hypotheses. Fortunately there is a much easier approach. According to the formula for the t-statistic in Equation (3.13), a trial value of $\mu_{Y,0}$ is rejected at the 5% level if it is more than 1.96 standard errors away from $\overline{Y}$. Thus the set of values of μ_Y that are not rejected at the 5% level consists of those values within $\pm 1.96 SE(\overline{Y})$ of $\overline{Y}$. That is, a 95% confidence interval for μ_Y is $\overline{Y} - 1.96 SE(\overline{Y}) \leq \mu_Y \leq \overline{Y} + 1.96 SE(\overline{Y})$. Key Concept 3.7 summarizes this approach.

As an example, consider the problem of constructing a 95% confidence interval for the mean hourly earnings of recent college graduates using a hypothetical random sample of 200 recent college graduates where $\overline{Y} = \$22.64$ and $SE(\overline{Y}) = 1.28$. The 95% confidence interval for mean hourly earnings is $22.64 \pm 1.96 \times 1.28 = 22.64 \pm 2.51 = [\$20.13, \$25.15]$.

This discussion so far has focused on two-sided confidence intervals. One could instead construct a one-sided confidence interval as the set of values of μ_Y that cannot be rejected by a one-sided hypothesis test. Although one-sided confidence intervals have applications in some branches of statistics, they are uncommon in applied econometric analysis.

Coverage probabilities. The **coverage probability** of a confidence interval for the population mean is the probability, computed over all possible random samples, that it contains the true population mean.

3.4 Comparing Means from Different Populations

Do recent male and female college graduates earn the same amount on average? This question involves comparing the means of two different population distributions. This section summarizes how to test hypotheses and how to construct confidence intervals for the difference in the means from two different populations.

Hypothesis Tests for the Difference Between Two Means

Let μ_w be the mean hourly earning in the population of women recently graduated from college and let μ_m be the population mean for recently graduated men. Consider the null hypothesis that earnings for these two populations differ by a certain amount, say d_0. Then the null hypothesis and the two-sided alternative hypothesis are

$$H_0: \mu_m - \mu_w = d_0 \text{ vs. } H_1: \mu_m - \mu_w \neq d_0. \tag{3.18}$$

The null hypothesis that men and women in these populations have the same earnings corresponds to H_0 in Equation (3.18) with $d_0 = 0$.

Because these population means are unknown, they must be estimated from samples of men and women. Suppose we have samples of n_m men and n_w women drawn at random from their populations. Let the sample average annual earnings be $\overline{Y}_m$ for men and $\overline{Y}_w$ for women. Then an estimator of $\mu_m - \mu_w$ is $\overline{Y}_m - \overline{Y}_w$.

To test the null hypothesis that $\mu_m - \mu_w = d_0$ using $\overline{Y}_m - \overline{Y}_w$, we need to know the distribution of $\overline{Y}_m - \overline{Y}_w$. Recall that $\overline{Y}_m$ is, according to the central limit theorem, approximately distributed $N(\mu_m, \sigma_m^2/n_m)$, where σ_m^2 is the population variance of earnings for men. Similarly, $\overline{Y}_w$ is approximately distributed $N(\mu_w, \sigma_w^2/n_w)$, where σ_w^2 is the population variance of earnings for women. Also, recall from Section 2.4 that a weighted average of two normal random variables is itself normally distributed. Because $\overline{Y}_m$ and $\overline{Y}_w$ are constructed from different randomly selected samples, they are independent random variables. Thus, $\overline{Y}_m - \overline{Y}_w$ is distributed $N[\mu_m - \mu_w, (\sigma_m^2/n_m) + (\sigma_w^2/n_w)]$.

If σ_m^2 and σ_w^2 are known, then this approximate normal distribution can be used to compute p-values for the test of the null hypothesis that $\mu_m - \mu_w = d_0$. In practice, however, these population variances are typically unknown so they must be estimated. As before, they can be estimated using the sample variances, s_m^2 and s_w^2, where s_m^2 is defined as in Equation (3.7), except that the statistic is computed only for the men in the sample, and s_w^2 is defined similarly for the women. Thus the standard error of $\overline{Y}_m - \overline{Y}_w$ is

$$SE(\overline{Y}_m - \overline{Y}_w) = \sqrt{\frac{s_m^2}{n_m} + \frac{s_w^2}{n_w}}. \tag{3.19}$$

The t-statistic for testing the null hypothesis is constructed analogously to the t-statistic for testing a hypothesis about a single population mean, by subtracting the null hypothesized value of $\mu_m - \mu_w$ from the estimator $\overline{Y}_m - \overline{Y}_w$ and dividing the result by the standard error of $\overline{Y}_m - \overline{Y}_w$:

$$t = \frac{(\overline{Y}_m - \overline{Y}_w) - d_0}{SE(\overline{Y}_m - \overline{Y}_w)} \quad (t\text{-statistic for comparing two means}). \tag{3.20}$$

If both n_m and n_w are large, then this t-statistic has a standard normal distribution.

Because the t-statistic in Equation (3.20) has a standard normal distribution under the null hypothesis when n_m and n_w are large, the p-value of the two-sided test is computed exactly as it was in the case of a single population; that is, the p-value is computed using Equation (3.14).

To conduct a test with a prespecified significance level, simply calculate the t-statistic in Equation (3.20) and compare it to the appropriate critical value. For example, the null hypothesis is rejected at the 5% significance level if the absolute value of the t-statistic exceeds 1.96.

If the alternative is one-sided rather than two-sided (that is, if the alternative is that $\mu_m - \mu_w > d_0$), then the test is modified as outlined in Section 3.2. The p-value is computed using Equation (3.17), and a test with a 5% significance level rejects when $t > 1.65$.

Confidence Intervals for the Difference Between Two Population Means

The method for constructing confidence intervals summarized in Section 3.3 extends to constructing a confidence interval for the difference between the means, $d = \mu_m - \mu_w$. Because the hypothesized value d_0 is rejected at the 5% level if $|t| > 1.96$, d_0 will be in the confidence set if $|t| \leq 1.96$. But $|t| \leq 1.96$ means that the estimated difference, $\overline{Y}_m - \overline{Y}_w$, is less than 1.96 standard errors away from d_0. Thus, the 95% two-sided confidence interval for d consists of those values of d within ± 1.96 standard errors of $\overline{Y}_m - \overline{Y}_w$:

$$\text{95\% confidence interval for } d = \mu_m - \mu_w \text{ is}$$
$$(\overline{Y}_m - \overline{Y}_w) \pm 1.96 SE(\overline{Y}_m - \overline{Y}_w). \tag{3.21}$$

With these formulas in hand, the box "The Gender Gap of Earnings of College Graduates in the U.S." contains an empirical investigation of gender differences in earnings of U.S. college graduates.

3.5   Differences-of-Means Estimation of Causal Effects Using Experimental Data

Recall from Section 1.2 that a randomized controlled experiment randomly selects subjects (individuals or, more generally, entities) from a population of interest, then randomly assigns them either to a treatment group, which receives the experimental treatment, or to a control group, which does not receive the treatment. The difference between the sample means of the treatment and control groups is an estimator of the causal effect of the treatment.

The Causal Effect as a Difference of Conditional Expectations

The causal effect of a treatment is the expected effect on the outcome of interest of the treatment as measured in an ideal randomized controlled experiment. This effect can be expressed as the difference of two conditional expectations. Specifically, the **causal effect** on Y of treatment level x is the difference in the conditional expectations, $E(Y|X = x) - E(Y|X = 0)$, where $E(Y|X = x)$ is the expected value of Y for the treatment group (which receives treatment level $X = x$) in an ideal randomized controlled experiment and $E(Y|X = 0)$ is the expected value of Y for the control group (which receives treatment level $X = 0$). In the context of experiments, the causal effect is also called the **treatment effect**. If there are only two treatment levels (that is, if the treatment is binary), then we can let $X = 0$ denote the control group and $X = 1$ denote the treatment group. If the treatment is binary treatment, then the causal effect (that is, the treatment effect) is $E(Y|X = 1) - E(Y|X = 0)$ in an ideal randomized controlled experiment.

The Gender Gap of Earnings of College Graduates in the U.S.

The box in Chapter 2, "The Distribution of Earnings in the United States in 2004," shows that, on average, male college graduates earn more than female college graduates. What are the recent trends in this "gender gap" in earnings? Social norms and laws governing gender discrimination in the workplace have changed substantially in the United States. Is the gender gap in earnings of college graduates stable or has it diminished over time?

Table 3.1 gives estimates of hourly earnings for college-educated full-time workers aged 25–34 in the United States in 1992, 1996, 2000, and 2004, using data collected by the Current Population Survey. Earnings for 1992, 1996, and 2000 were adjusted for inflation by putting them in 2004 dollars using the Consumer Price Index.[1] In 2004, the average hourly earnings of the 1,901 men surveyed was $21.99, and the standard deviation of earnings for men was $10.39. The average hourly earnings in 2004 of the

1739 women surveyed was $18.48, and the standard deviation of earnings was $8.16. Thus the estimate of the gender gap in earnings for 2004 is $3.52 (= $21.99 − $18.47), with a standard error of $0.31 (= $\sqrt{10.39^2/1901 + 8.16^2/1739}$). The 95% confidence interval for the gender gap in earnings in 2004 is $3.52 \pm 1.96 \times 0.31 = (\$2.91, \$4.12)$.

The results in Table 3.1 suggest four conclusions. First, the gender gap is large. An hourly gap of $3.52 might not sound like much, but over a year it adds up to $7,040, assuming a 40-hour work week and 50 paid weeks per year. Second, the estimated gender gap has increased by $0.79/hour in real terms over this sample, from $2.73/hour to $3.52/hour; however, this increase is not statistically significant at the 5% significance level (Exercise 3.17). Third, this gap is large if it is measured instead in percentage terms: According to the estimates in Table 3.1, in 2004 women

continued

TABLE 3.1   Trends in Hourly Earnings in the United States of Working College Graduates, Ages 25–34, 1992 to 2004, in 2004 Dollars

	Men			Women			Difference, Men vs. Women		
Year	$\bar{Y}_m$	s_m	n_m	$\bar{Y}_w$	s_w	n_w	$\bar{Y}_m - \bar{Y}_w$	$SE(\bar{Y}_m - \bar{Y}_w)$	95% Confidence Interval for d
1992	20.33	8.70	1592	17.60	6.90	1370	2.73**	0.29	2.16–3.30
1996	19.52	8.48	1377	16.72	7.03	1235	2.80**	0.30	2.22–3.40
2000	21.77	10.00	1300	18.21	8.20	1182	3.56**	0.37	2.83–4.29
2004	21.99	10.39	1901	18.47	8.16	1739	3.52**	0.31	2.91–4.13

These estimates are computed using data on all full-time workers aged 25–34 surveyed in the Current Population Survey conducted in March of the next year (for example, the data for 2004 were collected in March 2005). The difference is significantly different from zero at the **1% significance level.

earned 16% less per hour than men did ($3.52/ $21.99), more than the gap of 13% seen in 1992 ($2.73/$20.33). Fourth, the gender gap is smaller for young college graduates (the group analyzed in Table 3.1) than it is for all college graduates (analyzed in Table 2.4): As reported in Table 2.4, the mean earnings for all college-educated women working full-time in 2004 was $21.12, while for men this mean was $27.83, which corresponds to a gender gap of 24% [= (27.83 − 21.12)/27.83] among all full-time college-educated workers.

This empirical analysis documents that the "gender gap" in hourly earnings is large and has been fairly stable (or perhaps increased slightly) over the recent past. The analysis does not, however, tell us *why* this gap exists. Does it arise from gender discrimination in the labor market? Does it reflect differences in skills, experience, or education between men and women? Does it reflect differences in choice of jobs? Or is there some other cause? We return to these questions once we have in hand the tools of multiple regression analysis, the topic of Part II.

---

[1]Because of inflation, a dollar in 1992 was worth more than a dollar in 2004, in the sense that a dollar in 1992 could buy more goods and services than a dollar in 2004 could. Thus earnings in 1992 cannot be directly compared to earnings in 2004 without adjusting for inflation. One way to make this adjustment is to use the Consumer Price Index (CPI), a measure of the price of a "market basket" of consumer goods and services constructed by the Bureau of Labor Statistics. Over the twelve years from 1992 to 2004, the price of the CPI market basket rose by 34.6%; in other words, the CPI basket of goods and services that cost $100 in 1992 cost $134.60 in 2004. To make earnings in 1992 and 2004 comparable in Table 3.1, 1992 earnings are inflated by the amount of overall CPI price inflation, that is, by multiplying 1992 earnings by 1.346 to put them into "2004 dollars."

Estimation of the Causal Effect Using Differences of Means

If the treatment in a randomized controlled experiment is binary, then the causal effect can be estimated by the difference in the sample average outcomes between the treatment and control groups. The hypothesis that the treatment is ineffective is equivalent to the hypothesis that the two means are the same, which can be tested using the *t*-statistic for comparing two means, given in Equation (3.20). A 95% confidence interval for the difference in the means of the two groups is a 95% confidence interval for the causal effect, so a 95% confidence interval for the causal effect can be constructed using Equation (3.21).

A well-designed, well-run experiment can provide a compelling estimate of a causal effect. For this reason, randomized controlled experiments are commonly conducted in some fields, such as medicine. In economics, however, experiments tend to be expensive, difficult to administer, and, in some cases, ethically questionable, so they remain rare. For this reason, econometricians sometimes study "natural experiments," also called quasi-experiments, in which some event unrelated to the treatment or subject characteristics has the effect of assigning different treatments to different subjects *as if* they had been part of a randomized controlled experiment. The box, "A Novel Way to Boost Retirement Savings," provides an example of such a quasi-experiment that yielded some surprising conclusions.

3.6   Using the *t*-Statistic When the Sample Size Is Small

In Sections 3.2 through 3.5, the *t*-statistic is used in conjunction with critical values from the standard normal distribution for hypothesis testing and for the construction of confidence intervals. The use of the standard normal distribution is justified by the central limit theorem, which applies when the sample size is large. When the sample size is small, the standard normal distribution can provide a poor approximation to the distribution of the *t*-statistic. If, however, the population distribution is itself normally distributed, then the exact distribution (that is, the finite-sample distribution; see Section 2.6) of the *t*-statistic testing the mean of a single population is the Student *t* distribution with $n - 1$ degrees of freedom, and critical values can be taken from the Student *t* distribution.

The *t*-Statistic and the Student *t* Distribution

The t-statistic testing the mean.   Consider the *t*-statistic used to test the hypothesis that the mean of *Y* is $\mu_{Y,0}$, using data $Y_1, \ldots, Y_n$. The formula for this statistic is given by Equation (3.10), where the standard error of $\overline{Y}$ is given by Equation (3.8). Substitution of the latter expression into the former yields the formula for the *t*-statistic:

$$t = \frac{\overline{Y} - \mu_{Y,0}}{\sqrt{s_Y^2/n}},$$

(3.22)

where s_Y^2 is given in Equation (3.7).

As discussed in Section 3.2, under general conditions the *t*-statistic has a standard normal distribution if the sample size is large and the null hypothesis is true [see Equation (3.12)]. Although the standard normal approximation to the *t*-statistic is reliable for a wide range of distributions of *Y* if *n* is large, it can be unreliable if *n* is small. The exact distribution of the *t*-statistic depends on the distribution of *Y*, and it can be very complicated. There is, however, one special case in which the exact distribution of the *t*-statistic is relatively simple: If *Y* is normally distributed, then the *t*-statistic in Equation (3.22) has a Student *t* distribution with $n - 1$ degrees of freedom.

To verify this result, recall from Section 2.4 that the Student *t* distribution with $n - 1$ degrees of freedom is defined to be the distribution of $Z/\sqrt{W/(n - 1)}$, where Z is a random variable with a standard normal distribution, W is a random variable with a chi-squared distribution with $n - 1$ degrees of freedom, and Z and W are independently distributed. When $Y_1, \ldots, Y_n$ are i.i.d. and the population distribution of Y is $N(\mu_Y, \sigma_Y^2)$, the *t*-statistic can be written as such a ratio. Specifically, let $Z = (\overline{Y} - \mu_{Y,0})/\sqrt{\sigma_Y^2/n}$ and let $W = (n - 1)s_Y^2/\sigma_Y^2$; then some algebra[1] shows that the *t*-statistic in Equation (3.22) can be written as $t = Z/\sqrt{W/(n - 1)}$. Recall from Section 2.4 that if $Y_1, \ldots, Y_n$ are i.i.d. and the population distribution of Y is $N(\mu_Y, \sigma_Y^2)$, then the sampling distribution of $\overline{Y}$ is exactly $N(\mu_Y, \sigma_Y^2/n)$ for all n; thus, if the null hypothesis $\mu_Y = \mu_{Y,0}$ is correct, then $Z = (\overline{Y} - \mu_{Y,0})/\sqrt{\sigma_Y^2/n}$ has a standard normal distribution for all n. In addition, $W = (n - 1)s_Y^2/\sigma_Y^2$ has a χ_{n-1}^2 distribution for all n, and $\overline{Y}$ and s_Y^2 are independently distributed. It follows that, if the population distribution of Y is normal, then under the null hypothesis the *t*-statistic given in Equation (3.22) has an exact Student *t* distribution with $n - 1$ degrees of freedom.

If the population distribution is normally distributed, then critical values from the Student *t* distribution can be used to perform hypothesis tests and to construct confidence intervals. As an example, consider a hypothetical problem in which $t^{act} = 2.15$ and $n = 20$ so that the degrees of freedom is $n - 1 = 19$. From Appendix Table 2, the 5% two-sided critical value for the t_{19} distribution is 2.09. Because the *t*-statistic is larger in absolute value than the critical value (2.15 > 2.09), the null hypothesis would be rejected at the 5% significance level against the two-sided alternative. The 95% confidence interval for μ_Y, constructed using the t_{19} distribution, would be $\overline{Y} \pm 2.09 SE(\overline{Y})$. This confidence interval is somewhat wider than the confidence interval constructed using the standard normal critical value of 1.96.

The t-statistic testing differences of means.   The *t*-statistic testing the difference of two means, given in Equation (3.20), does not have a Student *t* distribution, even if the population distribution of Y is normal. The Student *t* distribution does not apply here because the variance estimator used to compute the standard error in Equation (3.19) does not produce a denominator in the *t*-statistic with a chi-squared distribution.

---

[1]The desired expression is obtained by multiplying and dividing by $\sqrt{\sigma_Y^2}$ and collecting terms:

$$t = \frac{\overline{Y} - \mu_{Y,0}}{\sqrt{s_Y^2/n}} = \frac{(\overline{Y} - \mu_{Y,0})}{\sqrt{\sigma_Y^2/n}} \div \sqrt{\frac{s_Y^2}{\sigma_Y^2}} = \frac{(\overline{Y} - \mu_{Y,0})}{\sqrt{\sigma_Y^2/n}} \div \sqrt{\frac{(n-1)s_Y^2/\sigma_Y^2}{n-1}} = Z \div \sqrt{W/(n-1)}.$$

A Novel Way to Boost Retirement Savings

Many economists think that workers tend not to save enough for their retirement. Conventional methods for encouraging retirement savings focus on financial incentives. Recently, however, economists have increasingly observed that behavior is not always in accord with conventional economic models. As a consequence, there has been an upsurge in interest in unconventional ways to influence economic decisions.

In an important study published in 2001, Brigitte Madrian and Dennis Shea considered one such unconventional method for stimulating retirement savings. Many firms offer retirement savings plans in which the firm matches, in full or in part, savings taken out of the paycheck of participating employees. Enrollment in such plans, called 401(k) plans after the applicable section of the U.S. tax code, is always optional. However, at some firms employees are automatically enrolled in such a plan unless they choose to opt out; at other firms employees are enrolled only if they choose to opt in. According to conventional economic models of behavior, the method of enrollment—opt out, or opt in—should scarcely matter: An employee who wants to change his or her enrollment status simply fills out a form, and the dollar value of the time required to fill out the form is very small compared with the financial implications of this decision. But, Madrian and Shea wondered, could this conventional reasoning be wrong? Does the *method of enrollment* in a savings plan directly affect its enrollment rate?

To measure the effect of the method of enrollment, Madrian and Shea studied a large firm that changed the default option for its 401(k) plan from nonparticipation to participation. They compared two groups of workers: those hired the year before the change and not automatically enrolled (but could opt in), and those hired in the year after the change and automatically enrolled (but could opt out). The financial aspects of the plan were the same. Madrian and Shea argued that there were no systematic differences between the workers hired before and after the change in the enrollment default. Thus, from an econometrician's perspective, the change was like a randomly assigned treatment and the causal effect of the change could be estimated by the difference in means between the two groups.

Madrian and Shea found that the default enrollment rule made a huge difference: The enrollment rate for the "opt-in" (control) group was 37.4% ($n = 4249$), whereas the enrollment rate for the "opt-out" (treatment) group was 85.9% ($n = 5801$). The estimate of the treatment effect is 48.5% ($= 85.9\% - 37.4\%$). Because their sample is large, the 95% confidence for the treatment effect is tight (46.8% to 50.2%).

To economists sympathetic to the enrollment default scheme should not matter. Maybe workers treated the default option as good advice (it was not), or maybe they just didn't want to think about growing old. Neither motive is economically rational—but both are consistent with the predictions of the growing field of "behavioral economics," and both could lead to accepting the default enrollment option.

This research had an important practical impact. In August 2006, Congress passed the Pension Protection Act, which (among other things) made it

continued

easier for firms to offer 401(k) plans in which enrollment is the default. The econometric findings of Madrian and Shea and others featured prominently in testimony on this aspect of the legislation.

To learn more about behavioral economics and the design of retirement savings plans, see Thaler and Benartzi (2004).

A modified version of the differences-of-means *t*-statistic, based on a different standard error formula—the "pooled" standard error formula—has an exact Student *t* distribution when *Y* is normally distributed; however, the pooled standard error formula applies only in the special case that the two groups have the same variance or that each group has the same number of observations (Exercise 3.21). Adopt the notation of Equation (3.19), so that the two groups are denoted as *m* and *w*. The pooled variance estimator is,

$$s_{pooled}^2 = \frac{1}{n_m + n_w - 2} \left[\underbrace{\sum_{i=1}^{n_m} (Y_i - \overline{Y}_m)^2}_{\text{group } m} + \underbrace{\sum_{i=1}^{n_w} (Y_i - \overline{Y}_w)^2}_{\text{group } w} \right], \quad (3.23)$$

where the first summation is for the observations in group *m* and the second summation is for the observations in group *w*. The pooled standard error of the difference in means is $SE_{pooled}(\overline{Y}_m - \overline{Y}_w) = s_{pooled} \times \sqrt{1/n_m + 1/n_w}$, and the pooled *t*-statistic is computed using Equation (3.20), where the standard error is the pooled standard error, $SE_{pooled}(\overline{Y}_m - \overline{Y}_w)$.

If the population distribution of *Y* in group *m* is $N(\mu_m, \sigma_m^2)$, if the population distribution of *Y* in group *w* is $N(\mu_w, \sigma_w^2)$, *and* if the two group variances are the same (that is, $\sigma_m^2 = \sigma_w^2$), then under the null hypothesis the *t*-statistic computed using the pooled standard error has a Student *t* distribution with $n_m + n_w - 2$ degrees of freedom.

The drawback of using the pooled variance estimator s_{pooled}^2 is that it applies only if the two population variances are the same (assuming $n_m \neq n_w$). If the population variances are different, the pooled variance estimator is biased and inconsistent. If the population variances are different but the pooled variance formula is used, the null distribution of the pooled *t*-statistic is not a Student *t* distribution, even if the data are normally distributed, in fact, it does not even have a standard normal distribution in large samples. Therefore, the pooled standard error and the pooled *t*-statistic should not be used unless you have a good reason to believe that the population variances are the same.

Use of the Student *t* Distribution in Practice

For the problem of testing the mean of Y, the Student t distribution is applicable if the underlying population distribution of Y is normal. For economic variables, however, normal distributions are the exception (for example, see the boxes in Chapter 2, "The Distribution of Earnings in the United States in 2004" and "A Bad Day on Wall Street"). Even if the underlying data are not normally distributed, the normal approximation to the distribution of the t-statistic is valid if the sample size is large. Therefore, inferences—hypothesis tests and confidence intervals—about the mean of a distribution should be based on the large-sample normal approximation.

When comparing two means, any economic reason for two groups having different means typically implies that the two groups also could have different variances. Accordingly, the pooled standard error formula is inappropriate and the correct standard error formula, which allows for different group variances, is as given in Equation (3.19). Even if the population distributions are normal, the t-statistic computed using the standard error formula in Equation (3.19) does not have a Student t distribution. In practice, therefore, inferences about differences in means should be based on Equation (3.19), used in conjunction with the large-sample standard normal approximation.

Even though the Student t distribution is rarely applicable in economics, some software uses the Student t distribution to compute p-values and confidence intervals. In practice, this does not pose a problem because the difference between the Student t distribution and the standard normal distribution is negligible if the sample size is large. For $n > 15$, the difference in the p-values computed using the Student t and standard normal distributions never exceed 0.01; for $n > 80$, they never exceed 0.002. In most modern applications, and in all applications in this textbook, the sample sizes are in the hundreds or thousands, large enough for the difference between the Student t distribution and the standard normal distribution to be negligible.

3.7 Scatterplots, the Sample Covariance, and the Sample Correlation

What is the relationship between age and earnings? This question, like many others, relates one variable, X (age), to another, Y (earnings). This section reviews three ways to summarize the relationship between variables: the scatterplot, the sample covariance, and the sample correlation coefficient.

FIGURE 3.2   **Scatterplot of Average Hourly Earnings vs. Age**

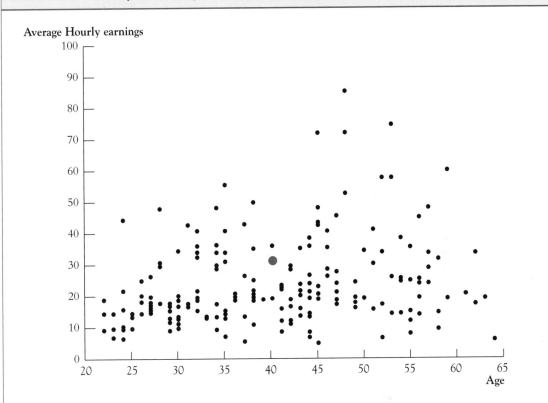

Each point in the plot represents the age and average earnings of one of the 200 workers in the sample. The colored dot corresponds to a 40-year-old worker who earns $31.25 per hour. The data are for technicians in the information industry from the March 2005 CPS.

Scatterplots

A **scatterplot** is a plot of n observations on X_i and Y_i, in which each observation is represented by the point (X_i, Y_i). For example, Figure 3.2 is a scatterplot of age (X) and hourly earnings (Y) for a sample of 200 workers in the information industry from the March 2005 CPS. Each dot in Figure 3.2 corresponds to an (X, Y) pair for one of the observations. For example one of the workers in this sample is 40 years old and earns $31.25 per hour; this worker's age and earnings are indicated by the colored dot in Figure 3.2. The scatterplot shows a positive relationship between age and earnings in this sample: Older workers tend to earn more than younger workers. This relationship is not exact, however, and earnings could not be predicted perfectly using only a person's age.

Sample Covariance and Correlation

The covariance and correlation were introduced in Section 2.3 as two properties of the joint probability distribution of the random variables X and Y. Because the population distribution is unknown, in practice we do not know the population covariance or correlation. The population covariance and correlation can, however, be estimated by taking a random sample of n members of the population and collecting the data (X_i, Y_i), $i = 1, \ldots, n$.

The sample covariance and correlation are estimators of the population covariance and correlation. Like the estimators discussed previously in this chapter, they are computed by replacing a population average (the expectation) with a sample average. The **sample covariance**, denoted s_{XY}, is

$$s_{XY} = \frac{1}{n-1} \sum_{i=1}^{n} (X_i - \overline{X})(Y_i - \overline{Y}). \tag{3.24}$$

Like the sample variance, the average in Equation (3.24) is computed by dividing by $n - 1$ instead of n; here, too, this difference stems from using $\overline{X}$ and $\overline{Y}$ to estimate the respective population means. When n is large, it makes little difference whether division is by n or $n - 1$.

The **sample correlation coefficient**, or **sample correlation**, is denoted r_{XY} and is the ratio of the sample covariance to the sample standard deviations:

$$r_{XY} = \frac{s_{XY}}{s_X s_Y}. \tag{3.25}$$

The sample correlation measures the strength of the linear association between X and Y in a sample of n observations. Like the population correlation, the sample correlation is unitless and lies between -1 and 1: $|r_{XY}| \leq 1$.

The sample correlation equals 1 if $X_i = Y_i$ for all i and equals -1 if $X_i = -Y_i$ for all i. More generally, the correlation is ± 1 if the scatterplot is a straight line. If the line slopes upward, then there is a positive relationship between X and Y and the correlation is 1. If the line slopes down, then there is a negative relationship and the correlation is -1. The closer the scatterplot is to a straight line, the closer is the correlation to ± 1. A high correlation coefficient does not necessarily mean that the line has a steep slope; rather, it means that the points in the scatterplot fall very close to a straight line.

Consistency of the sample covariance and correlation. Like the sample variance, the sample covariance is consistent. That is,

$$s_{XY} \xrightarrow{p} \sigma_{XY}. \tag{3.26}$$

In other words, in large samples the sample covariance is close to the population covariance with high probability.

The proof of the result in Equation (3.26) under the assumption that (X_i, Y_i) are i.i.d. and that X_i and Y_i have finite fourth moments is similar to the proof in Appendix 3.3 that the sample covariance is consistent, and is left as an exercise (Exercise 3.20).

Because the sample variance and sample covariance are consistent, the sample correlation coefficient is consistent, that is, $r_{XY} \xrightarrow{p} \text{corr}(X_i, Y_i)$.

Example.   As an example, consider the data on age and earnings in Figure 3.2. For these 200 workers, the sample standard deviation of age is $s_A = 10.75$ years and the sample standard deviation of earnings is $s_E = \$13.79$/hour. The covariance between age and earnings is $s_{AE} = 37.01$ (the units are years × dollars per hour, not readily interpretable). Thus, the correlation coefficient is $r_{AE} = 37.01/(10.75 \times 13.79) = 0.25$ or 25%. The correlation of 0.25 means that there is a positive relationship between age and earnings, but as is evident in the scatterplot, this relationship is far from perfect.

To verify that the correlation does not depend on the units of measurement, suppose that earnings had been reported in cents, in which case the sample standard deviations of earnings is 1379¢/hour and the covariance between age and earnings is 3701 (units are years × cents/hour); then the correlation is $3701/(10.75 \times 1379) = 0.25$ or 25%.

Figure 3.3 gives additional examples of scatterplots and correlation. Figure 3.3a shows a strong positive linear relationship between these variables, and the sample correlation is 0.9. Figure 3.3b shows a strong negative relationship with a sample correlation of -0.8. Figure 3.3c shows a scatterplot with no evident relationship, and the sample correlation is zero. Figure 3.3d shows a clear relationship: As X increases, Y initially increases but then decreases. Despite this discernable relationship between X and Y, the sample correlation is zero; the reason is that, for these data, small values of Y are associated with *both* large and small values of X.

This final example emphasizes an important point: The correlation coefficient is a measure of *linear* association. There is a relationship in Figure 3.3d, but it is not linear.

FIGURE 3.3 Scatterplots for Four Hypothetical Data Sets

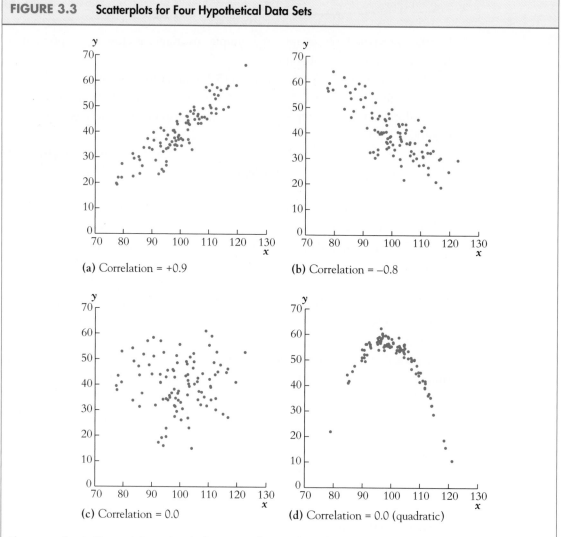

(a) Correlation = +0.9

(b) Correlation = −0.8

(c) Correlation = 0.0

(d) Correlation = 0.0 (quadratic)

The scatterplots in Figures 3.3a and 3.3b show strong linear relationships between X and Y. In Figure 3.3c, X is independent of Y and the two variables are uncorrelated. In Figure 3.3d, the two variables also are uncorrelated even though they are related nonlinearly.

Summary

1. The sample average, $\overline{Y}$, is an estimator of the population mean, μ_Y. When $Y_1, \ldots,$ Y_n are i.i.d.,

    a. the sampling distribution of $\overline{Y}$ has mean μ_Y and variance $\sigma_{\overline{Y}}^2 = \sigma_Y^2/n$;

    b. $\overline{Y}$ is unbiased;

   c. by the law of large numbers, $\overline{Y}$ is consistent; and

   d. by the central limit theorem, $\overline{Y}$ has an approximately normal sampling distribution when the sample size is large.

2. The t-statistic is used to test the null hypothesis that the population mean takes on a particular value. If n is large, the t-statistic has a standard normal sampling distribution when the null hypothesis is true.

3. The t-statistic can be used to calculate the p-value associated with the null hypothesis. A small p-value is evidence that the null hypothesis is false.

4. A 95% confidence interval for μ_Y is an interval constructed so that it contains the true value of μ_Y in 95% of repeated samples.

5. Hypothesis tests and confidence intervals for the difference in the means of two populations are conceptually similar to tests and intervals for the mean of a single population.

6. The sample correlation coefficient is an estimator of the population correlation coefficient and measures the linear relationship between two variables—that is, how well their scatterplot is approximated by a straight line.

Key Terms

estimator (65)

estimate (65)

bias, consistency, and efficiency (66)

BLUE (67)

least squares estimator (68)

hypothesis test (69)

null and alternative hypotheses (70)

two-sided alternative hypothesis (70)

p-value (significance probability) (71)

sample variance (73)

sample standard deviation (73)

degrees of freedom (73)

standard error of an estimator (74)

t-statistic (t-ratio) (75)

test statistic (75)

type I error (77)

type II error (77)

significance level (77)

critical value (77)

rejection region (77)

acceptance region (77)

size of a test (77)

power (77)

one-sided alternative hypothesis (78)

confidence set (79)

confidence level (79)

confidence interval (79)

coverage probability (81)

test for the difference between
    two means (81)

causal effect (83)

treatment effect (83)

scatterplot (91)

sample covariance (92)

sample correlation coefficient
    (sample correlation) (92)

Review the Concepts

3.1 Explain the difference between the sample average $\overline{Y}$ and the population mean.

3.2 Explain the difference between an estimator and an estimate. Provide an example of each.

3.3 A population distribution has a mean of 10 and a variance of 16. Determine the mean and variance of $\overline{Y}$ from an i.i.d. sample from this population for (a) $n = 10$; (b) $n = 100$; and (c) $n = 1000$. Relate your answers to the law of large numbers.

3.4 What role does the central limit theorem play in statistical hypothesis testing? In the construction of confidence intervals?

3.5 What is the difference between a null and alternative hypothesis? Among size, significance level, and power? Between a one-sided and two-sided alternative hypothesis?

3.6 Why does a confidence interval contain more information than the result of a single hypothesis test?

3.7 Explain why the differences-of-means estimator, applied to data from a randomized controlled experiment, is an estimator of the treatment effect.

3.8 Sketch a hypothetical scatterplot for a sample of size 10 for two random variables with a population correlation of (a) 1.0; (b) -1.0; (c) 0.9; (d) -0.5; (e) 0.0.

Exercises

3.1 In a population $\mu_Y = 100$ and $\sigma_Y^2 = 43$. Use the central limit theorem to answer the following questions:

a. In a random sample of size $n = 100$, find $\Pr(\overline{Y} < 101)$.

b. In a random sample of size $n = 64$, find $\Pr(101 < \overline{Y} < 103)$.

c. In a random sample of size $n = 165$, find $\Pr(\overline{Y} > 98)$.

3.2 Let Y be a Bernoulli random variable with success probability $\Pr(Y = 1) = p$, and let $Y_1, \ldots, Y_n$ be i.i.d. draws from this distribution. Let $\hat{p}$ be the fraction of successes (1s) in this sample.

a. Show that $\hat{p} = \overline{Y}$.

b. Show that $\hat{p}$ is an unbiased estimator of p.

c. Show that $\mathrm{var}(\hat{p}) = p(1 - p)/n$.

3.3 In a survey of 400 likely voters, 215 responded that they would vote for the incumbent and 185 responded that they would vote for the challenger. Let p denote the fraction of all likely voters who preferred the incumbent at the time of the survey, and let $\hat{p}$ be the fraction of survey respondents who preferred the incumbent.

  a. Use the survey results to estimate p.

  b. Use the estimator of the variance of $\hat{p}$, $\hat{p}(1 - \hat{p})/n$, to calculate the standard error of your estimator.

  c. What is the p-value for the test $H_0: p = 0.5$ vs. $H_1: p \neq 0.5$?

  d. What is the p-value for the test $H_0: p = 0.5$ vs. $H_1: p > 0.5$?

  e. Why do the results from (c) and (d) differ?

  f. Did the survey contain statistically significant evidence that the incumbent was ahead of the challenger at the time of the survey? Explain.

3.4 Using the data in Exercise 3.3:

  a. Construct a 95% confidence interval for p.

  b. Construct a 99% confidence interval for p.

  c. Why is the interval in (b) wider than the interval in (a)?

  d. Without doing any additional calculations, test the hypothesis $H_0: p = 0.50$ vs. $H_1: p \neq 0.50$ at the 5% significance level.

3.5 A survey of 1055 registered voters is conducted, and the voters are asked to choose between candidate A and candidate B. Let p denote the fraction of voters in the population who prefer candidate A, and let $\hat{p}$ denote the fraction of voters in the sample who prefer Candidate A.

  a. You are interested in the competing hypotheses: $H_0: p = 0.5$ vs. $H_1: p \neq 0.5$. Suppose that you decide to reject H_0 if $|\hat{p} - 0.5| > 0.02$.

   i. What is the size of this test?

   ii. Compute the power of this test if $p = 0.53$.

  b. In the survey $\hat{p} = 0.54$.

   i. Test $H_0: p = 0.5$ vs. $H_1: p \neq 0.5$ using a 5% significance level.

   ii. Test $H_0: p = 0.5$ vs. $H_1: p > 0.5$ using a 5% significance level.

   iii. Construct a 95% confidence interval for p.

   iv. Construct a 99% confidence interval for p.

   v. Construct a 50% confidence interval for p.

c. Suppose that the survey is carried out 20 times, using independently selected voters in each survey. For each of these 20 surveys, a 95% confidence interval for p is constructed.

   i. What is the probability that the true value of p is contained in all 20 of these confidence intervals?

   ii. How many of these confidence intervals do you expect to contain the true value of p?

d. In survey jargon, the "margin of error" is $1.96 \times SE(\hat{p})$; that is, it is $\frac{1}{2}$ times the length of 95% confidence interval. Suppose you wanted to design a survey that had a margin of error of at most 1%. That is, you wanted $\Pr(|\hat{p} - p| > 0.01) \leq 0.05$. How large should n be if the survey uses simple random sampling?

3.6 Let $Y_1, \ldots, Y_n$ be i.i.d. draws from a distribution with mean μ. A test of $H_0: \mu = 5$ versus $H_1: \mu \neq 5$ using the usual t-statistic yields a p-value of 0.03.

a. Does the 95% confidence interval contain $\mu = 5$? Explain.

b. Can you determine if $\mu = 6$ is contained in the 95% confidence interval? Explain.

3.7 In a given population, 11% of the likely voters are African American. A survey using a simple random sample of 600 land-line telephone numbers finds 8% African Americans. Is there evidence that the survey is biased? Explain.

3.8 A new version of the SAT test is given to 1000 randomly selected high school seniors. The sample mean test score is 1110 and the sample standard deviation is 123. Construct a 95% confidence interval for the population mean test score for high school seniors.

3.9 Suppose that a lightbulb manufacturing plant produces bulbs with a mean life of 2000 hours and a standard deviation of 200 hours. An inventor claims to have developed an improved process that produces bulbs with a longer mean life and the same standard deviation. The plant manager randomly selects 100 bulbs produced by the process. She says that she will believe the inventor's claim if the sample mean life of the bulbs is greater than 2100 hours; otherwise, she will conclude that the new process is no better than the old process. Let μ denote the mean of the new process. Consider the null and alternative hypothesis $H_0: \mu = 2000$ vs. $H_1: \mu > 2000$.

a. What is the size of the plant manager's testing procedure?

b. Suppose that the new process is in fact better and has a mean bulb life of 2150 hours. What is the power of the plant manager's testing procedure?

   c. What testing procedure should the plant manager use if she wants the size of her test to be 5%?

3.10 Suppose a new standardized test is given to 100 randomly selected third-grade students in New Jersey. The sample average score $\overline{Y}$ on the test is 58 points and the sample standard deviation, s_Y, is 8 points.

   a. The authors plan to administer the test to all third-grade students in New Jersey. Construct a 95% confidence interval for the mean score of all New Jersey third graders.

   b. Suppose the same test is given to 200 randomly selected third graders from Iowa, producing a sample average of 62 points and sample standard deviation of 11 points. Construct a 90% confidence interval for the difference in mean scores between Iowa and New Jersey.

   c. Can you conclude with a high degree of confidence that the population means for Iowa and New Jersey students are different? (What is the standard error of the difference in the two sample means? What is the p-value of the test of no difference in means versus some difference?)

3.11 Consider the estimator $\widetilde{Y}$, defined in Equation (3.1). Show that (a) $E(\widetilde{Y}) = \mu_Y$ and (b) $\text{var}(\widetilde{Y}) = 1.25\sigma_Y^2/n$.

3.12 To investigate possible gender discrimination in a firm, a sample of 100 men and 64 women with similar job descriptions are selected at random. A summary of the resulting monthly salaries follows:

	Average Salary ($\overline{Y}$)	Standard Deviation (s_Y)	n
Men	$3100	$200	100
Women	$2900	$320	64

   a. What do these data suggest about wage differences in the firm? Do they represent statistically significant evidence that wages of men and women are different? (To answer this question, first state the null and alternative hypothesis; second, compute the relevant t-statistic; third, compute the p-value associated with the t-statistic; and finally use the p-value to answer the question.)

   b. Do these data suggest that the firm is guilty of gender discrimination in its compensation policies? Explain.

3.13 Data on fifth-grade test scores (reading and mathematics) for 420 school districts in California yield $\overline{Y} = 646.2$ and standard deviation $s_Y = 19.5$.

a. Construct a 95% confidence interval for the mean test score in the population.

b. When the districts were divided into districts with small classes (<20 students per teacher) and large classes (≥ 20 students per teacher), the following results were found:

Class Size	Average Score ($\overline{Y}$)	Standard Deviation (s_Y)	n
Small	657.4	19.4	238
Large	650.0	17.9	182

Is there statistically significant evidence that the districts with smaller classes have higher average test scores? Explain.

3.14 Values of height in inches (X) and weight in pounds (Y) are recorded from a sample of 300 male college students. The resulting summary statistics are $\overline{X} = 70.5$ inches; $\overline{Y} = 158$ lbs; $s_X = 1.8$ inches; $s_Y = 14.2$ lbs; $s_{XY} = 21.73$ inches × lbs, and $r_{XY} = 0.85$. Convert these statistics to the metric system (meters and kilograms).

3.15 The CNN/USA Today/Gallup poll conducted on September 3–5, 2004, surveyed 755 likely voters; 405 reported a preference for President George W. Bush, and 350 reported a preference for Senator John Kerry. The CNN/USA Today/Gallup poll conducted on October 1–3, 2004, surveyed 756 likely voters; 378 reported a preference for Bush, and 378 reported a preference for Kerry.

a. Construct a 95% confidence interval for the fraction of likely voters in the population who favored Bush in early September 2004.

b. Construct a 95% confidence interval for the fraction of likely voters in the population who favored Bush in early October 2004.

c. Was there a statistically significant change in voters' opinions across the two dates?

3.16 Grades on a standardized test are known to have a mean of 1000 for students in the United States. The test is administered to 453 randomly selected students in Florida; in this sample, the mean is 1013 and the standard deviation (s) is 108.

a. Construct a 95% confidence interval for the average test score for Florida students.

b. Is there statistically significant evidence that Florida students perform differently than other students in the United States?

c. Another 503 students are selected at random from Florida. They are given a three-hour preparation course before the test is administered. Their average test score is 1019 with a standard deviation of 95.

    i. Construct a 95% confidence interval for the change in average test score associated with the prep course.

    ii. Is there statistically significant evidence that the prep course helped?

d. The original 453 students are given the prep course and then asked to take the test a second time. The average change in their test scores is 9 points, and the standard deviation of the change is 60 points.

    i. Construct a 95% confidence interval for the change in average test scores.

    ii. Is there statistically significant evidence that students will perform better on their second attempt after taking the prep course?

    iii. Students may have performed better in their second attempt because of the prep course or because they gained test-taking experience in their first attempt. Describe an experiment that would quantify these two effects.

3.17 Read the box "The Gender Gap in Earnings of College Graduates in the United States."

    a. Construct a 95% confidence interval for the change in men's average hourly earnings between 1992 and 2004.

    b. Construct a 95% confidence interval for the change in women's average hourly earnings between 1992 and 2004.

    c. Construct a 95% confidence interval for the change in the gender gap in average hourly earnings between 1992 and 2004. (*Hint:* $\overline{Y}_{m,1992} - \overline{Y}_{w,1992}$ is independent of $\overline{Y}_{m,2004} - \overline{Y}_{w,2004}$.)

3.18 This exercise shows that the sample variance is an unbiased estimator of the population variance when $Y_1, \ldots, Y_n$ are i.i.d. with mean μ_Y and variance σ_Y^2.

    a. Use Equation (2.31) to show that $E[(Y_i - \overline{Y})^2] = \text{var}(Y_i) - 2\text{cov}(Y_i, \overline{Y}) + \text{var}(\overline{Y})$.

  b. Use Equation (2.33) to show that $\text{cov}(\overline{Y}, Y_i) = \sigma_Y^2/n$.

  c. Use the results in parts (a) and (b) to show that $E(s_Y^2) = \sigma_Y^2$.

3.19 **a.** $\overline{Y}$ is an unbiased estimator of μ_Y. Is $\overline{Y}^2$ an unbiased estimator of μ_Y^2?

  b. $\overline{Y}$ is a consistent estimator of μ_Y. Is $\overline{Y}^2$ a consistent estimator of μ_Y^2?

3.20 Suppose that (X_i, Y_i) are i.i.d. with finite fourth moments. Prove that the sample covariance is a consistent estimator of the population covariance, that is, $s_{XY} \xrightarrow{p} \sigma_{XY}$, where s_{XY} is defined in Equation (3.24). (*Hint:* Use the strategy of Appendix 3.3 and the Cauchy-Schwartz inequality.)

3.21 Show that the pooled standard error $[SE_{pooled}(\overline{Y}_m - \overline{Y}_w)]$ given following Equation (3.23) equals the usual standard error for the difference in means in Equation (3.19) when the two group sizes are the same ($n_m = n_w$).

Empirical Exercise

E3.1   On the text Web site **www.aw-bc.com/stock_watson** you will find a data file **CPS92_04** that contains an extended version of the dataset used in Table 3.1 of the text for the years 1992 and 2004. It contains data on full-time, full-year workers, age 25–34, with a high school diploma or B.A./B.S. as their highest degree. A detailed description is given in **CPS92_04_Description**, available on the Web site. Use these data to answer the following questions.

  a. Compute the sample mean for average hourly earnings (AHE) in 1992 and in 2004. Construct a 95% confidence interval for the population means of AHE in 1992 and 2004 and the change between 1992 and 2004.

  b. In 2004, the value of the Consumer Price Index (CPI) was 188.9. In 1992, the value of the CPI was 140.3. Repeat (a) but use AHE measured in real 2004 dollars ($2004); that is, adjust the 1992 data for the price inflation that occurred between 1992 and 2004.

  c. If you were interested in the change in workers' purchasing power from 1992 to 2004, would you use the results from (a) or from (b)? Explain.

  d. Use the 2004 data to construct a 95% confidence interval for the mean of AHE for high school graduates. Construct a 95% confidence interval for the mean of AHE for workers with a college degree. Construct a 95% confidence interval for the difference between the two means.

e. Repeat (d) using the 1992 data expressed in $2004.

f. Did real (inflation-adjusted) wages of high school graduates increase from 1992 to 2004? Explain. Did real wages of college graduates increase? Did the gap between earnings of college and high school graduates increase? Explain, using appropriate estimates, confidence intervals, and test statistics.

g. Table 3.1 presents information on the gender gap for college graduates. Prepare a similar table for high school graduates using the 1992 and 2004 data. Are there any notable differences between the results for high school and college graduates?

APPENDIX
3.1 | The U.S. Current Population Survey

Each month the Bureau of Labor Statistics in the U.S. Department of Labor conducts the "Current Population Survey" (CPS), which provides data on labor force characteristics of the population, including the level of employment, unemployment, and earnings. More than 50,000 U.S. households are surveyed each month. The sample is chosen by randomly selecting addresses from a database of addresses from the most recent decennial census augmented with data on new housing units constructed after the last census. The exact random sampling scheme is rather complicated (first, small geographical areas are randomly selected, then housing units within these areas are randomly selected); details can be found in the *Handbook of Labor Statistics* and on the Bureau of Labor Statistics Web site (www.bls.gov).

The survey conducted each March is more detailed than in other months and asks questions about earnings during the previous year. The statistics in Table 3.1 were computed using the March surveys. The CPS earnings data are for full-time workers, defined to be somebody employed more than 35 hours per week for at least 48 weeks in the previous year.

Two Proofs That $\overline{Y}$ Is the Least Squares Estimator of μ_Y

This appendix provides two proofs, one using calculus and one not, that $\overline{Y}$ minimizes the sum of squared prediction mistakes in Equation (3.2)—that is, that $\overline{Y}$ is the least squares estimator of $E(Y)$.

Calculus Proof

To minimize the sum of squared prediction mistakes, take its derivative and set it to zero:

$$\frac{d}{dm} \sum_{i=1}^{n} (Y_i - m)^2 = -2 \sum_{i=1}^{n} (Y_i - m) = -2 \sum_{i=1}^{n} Y_i + 2nm = 0. \tag{3.27}$$

Solving for the final equation for m shows that $\sum_{i=1}^{n}(Y_i - m)^2$ is minimized when $m = \overline{Y}$.

Non-calculus Proof

The strategy is to show that the difference between the least squares estimator and $\overline{Y}$ must be zero, from which it follows that $\overline{Y}$ is the least squares estimator. Let $d = \overline{Y} - m$, so that $m = \overline{Y} - d$. Then $(Y_i - m)^2 = (Y_i - [\overline{Y} - d])^2 = ([Y_i - \overline{Y}] + d)^2 = (Y_i - \overline{Y})^2 + 2d(Y_i - \overline{Y}) + d^2$. Thus, the sum of squared prediction mistakes [Equation (3.2)] is

$$\sum_{i=1}^{n} (Y_i - m)^2 = \sum_{i=1}^{n} (Y_i - \overline{Y})^2 + 2d \sum_{i=1}^{n} (Y_i - \overline{Y}) + nd^2 = \sum_{i=1}^{n} (Y_i - \overline{Y})^2 + nd^2, \tag{3.28}$$

where the second equality uses the fact that $\sum_{i=1}^{n}(Y_i - \overline{Y}) = 0$. Because both terms in the final line of Equation (3.28) are nonnegative and because the first term does not depend on d, $\sum_{i=1}^{n}(Y_i - m)^2$ is minimized by choosing d to make the second term, nd^2, as small as possible. This is done by setting $d = 0$, that is, by setting $m = \overline{Y}$, so that $\overline{Y}$ is the least squares estimator of $E(Y)$.

APPENDIX

3.3 | A Proof That the Sample Variance Is Consistent

This appendix uses the law of large numbers to prove that the sample variance s_Y^2 is a consistent estimator of the population variance σ_Y^2, as stated in Equation (3.9), when $Y_1, \ldots, Y_n$ are i.i.d. and $E(Y_i^4) < \infty$.

First, add and subtract μ_Y to write $(Y_i - \overline{Y})^2 = [(Y_i - \mu_Y) - (\overline{Y} - \mu_Y)]^2 = (Y_i - \mu_Y)^2 - 2(Y_i - \mu_Y)(\overline{Y} - \mu_Y) + (\overline{Y} - \mu_Y)^2$. Substituting this expression for $(Y_i - \overline{Y})^2$ into the definition of s_Y^2 [Equation (3.7)], we have that

$$s_Y^2 = \frac{1}{n-1} \sum_{i=1}^{n} (Y_i - \overline{Y})^2$$

$$= \frac{1}{n-1} \sum_{i=1}^{n} (Y_i - \mu_Y)^2 - \frac{2}{n-1} \sum_{i=1}^{n} (Y_i - \mu_Y)(\overline{Y} - \mu_Y) + \frac{1}{n-1} \sum_{i=1}^{n} (\overline{Y} - \mu_Y)^2$$

$$= \left(\frac{n}{n-1}\right) \left[\frac{1}{n} \sum_{i=1}^{n} (Y_i - \mu_Y)^2\right] - \left(\frac{n}{n-1}\right)(\overline{Y} - \mu_Y)^2, \tag{3.29}$$

where the final equality follows from the definition of $\overline{Y}$ [which implies that $\sum_{i=1}^{n}(Y_i - \mu_Y) = n(\overline{Y} - \mu_Y)$] and by collecting terms.

The law of large numbers can now be applied to the two terms in the final line of Equation (3.29). Define $W_i = (Y_i - \mu_Y)^2$. Now $E(W_i) = \sigma_Y^2$ (by the definition of the variance). Because the random variables $Y_1, \ldots, Y_n$ are i.i.d., the random variables $W_1, \ldots, W_n$ are i.i.d. In addition, $E(W_i^2) = E[(Y_i - \mu_Y)^4] < \infty$ because, by assumption, $E(Y_i^4) < \infty$. Thus $W_1, \ldots, W_n$ are i.i.d. and $\text{var}(W_i) < \infty$, so $\overline{W}$ satisfies the conditions for the law of large numbers in Key Concept 2.6 and $\overline{W} \xrightarrow{p} E(W_i)$. But $\overline{W} = \frac{1}{n}\sum_{i=1}^{n}(Y_i - \mu_Y)^2$ and $E(W_i) = \sigma_Y^2$, so $\frac{1}{n}\sum_{i=1}^{n}(Y_i - \mu_Y)^2 \xrightarrow{p} \sigma_Y^2$. Also, $n/(n-1) \longrightarrow 1$, so the first term in Equation (3.29) converges in probability to σ_Y^2. Because $\overline{Y} \xrightarrow{p} \mu_Y$, $(\overline{Y} - \mu_Y)^2 \xrightarrow{p} 0$ so the second term converges in probability to zero. Combining these results yields $s_Y^2 \xrightarrow{p} \sigma_Y^2$.

PART TWO | # Fundamentals of Regression Analysis

CHAPTER **4**

Linear Regression
with One Regressor

A state implements tough new penalties on drunk drivers: What is the effect on highway fatalities? A school district cuts the size of its elementary school classes: What is the effect on its students' standardized test scores? You successfully complete one more year of college classes: What is the effect on your future earnings?

All three of these questions are about the unknown effect of changing one variable, X (X being penalties for drunk driving, class size, or years of schooling), on another variable, Y (Y being highway deaths, student test scores, or earnings).

This chapter introduces the linear regression model relating one variable, X, to another, Y. This model postulates a linear relationship between X and Y; the slope of the line relating X and Y is the effect of a one-unit change in X on Y. Just as the mean of Y is an unknown characteristic of the population distribution of Y, the slope of the line relating X and Y is an unknown characteristic of the population joint distribution of X and Y. The econometric problem is to estimate this slope—that is, to estimate the effect on Y of a unit change in X—using a sample of data on these two variables.

This chapter describes methods for estimating this slope using a random sample of data on X and Y. For instance, using data on class sizes and test scores from different school districts, we show how to estimate the expected effect on test scores of reducing class sizes by, say, one student per class. The slope and the intercept of the line relating X and Y can be estimated by a method called ordinary least squares (OLS).

4.1 The Linear Regression Model

The superintendent of an elementary school district must decide whether to hire additional teachers and she wants your advice. If she hires the teachers, she will reduce the number of students per teacher (the student–teacher ratio) by two. She faces a tradeoff. Parents want smaller classes so that their children can receive more individualized attention. But hiring more teachers means spending more money, which is not to the liking of those paying the bill! So she asks you: If she cuts class sizes, what will the effect be on student performance?

In many school districts, student performance is measured by standardized tests, and the job status or pay of some administrators can depend in part on how well their students do on these tests. We therefore sharpen the superintendent's question: If she reduces the average class size by two students, what will the effect be on standardized test scores in her district?

A precise answer to this question requires a quantitative statement about changes. If the superintendent *changes* the class size by a certain amount, what would she expect the *change* in standardized test scores to be? We can write this as a mathematical relationship using the Greek letter beta, $\beta_{ClassSize}$, where the subscript "ClassSize" distinguishes the effect of changing the class size from other effects. Thus,

$$\beta_{ClassSize} = \frac{\text{change in TestScore}}{\text{change in ClassSize}} = \frac{\Delta \text{TestScore}}{\Delta \text{ClassSize}}, \tag{4.1}$$

where the Greek letter Δ (delta) stands for "change in." That is, $\beta_{ClassSize}$ is the change in the test score that results from changing the class size, divided by the change in the class size.

If you were lucky enough to know $\beta_{ClassSize}$, you would be able to tell the superintendent that decreasing class size by one student would change districtwide test scores by $\beta_{ClassSize}$. You could also answer the superintendent's actual question, which concerned changing class size by two students per class. To do so, rearrange Equation (4.1) so that

$$\Delta TestScore = \beta_{ClassSize} \times \Delta ClassSize. \tag{4.2}$$

Suppose that $\beta_{ClassSize} = -0.6$. Then a reduction in class size of two students per class would yield a predicted change in test scores of $(-0.6) \times (-2) = 1.2$; that is, you would predict that test scores would *rise* by 1.2 points as a result of the *reduction* in class sizes by two students per class.

Equation (4.1) is the definition of the slope of a straight line relating test scores and class size. This straight line can be written

$$TestScore = \beta_0 + \beta_{ClassSize} \times ClassSize, \qquad (4.3)$$

where β_0 is the intercept of this straight line, and, as before, $\beta_{ClassSize}$ is the slope. According to Equation (4.3), if you knew β_0 and $\beta_{ClassSize}$, not only would you be able to determine the *change* in test scores at a district associated with a *change* in class size, but you also would be able to predict the average test score itself for a given class size.

When you propose Equation (4.3) to the superintendent, she tells you that something is wrong with this formulation. She points out that class size is just one of many facets of elementary education, and that two districts with the same class sizes will have different test scores for many reasons. One district might have better teachers or it might use better textbooks. Two districts with comparable class sizes, teachers, and textbooks still might have very different student populations; perhaps one district has more immigrants (and thus fewer native English speakers) or wealthier families. Finally, she points out that, even if two districts are the same in all these ways, they might have different test scores for essentially random reasons having to do with the performance of the individual students on the day of the test. She is right, of course; for all these reasons, Equation (4.3) will not hold exactly for all districts. Instead, it should be viewed as a statement about a relationship that holds *on average* across the population of districts.

A version of this linear relationship that holds for *each* district must incorporate these other factors influencing test scores, including each district's unique characteristics (for example, quality of their teachers, background of their students, how lucky the students were on test day). One approach would be to list the most important factors and to introduce them explicitly into Equation (4.3) (an idea we return to in Chapter 6). For now, however, we simply lump all these "other factors" together and write the relationship for a given district as

$$TestScore = \beta_0 + \beta_{ClassSize} \times ClassSize + \text{other factors.} \qquad (4.4)$$

Thus, the test score for the district is written in terms of one component, $\beta_0 + \beta_{ClassSize} \times ClassSize,$ that represents the average effect of class size on scores in the population of school districts and a second component that represents all other factors.

Although this discussion has focused on test scores and class size, the idea expressed in Equation (4.4) is much more general, so it is useful to introduce more general notation. Suppose you have a sample of n districts. Let Y_i be the average test score in the ith district, let X_i be the average class size in the ith district, and let u_i denote the other factors influencing the test score in the ith district. Then Equation (4.4) can be written more generally as

$$Y_i = \beta_0 + \beta_1 X_i + u_i, \tag{4.5}$$

for each district, (that is, $i = 1, \ldots, n$), where β_0 is the intercept of this line and β_1 is the slope. [The general notation "β_1" is used for the slope in Equation (4.5) instead of "$\beta_{ClassSize}$" because this equation is written in terms of a general variable X_i.]

Equation (4.5) is the **linear regression model with a single regressor**, in which Y is the **dependent variable** and X is the **independent variable** or the **regressor**.

The first part of Equation (4.5), $\beta_0 + \beta_1 X_i$, is the **population regression line** or the **population regression function**. This is the relationship that holds between Y and X on average over the population. Thus, if you knew the value of X, according to this population regression line you would predict that the value of the dependent variable, Y, is $\beta_0 + \beta_1 X$.

The **intercept** β_0 and the **slope** β_1 are the **coefficients** of the population regression line, also known as the **parameters** of the population regression line. The slope β_1 is the change in Y associated with a unit change in X. The intercept is the value of the population regression line when $X = 0$; it is the point at which the population regression line intersects the Y axis. In some econometric applications, the intercept has a meaningful economic interpretation. In other applications, the intercept has no real-world meaning; for example, when X is the class size, strictly speaking the intercept is the predicted value of test scores when there are no students in the class! When the real-world meaning of the intercept is nonsensical it is best to think of it mathematically as the coefficient that determines the level of the regression line.

The term u_i in Equation (4.5) is the **error term**. The error term incorporates all of the factors responsible for the difference between the ith district's average test score and the value predicted by the population regression line. This error term contains all the other factors besides X that determine the value of the dependent variable, Y, for a specific observation, i. In the class size example, these other factors include all the unique features of the ith district that affect the performance of its students on the test, including teacher quality, student economic background, luck, and even any mistakes in grading the test.

The linear regression model and its terminology are summarized in Key Concept 4.1.

TERMINOLOGY FOR THE LINEAR REGRESSION MODEL WITH A SINGLE REGRESSOR	**KEY CONCEPT** 4.1

The linear regression model is

$$Y_i = \beta_0 + \beta_1 X_i + u_i,$$

where

the subscript i runs over observations, $i = 1, \ldots, n$;

Y_i is the *dependent variable*, the *regressand*, or simply the *left-hand variable*;

X_i is the *independent variable*, the *regressor*, or simply the *right-hand variable*;

$\beta_0 + \beta_1 X$ is the *population regression line* or *population regression function*;

β_0 is the *intercept* of the population regression line;

β_1 is the *slope* of the population regression line; and

u_i is the *error term*.

Figure 4.1 summarizes the linear regression model with a single regressor for seven hypothetical observations on test scores (Y) and class size (X). The population regression line is the straight line $\beta_0 + \beta_1 X$. The population regression line slopes down ($\beta_1 < 0$), which means that districts with lower student–teacher ratios (smaller classes) tend to have higher test scores. The intercept β_0 has a mathematical meaning as the value of the Y axis intersected by the population regression line, but, as mentioned earlier, it has no real-world meaning in this example.

Because of the other factors that determine test performance, the hypothetical observations in Figure 4.1 do not fall exactly on the population regression line. For example, the value of Y for district #1, Y_1, is above the population regression line. This means that test scores in district #1 were better than predicted by the population regression line, so the error term for that district, u_1, is positive. In contrast, Y_2 is below the population regression line, so test scores for that district were worse than predicted, and $u_2 < 0$.

Now return to your problem as advisor to the superintendent: What is the expected effect on test scores of reducing the student–teacher ratio by two students per teacher? The answer is easy: The expected change is $(-2) \times \beta_{ClassSize}$. But what is the value of $\beta_{ClassSize}$?

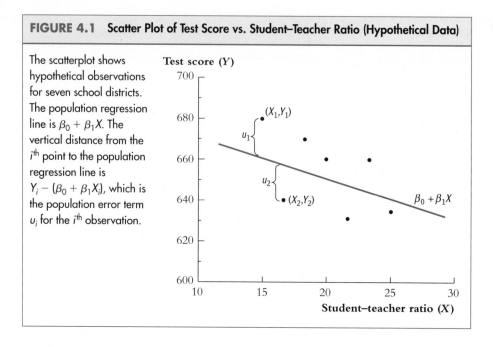

FIGURE 4.1 Scatter Plot of Test Score vs. Student–Teacher Ratio (Hypothetical Data)

The scatterplot shows hypothetical observations for seven school districts. The population regression line is $\beta_0 + \beta_1 X$. The vertical distance from the ith point to the population regression line is $Y_i - (\beta_0 + \beta_1 X_i)$, which is the population error term u_i for the ith observation.

4.2 Estimating the Coefficients of the Linear Regression Model

In a practical situation, such as the application to class size and test scores, the intercept β_0 and slope β_1 of the population regression line are unknown. Therefore, we must use data to estimate the unknown slope and intercept of the population regression line.

This estimation problem is similar to others you have faced in statistics. For example, suppose you want to compare the mean earnings of men and women who recently graduated from college. Although the population mean earnings are unknown, we can estimate the population means using a random sample of male and female college graduates. Then the natural estimator of the unknown population mean earnings for women, for example, is the average earnings of the female college graduates in the sample.

The same idea extends to the linear regression model. We do not know the population value of $\beta_{ClassSize}$, the slope of the unknown population regression line relating X (class size) and Y (test scores). But just as it was possible to learn about the population mean using a sample of data drawn from that

TABLE 4.1 Summary of the Distribution of Student–Teacher Ratios and Fifth-Grade Test Scores for 420 K–8 Districts in California in 1998

| | Average | Standard Deviation | Percentile | | | | | | |
			10%	25%	40%	50% (median)	60%	75%	90%
Student–teacher ratio	19.6	1.9	17.3	18.6	19.3	19.7	20.1	20.9	21.9
Test score	665.2	19.1	630.4	640.0	649.1	654.5	659.4	666.7	679.1

population, so is it possible to learn about the population slope $\beta_{ClassSize}$ using a sample of data.

The data we analyze here consist of test scores and class sizes in 1999 in 420 California school districts that serve kindergarten through eighth grade. The test score is the districtwide average of reading and math scores for fifth graders. Class size can be measured in various ways. The measure used here is one of the broadest, which is the number of students in the district divided by the number of teachers—that is, the districtwide student–teacher ratio. These data are described in more detail in Appendix 4.1.

Table 4.1 summarizes the distributions of test scores and class sizes for this sample. The average student–teacher ratio is 19.6 students per teacher and the standard deviation is 1.9 students per teacher. The 10th percentile of the distribution of the student–teacher ratio is 17.3 (that is, only 10% of districts have student–teacher ratios below 17.3), while the district at the 90th percentile has a student–teacher ratio of 21.9.

A scatterplot of these 420 observations on test scores and the student–teacher ratio is shown in Figure 4.2. The sample correlation is -0.23, indicating a weak negative relationship between the two variables. Although larger classes in this sample tend to have lower test scores, there are other determinants of test scores that keep the observations from falling perfectly along a straight line.

Despite this low correlation, if one could somehow draw a straight line through these data, then the slope of this line would be an estimate of $\beta_{ClassSize}$ based on these data. One way to draw the line would be to take out a pencil and a ruler and to "eyeball" the best line you could. While this method is easy, it is very unscientific and different people will create different estimated lines.

How, then, should you choose among the many possible lines? By far the most common way is to choose the line that produces the "least squares" fit to these data—that is, to use the ordinary least squares (OLS) estimator.

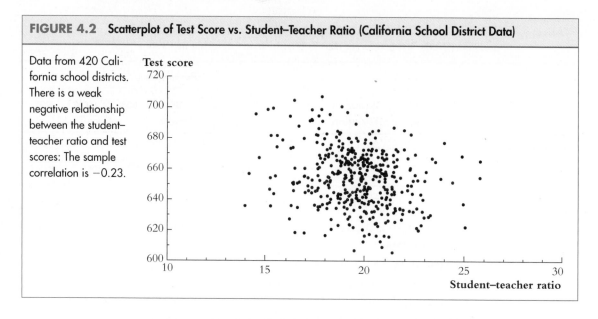

FIGURE 4.2   Scatterplot of Test Score vs. Student–Teacher Ratio (California School District Data)

Data from 420 California school districts. There is a weak negative relationship between the student–teacher ratio and test scores: The sample correlation is −0.23.

The Ordinary Least Squares Estimator

The OLS estimator chooses the regression coefficients so that the estimated regression line is as close as possible to the observed data, where closeness is measured by the sum of the squared mistakes made in predicting Y given X.

As discussed in Section 3.1, the sample average, $\overline{Y}$, is the least squares estimator of the population mean, $E(Y)$; that is, $\overline{Y}$ minimizes the total squared estimation mistakes $\sum_{i=1}^{n}(Y_i - m)^2$ among all possible estimators m [see expression (3.2)].

The OLS estimator extends this idea to the linear regression model. Let b_0 and b_1 be some estimators of β_0 and β_1. The regression line based on these estimators is $b_0 + b_1 X$, so the value of Y_i predicted using this line is $b_0 + b_1 X_i$. Thus, the mistake made in predicting the ith observation is $Y_i - (b_0 + b_1 X_i) = Y_i - b_0 - b_1 X_i$. The sum of these squared prediction mistakes over all n observations is

$$\sum_{i=1}^{n}(Y_i - b_0 - b_1 X_i)^2. \tag{4.6}$$

The sum of the squared mistakes for the linear regression model in expression (4.6) is the extension of the sum of the squared mistakes for the problem of estimating the mean in expression (3.2). In fact, if there is no regressor, then b_1 does not enter expression (4.6) and the two problems are identical except for the different notation [m in expression (3.2), b_0 in expression (4.6)]. Just as there is a unique estimator, $\overline{Y}$, that minimizes the expression (3.2), so is there a unique pair of estimators of β_0 and β_1 that minimize expression (4.6).

THE OLS ESTIMATOR, PREDICTED VALUES, AND RESIDUALS

The OLS estimators of the slope β_1 and the intercept β_0 are

$$\hat{\beta}_1 = \frac{\sum_{i=1}^{n}(X_i - \overline{X})(Y_i - \overline{Y})}{\sum_{i=1}^{n}(X_i - \overline{X})^2} = \frac{s_{XY}}{s_X^2} \tag{4.7}$$

$$\hat{\beta}_0 = \overline{Y} - \hat{\beta}_1 \overline{X}. \tag{4.8}$$

The OLS predicted values $\hat{Y}_i$ and residuals $\hat{u}_i$ are

$$\hat{Y}_i = \hat{\beta}_0 + \hat{\beta}_1 X_i, \ i = 1, \ldots, n \tag{4.9}$$

$$\hat{u}_i = Y_i - \hat{Y}_i, \ i = 1, \ldots, n. \tag{4.10}$$

The estimated intercept $(\hat{\beta}_0)$, slope $(\hat{\beta}_1)$, and residual $(\hat{u}_i)$ are computed from a sample of n observations of X_i and $Y_i, i = 1, \ldots, n$. These are estimates of the unknown true population intercept (β_0), slope (β_1), and error term (u_i).

The estimators of the intercept and slope that minimize the sum of squared mistakes in expression (4.6) are called the **ordinary least squares (OLS) estimators** of β_0 and β_1.

OLS has its own special notation and terminology. The OLS estimator of β_0 is denoted $\hat{\beta}_0$, and the OLS estimator of β_1 is denoted $\hat{\beta}_1$. The **OLS regression line** is the straight line constructed using the OLS estimators: $\hat{\beta}_0 + \hat{\beta}_1 X$. The **predicted value** of Y_i given X_i, based on the OLS regression line, is $\hat{Y}_i = \hat{\beta}_0 + \hat{\beta}_1 X_i$. The **residual** for the ith observation is the difference between Y_i and its predicted value: $\hat{u}_i = Y_i - \hat{Y}_i$.

You could compute the OLS estimators $\hat{\beta}_0$ and $\hat{\beta}_1$ by trying different values of b_0 and b_1 repeatedly until you find those that minimize the total squared mistakes in expression (4.6); they are the least squares estimates. This method would be quite tedious, however. Fortunately there are formulas, derived by minimizing expression (4.6) using calculus, that streamline the calculation of the OLS estimators.

The OLS formulas and terminology are collected in Key Concept 4.2. These formulas are implemented in virtually all statistical and spreadsheet programs. These formulas are derived in Appendix 4.2

OLS Estimates of the Relationship Between Test Scores and the Student–Teacher Ratio

When OLS is used to estimate a line relating the student–teacher ratio to test scores using the 420 observations in Figure 4.2, the estimated slope is −2.28 and the estimated intercept is 698.9. Accordingly, the OLS regression line for these 420 observations is

$$\widehat{TestScore} = 698.9 - 2.28 \times STR, \tag{4.11}$$

where *TestScore* is the average test score in the district and *STR* is the student–teacher ratio. The symbol "^" over *TestScore* in Equation (4.7) indicates that this is the predicted value based on the OLS regression line. Figure 4.3 plots this OLS regression line superimposed over the scatterplot of the data previously shown in Figure 4.2.

The slope of −2.28 means that an increase in the student–teacher ratio by one student per class is, on average, associated with a decline in districtwide test scores by 2.28 points on the test. A decrease in the student–teacher ratio by 2 students per class is, on average, associated with an increase in test scores of 4.56 points [= −2 × (−2.28)]. The negative slope indicates that more students per teacher (larger classes) is associated with poorer performance on the test.

It is now possible to predict the districtwide test score given a value of the student–teacher ratio. For example, for a district with 20 students per teacher, the

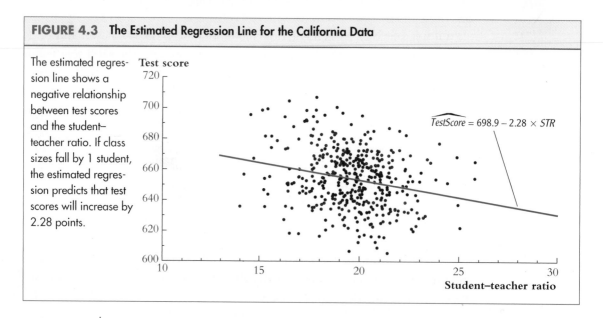

FIGURE 4.3   The Estimated Regression Line for the California Data

The estimated regression line shows a negative relationship between test scores and the student–teacher ratio. If class sizes fall by 1 student, the estimated regression predicts that test scores will increase by 2.28 points.

$\widehat{TestScore} = 698.9 - 2.28 \times STR$

predicted test score is $698.9 - 2.28 \times 20 = 653.3$. Of course, this prediction will not be exactly right because of the other factors that determine a district's performance. But the regression line does give a prediction (the OLS prediction) of what test scores would be for that district, based on their student–teacher ratio, absent those other factors.

Is this estimate of the slope large or small? To answer this, we return to the superintendent's problem. Recall that she is contemplating hiring enough teachers to reduce the student–teacher ratio by 2. Suppose her district is at the median of the California districts. From Table 4.1, the median student–teacher ratio is 19.7 and the median test score is 654.5. A reduction of 2 students per class, from 19.7 to 17.7, would move her student–teacher ratio from the 50th percentile to very near the 10th percentile. This is a big change, and she would need to hire many new teachers. How would it affect test scores?

According to Equation (4.11), cutting the student–teacher ratio by 2 is predicted to increase test scores by approximately 4.6 points; if her district's test scores are at the median, 654.5, they are predicted to increase to 659.1. Is this improvement large or small? According to Table 4.1, this improvement would move her district from the median to just short of the 60th percentile. Thus, a decrease in class size that would place her district close to the 10% with the smallest classes would move her test scores from the 50th to the 60th percentile. According to these estimates, at least, cutting the student–teacher ratio by a large amount (2 students per teacher) would help and might be worth doing depending on her budgetary situation, but it would not be a panacea.

What if the superintendent were contemplating a far more radical change, such as reducing the student–teacher ratio from 20 students per teacher to 5? Unfortunately, the estimates in Equation (4.11) would not be very useful to her. This regression was estimated using the data in Figure 4.2, and as the figure shows, the smallest student–teacher ratio in these data is 14. These data contain no information on how districts with extremely small classes perform, so these data alone are not a reliable basis for predicting the effect of a radical move to such an extremely low student–teacher ratio.

Why Use the OLS Estimator?

There are both practical and theoretical reasons to use the OLS estimators $\hat{\beta}_0$ and $\hat{\beta}_1$. Because OLS is the dominant method used in practice, it has become the common language for regression analysis throughout economics, finance (see the box), and the social sciences more generally. Presenting results using OLS (or its variants discussed later in this book) means that you are "speaking the same language"

The "Beta" of a Stock

A fundamental idea of modern finance is that an investor needs a financial incentive to take a risk. Said differently, the expected return[1] on a risky investment, R, must exceed the return on a safe, or risk-free, investment, R_f. Thus the expected excess return, $R - R_f$, on a risky investment, like owning stock in a company, should be positive.

At first it might seem like the risk of a stock should be measured by its variance. Much of that risk, however, can be reduced by holding other stocks in a "portfolio"—in other words, by diversifying your financial holdings. This means that the right way to measure the risk of a stock is not by its *variance* but rather by its *covariance* with the market.

The capital asset pricing model (CAPM) formalizes this idea. According to the CAPM, the expected excess return on an asset is proportional to the expected excess return on a portfolio of all available assets (the "market portfolio"). That is, the CAPM says that

$$R - R_f = \beta(R_m - R_f), \qquad (4.12)$$

where R_m is the expected return on the market portfolio and β is the coefficient in the population regression of $R - R_f$ on $R_m - R_f$. In practice, the risk-free return is often taken to be the rate of interest on short-term U.S. government debt. According to the CAPM, a stock with a $\beta < 1$ has less risk than the market portfolio and therefore has a lower expected excess return than the market portfolio. In contrast, a stock with a $\beta > 1$ is riskier than the market portfolio and thus comands a higher expected excess return.

The "beta" of a stock has become a workhorse of the investment industry, and you can obtain estimated β's for hundreds of stocks on investment firm Web sites. Those β's typically are estimated by OLS regression of the actual excess return on the stock against the actual excess return on a broad market index.

The table below gives estimated β's for six U.S. stocks. Low-risk consumer products firms like Kellogg have stocks with low β's; riskier technology stocks have high β's.

Company	Estimated β
Kellogg (breakfast cereal)	−0.03
Wal-Mart (discount retailer)	0.65
Waste Management (waste disposal)	0.70
Sprint Nextel (telecommunications)	0.78
Barnes and Noble (book retailer)	1.02
Microsoft (software)	1.27
Best Buy (electronic equipment retailer)	2.15
Amazon (online retailer)	2.65

Source: SmartMoney.com

---

[1] The return on an investment is the change in its price plus any payout (dividend) from the investment as a percentage of its initial price. For example, a stock bought on January 1 for $100, which then paid a $2.50 dividend during the year and sold on December 31 for $105, would have a return of $R = [(\$105 - \$100) + \$2.50]/\$100 = 7.5\%$.

as other economists and statisticians. The OLS formulas are built into virtually all spreadsheet and statistical software packages, making OLS easy to use.

The OLS estimators also have desirable theoretical properties. These are analogous to the desirable properties, studied in Section 3.1, of $\overline{Y}$ as an estimator of the population mean. Under the assumptions introduced in Section 4.4, the OLS estimator is unbiased and consistent. The OLS estimator is also efficient among a certain class of unbiased estimators; however, this efficiency result holds under some additional special conditions, and further discussion of this result is deferred until Section 5.5.

4.3 Measures of Fit

Having estimated a linear regression, you might wonder how well that regression line describes the data. Does the regressor account for much or for little of the variation in the dependent variable? Are the observations tightly clustered around the regression line, or are they spread out?

The R^2 and the standard error of the regression measure how well the OLS regression line fits the data. The R^2 ranges between 0 and 1 and measures the fraction of the variance of Y_i that is explained by X_i. The standard error of the regression measures how far Y_i typically is from its predicted value.

The R^2

The **regression R^2** is the fraction of the sample variance of Y_i explained by (or predicted by) X_i. The definitions of the predicted value and the residual (see Key Concept 4.2) allow us to write the dependent variable Y_i as the sum of the predicted value, $\hat{Y}_i$, plus the residual $\hat{u}_i$:

$$Y_i = \hat{Y}_i + \hat{u}_i. \tag{4.13}$$

In this notation, the R^2 is the ratio of the sample variance of $\hat{Y}_i$ to the sample variance of Y_i.

Mathematically, the R^2 can be written as the ratio of the explained sum of squares to the total sum of squares. The **explained sum of squares (ESS)** is the sum of squared deviations of the predicted values of Y_i, $\hat{Y}_i$, from their average, and the **total sum of squares (TSS)** is the sum of squared deviations of Y_i from its average:

$$ESS = \sum_{i=1}^{n} (\hat{Y}_i - \overline{Y})^2 \tag{4.14}$$

$$TSS = \sum_{i=1}^{n} (Y_i - \overline{Y})^2. \tag{4.15}$$

Equation (4.14) uses the fact that the sample average OLS predicted value equals $\overline{Y}$ (proven in Appendix 4.3).

The R^2 is the ratio of the explained sum of squares to the total sum of squares:

$$R^2 = \frac{ESS}{TSS}. \tag{4.16}$$

Alternatively, the R^2 can be written in terms of the fraction of the variance of Y_i *not* explained by X_i. The **sum of squared residuals**, or **SSR**, is the sum of the squared OLS residuals:

$$SSR = \sum_{i=1}^{n} \hat{u}_i^2. \tag{4.17}$$

It is shown in Appendix 4.3 that $TSS = ESS + SSR$. Thus the R^2 also can be expressed as 1 minus the ratio of the sum of squared residuals to the total sum of squares:

$$R^2 = 1 - \frac{SSR}{TSS}. \tag{4.18}$$

Finally, the R^2 of the regression of Y on the single regressor X is the square of the correlation coefficient between Y and X.

The R^2 ranges between 0 and 1. If $\hat{\beta}_1 = 0$, then X_i explains none of the variation of Y_i and the predicted value of Y_i based on the regression is just the sample average of Y_i. In this case, the explained sum of squares is zero and the sum of squared residuals equals the total sum of squares; thus the R^2 is zero. In contrast, if X_i explains all of the variation of Y_i, then $Y_i = \hat{Y}_i$ for all i and every residual is zero (that is, $\hat{u}_i = 0$), so that $ESS = TSS$ and $R^2 = 1$. In general, the R^2 does not take on the extreme values of 0 or 1 but falls somewhere in between. An R^2 near 1 indicates that the regressor is good at predicting Y_i, while an R^2 near 0 indicates that the regressor is not very good at predicting Y_i.

The Standard Error of the Regression

The **standard error of the regression (SER)** is an estimator of the standard deviation of the regression error u_i. The units of u_i and Y_i are the same, so the SER is a measure of the spread of the observations around the regression line, measured in the units of the dependent variable. For example, if the units of the dependent variable are dollars, then the SER measures the magnitude of a typical deviation from the regression line—that is, the magnitude of a typical regression error—in dollars.

Because the regression errors $u_1, \ldots, u_n$ are unobserved, the *SER* is computed using their sample counterparts, the OLS residuals $\hat{u}_1, \ldots, \hat{u}_n$. The formula for the *SER* is

$$SER = s_{\hat{u}}, \text{ where } s_{\hat{u}}^2 = \frac{1}{n-2}\sum_{i=1}^{n}\hat{u}_i^2 = \frac{SSR}{n-2}, \qquad (4.19)$$

where the formula for $s_{\hat{u}}^2$ uses the fact (proven in Appendix 4.3) that the sample average of the OLS residuals is zero.

The formula for the *SER* in Equation (4.19) is similar to the formula for the sample standard deviation of Y given in Equation (3.7) in Section 3.2, except that $Y_i - \overline{Y}$ in Equation (3.7) is replaced by $\hat{u}_i$, and the divisor in Equation (3.7) is $n - 1$, whereas here it is $n - 2$. The reason for using the divisor $n - 2$ here (instead of n) is the same as the reason for using the divisor $n - 1$ in Equation (3.7): It corrects for a slight downward bias introduced because two regression coefficients were estimated. This is called a "degrees of freedom" correction; because two coefficients were estimated (β_0 and β_1), two "degrees of freedom" of the data were lost, so the divisor in this factor is $n - 2$. (The mathematics behind this is discussed in Section 5.6.) When n is large, the difference between dividing by n, by $n - 1$, or by $n - 2$ is negligible.

Application to the Test Score Data

Equation (4.11) reports the regression line, estimated using the California test score data, relating the standardized test score (*TestScore*) to the student–teacher ratio (*STR*). The R^2 of this regression is 0.051, or 5.1%, and the *SER* is 18.6.

The R^2 of 0.051 means that the regressor *STR* explains 5.1% of the variance of the dependent variable *TestScore*. Figure 4.3 superimposes this regression line on the scatterplot of the *TestScore* and *STR* data. As the scatterplot shows, the student–teacher ratio explains some of the variation in test scores, but much variation remains unaccounted for.

The *SER* of 18.6 means that standard deviation of the regression residuals is 18.6, where the units are points on the standardized test. Because the standard deviation is a measure of spread, the *SER* of 18.6 means that there is a large spread of the scatterplot in Figure 4.3 around the regression line as measured in points on the test. This large spread means that predictions of test scores made using only the student–teacher ratio for that district will often be wrong by a large amount.

What should we make of this low R^2 and large *SER*? The fact that the R^2 of this regression is low (and the *SER* is large) does not, by itself, imply that this regression is either "good" or "bad." What the low R^2 *does* tell us is that other important factors influence test scores. These factors could include differences in the student body across districts, differences in school quality unrelated to the student–teacher ratio, or luck on the test. The low R^2 and high *SER* do not tell us what these factors are, but they do indicate that the student–teacher ratio alone explains only a small part of the variation in test scores in these data.

4.4 The Least Squares Assumptions

This section presents a set of three assumptions on the linear regression model and the sampling scheme under which OLS provides an appropriate estimator of the unknown regression coefficients, β_0 and β_1. Initially these assumptions might appear abstract. They do, however, have natural interpretations, and understanding these assumptions is essential for understanding when OLS will—and will not—give useful estimates of the regression coefficients.

Assumption #1: The Conditional Distribution of u_i Given X_i Has a Mean of Zero

The first **least squares assumption** is that the conditional distribution of u_i given X_i has a mean of zero. This assumption is a formal mathematical statement about the "other factors" contained in u_i and asserts that these other factors are unrelated to X_i in the sense that, given a value of X_i, the mean of the distribution of these other factors is zero.

This is illustrated in Figure 4.4. The population regression is the relationship that holds on average between class size and test scores in the population, and the error term u_i represents the other factors that lead test scores at a given district to differ from the prediction based on the population regression line. As shown in Figure 4.4, at a given value of class size, say 20 students per class, sometimes these other factors lead to better performance than predicted ($u_i > 0$) and sometimes to worse performance ($u_i < 0$), but on average over the population the prediction is right. In other words, given $X_i = 20$, the mean of the distribution of u_i is zero. In Figure 4.4, this is shown as the distribution of u_i being centered on the population regression line at $X_i = 20$ and, more generally, at other values x of X_i as well. Said differently, the distribution of u_i, conditional on $X_i = x$, has a mean of zero; stated mathematically, $E(u_i|X_i = x) = 0$ or, in somewhat simpler notation, $E(u_i|X_i) = 0$.

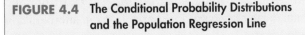

FIGURE 4.4   The Conditional Probability Distributions and the Population Regression Line

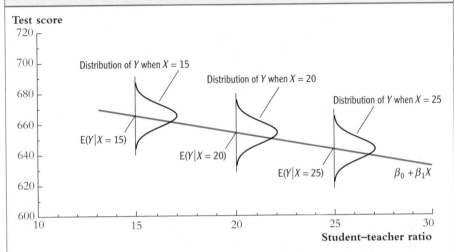

The figure shows the conditional probability of test scores for districts with class sizes of 15, 20, and 25 students. The mean of the conditional distribution of test scores, given the student–teacher ratio, $E(Y|X)$, is the population regression line $\beta_0 + \beta_1 X$. At a given value of X, Y is distributed around the regression line and the error, $u = Y - (\beta_0 + \beta_1 X)$, has a conditional mean of zero for all values of X.

As shown in Figure 4.4, the assumption that $E(u_i|X_i) = 0$ is equivalent to assuming that the population regression line is the conditional mean of Y_i given X_i (a mathematical proof of this is left as Exercise 4.6).

The conditional mean of u in a randomized controlled experiment.   In a randomized controlled experiment, subjects are randomly assigned to the treatment group ($X = 1$) or to the control group ($X = 0$). The random assignment typically is done using a computer program that uses no information about the subject, ensuring that X is distributed independently of all personal characteristics of the subject. Random assignment makes X and u independent, which in turn implies that the conditional mean of u given X is zero.

In observational data, X is not randomly assigned in an experiment. Instead, the best that can be hoped for is that X is *as if* randomly assigned, in the precise sense that $E(u_i|X_i) = 0$. Whether this assumption holds in a given empirical application with observational data requires careful thought and judgment, and we return to this issue repeatedly.

Correlation and conditional mean. Recall from Section 2.3 that if the conditional mean of one random variable given another is zero, then the two random variables have zero covariance and thus are uncorrelated [Equation (2.27)]. Thus, the conditional mean assumption $E(u_i|X_i) = 0$ implies that X_i and u_i are uncorrelated, or $\text{corr}(X_i, u_i) = 0$. Because correlation is a measure of linear association, this implication does not go the other way; even if X_i and u_i are uncorrelated, the conditional mean of u_i given X_i might be nonzero. However, if X_i and u_i are correlated, then it must be the case that $E(u_i|X_i)$ is nonzero. It is therefore often convenient to discuss the conditional mean assumption in terms of possible correlation between X_i and u_i. If X_i and u_i are correlated, then the conditional mean assumption is violated.

Assumption #2: (X_i, Y_i), $i = 1, \ldots, n$ Are Independently and Identically Distributed

The second least squares assumption is that (X_i, Y_i), $i = 1, \ldots, n$ are independently and identically distributed (i.i.d.) across observations. As discussed in Section 2.5 (Key Concept 2.5), this is a statement about how the sample is drawn. If the observations are drawn by simple random sampling from a single large population, then (X_i, Y_i), $i = 1, \ldots, n$ are i.i.d. For example, let X be the age of a worker and Y be his or her earnings, and imagine drawing a person at random from the population of workers. That randomly drawn person will have a certain age and earnings (that is, X and Y will take on some values). If a sample of n workers is drawn from this population, then (X_i, Y_i), $i = 1, \ldots, n$, necessarily have the same distribution. If they are drawn at random they are also distributed independently from one observation to the next; that is, they are i.i.d.

The i.i.d. assumption is a reasonable one for many data collection schemes. For example, survey data from a randomly chosen subset of the population typically can be treated as i.i.d.

Not all sampling schemes produce i.i.d. observations on (X_i, Y_i), however. One example is when the values of X are not drawn from a random sample of the population but rather are set by a researcher as part of an experiment. For example, suppose a horticulturalist wants to study the effects of different organic weeding methods (X) on tomato production (Y) and accordingly grows different plots of tomatoes using different organic weeding techniques. If she picks the techniques (the level of X) to be used on the ith plot and applies the same technique to the ith plot in all repetitions of the experiment, then the value of X_i does not change from one sample to the next. Thus X_i is nonrandom (although the outcome Y_i is random), so the sampling scheme is not i.i.d. The results presented in this chapter developed for i.i.d. regressors are also true if the regressors are nonrandom. The case of a nonrandom regressor is, however, quite special. For example, modern experimental protocols would have the horticulturalist assign the level of X to the different plots using a computerized random number generator, thereby circumventing any possible bias by the horticulturalist (she might use her favorite weeding method for the tomatoes in the sunniest plot). When this modern experimental protocol is used, the level of X is random and (X_i, Y_i) are i.i.d.

Another example of non-i.i.d. sampling is when observations refer to the same unit of observation over time. For example, we might have data on inventory levels (Y) at a firm and the interest rate at which the firm can borrow (X), where these data are collected over time from a specific firm; for example, they might be recorded four times a year (quarterly) for 30 years. This is an example of time series data, and a key feature of time series data is that observations falling close to each other in time are not independent but rather tend to be correlated with each other; if interest rates are low now, they are likely to be low next quarter. This pattern of correlation violates the "independence" part of the i.i.d. assumption. Time series data introduce a set of complications that are best handled after developing the basic tools of regression analysis.

Assumption #3: Large Outliers Are Unlikely

The third least squares assumption is that large outliers—that is, observations with values of X_i and/or Y_i far outside the usual range of the data—are unlikely. Large outliers can make OLS regression results misleading. This potential sensitivity of OLS to extreme outliers is illustrated in Figure 4.5 using hypothetical data.

In this book, the assumption that large outliers are unlikely is made mathematically precise by assuming that X and Y have nonzero finite fourth moments: $0 < E(X_i^4) < \infty$ and $0 < E(Y_i^4) < \infty$. Another way to state this assumption is that X and Y have finite kurtosis.

The assumption of finite kurtosis is used in the mathematics that justify the large-sample approximations to the distributions of the OLS test statistics. We encountered this assumption in Chapter 3 when discussing the consistency of the sample variance. Specifically, Equation (3.9) states that the sample variance s_Y^2 is a consistent estimator of the population variance σ_Y^2 ($s_Y^2 \xrightarrow{p} \sigma_Y^2$). If $Y_1, \ldots, Y_n$ are i.i.d. and the fourth moment of Y_i is finite, then the law of large numbers in Key Concept 2.6 applies to the average, $\frac{1}{n}\sum_{i=1}^{n}(Y_i - \mu_Y)^2$, a key step in the proof in Appendix 3.3 showing that s_Y^2 is consistent.

One source of large outliers is data entry errors, such as a typographical error or incorrectly using different units for different observations: Imagine collecting

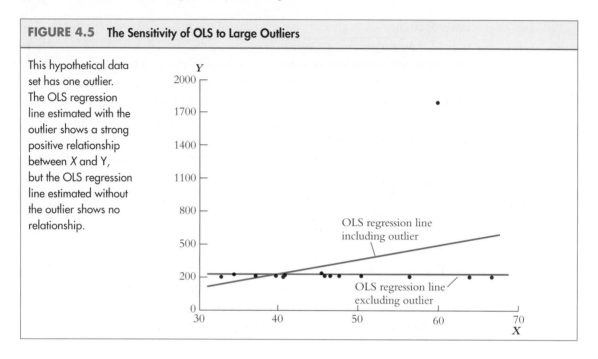

FIGURE 4.5   The Sensitivity of OLS to Large Outliers

This hypothetical data set has one outlier. The OLS regression line estimated with the outlier shows a strong positive relationship between X and Y, but the OLS regression line estimated without the outlier shows no relationship.

data on the height of students in meters, but inadvertently recording one student's height in centimeters instead. One way to find outliers is to plot your data. If you decide that an outlier is due to a data entry error, then you can either correct the error or, if that is impossible, drop the observation from your data set.

Data entry errors aside, the assumption of finite kurtosis is a plausible one in many applications with economic data. Class size is capped by the physical capacity of a classroom; the best you can do on a standardized test is to get all the questions right and the worst you can do is to get all the questions wrong. Because class size and test scores have a finite range, they necessarily have finite kurtosis. More generally, commonly used distributions such as the normal distribution have four moments. Still, as a mathematical matter, some distributions have infinite fourth moments, and this assumption rules out those distributions. If this assumption holds then it is unlikely that statistical inferences using OLS will be dominated by a few observations.

Use of the Least Squares Assumptions

The three least squares assumptions for the linear regression model are summarized in Key Concept 4.3. The least squares assumptions play twin roles, and we return to them repeatedly throughout this textbook.

THE LEAST SQUARES ASSUMPTIONS

$$Y_i = \beta_0 + \beta_1 X_i + u_i, i = 1, \ldots, n, \text{ where}$$

1. The error term u_i has conditional mean zero given X_i: $E(u_i|X_i) = 0$;
2. (X_i, Y_i), $i = 1, \ldots, n$ are independent and identically distributed (i.i.d.) draws from their joint distribution; and
3. Large outliers are unlikely: X_i and Y_i have nonzero finite fourth moments.

Their first role is mathematical: If these assumptions hold, then, as is shown in the next section, in large samples the OLS estimators have sampling distributions that are normal. In turn, this large-sample normal distribution lets us develop methods for hypothesis testing and constructing confidence intervals using the OLS estimators.

Their second role is to organize the circumstances that pose difficulties for OLS regression. As we will see, the first least squares assumption is the most important to consider in practice. One reason why the first least squares assumption might not hold in practice is discussed in Chapter 6, and additional reasons are discussed in Section 9.2.

It is also important to consider whether the second assumption holds in an application. Although it plausibly holds in many cross-sectional data sets, the independence assumption is inappropriate for time series data. Therefore, the regression methods developed under assumption 2 require modification for some applications with time series data.

The third assumption serves as a reminder that OLS, just like the sample mean, can be sensitive to large outliers. If your data set contains large outliers, you should examine those outliers carefully to make sure those observations are correctly recorded and belong in the data set.

4.5 Sampling Distribution of the OLS Estimators

Because the OLS estimators $\hat{\beta}_0$ and $\hat{\beta}_1$ are computed from a randomly drawn sample, the estimators themselves are random variables with a probability distribution—the sampling distribution—that describes the values they could take over different possible random samples. This section presents these sampling distributions. In small samples, these distributions are complicated, but in large samples, they are approximately normal because of the central limit theorem.

The Sampling Distribution of the OLS Estimators

Review of the sampling distribution of $\overline{Y}$.   Recall the discussion in Sections 2.5 and 2.6 about the sampling distribution of the sample average, $\overline{Y}$, an estimator of the unknown population mean of Y, μ_Y. Because $\overline{Y}$ is calculated using a randomly drawn sample, $\overline{Y}$ is a random variable that takes on different values from one sample to the next; the probability of these different values is summarized in its sampling distribution. Although the sampling distribution of $\overline{Y}$ can be complicated when the sample size is small, it is possible to make certain statements about it that hold for all n. In particular, the mean of the sampling distribution is μ_Y, that is, $E(\overline{Y}) = \mu_Y$, so $\overline{Y}$ is an unbiased estimator of μ_Y. If n is large, then more can be said about the sampling distribution. In particular, the central limit theorem (Section 2.6) states that this distribution is approximately normal.

The sampling distribution of $\hat{\beta}_0$ and $\hat{\beta}_1$.   These ideas carry over to the OLS estimators $\hat{\beta}_0$ and $\hat{\beta}_1$ of the unknown intercept β_0 and slope β_1 of the population regression line. Because the OLS estimators are calculated using a random sample, $\hat{\beta}_0$ and $\hat{\beta}_1$ are random variables that take on different values from one sample to the next; the probability of these different values is summarized in their sampling distributions.

   Although the sampling distribution of $\hat{\beta}_0$ and $\hat{\beta}_1$ can be complicated when the sample size is small, it is possible to make certain statements about it that hold for all n. In particular, the mean of the sampling distributions of $\hat{\beta}_0$ and $\hat{\beta}_1$ are β_0 and β_1. In other words, under the least squares assumptions in Key Concept 4.3,

$$E(\hat{\beta}_0) = \beta_0 \text{ and } E(\hat{\beta}_1) = \beta_1, \tag{4.20}$$

that is, $\hat{\beta}_0$ and $\hat{\beta}_1$ are unbiased estimators of β_0 and β_1. The proof that $\hat{\beta}_1$ is unbiased is given in Appendix 4.3 and the proof that $\hat{\beta}_0$ is unbiased is left as Exercise 4.7.

   If the sample is sufficiently large, by the central limit theorem the sampling distribution of $\hat{\beta}_0$ and $\hat{\beta}_1$ is well approximated by the bivariate normal distribution (Section 2.4.). This implies that the marginal distributions of $\hat{\beta}_0$ and $\hat{\beta}_1$ are normal in large samples.

LARGE-SAMPLE DISTRIBUTIONS OF $\hat{\beta}_0$ AND $\hat{\beta}_1$

If the least squares assumptions in Key Concept 4.3 hold, then in large samples $\hat{\beta}_0$ and $\hat{\beta}_1$ have a jointly normal sampling distribution. The large-sample normal distribution of $\hat{\beta}_1$ is $N(\beta_1, \sigma^2_{\hat{\beta}_1})$, where the variance of this distribution, $\sigma^2_{\hat{\beta}_1}$, is

$$\sigma^2_{\hat{\beta}_1} = \frac{1}{n} \frac{\text{var}[(X_i - \mu_X)u_i]}{[\text{var}(X_i)]^2}. \tag{4.21}$$

The large-sample normal distribution of $\hat{\beta}_0$ is $N(\beta_0, \sigma^2_{\hat{\beta}_0})$, where

$$\sigma^2_{\hat{\beta}_0} = \frac{1}{n} \frac{\text{var}(H_i u_i)}{[E(H_i^2)]^2}, \quad \text{where } H_i = 1 - \left(\frac{\mu_X}{E(X_i^2)}\right)X_i. \tag{4.22}$$

This argument invokes the central limit theorem. Technically, the central limit theorem concerns the distribution of averages (like $\overline{Y}$). If you examine the numerator in Equation (4.7) for $\hat{\beta}_1$, you will see that it, too, is a type of average—not a simple average, like $\overline{Y}$, but an average of the product, $(Y_i - \overline{Y})(X_i - \overline{X})$. As discussed further in Appendix 4.3, the central limit theorem applies to this average so that, like the simpler average $\overline{Y}$, it is normally distributed in large samples.

The normal approximation to the distribution of the OLS estimators in large samples is summarized in Key Concept 4.4. (Appendix 4.3 summarizes the derivation of these formulas.) A relevant question in practice is how large n must be for these approximations to be reliable. In Section 2.6 we suggested that $n = 100$ is sufficiently large for the sampling distribution of $\overline{Y}$ to be well approximated by a normal distribution, and sometimes smaller n suffices. This criterion carries over to the more complicated averages appearing in regression analysis. In virtually all modern econometric applications $n > 100$, so we will treat the normal approximations to the distributions of the OLS estimators as reliable unless there are good reasons to think otherwise.

The results in Key Concept 4.4 imply that the OLS estimators are consistent—that is, when the sample size is large, $\hat{\beta}_0$ and $\hat{\beta}_1$ will be close to the true population coefficients β_0 and β_1 with high probability. This is because the variances $\sigma^2_{\hat{\beta}_0}$ and $\sigma^2_{\hat{\beta}_1}$ of the estimators decrease to zero as n increases (n appears in the denominator of the formulas for the variances), so the distribution of the OLS estimators will be tightly concentrated around their means, β_0 and β_1, when n is large.

FIGURE 4.6 The Variance of $\hat{\beta}_1$ and the Variance of X

The colored dots represent a set of X_i's with a small variance. The black dots represent a set of X_i's with a large variance. The regression line can be estimated more accurately with the black dots than with the colored dots.

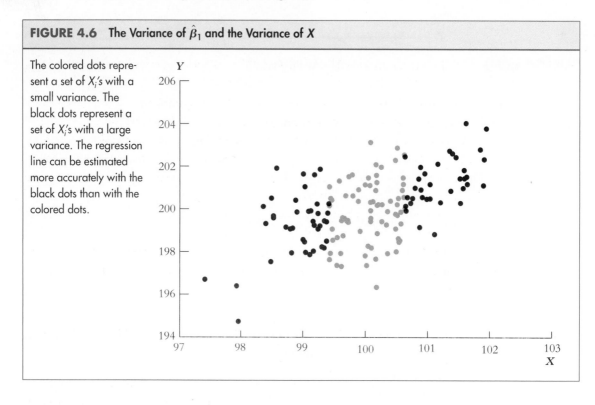

Another implication of the distributions in Key Concept 4.4 is that, in general, the larger the variance of X_i, the smaller the variance $\sigma^2_{\hat{\beta}_1}$ of $\hat{\beta}_1$. Mathematically, this arises because the variance of $\hat{\beta}_1$ in Equation (4.21) is inversely proportional to the square of the variance of X_i: the larger is var(X_i), the larger is the denominator in Equation (4.21) so the smaller is $\sigma^2_{\hat{\beta}_1}$. To get a better sense of why this is so, look at Figure 4.6, which presents a scatterplot of 150 artificial data points on X and Y. The data points indicated by the colored dots are the 75 observations closest to $\overline{X}$. Suppose you were asked to draw a line as accurately as possible through *either* the colored or the black dots—which would you choose? It would be easier to draw a precise line through the black dots, which have a larger variance than the colored dots. Similarly, the larger the variance of X, the more precise is $\hat{\beta}_1$.

The normal approximation to the sampling distribution of $\hat{\beta}_0$ and $\hat{\beta}_1$ is a powerful tool. With this approximation in hand, we are able to develop methods for making inferences about the true population values of the regression coefficients using only a sample of data.

4.6 Conclusion

This chapter has focused on the use of ordinary least squares to estimate the intercept and slope of a population regression line using a sample of n observations on a dependent variable, Y, and a single regressor, X. There are many ways to draw a straight line through a scatterplot, but doing so using OLS has several virtues. If the least squares assumptions hold, then the OLS estimators of the slope and intercept are unbiased, are consistent, and have a sampling distribution with a variance that is inversely proportional to the sample size n. Moreover, if n is large, then the sampling distribution of the OLS estimator is normal.

These important properties of the sampling distribution of the OLS estimator hold under the three least squares assumptions.

The first assumption is that the error term in the linear regression model has a conditional mean of zero, given the regressor X. This assumption implies that the OLS estimator is unbiased.

The second assumption is that (X_i, Y_i) are i.i.d., as is the case if the data are collected by simple random sampling. This assumption yields the formula, presented in Key Concept 4.4, for the variance of the sampling distribution of the OLS estimator.

The third assumption is that large outliers are unlikely. Stated more formally, X and Y have finite fourth moments (finite kurtosis). The reason for this assumption is that OLS can be unreliable if there are large outliers.

The results in this chapter describe the sampling distribution of the OLS estimator. By themselves, however, these results are not sufficient to test a hypothesis about the value of β_1 or to construct a confidence interval for β_1. Doing so requires an estimator of the standard deviation of the sampling distribution—that is, the standard error of the OLS estimator. This step—moving from the sampling distribution of $\hat{\beta}_1$ to its standard error, hypothesis tests, and confidence intervals—is taken in the next chapter.

Summary

1. The population regression line, $\beta_0 + \beta_1 X$, is the mean of Y as a function of the value of X. The slope, β_1, is the expected change in Y associated with a 1-unit change in X. The intercept, β_0, determines the level (or height) of the regression line. Key Concept 4.1 summarizes the terminology of the population linear regression model.

2. The population regression line can be estimated using sample observations $(Y_i, X_i), i = 1, \ldots, n$ by ordinary least squares (OLS). The OLS estimators of the regression intercept and slope are denoted by $\hat{\beta}_0$ and $\hat{\beta}_1$.

3. The R^2 and standard error of the regression (SER) are measures of how close the values of Y_i are to the estimated regression line. The R^2 is between 0 and 1, with a larger value indicating that the Y_i's are closer to the line. The standard error of the regression is an estimator of the standard deviation of the regression error.

4. There are three key assumptions for the linear regression model: (1) The regression errors, u_i, have a mean of zero conditional on the regressors X_i; (2) the sample observations are i.i.d. random draws from the population; and (3) large outliers are unlikely. If these assumptions hold, the OLS estimators $\hat{\beta}_0$ and $\hat{\beta}_1$ are (1) unbiased; (2) consistent; and (3) normally distributed when the sample is large.

Key Terms

linear regression model with a single
    regressor (112)
dependent variable (112)
independent variable (112)
regressor (112)
population regression line (112)
population regression function (112)
population intercept and slope (112)
population coefficients (112)
parameters (112)
error term (112)

ordinary least squares (OLS)
    estimator (117)
OLS regression line (117)
predicted value (117)
residual (117)
regression R^2 (121)
explained sum of squares (ESS) (121)
total sum of squares (TSS) (121)
sum of squared residuals (SSR) (122)
standard error of the regression
    (SER) (122)
least squares assumptions (124)

Review the Concepts

4.1 Explain the difference between $\hat{\beta}_1$ and β_1; between the residual $\hat{u}_i$ and the regression error u_i; and between the OLS predicted value $\hat{Y}_i$ and $E(Y_i | X_i)$.

4.2 For each least squares assumption, provide an example in which the assumption is valid, and then provide an example in which the assumption fails.

4.3 Sketch a hypothetical scatterplot of data for an estimated regression with $R^2 = 0.9$. Sketch a hypothetical scatterplot of data for a regression with $R^2 = 0.5$.

Exercises

4.1 Suppose that a researcher, using data on class size (CS) and average test scores from 100 third-grade classes, estimates the OLS regression,

$$\widehat{TestScore} = 520.4 - 5.82 \times CS, R^2 = 0.08, SER = 11.5.$$

a. A classroom has 22 students. What is the regression's prediction for that classroom's average test score?

b. Last year a classroom had 19 students, and this year it has 23 students. What is the regression's prediction for the change in the classroom average test score?

c. The sample average class size across the 100 classrooms is 21.4. What is the sample average of the test scores across the 100 classrooms? (*Hint:* Review the formulas for the OLS estimators.)

d. What is the sample standard deviation of test scores across the 100 classrooms? (*Hint:* Review the formulas for the R^2 and SER.)

4.2 Suppose that a random sample of 200 twenty-year-old men is selected from a population and that these men's height and weight are recorded. A regression of weight on height yields

$$\widehat{Weight} = -99.41 + 3.94 \times Height, R^2 = 0.81, SER = 10.2,$$

where *Weight* is measured in pounds and *Height* is measured in inches.

a. What is the regression's weight prediction for someone who is 70 inches tall? 65 inches tall? 74 inches tall?

b. A man has a late growth spurt and grows 1.5 inches over the course of a year. What is the regression's prediction for the increase in this man's weight?

c. Suppose that instead of measuring weight and height in pounds and inches, these variable are measured in centimeters and kilograms. What are the regression estimates from this new centimeter-kilogram regression? (Give all results, estimated coefficients, R^2, and SER.)

4.3 A regression of average weekly earnings (AWE, measured in dollars) on age (measured in years) using a random sample of college-educated full-time workers aged 25–65 yields the following:

$$\widehat{AWE} = 696.7 + 9.6 \times Age, R^2 = 0.023, SER = 624.1.$$

a. Explain what the coefficient values 696.7 and 9.6 mean.

b. The standard error of the regression (SER) is 624.1. What are the units of measurement for the SER (dollars? years? or is SER unit-free)?

c. The regression R^2 is 0.023. What are the units of measurement for the R^2 (dollars? years? or is R^2 unit-free)?

d. What is the regression's predicted earnings for a 25-year-old worker? A 45-year-old worker?

e. Will the regression give reliable predictions for a 99-year-old worker? Why or why not?

f. Given what you know about the distribution of earnings, do you think it is plausible that the distribution of errors in the regression is normal? (*Hint:* Do you think that the distribution is symmetric or skewed? What is the smallest value of earnings, and is it consistent with a normal distribution?)

g. The average age in this sample is 41.6 years. What is the average value of AWE in the sample? (*Hint:* Review Key Concept 4.2.)

4.4 Read the box "The 'Beta' of a Stock" in Section 4.2.

a. Suppose that the value of β is greater than 1 for a particular stock. Show that the variance of $(R - R_f)$ for this stock is greater than the variance of $(R_m - R_t)$.

b. Suppose that the value of β is less than 1 for a particular stock. Is it possible that variance of $(R - R_f)$ for this stock is greater than the variance of $(R_m - R_t)$? (*Hint:* Don't forget the regression error.)

c. In a given year, the rate of return on 3-month Treasury bills is 3.5% and the rate of return on a large diversified portfolio of stocks (the S&P 500) is 7.3%. For each company listed in the table at the end of the box, use the estimated value of β to estimate the stock's expected rate of return.

4.5 A professor decides to run an experiment to measure the effect of time pressure on final exam scores. He gives each of the 400 students in his course the same final exam, but some students have 90 minutes to complete the exam while others have 120 minutes. Each student is randomly assigned one of the examination times based on the flip of a coin. Let Y_i denote the number of points scored on the exam by the ith student ($0 \le Y_i \le 100$), let X_i denote the amount of time that the student has to complete the exam ($X_i = 90$ or 120), and consider the regression model $Y_i = \beta_0 + \beta_1 X_i + u_i$.

a. Explain what the term u_i represents. Why will different students have different values of u_i?

b. Explain why $E(u_i|X_i) = 0$ for this regression model.

c. Are the other assumptions in Key Concept 4.3 satisfied? Explain.

d. The estimated regression is $\hat{Y}_i = 49 + 0.24\,X_i$.

   i. Compute the estimated regression's prediction for the average score of students given 90 minutes to complete the exam; 120 minutes; and 150 minutes.

   ii. Compute the estimated gain in score for a student who is given an additional 10 minutes on the exam.

4.6 Show that the first least squares assumption, $E(u_i|X_i) = 0$, implies that $E(Y_i|X_i) = \beta_0 + \beta_1 X_i$.

4.7 Show that $\hat{\beta}_0$ is an unbiased estimator of β_0. (*Hint:* Use the fact that $\hat{\beta}_1$ is unbiased, which is shown in Appendix 4.3.)

4.8 Suppose that all of the regression assumptions in Key Concept 4.3 are satisfied except that the first assumption is replaced with $E(u_i|X_i) = 2$. Which parts of Key Concept 4.4 continue to hold? Which change? Why? (Is $\hat{\beta}_1$ normally distributed in large samples with mean and variance given in Key Concept 4.4? What about $\hat{\beta}_0$?)

4.9   **a.** A linear regression yields $\hat{\beta}_1 = 0$. Show that $R^2 = 0$.

   b. A linear regression yields $R^2 = 0$. Does this imply that $\hat{\beta}_1 = 0$?

4.10 Suppose that $Y_i = \beta_0 + \beta_1 X_i + u_i$, where (X_i, u_i) are i.i.d., and X_i is a Bernoulli random variable with $\Pr(X = 1) = 0.20$. When $X = 1, u_i$ is $N(0, 4)$; when $X = 0, u_i$ is $N(0, 1)$.

a. Show that the regression assumptions in Key Concept 4.3 are satisfied.

b. Derive an expression for the large-sample variance of $\hat{\beta}_1$. [*Hint:* Evaluate the terms in Equation (4.21).]

4.11 Consider the regression model $Y_i = \beta_0 + \beta_1 X_i + u_i$.

a. Suppose you know that $\beta_0 = 0$. Derive a formula for the least squares estimator of β_1.

b. Suppose you know that $\beta_0 = 4$. Derive a formula for the least squares estimator of β_1.

4.12 **a.** Show that the regression R^2 in the regression of Y on X is the squared value of the sample correlation between X and Y. That is, show that $R^2 = r_{XY}^2$.

b. Show that the R^2 from the regression of Y on X is the same as the R^2 from the regression of X on Y.

Empirical Exercises

E4.1 On the text Web site (**www.aw-bc.com/stock_watson**), you will find a data file **CPS04** that contains an extended version of the data set used in Table 3.1 for 2004. It contains data for full-time, full-year workers, age 25–34, with a high school diploma or B.A./B.S. as their highest degree. A detailed description is given in **CPS04_Description**, also available on the Web site. (These are the same data as in **CPS92_04** but are limited to the year 2004.) In this exercise you will investigate the relationship between a worker's age and earnings. (Generally, older workers have more job experience, leading to higher productivity and earnings.)

a. Run a regression of average hourly earnings (*AHE*) on age (*Age*). What is the estimated intercept? What is the estimated slope? Use the estimated regression to answer this question: How much do earnings increase as workers age by one year?

b. Bob is a 26-year-old worker. Predict Bob's earnings using the estimated regression. Alexis is a 30-year-old worker. Predict Alexis's earnings using the estimated regression.

c. Does age account for a large fraction of the variance in earnings across individuals? Explain.

E4.2 On the text Web site (**www.aw-bc.com/stock_watson**), you will find a data file **TeachingRatings** that contains data on course evaluations, course characteristics, and professor characteristics for 463 courses at the University of Texas at Austin.[1] A detailed description is given in **TeachingRatings_Description**, also available on the Web site. One of the characteristics is an index of the professor's "beauty" as rated by a panel of six judges. In this exercise you will investigate how course evaluations are related to the professor's beauty.

---

[1]These data were provided by Professor Daniel Hamermesh of the University of Texas at Austin and were used in his paper with Amy Parker, "Beauty in the Classroom: Instructors' Pulchritude and Putative Pedagogical Productivity," *Economics of Education Review*, August 2005, 24(4): pp. 369–376.

a. Construct a scatterplot of average course evaluations (*Course_Eval*) on the professor's beauty (*Beauty*). Does there appear to be a relationship between the variables?

b. Run a regression of average course evaluations (*Course_Eval*) on the professor's beauty (*Beauty*). What is the estimated intercept? What is the estimated slope? Explain why the estimated intercept is equal to the sample mean of *Course_Eval*. (*Hint:* What is the sample mean of *Beauty*?)

c. Professor Watson has an average value of *Beauty*, while Professor Stock's value of *Beauty* is one standard deviation above the average. Predict Professor Stock's and Professor Watson's course evaluations.

d. Comment on the size of the regression's slope. Is the estimated effect of *Beauty* on *Course_Eval* large or small? Explain what you mean by "large" and "small."

e. Does *Beauty* explain a large fraction of the variance in evaluations across courses? Explain.

E4.3 On the text Web site (**www.aw-bc.com/stock_watson**), you will find a data file **CollegeDistance** that contains data from a random sample of high school seniors interviewed in 1980 and re-interviewed in 1986. In this exercise you will use these data to investigate the relationship between the number of completed years of education for young adults and the distance from each student's high school to the nearest four-year college. (Proximity to college lowers the cost of education, so that students who live closer to a four-year college should, on average, complete more years of higher education.) A detailed description is given in **CollegeDistance_Description**, also available on the Web site.[2]

a. Run a regression of years of completed education (*ED*) on distance to the nearest college (*Dist*), where *Dist* is measured in tens of miles. (For example, *Dist* = 2 means that the distance is 20 miles.) What is the estimated intercept? What is the estimated slope? Use the estimated regression to answer this question: How does the average value of years of completed schooling change when colleges are built close to where students go to high school?

---

[2]These data were provided by Professor Cecilia Rouse of Princeton University and were used in her paper "Democratization or Diversion? The Effect of Community Colleges on Educational Attainment," *Journal of Business and Economic Statistics*, April 1995, 12(2): pp 217–224.

b. Bob's high school was 20 miles from the nearest college. Predict Bob's years of completed education using the estimated regression. How would the prediction change if Bob lived 10 miles from the nearest college?

c. Does distance to college explain a large fraction of the variance in educational attainment across individuals? Explain.

d. What is the value of the standard error of the regression? What are the units for the standard error (meters, grams, years, dollars, cents, or something else)?

E4.4 On the text Web site (**www.aw-bc.com/stock_watson**), you will find a data file **Growth** that contains data on average growth rates over 1960–1995 for 65 countries, along with variables that are potentially related to growth. A detailed description is given in **Growth_Description**, also available on the Web site. In this exercise you will investigate the relationship between growth and trade.[3]

a. Construct a scatterplot of average annual growth rate (*Growth*) on the average trade share (*TradeShare*). Does there appear to be a relationship between the variables?

b. One country, Malta, has a trade share much larger than the other countries. Find Malta on the scatterplot. Does Malta look like an outlier?

c. Using all observations, run a regression of *Growth* on *TradeShare*. What is the estimated slope? What is the estimated intercept? Use the regression to predict the growth rate for a country with trade share of 0.5 and with a trade share equal to 1.0.

d. Estimate the same regression excluding the data from Malta. Answer the same questions in (c).

e. Where is Malta? Why is the Malta trade share so large? Should Malta be included or excluded from the analysis?

---

[3]These data were provided by Professor Ross Levine of Brown University and were used in his paper with Thorsten Beck and Norman Loayza, "Finance and the Sources of Growth," *Journal of Financial Economics*, 2000, 58: 261–300.

APPENDIX
4.1 | The California Test Score Data Set

The California Standardized Testing and Reporting data set contains data on test performance, school characteristics, and student demographic backgrounds. The data used here
are from all 420 K–6 and K–8 districts in California with data available for 1998 and 1999.
Test scores are the average of the reading and math scores on the Stanford 9 Achievement
Test, a standardized test administered to fifth-grade students. School characteristics (averaged across the district) include enrollment, number of teachers (measured as "full-time
equivalents"), number of computers per classroom, and expenditures per student. The student–teacher ratio used here is the number of students in the district, divided by the number of full-time equivalent teachers. Demographic variables for the students also are
averaged across the district. The demographic variables include the percentage of students
who are in the public assistance program CalWorks (formerly AFDC), the percentage of
students who qualify for a reduced price lunch, and the percentage of students who are English learners (that is, students for whom English is a second language). All of these data
were obtained from the California Department of Education (www.cde.ca.gov).

APPENDIX
4.2 | Derivation of the OLS Estimators

This appendix uses calculus to derive the formulas for the OLS estimators given in Key
Concept 4.2. To minimize the sum of squared prediction mistakes $\sum_{i=1}^{n}(Y_i - b_0 - b_1X_i)^2$
[Equation (4.6)], first take the partial derivatives with respect to b_0 and b_1:

$$\frac{\partial}{\partial b_0} \sum_{i=1}^{n} (Y_i - b_0 - b_1X_i)^2 = -2\sum_{i=1}^{n} (Y_i - b_0 - b_1X_i) \text{ and} \qquad (4.23)$$

$$\frac{\partial}{\partial b_1} \sum_{i=1}^{n} (Y_i - b_0 - b_1X_i)^2 = -2\sum_{i=1}^{n} (Y_i - b_0 - b_1X_i)X_i. \qquad (4.24)$$

The OLS estimators, $\hat{\beta}_0$ and $\hat{\beta}_1$, are the values of b_0 and b_1 that minimize $\sum_{i=1}^{n}(Y_i - b_0 - b_1X_i)^2$ or, equivalently, the values of b_0 and b_1 for which the derivatives in Equations (4.23) and (4.24) equal zero. Accordingly, setting these derivatives equal to zero, collecting terms, and dividing by n shows that the OLS estimators, $\hat{\beta}_0$ and $\hat{\beta}_1$, must satisfy the two equations,

$$\overline{Y} - \hat{\beta}_0 - \hat{\beta}_1 \overline{X} = 0 \text{ and} \tag{4.25}$$

$$\frac{1}{n}\sum_{i=1}^{n} X_i Y_i - \hat{\beta}_0 \overline{X} - \hat{\beta}_1 \frac{1}{n}\sum_{i=1}^{n} X_i^2 = 0. \tag{4.26}$$

Solving this pair of equations for $\hat{\beta}_0$ and $\hat{\beta}_1$ yields

$$\hat{\beta}_1 = \frac{\dfrac{1}{n}\sum_{i=1}^{n} X_i Y_i - \overline{X}\,\overline{Y}}{\dfrac{1}{n}\sum_{i=1}^{n} X_i^2 - (\overline{X})^2} = \frac{\sum_{i=1}^{n}(X_i - \overline{X})(Y_i - \overline{Y})}{\sum_{i=1}^{n}(X_i - \overline{X})^2} \tag{4.27}$$

$$\hat{\beta}_0 = \overline{Y} - \hat{\beta}_1 \overline{X}. \tag{4.28}$$

Equations (4.27) and (4.28) are the formulas for $\hat{\beta}_0$ and $\hat{\beta}_1$ given in Key Concept 4.2; the formula $\hat{\beta}_1 = s_{XY}/s_X^2$ is obtained by dividing the numerator and denominator in Equation (4.27) by $n - 1$.

APPENDIX

4.3 | Sampling Distribution of the OLS Estimator

In this appendix, we show that the OLS estimator $\hat{\beta}_1$ is unbiased and, in large samples, has the normal sampling distribution given in Key Concept 4.4.

Representation of $\hat{\beta}_1$ in Terms of the Regressors and Errors

We start by providing an expression for $\hat{\beta}_1$ in terms of the regressors and errors. Because $Y_i = \beta_0 + \beta_1 X_i + u_i$, $Y_i - \overline{Y} = \beta_1(X_i - \overline{X}) + u_i - \overline{u}$, so the numerator of the formula for $\hat{\beta}_1$ in Equation (4.27) is

$$\sum_{i=1}^{n}(X_i - \overline{X})(Y_i - \overline{Y}) = \sum_{i=1}^{n}(X_i - \overline{X})[\beta_1(X_i - \overline{X}) + (u_i - \overline{u})]$$
$$= \beta_1\sum_{i=1}^{n}(X_i - \overline{X})^2 + \sum_{i=1}^{n}(X_i - \overline{X})(u_i - \overline{u}). \tag{4.29}$$

Now $\Sigma_{i=1}^{n}(X_i - \overline{X})(u_i - \overline{u}) = \Sigma_{i=1}^{n}(X_i - \overline{X})u_i - \Sigma_{i=1}^{n}(X_i - \overline{X})\overline{u} = \Sigma_{i=1}^{n}(X_i - \overline{X})u_i$, where the final equality follows from the definition of $\overline{X}$, which implies that $\Sigma_{i=1}^{n}(X_i - \overline{X})\overline{u} = [\Sigma_{i=1}^{n}X_i - n\overline{X}]\overline{u} = 0$. Substituting $\Sigma_{i=1}^{n}(X_i - \overline{X})(u_i - \overline{u}) = \Sigma_{i=1}^{n}(X_i - \overline{X})u_i$ into the final expression in Equation (4.29) yields $\Sigma_{i=1}^{n}(X_i - \overline{X})(Y_i - \overline{Y}) = \beta_1\Sigma_{i=1}^{n}(X_i - \overline{X})^2 + \Sigma_{i=1}^{n}(X_i - \overline{X})u_i$. Substituting this expression in turn into the formula for $\hat{\beta}_1$ in Equation (4.27) yields

$$\hat{\beta}_1 = \beta_1 + \frac{\dfrac{1}{n}\sum_{i=1}^{n}(X_i - \overline{X})u_i}{\dfrac{1}{n}\sum_{i=1}^{n}(X_i - \overline{X})^2}. \tag{4.30}$$

Proof That $\hat{\beta}_1$ Is Unbiased

The expectation of $\hat{\beta}_1$ is obtained by taking the expectation of both sides of Equation (4.30). Thus,

$$E(\hat{\beta}_1) = \beta_1 + E\left[\frac{\dfrac{1}{n}\sum_{i=1}^{n}(X_i - \overline{X})u_i}{\dfrac{1}{n}\sum_{i=1}^{n}(X_i - \overline{X})^2}\right]$$

$$= \beta_1 + E\left[\frac{\dfrac{1}{n}\sum_{i=1}^{n}(X_i - \overline{X})E(u_i|X_1, \ldots, X_n)}{\dfrac{1}{n}\sum_{i=1}^{n}(X_i - \overline{X})^2}\right] = \beta_1, \tag{4.31}$$

where the second equality in Equation (4.31) follows by using the law of iterated expectations (Section 2.3). By the second least squares assumption, u_i is distributed independently of X for all observations other than i, so $E(u_i|X_1, \ldots, X_n) = E(u_i|X_i)$. By the first least squares assumption, however, $E(u_i|X_i) = 0$. It follows that the conditional expectation in large brackets in the second line of Equation (4.31) is zero, so that $E(\hat{\beta}_1 - \beta_1|X_1, \ldots, X_n) = 0$. Equivalently, $E(\hat{\beta}_1|X_1, \ldots, X_n) = \beta_1$; that is, $\hat{\beta}_1$ is conditionally unbiased, given $X_1, \ldots, X_n$. By the law of iterated expectations $E(\hat{\beta}_1 - \beta_1) = E[E(\hat{\beta}_1 - \beta_1|X_1, \ldots, X_n)] = 0$, so that $E(\hat{\beta}_1) = \beta_1$; that is, $\hat{\beta}_1$ is unbiased.

Large-Sample Normal Distribution of the OLS Estimator

The large-sample normal approximation to the limiting distribution of $\hat{\beta}_1$ (Key Concept 4.4) is obtained by considering the behavior of the final term in Equation (4.30).

First consider the numerator of this term. Because $\overline{X}$ is consistent, if the sample size is large, $\overline{X}$ is nearly equal to μ_X. Thus, to a close approximation, the term in the numerator of Equation (4.30) is the sample average $\overline{v}$, where $v_i = (X_i - \mu_X)u_i$. By the first least squares assumption, v_i has a mean of zero. By the second least squares assumption, v_i is i.i.d. The variance of v_i is $\sigma_v^2 = \text{var}[(X_i - \mu_X)u_i]$ which, by the third least squares assumption, is nonzero and finite. Therefore, $\overline{v}$ satisfies all the requirements of the central limit theorem (Key Concept 2.7). Thus, $\overline{v}/\sigma_{\overline{v}}$ is, in large samples, distributed $N(0, 1)$, where $\sigma_{\overline{v}}^2 = \sigma_v^2/n$. Thus the distribution of $\overline{v}$ is well approximated by the $N(0, \sigma_v^2/n)$ distribution.

Next consider the expression in the denominator in Equation (4.30); this is the sample variance of X (except dividing by n rather than $n - 1$, which is inconsequential if n is large). As discussed in Section 3.2 [Equation (3.8)], the sample variance is a consistent estimator of the population variance, so in large samples it is arbitrarily close to the population variance of X.

Combining these two results, we have that, in large samples, $\hat{\beta}_1 - \beta_1 \cong \overline{v}/\text{var}(X_i)$, so that the sampling distribution of $\hat{\beta}_1$ is, in large samples, $N(\beta_1, \sigma_{\hat{\beta}_1}^2)$, where $\sigma_{\hat{\beta}_1}^2 = \text{var}(\overline{v})/[\text{var}(X_i)]^2 = \text{var}[(X_i - \mu_X)u_i]/\{n[\text{var}(X_i)]^2\}$, which is the expression in Equation (4.21).

Some Additional Algebraic Facts About OLS

The OLS residuals and predicted values satisfy:

$$\frac{1}{n}\sum_{i=1}^{n}\hat{u}_i = 0, \tag{4.32}$$

$$\frac{1}{n}\sum_{i=1}^{n}\hat{Y}_i = \overline{Y}, \tag{4.33}$$

$$\sum_{i=1}^{n}\hat{u}_iX_i = 0 \text{ and } s_{\hat{u}X} = 0, \text{ and} \tag{4.34}$$

$$TSS = SSR + ESS. \tag{4.35}$$

Equations (4.32) through (4.35) say that the sample average of the OLS residuals is zero; the sample average of the OLS predicted values equals $\overline{Y}$; the sample covariance $s_{\hat{u}X}$ between the OLS residuals and the regressors is zero; and the total sum of squares is the sum of the sum of squared residuals and the explained sum of squares [the *ESS*, *TSS*, and *SSR* are defined in Equations (4.14), (4.15), and (4.17)].

To verify Equation (4.32), note that the definition of $\hat{\beta}_0$ lets us write the OLS residuals as $\hat{u}_i = Y_i - \hat{\beta}_0 - \hat{\beta}_1 X_i = (Y_i - \overline{Y}) - \hat{\beta}_1(X_i - \overline{X})$; thus

$$\sum_{i=1}^n \hat{u}_i = \sum_{i=1}^n (Y_i - \overline{Y}) - \hat{\beta}_1 \sum_{i=1}^n (X_i - \overline{X}).$$

But the definition of $\overline{Y}$ and $\overline{X}$ imply that $\sum_{i=1}^n (Y_i - \overline{Y}) = 0$ and $\sum_{i=1}^n (X_i - \overline{X}) = 0$, so $\sum_{i=1}^n \hat{u}_i = 0$.

To verify Equation (4.33), note that $Y_i = \hat{Y}_i + \hat{u}_i$, so $\sum_{i=1}^n Y_i = \sum_{i=1}^n \hat{Y}_i + \sum_{i=1}^n \hat{u}_1 = \sum_{i=1}^n \hat{Y}_i$, where the second equality is a consequence of Equation (4.32).

To verify Equation (4.34), note that $\sum_{i=1}^n \hat{u}_i = 0$ implies $\sum_{i=1}^n \hat{u}_i X_i = \sum_{i=1}^n \hat{u}_i(X_i - \overline{X})$, so

$$\begin{aligned}
\sum_{i=1}^n \hat{u}_i X_i &= \sum_{i=1}^n [(Y_i - \overline{Y}) - \hat{\beta}_1(X_i - \overline{X})] (X_i - \overline{X}) \\
&= \sum_{i=1}^n (Y_i - \overline{Y})(X_i - \overline{X}) - \hat{\beta}_1 \sum_{i=1}^n (X_i - \overline{X})^2 = 0,
\end{aligned} \tag{4.36}$$

where the final equality in Equation (4.36) is obtained using the formula for $\hat{\beta}_1$ in Equation (4.27). This result, combined with the preceding results, implies that $s_{\hat{u}X} = 0$.

Equation (4.35) follows from the previous results and some algebra:

$$\begin{aligned}
TSS &= \sum_{i=1}^n (Y_i - \overline{Y})^2 = \sum_{i=1}^n (Y_i - \hat{Y}_i + \hat{Y}_i - \overline{Y})^2 \\
&= \sum_{i=1}^n (Y_i - \hat{Y}_i)^2 + \sum_{i=1}^n (\hat{Y}_i - \overline{Y})^2 + 2 \sum_{i=1}^n (Y_i - \hat{Y}_i)(\hat{Y}_i - \overline{Y}) \\
&= SSR + ESS + 2 \sum_{i=1}^n \hat{u}_i \hat{Y}_i = SSR + ESS,
\end{aligned} \tag{4.37}$$

where the final equality follows from $\sum_{i=1}^n \hat{u}_i \hat{Y}_i = \sum_{i=1}^n \hat{u}_i(\hat{\beta}_0 + \hat{\beta}_1 X_i) = \hat{\beta}_0 \sum_{i=1}^n \hat{u}_i + \hat{\beta}_1 \sum_{i=1}^n \hat{u}_i X_i = 0$ by the previous results.

CHAPTER 5

Regression with a Single Regressor: Hypothesis Tests and Confidence Intervals

This chapter continues the treatment of linear regression with a single regressor. Chapter 4 explained how the OLS estimator $\hat{\beta}_1$ of the slope coefficient β_1 differs from one sample to the next—that is, how $\hat{\beta}_1$ has a sampling distribution. In this chapter, we show how knowledge of this sampling distribution can be used to make statements about β_1 that accurately summarize the sampling uncertainty. The starting point is the standard error of the OLS estimator, which measures the spread of the sampling distribution of $\hat{\beta}_1$. Section 5.1 provides an expression for this standard error (and for the standard error of the OLS estimator of the intercept), then shows how to use $\hat{\beta}_1$ and its standard error to test hypotheses. Section 5.2 explains how to construct confidence intervals for β_1. Section 5.3 takes up the special case of a binary regressor.

Sections 5.1–5.3 assume that the three least squares assumptions of Chapter 4 hold. If, in addition, some stronger conditions hold, then some stronger results can be derived regarding the distribution of the OLS estimator. One of these stronger conditions is that the errors are homoskedastic, a concept introduced in Section 5.4. Section 5.5 presents the Gauss-Markov theorem, which states that, under certain conditions, OLS is efficient (has the smallest variance) among a certain class of estimators. Section 5.6 discusses the distribution of the OLS estimator when the population distribution of the regression errors is normal.

5.1   Testing Hypotheses About One of the Regression Coefficients

Your client, the superintendent, calls you with a problem. She has an angry tax-payer in her office who asserts that cutting class size will not help boost test scores, so that reducing them further is a waste of money. Class size, the taxpayer claims, has no effect on test scores.

The taxpayer's claim can be rephrased in the language of regression analysis. Because the effect on test scores of a unit change in class size is $\beta_{ClassSize}$, the taxpayer is asserting that the population regression line is flat—that is, the slope $\beta_{ClassSize}$ of the population regression line is zero. Is there, the superintedent asks, evidence in your sample of 420 observations on California school districts that this slope is nonzero? Can you reject the taxpayer's hypothesis that $\beta_{ClassSize} = 0$, or should you accept it, at least tentatively pending further new evidence?

This section discusses tests of hypotheses about the slope β_1 or intercept β_0 of the population regression line. We start by discussing two-sided tests of the slope β_1 in detail, then turn to one-sided tests and to tests of hypotheses regarding the intercept β_0.

Two-Sided Hypotheses Concerning β_1

The general approach to testing hypotheses about these coefficients is the same as to testing hypotheses about the population mean, so we begin with a brief review.

Testing hypotheses about the population mean.   Recall from Section 3.2 that the null hypothesis that the mean of Y is a specific value $\mu_{Y,0}$ can be written as $H_0: E(Y) = \mu_{Y,0}$, and the two-sided alternative is $H_1: E(Y) \neq \mu_{Y,0}$.

The test of the null hypothesis H_0 against the two-sided alternative proceeds as in the three steps summarized in Key Concept 3.6. The first is to compute the standard error of $\overline{Y}$, $SE(\overline{Y})$, which is an estimator of the standard deviation of the sampling distribution of $\overline{Y}$. The second step is to compute the t-statistic, which has the general form given in Key Concept 5.1; applied here, the t-statistic is $t = (\overline{Y} - \mu_{Y,0})/SE(\overline{Y})$.

The third step is to compute the p-value, which is the smallest significance level at which the null hypothesis could be rejected, based on the test statistic actually observed; equivalently, the p-value is the probability of obtaining a statistic, by random sampling variation, at least as different from the null hypothesis value as is the statistic actually observed, assuming that the null hypothesis is correct

KEY CONCEPT

5.1

GENERAL FORM OF THE *t*-STATISTIC

In general, the *t*-statistic has the form

$$t = \frac{\text{estimator} - \text{hypothesized value}}{\text{standard error of the estimator}}. \tag{5.1}$$

(Key Concept 3.5). Because the *t*-statistic has a standard normal distribution in large samples under the null hypothesis, the *p*-value for a two-sided hypothesis test is $2\Phi(-|t^{act}|)$, where t^{act} is the value of the *t*-statistic actually computed and Φ is the cumulative standard normal distribution tabulated in Appendix Table 1. Alternatively, the third step can be replaced by simply comparing the *t*-statistic to the critical value appropriate for the test with the desired significance level. For example, a two-sided test with a 5% significance level would reject the null hypothesis if $|t^{act}| > 1.96$. In this case, the population mean is said to be statistically significantly different than the hypothesized value at the 5% significance level.

Testing hypotheses about the slope β_1.   At a theoretical level, the critical feature justifying the foregoing testing procedure for the population mean is that, in large samples, the sampling distribution of $\overline{Y}$ is approximately normal. Because $\hat{\beta}_1$ also has a normal sampling distribution in large samples, hypotheses about the true value of the slope β_1 can be tested using the same general approach.

The null and alternative hypotheses need to be stated precisely before they can be tested. The angry taxpayer's hypothesis is that $\beta_{ClassSize} = 0$. More generally, under the null hypothesis the true population slope β_1 takes on some specific value, $\beta_{1,0}$. Under the two-sided alternative, β_1 does not equal $\beta_{1,0}$. That is, the **null hypothesis** and the **two-sided alternative hypothesis** are

$$H_0: \beta_1 = \beta_{1,0} \text{ vs. } H_1: \beta_1 \neq \beta_{1,0} \quad \text{(two-sided alternative).} \tag{5.2}$$

To test the null hypothesis H_0, we follow the same three steps as for the population mean.

The first step is to compute the **standard error of $\hat{\beta}_1$**, $SE(\hat{\beta}_1)$. The standard error of $\hat{\beta}_1$ is an estimator of $\sigma_{\hat{\beta}_1}$, the standard deviation of the sampling distribution of $\hat{\beta}_1$. Specifically,

$$SE(\hat{\beta}_1) = \sqrt{\hat{\sigma}^2_{\hat{\beta}_1}}, \tag{5.3}$$

where

$$\hat{\sigma}_{\hat{\beta}_1}^2 = \frac{1}{n} \times \frac{\dfrac{1}{n-2} \sum_{i=1}^{n} (X_i - \overline{X})^2 \hat{u}_i^2}{\left[\dfrac{1}{n} \sum_{i=1}^{n} (X_i - \overline{X})^2 \right]^2}. \tag{5.4}$$

The estimator of the variance in Equation (5.4) is discussed in Appendix 5.1. Although the formula for $\hat{\sigma}_{\hat{\beta}_1}^2$ is complicated, in applications the standard error is computed by regression software so that it is easy to use in practice.

The second step is to compute the **t-statistic**,

$$t = \frac{\hat{\beta}_1 - \beta_{1,0}}{SE(\hat{\beta}_1)}. \tag{5.5}$$

The third step is to compute the **p-value**, the probability of observing a value of $\hat{\beta}_1$ at least as different from $\beta_{1,0}$ as the estimate actually computed ($\hat{\beta}_1^{act}$), assuming that the null hypothesis is correct. Stated mathematically,

$$\begin{aligned} \text{p-value} &= \Pr_{H_0}[|\hat{\beta}_1 - \beta_{1,0}| > |\hat{\beta}_1^{act} - \beta_{1,0}|] \\ &= \Pr_{H_0}\left[\left| \frac{\hat{\beta}_1 - \beta_{1,0}}{SE(\hat{\beta}_1)} \right| > \left| \frac{\hat{\beta}_1^{act} - \beta_{1,0}}{SE(\hat{\beta}_1)} \right| \right] = \Pr_{H_0}(|t| > |t^{act}|), \end{aligned} \tag{5.6}$$

where $\Pr_{H_0}$ denotes the probability computed under the null hypothesis, the second equality follows by dividing by $SE(\hat{\beta}_1)$, and t^{act} is the value of the t-statistic actually computed. Because $\hat{\beta}_1$ is approximately normally distributed in large samples, under the null hypothesis the t-statistic is approximately distributed as a standard normal random variable, so in large samples,

$$\text{p-value} = \Pr(|Z| > |t^{act}|) = 2\Phi(-|t^{act}|). \tag{5.7}$$

A small value of the p-value, say less than 5%, provides evidence against the null hypothesis in the sense that the chance of obtaining a value of $\hat{\beta}_1$ by pure random variation from one sample to the next is less than 5% if, in fact, the null hypothesis is correct. If so, the null hypothesis is rejected at the 5% significance level.

Alternatively, the hypothesis can be tested at the 5% significance level simply by comparing the value of the t-statistic to ± 1.96, the critical value for a two-sided test, and rejecting the null hypothesis at the 5% level if $|t^{act}| > 1.96$.

These steps are summarized in Key Concept 5.2.

TESTING THE HYPOTHESIS $\beta_1 = \beta_{1,0}$
AGAINST THE ALTERNATIVE $\beta_1 \neq \beta_{1,0}$

1. Compute the standard error of $\hat{\beta}_1$, $SE(\hat{\beta}_1)$ [Equation (5.3)].
2. Compute the t-statistic [Equation (5.5)].
3. Compute the p-value [Equation (5.7)]. Reject the hypothesis at the 5% significance level if the p-value is less than 0.05 or, equivalently, if $|t^{act}| > 1.96$.

The standard error and (typically) the t-statistic and p-value testing $\beta_1 = 0$ are computed automatically by regression software.

Reporting regression equations and application to test scores.   The OLS regression of the test score against the student–teacher ratio, reported in Equation (4.11), yielded $\hat{\beta}_0 = 698.9$ and $\hat{\beta}_1 = -2.28$. The standard errors of these estimates are $SE(\hat{\beta}_0) = 10.4$ and $SE(\hat{\beta}_1) = 0.52$.

Because of the importance of the standard errors, by convention they are included when reporting the estimated OLS coefficients. One compact way to report the standard errors is to place them in parentheses below the respective coefficients of the OLS regression line:

$$\widehat{TestScore} = 698.9 - 2.28 \times STR, \ R^2 = 0.051, SER = 18.6. \quad (5.8)$$
$$\qquad\qquad (10.4) \ \ (0.52)$$

Equation (5.8) also reports the regression R^2 and the standard error of the regression (*SER*) following the estimated regression line. Thus Equation (5.8) provides the estimated regression line, estimates of the sampling uncertainty of the slope and the intercept (the standard errors), and two measures of the fit of this regression line (the R^2 and the *SER*). This is a common format for reporting a single regression equation, and it will be used throughout the rest of this book.

Suppose you wish to test the null hypothesis that the slope β_1 is zero in the population counterpart of Equation (5.8) at the 5% significance level. To do so, construct the t-statistic and compare it to 1.96, the 5% (two-sided) critical value taken from the standard normal distribution. The t-statistic is constructed by substituting the hypothesized value of β_1 under the null hypothesis (zero), the estimated slope, and its standard error from Equation (5.8) into the general formula

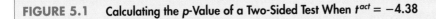

FIGURE 5.1 Calculating the *p*-Value of a Two-Sided Test When $t^{act} = -4.38$

The *p*-value of a two-sided test is the probability that $|Z| > |t^{act}|$, where Z is a standard normal random variable and t^{act} is the value of the *t*-statistic calculated from the sample. When $t^{act} = -4.38$, the *p*-value is only 0.00001.

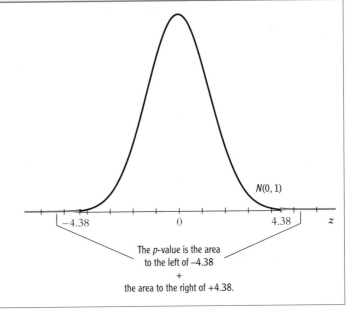

$N(0, 1)$

-4.38 0 4.38 z

The *p*-value is the area
to the left of –4.38
+
the area to the right of +4.38.

---

in Equation (5.5); the result is $t^{act} = (-2.28 - 0)/0.52 = -4.38$. This *t*-statistic exceeds (in absolute value) the 5% two-sided critical value of 1.96, so the null hypothesis is rejected in favor of the two-sided alternative at the 5% significance level.

Alternatively, we can compute the *p*-value associated with $t^{act} = -4.38$. This probability is the area in the tails of standard normal distribution, as shown in Figure 5.1. This probability is extremely small, approximately 0.00001, or 0.001%. That is, if the null hypothesis $\beta_{ClassSize} = 0$ is true, the probability of obtaining a value of $\hat{\beta}_1$ as far from the null as the value we actually obtained is extremely small, less than 0.001%. Because this event is so unlikely, it is reasonable to conclude that the null hypothesis is false.

One-Sided Hypotheses Concerning β_1

The discussion so far has focused on testing the hypothesis that $\beta_1 = \beta_{1,0}$ against the hypothesis that $\beta_1 \neq \beta_{1,0}$. This is a two-sided hypothesis test, because under the alternative β_1 could be either larger or smaller than $\beta_{1,0}$. Sometimes, however, it is appropriate to use a one-sided hypothesis test. For example, in the student–teacher ratio/test score problem, many people think that smaller classes provide a better learning environment. Under that hypothesis, β_1 is negative: Smaller classes lead to higher scores. It might make sense, therefore, to test the null hypothesis that $\beta_1 = 0$ (no effect) against the one-sided alternative that $\beta_1 < 0$.

For a one-sided test, the null hypothesis and the one-sided alternative hypothesis are

$$H_0: \beta_1 = \beta_{1,0} \text{ vs. } H_1: \beta_1 < \beta_{1,0}, \quad \text{(one-sided alternative).} \qquad (5.9)$$

where $\beta_{1,0}$ is the value of β_1 under the null (0 in the student–teacher ratio example) and the alternative is that β_1 is less than $\beta_{1,0}$. If the alternative is that β_1 is greater than $\beta_{1,0}$, the inequality in Equation (5.9) is reversed.

Because the null hypothesis is the same for a one- and a two-sided hypothesis test, the construction of the t-statistic is the same. The only difference between a one- and two-sided hypothesis test is how you interpret the t-statistic. For the one-sided alternative in Equation (5.9), the null hypothesis is rejected against the one-sided alternative for large negative, but not large positive, values of the t-statistic: Instead of rejecting if $|t^{act}| > 1.96$, the hypothesis is rejected at the 5% significance level if $t^{act} < -1.645$.

The p-value for a one-sided test is obtained from the cumulative standard normal distribution as

$$p\text{-value} = \Pr(Z < t^{act}) = \Phi(t^{act}) \ (p\text{-value, one-sided left-tail test}). \quad (5.10)$$

If the alternative hypothesis is that β_1 is greater than $\beta_{1,0}$, the inequalities in Equations (5.9) and (5.10) are reversed, so the p-value is the right-tail probability, $\Pr(Z > t^{act})$.

When should a one-sided test be used?   In practice, one-sided alternative hypotheses should be used only when there is a clear reason for doing so. This reason could come from economic theory, prior empirical evidence, or both. However, even if it initially seems that the relevant alternative is one-sided, upon reflection this might not necessarily be so. A newly formulated drug undergoing clinical trials actually could prove harmful because of previously unrecognized side effects. In the class size example, we are reminded of the graduation joke that a university's secret of success is to admit talented students and then make sure that the faculty stays out of their way and does as little damage as possible. In practice, such ambiguity often leads econometricians to use two-sided tests.

Application to test scores. The t-statistic testing the hypothesis that there is no effect of class size on test scores [so $\beta_{1,0} = 0$ in Equation (5.9)] is $t^{act} = -4.38$. This is less than -2.33 (the critical value for a one-sided test with a 1% significance level), so the null hypothesis is rejected against the one-sided alternative at the 1% level. In fact, the p-value is less than 0.0006%. Based on these data, you can reject the angry taxpayer's assertion that the negative estimate of the slope arose purely because of random sampling variation at the 1% significance level.

Testing Hypotheses About the Intercept β_0

This discussion has focused on testing hypotheses about the slope, β_1. Occasionally, however, the hypothesis concerns the intercept, β_0. The null hypothesis concerning the intercept and the two-sided alternative are

$$H_0\colon \beta_0 = \beta_{0,0} \text{ vs. } H_1\colon \beta_0 \neq \beta_{0,0} \quad \text{(two-sided alternative).} \qquad (5.11)$$

The general approach to testing this null hypothesis consists of the three steps in Key Concept 5.2, applied to β_0 (the formula for the standard error of $\hat{\beta}_0$ is given in Appendix 5.1). If the alternative is one-sided, this approach is modified as was discussed in the previous subsection for hypotheses about the slope.

Hypothesis tests are useful if you have a specific null hypothesis in mind (as did our angry taxpayer). Being able to accept or to reject this null hypothesis based on the statistical evidence provides a powerful tool for coping with the uncertainty inherent in using a sample to learn about the population. Yet, there are many times that no single hypothesis about a regression coefficient is dominant, and instead one would like to know a range of values of the coefficient that are consistent with the data. This calls for constructing a confidence interval.

5.2 Confidence Intervals for a Regression Coefficient

Because any statistical estimate of the slope β_1 necessarily has sampling uncertainty, we cannot determine the true value of β_1 exactly from a sample of data. It is, however, possible to use the OLS estimator and its standard error to construct a confidence interval for the slope β_1 or for the intercept β_0.

Confidence interval for β_1.   Recall that a 95% **confidence interval for β_1** has two equivalent definitions. First, it is the set of values that cannot be rejected using a two-sided hypothesis test with a 5% significance level. Second, it is an interval that has a 95% probability of containing the true value of β_1; that is, in 95% of possible samples that might be drawn, the confidence interval will contain the true value of β_1. Because this interval contains the true value in 95% of all samples, it is said to have a **confidence level** of 95%.

The reason these two definitions are equivalent is as follows. A hypothesis test with a 5% significance level will, by definition, reject the true value of β_1 in only 5% of all possible samples; that is, in 95% of all possible samples the true value of β_1 will *not* be rejected. Because the 95% confidence interval (as defined in the first definition) is the set of all values of β_1 that are *not* rejected at the 5% significance level, it follows that the true value of β_1 will be contained in the confidence interval in 95% of all possible samples.

As in the case of a confidence interval for the population mean (Section 3.3), in principle a 95% confidence interval can be computed by testing all possible values of β_1 (that is, testing the null hypothesis $\beta_1 = \beta_{1,0}$ for all values of $\beta_{1,0}$) at the 5% significance level using the t-statistic. The 95% confidence interval is then the collection of all the values of β_1 that are not rejected. But constructing the t-statistic for all values of β_1 would take forever.

An easier way to construct the confidence interval is to note that the t-statistic will reject the hypothesized value $\beta_{1,0}$ whenever $\beta_{1,0}$ is outside the range $\hat{\beta}_1 \pm 1.96SE(\hat{\beta}_1)$. That is, the 95% confidence interval for β_1 is the interval $[\hat{\beta}_1 - 1.96SE(\hat{\beta}_1), \hat{\beta}_1 + 1.96SE(\hat{\beta}_1)]$. This argument parallels the argument used to develop a confidence interval for the population mean.

The construction of a confidence interval for β_1 is summarized as Key Concept 5.3.

Confidence interval for β_0.   A 95% confidence interval for β_0 is constructed as in Key Concept 5.3, with $\hat{\beta}_0$ and $SE(\hat{\beta}_0)$ replacing $\hat{\beta}_1$ and $SE(\hat{\beta}_1)$.

Application to test scores.   The OLS regression of the test score against the student–teacher ratio, reported in Equation (5.8), yielded $\hat{\beta}_1 = -2.28$ and $SE(\hat{\beta}_1) = 0.52$. The 95% two-sided confidence interval for β_1 is $\{-2.28 \pm 1.96 \times 0.52\}$, or $-3.30 \le \beta_1 \le -1.26$. The value $\beta_1 = 0$ is not contained in this confidence interval,

CONFIDENCE INTERVAL FOR β_1 KEY CONCEPT

5.3

A 95% two-sided confidence interval for β_1 is an interval that contains the true value of β_1 with a 95% probability; that is, it contains the true value of β_1 in 95% of all possible randomly drawn samples. Equivalently, it is the set of values of β_1 that cannot be rejected by a 5% two-sided hypothesis test. When the sample size is large, it is constructed as

$$95\% \text{ confidence interval for } \beta_1 =$$
$$[\hat{\beta}_1 - 1.96SE(\hat{\beta}_1), \hat{\beta}_1 + 1.96SE(\hat{\beta}_1)]. \tag{5.12}$$

so (as we knew already from Section 5.1) the hypothesis $\beta_1 = 0$ can be rejected at the 5% significance level.

Confidence intervals for predicted effects of changing X. The 95% confidence interval for β_1 can be used to construct a 95% confidence interval for the predicted effect of a general change in X.

Consider changing X by a given amount, Δx. The predicted change in Y associated with this change in X is $\beta_1 \Delta x$. The population slope β_1 is unknown, but because we can construct a confidence interval for β_1, we can construct a confidence interval for the predicted effect $\beta_1 \Delta x$. Because one end of a 95% confidence interval for β_1 is $\hat{\beta}_1 - 1.96SE(\hat{\beta}_1)$, the predicted effect of the change Δx using this estimate of β_1 is $[\hat{\beta}_1 - 1.96SE(\hat{\beta}_1)] \times \Delta x$. The other end of the confidence interval is $\hat{\beta}_1 + 1.96SE(\hat{\beta}_1)$, and the predicted effect of the change using that estimate is $[\hat{\beta}_1 + 1.96SE(\hat{\beta}_1)] \times \Delta x$. Thus a 95% confidence interval for the effect of changing x by the amount Δx can be expressed as

$$95\% \text{ confidence interval for } \beta_1 \Delta x =$$
$$[\hat{\beta}_1 \Delta x - 1.96SE(\hat{\beta}_1) \times \Delta x, \hat{\beta}_1 \Delta x + 1.96SE(\hat{\beta}_1) \times \Delta x]. \tag{5.13}$$

For example, our hypothetical superintendent is contemplating reducing the student–teacher ratio by 2. Because the 95% confidence interval for β_1 is $[-3.30, -1.26]$, the effect of reducing the student–teacher ratio by 2 could be as great as $-3.30 \times (-2) = 6.60$, or as little as $-1.26 \times (-2) = 2.52$. Thus decreasing the student–teacher ratio by 2 is predicted to increase test scores by between 2.52 and 6.60 points, with a 95% confidence level.

5.3 Regression When X Is a Binary Variable

The discussion so far has focused on the case that the regressor is a continuous variable. Regression analysis can also be used when the regressor is binary—that is, when it takes on only two values, 0 or 1. For example, X might be a worker's gender (= 1 if female, = 0 if male), whether a school district is urban or rural (= 1 if urban, = 0 if rural), or whether the district's class size is small or large (= 1 if small, = 0 if large). A binary variable is also called an **indicator variable** or sometimes a **dummy variable**.

Interpretation of the Regression Coefficients

The mechanics of regression with a binary regressor are the same as if it is continuous. The interpretation of β_1, however, is different, and it turns out that regression with a binary variable is equivalent to performing a difference of means analysis, as described in Section 3.4.

To see this, suppose you have a variable D_i that equals either 0 or 1, depending on whether the student–teacher ratio is less than 20:

$$D_i = \begin{cases} 1 \text{ if the student–teacher ratio in } i^{\text{th}} \text{ district} < 20 \\ 0 \text{ if the student–teacher ratio in } i^{\text{th}} \text{ district} \geq 20. \end{cases} \qquad (5.14)$$

The population regression model with D_i as the regressor is

$$Y_i = \beta_0 + \beta_1 D_i + u_i, \quad i = 1, \ldots, n. \qquad (5.15)$$

This is the same as the regression model with the continuous regressor X_i, except that now the regressor is the binary variable D_i. Because D_i is not continuous, it is not useful to think of β_1 as a slope; indeed, because D_i can take on only two values, there is no "line" so it makes no sense to talk about a slope. Thus we will not refer to β_1 as the slope in Equation (5.15); instead we will simply refer to β_1 as the **coefficient multiplying D_i** in this regression or, more compactly, the **coefficient on D_i**.

If β_1 in Equation (5.15) is not a slope, then what is it? The best way to interpret β_0 and β_1 in a regression with a binary regressor is to consider, one at a time, the two possible cases, $D_i = 0$ and $D_i = 1$. If the student–teacher ratio is high, then $D_i = 0$ and Equation (5.15) becomes

$$Y_i = \beta_0 + u_i \ (D_i = 0). \qquad (5.16)$$

Because $E(u_i|D_i) = 0$, the conditional expectation of Y_i when $D_i = 0$ is $E(Y_i|D_i = 0) = \beta_0$; that is, β_0 is the population mean value of test scores when the student–teacher ratio is high. Similarly, when $D_i = 1$,

$$Y_i = \beta_0 + \beta_1 + u_i \quad (D_i = 1). \tag{5.17}$$

Thus, when $D_i = 1$, $E(Y_i|D_i = 1) = \beta_0 + \beta_1$; that is, $\beta_0 + \beta_1$ is the population mean value of test scores when the student–teacher ratio is low.

Because $\beta_0 + \beta_1$ is the population mean of Y_i when $D_i = 1$ and β_0 is the population mean of Y_i when $D_i = 0$, the difference $(\beta_0 + \beta_1) - \beta_0 = \beta_1$ is the difference between these two means. In other words, β_1 is the difference between the conditional expectation of Y_i when $D_i = 1$ and when $D_i = 0$, or $\beta_1 = E(Y_i|D_i = 1) - E(Y_i|D_i = 0)$. In the test score example, β_1 is the difference between mean test score in districts with low student–teacher ratios and the mean test score in districts with high student–teacher ratios.

Because β_1 is the difference in the population means, it makes sense that the OLS estimator β_1 is the difference between the sample averages of Y_i in the two groups, and in fact this is the case.

Hypothesis tests and confidence intervals.   If the two population means are the same, then β_1 in Equation (5.15) is zero. Thus, the null hypothesis that the two population means are the same can be tested against the alternative hypothesis that they differ by testing the null hypothesis $\beta_1 = 0$ against the alternative $\beta_1 \neq 0$. This hypothesis can be tested using the procedure outlined in Section 5.1. Specifically, the null hypothesis can be rejected at the 5% level against the two-sided alternative when the OLS t-statistic $t = \hat{\beta}_1/SE(\hat{\beta}_1)$ exceeds 1.96 in absolute value. Similarly, a 95% confidence interval for β_1, constructed as $\hat{\beta}_1 \pm 1.96SE(\hat{\beta}_1)$ as described in Section 5.2, provides a 95% confidence interval for the difference between the two population means.

Application to test scores.   As an example, a regression of the test score against the student–teacher ratio binary variable D defined in Equation (5.14) estimated by OLS using the 420 observations in Figure 4.2, yields

$$\widehat{TestScore} = 650.0 + 7.4D, \; R^2 = 0.037, \; SER = 18.7, \tag{5.18}$$
$$\qquad\qquad\quad (1.3) \quad (1.8)$$

where the standard errors of the OLS estimates of the coefficients β_0 and β_1 are given in parentheses below the OLS estimates. Thus the average test score for the subsample with student–teacher ratios greater than or equal to 20 (that is, for which $D = 0$) is 650.0, and the average test score for the subsample with student–teacher ratios less than 20 (so $D = 1$) is $650.0 + 7.4 = 657.4$. The difference between the sample average test scores for the two groups is 7.4. This is the OLS estimate of β_1, the coefficient on the student–teacher ratio binary variable D.

Is the difference in the population mean test scores in the two groups statistically significantly different from zero at the 5% level? To find out, construct the t-statistic on β_1: $t = 7.4/1.8 = 4.04$. This exceeds 1.96 in absolute value, so the hypothesis that the population mean test scores in districts with high and low student–teacher ratios is the same can be rejected at the 5% significance level.

The OLS estimator and its standard error can be used to construct a 95% confidence interval for the true difference in means. This is $7.4 \pm 1.96 \times 1.8 = (3.9, 10.9)$. This confidence interval excludes $\beta_1 = 0$, so that (as we know from the previous paragraph) the hypothesis $\beta_1 = 0$ can be rejected at the 5% significance level.

5.4 Heteroskedasticity and Homoskedasticity

Our only assumption about the distribution of u_i conditional on X_i is that it has a mean of zero (the first least squares assumption). If, furthermore, the *variance* of this conditional distribution does not depend on X_i, then the errors are said to be homoskedastic. This section discusses homoskedasticity, its theoretical implications, the simplified formulas for the standard errors of the OLS estimators that arise if the errors are homoskedastic, and the risks you run if you use these simplified formulas in practice.

What Are Heteroskedasticity and Homoskedasticity?

Definitions of heteroskedasticity and homoskedasticity. The error term u_i is **homoskedastic** if the variance of the conditional distribution of u_i given X_i is constant for $i = 1, \ldots, n$ and in particular does not depend on X_i. Otherwise, the error term is **heteroskedastic**.

FIGURE 5.2 **An Example of Heteroskedasticity**

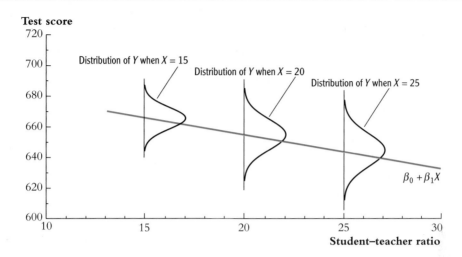

Like Figure 4.4, this shows the conditional distribution of test scores for three different class sizes. Unlike Figure 4.4, these distributions become more spread out (have a larger variance) for larger class sizes. Because the variance of the distribution of u given X, $\text{var}(u|X)$, depends on X, u is heteroskedastic.

As an illustration, return to Figure 4.4. The distribution of the errors u_i is shown for various values of x. Because this distribution applies specifically for the indicated value of x, this is the conditional distribution of u_i given $X_i = x$. As drawn in that figure, all these conditional distributions have the same spread; more precisely, the variance of these distributions is the same for the various values of x. That is, in Figure 4.4, the conditional variance of u_i given $X_i = x$ does not depend on x, so the errors illustrated in Figure 4.4 are homoskedastic.

In contrast, Figure 5.2 illustrates a case in which the conditional distribution of u_i spreads out as x increases. For small values of x, this distribution is tight, but for larger values of x, it has a greater spread. Thus, in Figure 5.2 the variance of u_i given $X_i = x$ increases with x, so that the errors in Figure 5.2 are heteroskedastic.

The definitions of heteroskedasticity and homoskedasticity are summarized in Key Concept 5.4.

HETEROSKEDASTICITY AND HOMOSKEDASTICITY

The error term u_i is homoskedastic if the variance of the conditional distribution of u_i given X_i, $\mathrm{var}(u_i|X_i = x)$, is constant for $i = 1, \ldots, n$, and in particular does not depend on x. Otherwise, the error term is heteroskedastic.

Example.   These terms are a mouthful and the definitions might seem abstract. To help clarify them with an example, we digress from the student–teacher ratio/test score problem and instead return to the example of earnings of male versus female college graduates considered in the box in Chapter 3, "The Gender Gap in Earnings of College Graduates in the United States." Let $MALE_i$ be a binary variable that equals 1 for male college graduates and equals 0 for female graduates. The binary variable regression model relating someone's earnings to his or her gender is

$$Earnings_i = \beta_0 + \beta_1 MALE_i + u_i \qquad (5.19)$$

for $i = 1, \ldots, n$. Because the regressor is binary, β_1 is the difference in the population means of the two groups—in this case, the difference in mean earnings between men and women who graduated from college.

The definition of homoskedasticity states that the variance of u_i does not depend on the regressor. Here the regressor is $MALE_i$, so at issue is whether the variance of the error term depends on $MALE_i$. In other words, is the variance of the error term the same for men and for women? If so, the error is homoskedastic; if not, it is heteroskedastic.

Deciding whether the variance of u_i depends on $MALE_i$ requires thinking hard about what the error term actually is. In this regard, it is useful to write Equation (5.19) as two separate equations, one for men and one for women:

$$Earnings_i = \beta_0 + u_i \quad \text{(women) and} \qquad (5.20)$$

$$Earnings_i = \beta_0 + \beta_1 + u_i \quad \text{(men).} \qquad (5.21)$$

Thus, for women, u_i is the deviation of the ith woman's earnings from the population mean earnings for women (β_0), and for men, u_i is the deviation of the ith man's earnings from the population mean earnings for men ($\beta_0 + \beta_1$). It follows that the statement, "the variance of u_i does not depend on *MALE*," is equivalent to the statement, "the variance of earnings is the same for men as it is for women." In other words, in this example, the error term is homoskedastic if the variance of the population distribution of earnings is the same for men and women; if these variances differ, the error term is heteroskedastic.

Mathematical Implications of Homoskedasticity

The OLS estimators remain unbiased and asymptotically normal. Because the least squares assumptions in Key Concept 4.3 place no restrictions on the conditional variance, they apply to both the general case of heteroskedasticity and the special case of homoskedasticity. Therefore, the OLS estimators remain unbiased and consistent even if the errors are homoskedastic. In addition, the OLS estimators have sampling distributions that are normal in large samples even if the errors are homoskedastic. Whether the errors are homoskedastic or heteroskedastic, the OLS estimator is unbiased, consistent, and asymptotically normal.

Efficiency of the OLS estimator when the errors are homoskedastic. If the least squares assumptions in Key Concept 4.3 hold and the errors are homoskedastic, then the OLS estimators $\hat{\beta}_0$ and $\hat{\beta}_1$ are efficient among all estimators that are linear in $Y_1, \ldots, Y_n$ and are unbiased, conditional on $X_1, \ldots, X_n$. This result, which is called the Gauss-Markov theorem, is discussed in Section 5.5.

Homoskedasticity-only variance formula. If the error term is homoskedastic, then the formulas for the variances of $\hat{\beta}_0$ and $\hat{\beta}_1$ in Key Concept 4.4 simplify. Consequently, if the errors are homoskedastic, then there is a specialized formula that can be used for the standard errors of $\hat{\beta}_0$ and $\hat{\beta}_1$. The **homoskedasticity-only standard error** of $\hat{\beta}_1$, derived in Appendix 5.1, is $SE(\hat{\beta}_1) = \sqrt{\tilde{\sigma}^2_{\hat{\beta}_1}}$, where $\tilde{\sigma}^2_{\hat{\beta}_1}$ is the homoskedasticity-only estimator of the variance of $\hat{\beta}_1$:

$$\tilde{\sigma}^2_{\hat{\beta}_1} = \frac{s^2_{\hat{u}}}{\sum_{i=1}^{n}(X_i - \overline{X})^2} \quad \text{(homoskedasticity-only)}, \tag{5.22}$$

where $s^2_{\hat{u}}$ is given in Equation (4.19). The homoskedasticity-only formula for the standard error of $\hat{\beta}_0$ is given in Appendix 5.1. In the special case that X is a binary variable, the estimator of the variance of $\hat{\beta}_1$ under homoskedasticity (that is, the square of the standard error of $\hat{\beta}_1$ under homoskedasticity) is the so-called pooled variance formula for the difference in means, given in Equation (3.23).

Because these alternative formulas are derived for the special case that the errors are homoskedastic and do not apply if the errors are heteroskedastic, they will be referred to as the "homoskedasticity-only" formulas for the variance and standard error of the OLS estimators. As the name suggests, if the errors are heteroskedastic, then the homoskedasticity-only standard errors are inappropriate. Specifically, if the errors are heteroskedastic, then the t-statistic computed using the homoskedasticity-only standard error does not have a standard normal distribution, even in large samples. In fact, the correct critical values to use for this homoskedasticity-only t-statistic depend on the precise nature of the heteroskedasticity, so those critical values cannot be tabulated. Similarly, if the errors are heteroskedastic but a confidence interval is constructed as ± 1.96 homoskedasticity-only standard errors, in general the probability that this interval contains the true value of the coefficient is not 95%, even in large samples.

In contrast, because homoskedasticity is a special case of heteroskedasticity, the estimators $\hat{\sigma}^2_{\hat{\beta}_1}$ and $\hat{\sigma}^2_{\hat{\beta}_0}$ of the variances of $\hat{\beta}_1$ and $\hat{\beta}_0$ given in Equations (5.4) and (5.26) produce valid statistical inferences whether the errors are heteroskedastic or homoskedastic. Thus hypothesis tests and confidence intervals based on those standard errors are valid whether or not the errors are heteroskedastic. Because the standard errors we have used so far [i.e., those based on Equations (5.4) and (5.26)] lead to statistical inferences that are valid whether or not the errors are heteroskedastic, they are called **heteroskedasticity-robust standard errors**. Because such formulas were proposed by Eicker (1967), Huber (1967), and White (1980), they are also referred to as Eicker-Huber-White standard errors.

What Does This Mean in Practice?

Which is more realistic, heteroskedasticity or homoskedasticity?   The answer to this question depends on the application. However, the issues can be clarified by returning to the example of the gender gap in earnings among college graduates. Familiarity with how people are paid in the world around us gives some clues as to which assumption is more sensible. For many years—and, to a lesser extent, today—women were not found in the top-paying jobs: There have always been poorly paid men, but there have rarely been highly paid women. This suggests that the distribution of earnings among women is tighter than among men (See the box in Chapter 3, "The Gender Gap in Earnings of College Graduates in the United States"). In other words, the variance of the error term in Equa-

The Economic Value of a Year of Education: Homoskedasticity or Heteroskedasticity?

On average, workers with more education have higher earnings than workers with less education. But if the best-paying jobs mainly go to the college educated, it might also be that the *spread* of the distribution of earnings is greater for workers with more education. Does the distribution of earnings spread out as education increases?

This is an empirical question, so answering it requires analyzing data. Figure 5.3 is a scatterplot of the hourly earnings and the number of years of education for a sample of 2950 full-time workers in the United States in 2004, ages 29 and 30, with between 6 and 18 years of education. The data come from the March 2005 Current Population Survey, which is described in Appendix 3.1.

Figure 5.3 has two striking features. The first is that the mean of the distribution of earnings increases with the number of years of education. This increase is summarized by the OLS regression line,

$$\widehat{Earnings} = -3.13 + 1.47 \, Years \, Education,$$
$$(0.93) \quad (0.07)$$
$$R^2 = 0.130, SER = 8.77. \tag{5.23}$$

This line is plotted in Figure 5.3. The coefficient of 1.47 in the OLS regression line means that, on

average, hourly earnings increase by $1.47 for each additional year of education. The 95% confidence interval for this coefficient is $1.47 \pm 1.96 \times 0.07$, or 1.33 to 1.61.

The second striking feature of Figure 5.3 is that the spread of the distribution of earnings increases with the years of education. While some workers with many years of education have low-paying jobs, very few workers with low levels of education have high-paying jobs. This can be stated more precisely by looking at the spread of the residuals around the OLS regression line. For workers with ten years of education, the standard deviation of the residuals is $5.46; for workers with a high school diploma, this standard deviation is $7.43; and for workers with a college degree, this standard deviation increases to $10.78. Because these standard deviations differ for different levels of education, the variance of the residuals in the regression of Equation (5.23) depends on the value of the regressor (the years of education); in other words, the regression errors are heteroskedastic. In real-world terms, not all college graduates will be earning $50/hour by the time they are 29, but some will, and workers with only ten years of education have no shot at those jobs.

FIGURE 5.3 Scatterplot of Hourly Earnings and Years of Education for 29- to 30-Year Olds in the United States in 2004

Hourly earnings are plotted against years of education for 2950 full-time, 29- to 30-year-old workers. The spread around the regression line increases with the years of education, indicating that the regression errors are heteroskedastic.

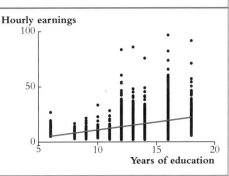

tion (5.20) for women is plausibly less than the variance of the error term in Equation (5.21) for men. Thus, the presence of a "glass ceiling" for women's jobs and pay suggests that the error term in the binary variable regression model in Equation (5.19) is heteroskedastic. Unless there are compelling reasons to the contrary—and we can think of none—it makes sense to treat the error term in this example as heteroskedastic.

As this example of modeling earnings illustrates, heteroskedasticity arises in many econometric applications. At a general level, economic theory rarely gives any reason to believe that the errors are homoskedastic. It therefore is prudent to assume that the errors might be heteroskedastic unless you have compelling reasons to believe otherwise.

Practical implications.   The main issue of practical relevance in this discussion is whether one should use heteroskedasticity-robust or homoskedasticity-only standard errors. In this regard, it is useful to imagine computing both, then choosing between them. If the homoskedasticity-only and heteroskedasticity-robust standard errors are the same, nothing is lost by using the heteroskedasticity-robust standard errors; if they differ, however, then you should use the more reliable ones that allow for heteroskedasticity. The simplest thing, then, is always to use the heteroskedasticity-robust standard errors.

For historical reasons, many software programs use the homoskedasticity-only standard errors as their default setting, so it is up to the user to specify the option of heteroskedasticity-robust standard errors. The details of how to implement heteroskedasticity-robust standard errors depend on the software package you use.

All of the empirical examples in this book employ heteroskedasticity-robust standard errors unless explicitly stated otherwise.[1]

*5.5   The Theoretical Foundations of Ordinary Least Squares

As discussed in Section 4.5, the OLS estimator is unbiased, is consistent, has a variance that is inversely proportional to n, and has a normal sampling distribution

---

[1]In case this book is used in conjunction with other texts, it might be helpful to note that some textbooks add homoskedasticity to the list of least squares assumptions. As just discussed, however, this additional assumption is not needed for the validity of OLS regression analysis as long as heteroskedasticity-robust standard errors are used.

*This section is optional and is not used in later chapters.

when the sample size is large. In addition, under certain conditions the OLS estimator is more efficient than some other candidate estimators. Specifically, if the least squares assumptions hold and if the errors are homoskedastic, then the OLS estimator has the smallest variance of all conditionally unbiased estimators that are linear functions of $Y_1, \ldots, Y_n$. This section explains and discusses this result, which is a consequence of the Gauss-Markov theorem. The section concludes with a discussion of alternative estimators that are more efficient than OLS when the conditions of the Gauss-Markov theorem do not hold.

Linear Conditionally Unbiased Estimators and the Gauss-Markov Theorem

If the three least squares assumptions (Key Concept 4.3) hold and if the error is homoskedastic, then the OLS estimator has the smallest variance, conditional on $X_1, \ldots, X_n$, among all estimators in the class of linear conditionally unbiased estimators. In other words, the OLS estimator is the **B**est **L**inear conditionally **U**nbiased **E**stimator—that is, it is BLUE. This result extends to regression the result, summarized in Key Concept 3.3, that the sample average $\overline{Y}$ is the most efficient estimator of the population mean among the class of all estimators that are unbiased and are linear functions (weighted averages) of $Y_1, \ldots, Y_n$.

Linear conditionally unbiased estimators.   The class of linear conditionally unbiased estimators consists of all estimators of β_1 that are linear functions of $Y_1, \ldots, Y_n$ and that are unbiased, conditional on $X_1, \ldots, X_n$. That is, if $\tilde{\beta}_1$ is a linear estimator, then it can be written as

$$\tilde{\beta}_1 = \sum_{i=1}^{n} a_i Y_i \quad (\tilde{\beta}_1 \text{ is linear}), \tag{5.24}$$

where the weights $a_1, \ldots, a_n$ can depend on $X_1, \ldots, X_n$ but *not* on $Y_1, \ldots, Y_n$. The estimator $\tilde{\beta}_1$ is conditionally unbiased if the mean of its conditional sampling distribution, given $X_1, \ldots, X_n$, is β_1. That is, the estimator $\tilde{\beta}_1$ is conditionally unbiased if

$$E(\tilde{\beta}_1 | X_1, \ldots, X_n) = \beta_1 \quad (\tilde{\beta}_1 \text{ is conditionally unbiased}). \tag{5.25}$$

The estimator $\tilde{\beta}_1$ is a linear conditionally unbiased estimator if it can be written in the form of Equation (5.24) (it is linear) and if Equation (5.25) holds (it is

THE GAUSS-MARKOV THEOREM FOR $\hat{\beta}_1$

If the three least squares assumptions in Key Concept 4.3 hold *and* if errors are homoskedastic, then the OLS estimator $\hat{\beta}_1$ is the **B**est (most efficient) **L**inear conditionally **U**nbiased **E**stimator (is **BLUE**).

conditionally unbiased). It is shown in Appendix 5.2 that the OLS estimator is linear and conditionally unbiased.

The Gauss-Markov theorem. The **Gauss-Markov** theorem states that, under a set of conditions known as the Gauss-Markov conditions, the OLS estimator $\hat{\beta}_1$ has the smallest conditional variance, given $X_1, \ldots, X_n$, of all linear conditionally unbiased estimators of β_1; that is, the OLS estimator is BLUE. The Gauss-Markov conditions, which are stated in Appendix 5.2, are implied by the three least squares assumptions plus the assumption that the errors are homoskedastic. Consequently, if the three least squares assumptions hold and the errors are homoskedastic, then OLS is BLUE. The Gauss-Markov theorem is stated in Key Concept 5.5 and proven in Appendix 5.2.

Limitations of the Gauss-Markov theorem. The Gauss-Markov theorem provides a theoretical justification for using OLS. However, the theorem has two important limitations. First, its conditions might not hold in practice. In particular, if the error term is heteroskedastic—as it often is in economic applications—then the OLS estimator is no longer BLUE. As discussed in Section 5.4, the presence of heteroskedasticity does not pose a threat to inference based on heteroskedasticity-robust standard errors, but it does mean that OLS is no longer the efficient linear conditionally unbiased estimator. An alternative to OLS when there is heteroskedasticity of a known form, called the weighted least squares estimator, is discussed below.

The second limitation of the Gauss-Markov theorem is that even if the conditions of the theorem hold, there are other candidate estimators that are not linear and conditionally unbiased; under some conditions, these other estimators are more efficient than OLS.

Regression Estimators Other Than OLS

Under certain conditions, some regression estimators are more efficient than OLS.

The weighted least squares estimator.   If the errors are heteroskedastic, then OLS is no longer BLUE. If the nature of the heteroskedastic is known—specifically, if the conditional variance of u_i given X_i is known up to a constant factor of proportionality—then it is possible to construct an estimator that has a smaller variance than the OLS estimator. This method, called **weighted least squares** (WLS), weights the ith observation by the inverse of the square root of the conditional variance of u_i given X_i. Because of this weighting, the errors in this weighted regression are homoskedastic, so OLS, when applied to the weighted data, is BLUE. Although theoretically elegant, the practical problem with weighted least squares is that you must know how the conditional variance of u_i depends on X_i —something that is rarely known in applications.

The least absolute deviations estimator.   As discussed in Section 4.3, the OLS estimator can be sensitive to outliers. If extreme outliers are not rare, then other estimators can be more efficient than OLS and can produce inferences that are more reliable. One such estimator is the least absolute deviations (LAD) estimator, in which the regression coefficients β_0 and β_1 are obtained by solving a minimization like that in Equation (4.6), except that the absolute value of the prediction "mistake" is used instead of its square. That is, the least absolute deviations estimators of β_0 and β_1 are the values of b_0 and b_1 that minimize $\sum_{i=1}^{n} |Y_i - b_0 - b_1 X_i|$. In practice, this estimator is less sensitive to large outliers in u than is OLS.

In many economic data sets, severe outliers in u are rare, so use of the LAD estimator, or other estimators with reduced sensitivity to outliers, is uncommon in applications. Thus the treatment of linear regression throughout the remainder of this text focuses exclusively on least squares methods.

*5.6   Using the *t*-Statistic in Regression When the Sample Size Is Small

When the sample size is small, the exact distribution of the *t*-statistic is complicated and depends on the unknown population distribution of the data. If, however, the three least squares assumptions hold, the regression errors are homoskedastic, *and* the regression errors are normally distributed, then the OLS

---

*This section is optional and is not used in later chapters.

estimator is normally distributed and the homoskedasticity-only t-statistic has a Student t distribution. These five assumptions—the three least squares assumptions, that the errors are homoskedastic, and that the errors are normally distributed—are collectively called the **homoskedastic normal regression assumptions**.

The t-Statistic and the Student t Distribution

Recall from Section 2.4 that the Student t distribution with m degrees of freedom is defined to be the distribution of $Z/\sqrt{W/m}$, where Z is a random variable with a standard normal distribution, W is a random variable with a chi-squared distribution with m degrees of freedom, and Z and W are independent. Under the null hypothesis, the t-statistic computed using the homoskedasticity-only standard error can be written in this form.

The homoskedasticity-only t-statistic testing $\beta_1 = \beta_{1,0}$ is $\tilde{t} = (\hat{\beta}_1 - \beta_{1,0})/\tilde{\sigma}_{\hat{\beta}_1}$, where $\tilde{\sigma}_{\hat{\beta}_1}^2$ is defined in Equation (5.22). Under the homoskedastic normal regression assumptions, Y has a normal distribution, conditional on $X_1, \ldots, X_n$. As discussed in Section 5.5, the OLS estimator is a weighted average of $Y_1, \ldots, Y_n$, where the weights depend on $X_1, \ldots, X_n$ [see Equation (5.32) in Appendix 5.2]. Because a weighted average of independent normal random variables is normally distributed, $\hat{\beta}_1$ has a normal distribution, conditional on $X_1, \ldots, X_n$. Thus $(\hat{\beta}_1 - \beta_{1,0})$ has a normal distribution under the null hypothesis, conditional on $X_1, \ldots, X_n$. In addition, the (normalized) homoskedasticity-only variance estimator has a chi-squared distribution with $n - 2$ degrees of freedom, divided by $n - 2$, and $\tilde{\sigma}_{\hat{\beta}_1}^2$ and $\hat{\beta}_1$ are independently distributed. Consequently, the homoskedasticity-only t-statistic has a Student t distribution with $n - 2$ degrees of freedom.

This result is closely related to a result discussed in Section 3.5 in the context of testing for the equality of the means in two samples. In that problem, if the two population distributions are normal with the same variance and if the t-statistic is constructed using the pooled standard error formula [Equation (3.23)], then the (pooled) t-statistic has a Student t distribution. When X is binary, the homoskedasticity-only standard error for $\hat{\beta}_1$ simplifies to the pooled standard error formula for the difference of means. It follows that the result of Section 3.5 is a special case of the result that, if the homoskedastic normal regression assumptions hold, then the homoskedasticity-only regression t-statistic has a Student t distribution (see Exercise 5.10).

Use of the Student t Distribution in Practice

If the regression errors are homoskedastic and normally distributed and if the homoskedasticity-only t-statistic is used, then critical values should be taken from the Student t distribution (Appendix Table 2) instead of the standard normal distribution. Because the difference between the Student t distribution and the normal distribution is negligible if n is moderate or large, this distinction is relevant only if the sample size is small.

In econometric applications, there is rarely a reason to believe that the errors are homoskedastic and normally distributed. Because sample sizes typically are large, however, inference can proceed as described in Sections 5.1 and 5.2—that is, by first computing heteroskedasticity-robust standard errors, and then using the standard normal distribution to compute p-values, hypothesis tests, and confidence intervals.

5.7 Conclusion

Return for a moment to the problem that started Chapter 4: the superintendent who is considering hiring additional teachers to cut the student–teacher ratio. What have we learned that she might find useful?

Our regression analysis, based on the 420 observations for 1998 in the California test score data set, showed that there was a negative relationship between the student–teacher ratio and test scores: Districts with smaller classes have higher test scores. The coefficient is moderately large, in a practical sense: Districts with 2 fewer students per teacher have, on average, test scores that are 4.6 points higher. This corresponds to moving a district at the 50th percentile of the distribution of test scores to approximately the 60th percentile.

The coefficient on the student–teacher ratio is statistically significantly different from 0 at the 5% significance level. The population coefficient might be 0, and we might simply have estimated our negative coefficient by random sampling variation. However, the probability of doing so (and of obtaining a t-statistic on β_1 as large as we did) purely by random variation over potential samples is exceedingly small, approximately 0.001%. A 95% confidence interval for β_1 is $-3.30 \le \beta_1 \le -1.26$.

This represents considerable progress toward answering the superintendent's question. Yet, a nagging concern remains. There is a negative relationship between the student–teacher ratio and test scores, but is this relationship necessarily the *causal* one that the superintendent needs to make her decision? Districts with lower student–teacher ratios have, on average, higher test scores. But does this mean that reducing the student–teacher ratio will, in fact, increase scores?

There is, in fact, reason to worry that it might not. Hiring more teachers, after all, costs money, so wealthier school districts can better afford smaller classes. But students at wealthier schools also have other advantages over their poorer neighbors, including better facilities, newer books, and better-paid teachers. Moreover, students at wealthier schools tend themselves to come from more affluent families, and thus have other advantages not directly associated with their school. For example, California has a large immigrant community; these immigrants tend to be poorer than the overall population and, in many cases, their children are not native English speakers. It thus might be that our negative estimated relationship between test scores and the student–teacher ratio is a consequence of large classes being found in conjunction with many other factors that are, in fact, the real cause of the lower test scores.

These other factors, or "omitted variables," could mean that the OLS analysis done so far has little value to the superintendent. Indeed, it could be misleading: Changing the student–teacher ratio alone would not change these other factors that determine a child's performance at school. To address this problem, we need a method that will allow us to isolate the effect on test scores of changing the student–teacher ratio, *holding these other factors constant*. That method is multiple regression analysis, the topic of Chapters 6 and 7.

Summary

1. Hypothesis testing for regression coefficients is analogous to hypothesis testing for the population mean: Use the *t*-statistic to calculate the *p*-values and either accept or reject the null hypothesis. Like a confidence interval for the population mean, a 95% confidence interval for a regression coefficient is computed as the estimator $\pm$ 1.96 standard errors.

2. When X is binary, the regression model can be used to estimate and test hypotheses about the difference between the population means of the "$X = 0$" group and the "$X = 1$" group.

3. In general the error u_i is heteroskedastic—that is, the variance of u_i at a given value of X_i, $\text{var}(u_i | X_i = x)$ depends on x. A special case is when the error is homoskedastic, that is, $\text{var}(u_i | X_i = x)$ is constant. Homoskedasticity-only standard errors do not produce valid statistical inferences when the errors are heteroskedastic, but heteroskedasticity-robust standard errors do.

4. If the three least squares assumption hold *and* if the regression errors are homoskedastic, then, as a result of the Gauss-Markov theorem, the OLS estimator is BLUE.

5. If the three least squares assumptions hold, if the regression errors are homoskedastic, *and* if the regression errors are normally distributed, then the OLS t-statistic computed using homoskedasticity-only standard errors has a Student t distribution when the null hypothesis is true. The difference between the Student t distribution and the normal distribution is negligible if the sample size is moderate or large.

Key Terms

null hypothesis (148)
two-sided alternative hypothesis (148)
standard error of $\hat{\beta}_1$ (148)
t-statistic (149)
p-value (149)
confidence interval for β_1 (154)
confidence level (154)
indicator variable (156)
dummy variable (156)
coefficient multiplying variable D_i (156)
coefficient on D_i (156)
heteroskedasticity and
    homoskedasticity (158)

homoskedasticity-only standard
    errors (161)
heteroskedasticity-robust standard
    errors (162)
best linear unbiased estimator
    (BLUE) (166)
Gauss-Markov theorem (166)
weighted least squares (167)
homoskedastic normal regression
    assumptions (168)
Gauss-Markov conditions (180)

Review the Concepts

5.1 Outline the procedures for computing the p-value of a two-sided test of $H_0: \mu_Y = 0$ using an i.i.d. set of observations $Y_i, i = 1, \ldots, n$. Outline the procedures for computing the p-value of a two-sided test of $H_0: \beta_1 = 0$ in a regression model using an i.i.d. set of observations $(Y_i, X_i), i = 1, \ldots, n$.

5.2 Explain how you could use a regression model to estimate the wage gender gap using the data on earnings of men and women. What are the dependent and independent variables?

5.3 Define *homoskedasticity* and *heteroskedasticity*. Provide a hypothetical empirical example in which you think the errors would be heteroskedastic, and explain you reasoning.

Exercises

5.1 Suppose that a researcher, using data on class size (CS) and average test scores from 100 third-grade classes, estimates the OLS regression,

$$\widehat{TestScore} = 520.4 - 5.82 \times CS, \ R^2 = 0.08, SER = 11.5.$$
$$(20.4) \ \ (2.21)$$

  a. Construct a 95% confidence interval for β_1, the regression slope coefficient.

  b. Calculate the p-value for the two-sided test of the null hypothesis $H_0: \beta_1 = 0$. Do you reject the null hypothesis at the 5% level? At the 1% level?

  c. Calculate the p-value for the two-sided test of the null hypothesis $H_0: \beta_1 = -5.6$. Without doing any additional calculations, determine whether -5.6 is contained in the 95% confidence interval for β_1.

  d. Construct a 99% confidence interval for β_0.

5.2 Suppose that a researcher, using wage data on 250 randomly selected male workers and 280 female workers, estimates the OLS regression,

$$\widehat{Wage} = 12.52 + 2.12 \times Male, \ R^2 = 0.06, SER = 4.2,$$
$$(.23) \ \ (0.36)$$

where *Wage* is measured in $/hour and *Male* is a binary variable that is equal to 1 if the person is a male and 0 if the person is a female. Define the wage gender gap as the difference in mean earnings between men and women.

  a. What is the estimated gender gap?

  b. Is the estimated gender gap significantly different from zero? (Compute the *p*-value for testing the null hypothesis that there is no gender gap.)

  c. Construct a 95% confidence interval for the gender gap.

  d. In the sample, what is the mean wage of women? Of men?

  e. Another researcher uses these same data, but regresses *Wages* on *Female,* a variable that is equal to 1 if the person is female and 0 if the person a male. What are the regression estimates calculated from this regression?

$$\widehat{Wage} = \underline{\hspace{1cm}} + \underline{\hspace{1cm}} \times Female, R^2 = \underline{\hspace{1cm}}, SER = \underline{\hspace{1cm}}.$$

5.3 Suppose that a random sample of 200 twenty-year-old men is selected from a population and their heights and weights are recorded. A regression of weight on height yields

$$\widehat{Weight} = -99.41 + 3.94 \times Height, R^2 = 0.81, SER = 10.2,$$
$$(2.15)\quad(0.31)$$

where *Weight* is measured in pounds and *Height* is measured in inches. A man has a late growth spurt and grows 1.5 inches over the course of a year. Construct a 99% confidence interval for the person's weight gain.

5.4 Read the box "The Economic Value of a Year of Education: Heteroskedasticity or Homoskedasticity?" in Section 5.4. Use the regression reported in Equation (5.23) to answer the following.

  a. A randomly selected 30-year-old worker reports an education level of 16 years. What is the worker's expected average hourly earnings?

  b. A high school graduate (12 years of education) is contemplating going to a community college for a two-year degree. How much is this worker's average hourly earnings expected to increase?

c. A high school counselor tells a student that, on average, college gradu-ates earn $10 per hour more than high school graduates. Is this state-ment consistent with the regression evidence? What range of values is consistent with the regression evidence?

5.5 In the 1980s, Tennessee conducted an experiment in which kindergarten stu-dents were randomly assigned to "regular" and "small" classes, and given standardized tests at the end of the year. (Regular classes contained approx-imately 24 students and small classes contained approximately 15 students.) Suppose that, in the population, the standardized tests have a mean score of 925 points and a standard deviation of 75 points. Let *SmallClass* denote a binary variable equal to 1 if the student is assigned to a small class and equal to 0 otherwise. A regression of *Testscore* on *SmallClass* yields

$$\widehat{TestScore} = 918.0 + 13.9 \times SmallClass, R^2 = 0.01, SER = 74.6.$$
$$(1.6) \quad (2.5)$$

a. Do small classes improve test scores? By how much? Is the effect large? Explain.

b. Is the estimated effect of class size on test scores statistically signifi-cant? Carry out a test at the 5% level.

c. Construct a 99% confidence interval for the effect of *SmallClass* on test score.

5.6 Refer to the regression described in Exercise 5.5.

a. Do you think that the regression errors plausibly are homoskedastic? Explain.

b. $SE(\hat{\beta}_1)$ was computed using Equation (5.3). Suppose that the regres-sion errors were homoskedastic: Would this affect the validity of the confidence interval constructed in Exercise 5.5(c)? Explain.

5.7 Suppose that (Y_i, X_i) satisfy the assumptions in Key Concept 4.3. A random sample of size $n = 250$ is drawn and yields

$$\hat{Y} = 5.4 + 3.2X, R^2 = 0.26, SER = 6.2.$$
$$(3.1) \quad (1.5)$$

a. Test $H_0: \beta_1 = 0$ vs. $H_1: \beta_1 \neq 0$ at the 5% level.

b. Construct a 95% confidence interval for β_1.

c. Suppose you learned that Y_i and X_i were independent. Would you be surprised? Explain.

d. Suppose that Y_i and X_i are independent and many samples of size $n = 250$ are drawn, regressions estimated, and (a) and (b) answered. In what fraction of the samples would H_0 from (a) be rejected? In what fraction of samples would the value $\beta_1 = 0$ be included in the confidence interval from (b)?

5.8 Suppose that (Y_i, X_i) satisfy the assumptions in Key Concept 4.3 and, in addition, u_i is $N(0, \sigma_u^2)$ and is independent of X_i. A sample of size $n = 30$ yields

$$\hat{Y} = 43.2 + 61.5X, R^2 = 0.54, SER = 1.52,$$
$$(10.2) \quad (7.4)$$

where the numbers in parentheses are the homoskedastic-only standard errors for the regression coefficients.

a. Construct a 95% confidence interval for β_0.

b. Test $H_0: \beta_1 = 55$ vs. $H_1: \beta_1 \neq 55$ at the 5% level.

c. Test $H_0: \beta_1 = 55$ vs. $H_1: \beta_1 > 55$ at the 5% level.

5.9 Consider the regression model

$$Y_i = \beta X_i + u_i,$$

where u_i and X_i satisfy the assumptions in Key Concept 4.3. Let $\bar{\beta}$ denote an estimator of β that is constructed as $\bar{\beta} = \frac{\bar{Y}}{\bar{X}}$, where $\bar{Y}$ and $\bar{X}$ are the sample means of Y_i and X_i, respectively.

a. Show that $\bar{\beta}$ is a linear function of $Y_1, Y_2, \ldots, Y_n$.

b. Show that $\bar{\beta}$ is conditionally unbiased.

5.10 Let X_i denote a binary variable and consider the regression $Y_i = \beta_0 + \beta_1 X_i + u_i$. Let $\bar{Y}_0$ denote the sample mean for observations with $X = 0$ and $\bar{Y}_1$

denote the sample mean for observations with $X = 1$. Show that $\hat{\beta}_0 = \overline{Y}_0$, $\hat{\beta}_0 + \hat{\beta}_1 = \overline{Y}_1$, and $\hat{\beta}_1 = \overline{Y}_1 - \overline{Y}_0$.

5.11 A random sample of workers contains $n_m = 120$ men and $n_w = 131$ women. The sample average of men's weekly earnings $(\overline{Y}_m = \frac{1}{n_m}\sum_{i=1}^{n_m}Y_{m,i})$ is \$523.10, and the sample standard deviation $(s_m = \sqrt{\frac{1}{n_m - 1}\sum_{i=1}^{n_m}(Y_{m,i} - \overline{Y}_m)^2})$ is \$68.1. The corresponding values for women are $\overline{Y}_w = \$485.10$ and $s_w = \$51.10$. Let *Women* denote an indicator variable that is equal to 1 for women and 0 for men, and suppose that all 251 observations are used in the regression $Y_i = \beta_0 + \beta_1$ *Women*$_i + u_i$ is run. Find the OLS estimates of β_0 and β_1 and their corresponding standard errors.

5.12 Starting from Equation (4.22), derive the variance of $\hat{\beta}_0$ under homoskedasticity given in Equation (5.28) in Appendix 5.1.

5.13 Suppose that (Y_i, X_i) satisfy the assumptions in Key Concept 4.3 and, in addition, u_i is $N(0, \sigma_u^2)$ and is independent of X_i.

a. Is $\hat{\beta}_1$ conditionally unbiased?

b. Is $\hat{\beta}_1$ the best linear conditionally unbiased estimator of β_1?

c. How would your answers to (a) and (b) change if you assumed only that (Y_i, X_i) satisfied the assumptions in Key Concept 4.3 and $var(u_i | X_i = x)$ is constant?

d. How would your answers to (a) and (b) change if you assumed only that (Y_i, X_i) satisfied the assumptions in Key Concept 4.3?

5.14 Suppose that $Y_i = \beta X_i + u_i$, where (u_i, X_i) satisfy the Gauss-Markov conditions given in Equation (5.31).

a. Derive the least squares estimator of β and show that it is a linear function of $Y_1, \ldots, Y_n$.

b. Show that the estimator is conditionally unbiased.

c. Derive the conditional variance of the estimator.

d. Prove that the estimator is BLUE.

5.15 A researcher has two independent samples of observations on (Y_i, X_i). To be specific, suppose that Y_i denotes earnings, X_i denotes years of schooling, and the independent samples are for men and women. Write the regression for men as $Y_{m,i} = \beta_{m,0} + \beta_{m,1}X_{m,i} + u_{m,i}$, and the regression for women as $Y_{w,i} = \beta_{w,0} + \beta_{w,1}X_{w,i} + u_{w,i}$. Let $\hat{\beta}_{m,1}$ denote the OLS estimator constructed using the sample of men, $\hat{\beta}_{w,1}$ denote the OLS estimator constructed from the sample of women, and $SE(\hat{\beta}_{m,1})$ and $SE(\hat{\beta}_{w,1})$ denote the corresponding standard errors. Show that the standard error of $\hat{\beta}_{m,1} - \hat{\beta}_{w,1}$ is given by $SE(\hat{\beta}_{m,1} - \hat{\beta}_{w,1}) = \sqrt{[SE(\hat{\beta}_{m,1})]^2 + [SE(\hat{\beta}_{w,1})]^2}$.

Empirical Exercises

E5.1 Using the data set **CPS04** described in Empirical Exercise 4.1, run a regression of average hourly earnings (AHE) on Age and carry out the following exercises.

a. Is the estimated regression slope coefficient statistically significant? That is, can you reject the null hypothesis $H_0: \beta_1 = 0$ versus a two-sided alternative at the 10%, 5%, or 1% significance level? What is the p-value associated with coefficient's t-statistic?

b. Construct a 95% confidence interval for the slope coefficient.

c. Repeat (a) using only the data for high school graduates.

d. Repeat (a) using only the data for college graduates.

e. Is the effect of age on earnings different for high school graduates than for college graduates? Explain. (*Hint:* See Exercise 5.15.)

E5.2 Using the data set **TeachingRatings** described in Empirical Exercise 4.2, run a regression of *Course_Eval* on *Beauty*. Is the estimated regression slope coefficient statistically significant? That is, can you reject the null hypothesis $H_0: \beta_1 = 0$ versus a two-sided alternative at the 10%, 5%, or 1% significance level? What is the p-value associated with coefficient's t-statistic?

E5.3 Using the data set **CollegeDistance** described in Empirical Exercise 4.3, run a regression of years of completed education (ED) on distance to the nearest college (*Dist*) and carry out the following exercises.

a. Is the estimated regression slope coefficient statistically significant? That is, can you reject the null hypothesis $H_0: \beta_1 = 0$ versus a two-sided alternative at the 10%, 5%, or 1% significance level? What is the p-value associated with coefficient's t-statistic?

b. Construct a 95% confidence interval for the slope coefficient.

c. Run the regression using data only on females and repeat (b).

d. Run the regression using data only on males and repeat (b).

e. Is the effect of distance on completed years of education different for men than for women? (*Hint:* See Exercise 5.15.)

Formulas for OLS Standard Errors

This appendix discusses the formulas for OLS standard errors. These are first presented under the least squares assumptions in Key Concept 4.3, which allow for heteroskedasticity; these are the "heteroskedasticity-robust" standard errors. Formulas for the variance of the OLS estimators and the associated standard errors are then given for the special case of homoskedasticity.

Heteroskedasticity-Robust Standard Errors

The estimator $\hat{\sigma}^2_{\hat{\beta}_1}$ defined in Equation (5.4) is obtained by replacing the population variances in Equation (4.21) by the corresponding sample variances, with a modification. The variance in the numerator of Equation (4.21) is estimated by $\frac{1}{n-2}\Sigma^n_{i=1}(X_i - \overline{X})^2\hat{u}^2_i$, where the divisor $n - 2$ (instead of n) incorporates a degrees-of-freedom adjustment to correct for downward bias, analogously to the degrees-of-freedom adjustment used in the definition of the *SER* in Section 4.3. The variance in the denominator is estimated by $\frac{1}{n}\Sigma^n_{i=1}(X_i - \overline{X})^2$. Replacing $\text{var}[(X_i - \mu_X)u_i]$ and $\text{var}(X_i)$ in Equation (4.21) by these two estimators yields $\hat{\sigma}^2_{\hat{\beta}_1}$ in Equation (5.4).

The estimator of the variance of $\hat{\beta}_0$ is

$$\hat{\sigma}^2_{\hat{\beta}_0} = \frac{1}{n} \times \frac{\dfrac{1}{n-2}\sum_{i=1}^{n}\hat{H}^2_i\hat{u}^2_i}{\left(\dfrac{1}{n}\sum_{i=1}^{n}\hat{H}^2_i\right)^2}, \tag{5.26}$$

where $\hat{H}_i = 1 - [\overline{X}/\frac{1}{n}\sum_{i=1}^{n}X_i^2]X_i$. The standard error of $\hat{\beta}_0$ is $SE(\hat{\beta}_0) = \sqrt{\hat{\sigma}_{\hat{\beta}_0}^2}$. The reasoning behind the estimator $\hat{\sigma}_{\hat{\beta}_0}^2$ is the same as behind $\hat{\sigma}_{\hat{\beta}_1}^2$ and stems from replacing population expectations with sample averages.

Homoskedasticity-Only Variances

Under homoskedasticity, the conditional variance of u_i given X_i is a constant: $\text{var}(u_i|X_i) = \sigma_u^2$. If the errors are homoskedastic, the formulas in Key Concept 4.4 simplify to

$$\sigma_{\hat{\beta}_1}^2 = \frac{\sigma_u^2}{n\sigma_X^2} \text{ and} \tag{5.27}$$

$$\sigma_{\hat{\beta}_0}^2 = \frac{E(X_i^2)}{n\sigma_X^2}\sigma_u^2. \tag{5.28}$$

To derive Equation (5.27), write the numerator in Equation (4.21) as $\text{var}[(X_i - \mu_X)u_i]$ $= E(\{(X_i - \mu_X)u_i - E[(X_i - \mu_X)u_i]\}^2) = E\{[(X_i - \mu_X)u_i]^2\} = E[(X_i - \mu_X)^2u_i^2] = E[(X_i - \mu_X)^2\text{var}(u_i|X_i)]$, where the second equality follows because $E[(X_i - \mu_X)u_i] = 0$ (by the first least squares assumption) and where the final equality follows from the law of iterated expectations (Section 2.3). If u_i is homoskedastic, then $\text{var}(u_i|X_i) = \sigma_u^2$ so $E[(X_i - \mu_X)^2\text{var}(u_i|X_i)] = \sigma_u^2 E[(X_i - \mu_X)^2] = \sigma_u^2\sigma_X^2$. The result in Equation (5.27) follows by substituting this expression into the numerator of Equation (4.21) and simplifying. A similar calculation yields Equation (5.28).

Homoskedasticity-Only Standard Errors

The homoskedasticity-only standard errors are obtained by substituting sample means and variances for the population means and variances in Equations (5.27) and (5.28), and by estimating the variance of u_i by the square of the *SER*. The homoskedasticity-only estimators of these variances are

$$\tilde{\sigma}_{\hat{\beta}_1}^2 = \frac{s_{\hat{u}}^2}{\sum_{i=1}^{n}(X_i - \overline{X})^2} \quad \text{(homoskedasticity-only) and} \tag{5.29}$$

$$\tilde{\sigma}_{\hat{\beta}_0}^2 = \frac{\left(\frac{1}{n}\sum_{i=1}^{n}X_i^2\right)s_{\hat{u}}^2}{\sum_{i=1}^{n}(X_i - \overline{X})^2} \quad \text{(homoskedasticity-only)}, \tag{5.30}$$

where $s_{\hat{u}}^2$ is given in Equation (4.19). The homoskedasticity-only standard errors are the square roots of $\tilde{\sigma}_{\hat{\beta}_0}^2$ and $\tilde{\sigma}_{\hat{\beta}_1}^2$.

The Gauss-Markov Conditions and a Proof of the Gauss-Markov Theorem

As discussed in Section 5.5, the Gauss-Markov theorem states that if the Gauss-Markov conditions hold, then the OLS estimator is the best (most efficient) conditionally linear unbiased estimator (is BLUE). This appendix begins by stating the Gauss-Markov conditions and showing that they are implied by the three least squares condition plus homoskedasticity. We next show that the OLS estimator is a linear conditionally unbiased estimator. Finally, we turn to the proof of the theorem.

The Gauss-Markov Conditions

The three **Gauss-Markov conditions** are

$$
\begin{align}
&\text{(i)} \quad E(u_i | X_1, \ldots, X_n) = 0 \\
&\text{(ii)} \quad \mathrm{var}(u_i | X_1, \ldots, X_n) = \sigma_u^2, \ 0 < \sigma_u^2 < \infty \qquad\qquad (5.31)\\
&\text{(iii)} \quad E(u_i u_j | X_1, \ldots, X_n) = 0, i \neq j
\end{align}
$$

where the conditions hold for $i, j = 1, \ldots, n$. The three conditions, respectively, state that u_i has mean zero, that u_i has a constant variance, and that the errors are uncorrelated for different observations, where all these statements hold conditionally on all observed X's $(X_1, \ldots, X_n)$.

The Gauss-Markov conditions are implied by the three least squares assumptions (Key Concept 4.3), plus the additional assumptions that the errors are homoskedastic. Because the observations are i.i.d. (Assumption 2), $E(u_i | X_1, \ldots, X_n) = E(u_i | X_i)$, and by Assumption 1, $E(u_i | X_i) = 0$; thus condition (i) holds. Similarly, by Assumption 2, $\mathrm{var}(u_i | X_1, \ldots, X_n)$ $= \mathrm{var}(u_i | X_i)$, and because the errors are assumed to be homoskedastic, $\mathrm{var}(u_i | X_i) = \sigma_u^2$, which is constant. Assumption 3 (nonzero finite fourth moments) ensures that $0 < \sigma_u^2 < \infty$, so condition (ii) holds. To show that condition (iii) is implied by the least squares assumptions, note that $E(u_i u_j | X_1, \ldots, X_n) = E(u_i u_j | X_i, X_j)$ because (X_i, Y_i) are i.i.d. by Assumption 2. Assumption 2 also implies that $E(u_i u_j | X_i, X_j) = E(u_i | X_i) E(u_j | X_j)$ for $i \neq j$; because $E(u_i | X_i) = 0$ for all i, it follows that $E(u_i u_j | X_1, \ldots, X_n) = 0$ for all $i \neq j$, so condition (iii) holds. Thus, the least squares assumptions in Key Concept 4.3, plus homoskedasticity of the errors, imply the Gauss-Markov conditions in Equation (5.31).

The OLS Estimator $\hat{\beta}_1$ Is a Linear Conditionally Unbiased Estimator

To show that $\hat{\beta}_1$ is linear, first note that, because $\sum_{i=1}^{n}(X_i - \overline{X}) = 0$ (by the definition of $\overline{X}$), $\sum_{i=1}^{n}(X_i - \overline{X})(Y_i - \overline{Y}) = \sum_{i=1}^{n}(X_i - \overline{X})Y_i - \overline{Y}\sum_{i=1}^{n}(X_i - \overline{X}) = \sum_{i=1}^{n}(X_i - \overline{X})Y_i$. Substituting this result into the formula for $\hat{\beta}_1$ in Equation (4.7) yields

$$\hat{\beta}_1 = \frac{\sum_{i=1}^{n}(X_i - \overline{X})Y_i}{\sum_{j=1}^{n}(X_j - \overline{X})^2} = \sum_{i=1}^{n}\hat{a}_i Y_i, \text{ where } \hat{a}_i = \frac{(X_i - \overline{X})}{\sum_{j=1}^{n}(X_j - \overline{X})^2} \tag{5.32}$$

Because the weights $\hat{a}_i, i = 1, \ldots, n$ in Equation (5.32) depend on $X_1, \ldots, X_n$ but not on $Y_1, \ldots, Y_n$, the OLS estimator $\hat{\beta}_1$ is a linear estimator.

Under the Gauss-Markov conditions, $\hat{\beta}_1$ is conditionally unbiased, and the variance of the conditional distribution of $\hat{\beta}_1$, given $X_1, \ldots, X_n$, is

$$\text{var}(\hat{\beta}_1 | X_1, \ldots, X_n) = \frac{\sigma_u^2}{\sum_{i=1}^{n}(X_i - \overline{X})^2}. \tag{5.33}$$

The result that $\hat{\beta}_1$ is conditionally unbiased was previously shown in Appendix 4.3.

Proof of the Gauss-Markov Theorem

We start by deriving some facts that hold for all linear conditionallly unbiased estimators—that is, for all estimators $\tilde{\beta}_1$ satisfying Equations (5.24) and (5.25). Substituting $Y_i = \beta_0 + \beta_1 X_i + u_i$ into $\tilde{\beta}_1 = \sum_{i=1}^{n}a_i Y_i$ and collecting terms, we have that

$$\tilde{\beta}_1 = \beta_0\left(\sum_{i=1}^{n}a_i\right) + \beta_1\left(\sum_{i=1}^{n}a_i X_i\right) + \sum_{i=1}^{n}a_i u_i. \tag{5.34}$$

By the first Gauss-Markov condition, $E(\sum_{i=1}^{n}a_i u_i | X_1, \ldots, X_n) = \sum_{i=1}^{n}a_i E(u_i | X_1, \ldots, X_n) = 0$; thus, taking conditional expectations of both sides of Equation (5.34) yields $E(\tilde{\beta}_1 | X_1, \ldots, X_n) = \beta_0(\sum_{i=1}^{n}a_i) + \beta_1(\sum_{i=1}^{n}a_i X_i)$. Because $\tilde{\beta}_1$ is conditionally unbiased by assumption, it must be that $\beta_0(\sum_{i=1}^{n}a_i) + \beta_1(\sum_{i=1}^{n}a_i X_i) = \beta_1$, but for this equality to hold for all values of β_0 and β_1 it must be the case that, for $\tilde{\beta}_1$ to be conditionally unbiased,

$$\sum_{i=1}^{n}a_i = 0 \text{ and } \sum_{i=1}^{n}a_i X_i = 1. \tag{5.35}$$

Under the Gauss-Markov conditions, the variance of $\widetilde{\beta}_1$, conditional on $X_1, \ldots, X_n$, has a simple form. Substituting Equation (5.35) into Equation (5.34) yields $\widetilde{\beta}_1 - \beta_1 = \sum_{i=1}^{n} a_i u_i$. Thus, $\text{var}(\widetilde{\beta}_1 | X_1, \ldots, X_n) = \text{var}(\sum_{i=1}^{n} a_i u_i | X_1, \ldots, X_n) = \sum_{i=1}^{n} \sum_{j=1}^{n} a_i a_j \text{cov}(u_i, u_j | X_1, \ldots, X_n)$; applying the second and third Gauss-Markov conditions, the cross terms in the double summation vanish and the expression for the conditional variance simplifies to

$$\text{var}(\widetilde{\beta}_1 | X_1, \ldots, X_n) = \sigma_u^2 \sum_{i=1}^{n} a_i^2. \tag{5.36}$$

Note that Equations (5.35) and (5.36) apply to $\hat{\beta}_1$ with weights $a_i = \hat{a}_i$, given in Equation (5.32).

We now show that the two restrictions in Equation (5.35) and the expression for the conditional variance in Equation (5.36) imply that the conditional variance of $\widetilde{\beta}_1$ exceeds the conditional variance of $\hat{\beta}_1$ unless $\widetilde{\beta}_1 = \hat{\beta}_1$. Let $a_i = \hat{a}_i + d_i$ so $\sum_{i=1}^{n} a_i^2 = \sum_{i=1}^{n}(\hat{a}_i^2 + d_i)^2 = \sum_{i=1}^{n} \hat{a}_i^2 + 2\sum_{i=1}^{n} \hat{a}_i d_i + \sum_{i=1}^{n} d_i^2$.

Using the definition of $\hat{a}_i$, we have that

$$\sum_{i=1}^{n} \hat{a}_i d_i = \sum_{i=1}^{n}(X_i - \overline{X})d_i \Big/ \sum_{j=1}^{n}(X_j - \overline{X})^2 = \left(\sum_{i=1}^{n} d_i X_i - \overline{X}\sum_{i=1}^{n} d_i\right) \Big/ \sum_{j=1}^{n}(X_j - \overline{X})^2$$

$$= \left[\left(\sum_{i=1}^{n} a_i X_i - \sum_{i=1}^{n} \hat{a}_i X_i\right) - \overline{X}\left(\sum_{i=1}^{n} a_i - \sum_{i=1}^{n} \hat{a}_i\right)\right] \Big/ \sum_{j=1}^{n}(X_j - \overline{X})^2 = 0,$$

where the final equality follows from Equation (5.35) (which holds for both a_i and $\hat{a}_i$). Thus $\sigma_u^2 \sum_{i=1}^{n} a_i^2 = \sigma_u^2 \sum_{i=1}^{n} \hat{a}_i + \sigma_u^2 \sum_{i=1}^{n} d_i^2 = \text{var}(\hat{\beta}_1 | X_1, \ldots, X_n) + \sigma_u^2 \sum_{i=1}^{n} d_i^2$; substituting this result into Equation (5.36) yields

$$\text{var}(\widetilde{\beta}_1 | X_1, \ldots, X_n) - \text{var}(\hat{\beta}_1 | X_1, \ldots, X_n) = \sigma_u^2 \sum_{i=1}^{n} d_i^2. \tag{5.37}$$

Thus $\widetilde{\beta}_1$ has a greater conditional variance than $\hat{\beta}_1$ if d_i is nonzero for any $i = 1, \ldots, n$. But if $d_i = 0$ for all i, then $a_i = \hat{a}_i$ and $\widetilde{\beta}_1 = \hat{\beta}_1$, which proves that OLS is BLUE.

The Gauss-Markov Theorem When X Is Nonrandom

With a minor change in interpretation, the Gauss-Markov theorem also applies to nonrandom regressors; that is, it applies to regressors that do not change their values over repeated samples. Specifically, if the second least squares assumption is replaced by the assumption that $X_1, \ldots, X_n$ are nonrandom (fixed over repeated samples) and $u_1, \ldots, u_n$ are i.i.d., then the foregoing statement and proof of the Gauss-Markov theorem apply directly, except that all of the "conditional on $X_1, \ldots, X_n$" statements are unnecessary because $X_1, \ldots, X_n$ take on the same values from one sample to the next.

The Sample Average is the Efficient Linear Estimator of $E(Y)$

An implication of the Gauss-Markov theorem is that the sample average, $\overline{Y}$, is the most efficient linear estimator of $E(Y_i)$ when $Y_i, \ldots, Y_n$ are i.i.d. To see this, consider the case of regression without an "X," so that the only regressor is the constant regressor $X_{0i} = 1$. Then the OLS estimator $\hat{\beta}_0 = \overline{Y}$. It follows that, under the Gauss-Markov assumptions, $\overline{Y}$ is BLUE. Note that the Gauss-Markov requirement that the error be homoskedastic is irrelevant in this case because there is no regressor, so it follows that $\overline{Y}$ is BLUE if $Y_1, \ldots, Y_n$ are i.i.d. This result was stated previously in Key Concept 3.3.

CHAPTER 6

Linear Regression with Multiple Regressors

Chapter 5 ended on a worried note. Although school districts with lower student–teacher ratios tend to have higher test scores in the California data set, perhaps students from districts with small classes have other advantages that help them perform well on standardized tests. Could this have produced misleading results and, if so, what can be done?

Omitted factors, such as student characteristics, can in fact make the ordinary least squares (OLS) estimator of the effect of class size on test scores misleading or, more precisely, biased. This chapter explains this "omitted variable bias" and introduces multiple regression, a method that can eliminate omitted variable bias. The key idea of multiple regression is that, if we have data on these omitted variables, then we can include them as additional regressors and thereby estimate the effect of one regressor (the student–teacher ratio) while holding constant the other variables (such as student characteristics).

This chapter explains how to estimate the coefficients of the multiple linear regression model. Many aspects of multiple regression parallel those of regression with a single regressor, studied in Chapters 4 and 5. The coefficients of the multiple regression model can be estimated from data using OLS; the OLS estimators in multiple regression are random variables because they depend on data from a random sample; and in large samples the sampling distributions of the OLS estimators are approximately normal.

6.1 Omitted Variable Bias

By focusing only on the student–teacher ratio, the empirical analysis in Chapters 4 and 5 ignored some potentially important determinants of test scores by collecting their influences in the regression error term. These omitted factors include school characteristics, such as teacher quality and computer usage, and student characteristics, such as family background. We begin by considering an omitted student characteristic that is particularly relevant in California because of its large immigrant population: the prevalence in the school district of students who are still learning English.

By ignoring the percentage of English learners in the district, the OLS estimator of the slope in the regression of test scores on the student–teacher ratio could be biased; that is, the mean of the sampling distribution of the OLS estimator might not equal the true effect on test scores of a unit change in the student–teacher ratio. Here is the reasoning. Students who are still learning English might perform worse on standardized tests than native English speakers. If districts with large classes also have many students still learning English, then the OLS regression of test scores on the student–teacher ratio could erroneously find a correlation and produce a large estimated coefficient, when in fact the true causal effect of cutting class sizes on test scores is small, even zero. Accordingly, based on the analysis of Chapters 4 and 5, the superintendent might hire enough new teachers to reduce the student–teacher ratio by two, but her hoped-for improvement in test scores will fail to materialize if the true coefficient is small or zero.

A look at the California data lends credence to this concern. The correlation between the student–teacher ratio and the percentage of English learners (students who are not native English speakers and who have not yet mastered English) in the district is 0.19. This small but positive correlation suggests that districts with more English learners tend to have a higher student–teacher ratio (larger classes). If the student–teacher ratio were unrelated to the percentage of English learners, then it would be safe to ignore English proficiency in the regression of test scores against the student–teacher ratio. But because the student–teacher ratio and the percentage of English learners are correlated, it is possible that the OLS coefficient in the regression of test scores on the student–teacher ratio reflects that influence.

Definition of Omitted Variable Bias

If the regressor (the student–teacher ratio) is correlated with a variable that has been omitted from the analysis (the percentage of English learners) and that determines, in part, the dependent variable (test scores), then the OLS estimator will have **omitted variable bias**.

Omitted variable bias occurs when two conditions are true: (1) the omitted variable is correlated with the included regressor; and (2) the omitted variable is a determinant of the dependent variable. To illustrate these conditions, consider three examples of variables that are omitted from the regression of test scores on the student–teacher ratio.

Example #1: Percentage of English learners.   Because the percentage of English learners is correlated with the student–teacher ratio, the first condition for omitted variable bias holds. It is plausible that students who are still learning English will do worse on standardized tests than native English speakers, in which case the percentage of English learners is a determinant of test scores and the second condition for omitted variable bias holds. Thus, the OLS estimator in the regression of test scores on the student–teacher ratio could incorrectly reflect the influence of the omitted variable, the percentage of English learners. That is, omitting the percentage of English learners may introduce omitted variable bias.

Example #2: Time of day of the test.   Another variable omitted from the analysis is the time of day that the test was administered. For this omitted variable, it is plausible that the first condition for omitted variable bias does not hold but the second condition does. For example, if the time of day of the test varies from one district to the next in a way that is unrelated to class size, then the time of day and class size would be uncorrelated so the first condition does not hold. Conversely, the time of day of the test could affect scores (alertness varies through the school day), so the second condition holds. However, because in this example the time that the test is administered is uncorrelated with the student–teacher ratio, the student–teacher ratio could not be incorrectly picking up the "time of day" effect. Thus omitting the time of day of the test does not result in omitted variable bias.

Example #3: Parking lot space per pupil.   Another omitted variable is parking lot space per pupil (the area of the teacher parking lot divided by the number of students). This variable satisfies the first but not the second condition for omitted variable bias. Specifically, schools with more teachers per pupil probably have more teacher parking space, so the first condition would be satisfied. However, under the assumption that learning takes place in the classroom, not the parking lot, parking lot space has no direct effect on learning; thus the second condition does not hold. Because parking lot space per pupil is not a determinant of test scores, omitting it from the analysis does not lead to omitted variable bias.

Omitted variable bias is summarized in Key Concept 6.1.

Omitted variable bias and the first least squares assumption.   Omitted variable bias means that the first least squares assumption—that $E(u_i \mid X_i) = 0$, as listed in Key Concept 4.3—is incorrect. To see why, recall that the error term u_i in the linear regression model with a single regressor represents all factors, other than X_i, that are determinants of Y_i. If one of these other factors is correlated with X_i,

---

OMITTED VARIABLE BIAS IN REGRESSION WITH A SINGLE REGRESSOR	KEY CONCEPT 6.1

Omitted variable bias is the bias in the OLS estimator that arises when the regressor, X, is correlated with an omitted variable. For omitted variable bias to occur, two conditions must be true:

1. X is correlated with the omitted variable.
2. The omitted variable is a determinant of the dependent variable, Y.

---

this means that the error term (which contains this factor) is correlated with X_i. In other words, if an omitted variable is a determinant of Y_i, then it is in the error term, and if it is correlated with X_i, then the error term is correlated with X_i. Because u_i and X_i are correlated, the conditional mean of u_i given X_i is nonzero. This correlation therefore violates the first least squares assumption, and the consequence is serious: The OLS estimator is biased. This bias does not vanish even in very large samples, and the OLS estimator is inconsistent.

A Formula for Omitted Variable Bias

The discussion of the previous section about omitted variable bias can be summarized mathematically by a formula for this bias. Let the correlation between X_i and u_i be $\mathrm{corr}(X_i, u_i) = \rho_{Xu}$. Suppose that the second and third least squares assumptions hold, but the first does not because ρ_{Xu} is nonzero. Then the OLS estimator has the limit (derived in Appendix 6.1)

$$\hat{\beta}_1 \xrightarrow{p} \beta_1 + \rho_{Xu}\frac{\sigma_u}{\sigma_X}. \tag{6.1}$$

That is, as the sample size increases, $\hat{\beta}_1$ is close to $\beta_1 + \rho_{Xu}(\sigma_u/\sigma_X)$ with increasingly high probability.

The formula in Equation (6.1) summarizes several of the ideas discussed above about omitted variable bias:

1. Omitted variable bias is a problem whether the sample size is large or small. Because $\hat{\beta}_1$ does not converge in probability to the true value β_1, $\hat{\beta}_1$ is inconsistent; that is, $\hat{\beta}_1$ is not a consistent estimator of β_1 when there is omitted variable bias. The term $\rho_{Xu}(\sigma_u/\sigma_X)$ in Equation (6.1) is the bias in $\hat{\beta}_1$ that persists even in large samples.

The Mozart Effect: Omitted Variable Bias?

A study published in *Nature* in 1993 (Rauscher, Shaw and Ky, 1993) suggested that listening to Mozart for 10–15 minutes could temporarily raise your IQ by 8 or 9 points. That study made big news—and politicians and parents saw an easy way to make their children smarter. For a while, the state of Georgia even distributed classical music CDs to all infants in the state.

What is the evidence for the "Mozart effect"? A review of dozens of studies found that students who take optional music or arts courses in high school do in fact have higher English and math test scores than those who don't.[1] A closer look at these studies, however, suggests that the real reason for the better test performance has little to do with those courses. Instead, the authors of the review suggested that the correlation between testing well and taking art or music could arise from any number of things. For example, the academically better students might have more time to take optional music courses or more interest in doing so, or those schools with a deeper music curriculum might just be better schools across the board.

In the terminology of regression, the estimated relationship between test scores and taking optional music courses appears to have omitted variable bias. By omitting factors such as the student's innate ability or the overall quality of the school, studying music appears to have an effect on test scores when in fact it has none.

So is there a Mozart effect? One way to find out is to do a randomized controlled experiment. (As discussed in Chapter 4, randomized controlled experiments eliminate omitted variable bias by randomly assigning participants to "treatment" and "control" groups.) Taken together, the many controlled experiments on the Mozart effect fail to show that listening to Mozart improves IQ or general test performance. For reasons not fully understood, however, it seems that listening to classical music *does* help temporarily in one narrow area: folding paper and visualizing shapes. So the next time you cram for an origami exam, try to fit in a little Mozart, too.

---

[1] See the *Journal of Aesthetic Education* 34: 3–4 (Fall/Winter 2000), especially the article by Ellen Winner and Monica Cooper, (pp. 11–76) and the one by Lois Hetland (pp. 105–148).

2. Whether this bias is large or small in practice depends on the correlation ρ_{Xu} between the regressor and the error term. The larger is $|\rho_{Xu}|$, the larger is the bias.

3. The direction of the bias in $\hat{\beta}_1$ depends on whether X and u are positively or negatively correlated. For example, we speculated that the percentage of students learning English has a *negative* effect on district test scores (students still learning English have lower scores), so that the percentage of English learners enters the error term with a negative sign. In our data, the fraction of English learners is *positively* correlated with the student–teacher ratio

(districts with more English learners have larger classes). Thus the student–teacher ratio (X) would be *negatively* correlated with the error term (u), so $\rho_{Xu} < 0$ and the coefficient on the student–teacher ratio $\hat{\beta}_1$ would be biased toward a negative number. In other words, having a small percentage of English learners is associated both with *high* test scores and *low* student–teacher ratios, so one reason that the OLS estimator suggests that small classes improve test scores may be that the districts with small classes have fewer English learners.

Addressing Omitted Variable Bias by Dividing the Data into Groups

What can you do about omitted variable bias? Our superintendent is considering increasing the number of teachers in her district, but she has no control over the fraction of immigrants in her community. As a result, she is interested in the effect of the student–teacher ratio on test scores, *holding constant* other factors, including the percentage of English learners. This new way of posing her question suggests that, instead of using data for all districts, perhaps we should focus on districts with percentages of English learners comparable to hers. Among this subset of districts, do those with smaller classes do better on standardized tests?

Table 6.1 reports evidence on the relationship between class size and test scores within districts with comparable percentages of English learners. Districts

TABLE 6.1	Differences in Test Scores for California School Districts with Low and High Student–Teacher Ratios, by the Percentage of English Learners in the District					
	Student–Teacher Ratio < 20		**Student–Teacher Ratio ≥ 20**		**Difference in Test Scores, Low vs. High STR**	
	Average Test Score	**n**	**Average Test Score**	**n**	**Difference**	**t-statistic**
All districts	657.4	238	650.0	182	7.4	4.04
Percentage of English learners						
< 1.9%	664.5	76	665.4	27	−0.9	−0.30
1.9–8.8%	665.2	64	661.8	44	3.3	1.13
8.8–23.0%	654.9	54	649.7	50	5.2	1.72
> 23.0%	636.7	44	634.8	61	1.9	0.68

are divided into eight groups. First, the districts are broken into four categories that correspond to the quartiles of the distribution of the percentage of English learners across districts. Second, within each of these four categories, districts are further broken down into two groups, depending on whether the student–teacher ratio is small ($STR < 20$) or large ($STR \geq 20$).

The first row in Table 6.1 reports the overall difference in average test scores between districts with low and high student–teacher ratios, that is, the difference in test scores between these two groups without breaking them down further into the quartiles of English learners. (Recall that this difference was previously reported in regression form in Equation (5.18) as the OLS estimate of the coefficient on D_i in the regression of *TestScore* on D_i, where D_i is a binary regressor that equals 1 if $STR_i < 20$ and equals 0 otherwise.) Over the full sample of 420 districts, the average test score is 7.4 points higher in districts with a low student–teacher ratio than a high one; the t-statistic is 4.04, so the null hypothesis that the mean test score is the same in the two groups is rejected at the 1% significance level.

The final four rows in Table 6.1 report the difference in test scores between districts with low and high student–teacher ratios, broken down by the quartile of the percentage of English learners. This evidence presents a different picture. Of the districts with the fewest English learners ($< 1.9\%$), the average test score for those 76 with low student–teacher ratios is 664.5 and the average for the 27 with high student–teacher ratios is 665.4. Thus, for the districts with the fewest English learners, test scores were on average 0.9 points *lower* in the districts with low student–teacher ratios! In the second quartile, districts with low student–teacher ratios had test scores that averaged 3.3 points higher than those with high student–teacher ratios; this gap was 5.2 points for the third quartile and only 1.9 points for the quartile of districts with the most English learners. Once we hold the percentage of English learners constant, the difference in performance between districts with high and low student–teacher ratios is perhaps half (or less) of the overall estimate of 7.4 points.

At first this finding might seem puzzling. How can the overall effect of test scores be twice the effect of test scores within any quartile? The answer is that the districts with the most English learners tend to have *both* the highest student–teacher ratios *and* the lowest test scores. The difference in the average test score between districts in the lowest and highest quartile of the percentage of English learners is large, approximately 30 points. The districts with few English learners tend to have lower student–teacher ratios: 74% (76 of 103) of the districts in the first quartile of English learners have small classes ($STR < 20$), while only 42% (44 of 105) of the districts in the quartile with the most English learners have small classes. So, the districts with the most English learners have both lower test scores and higher student–teacher ratios than the other districts.

This analysis reinforces the superintendent's worry that omitted variable bias is present in the regression of test scores against the student–teacher ratio. By looking within quartiles of the percentage of English learners, the test score differences in the second part of Table 6.1 improve upon the simple difference-of-means analysis in the first line of Table 6.1. Still, this analysis does not yet provide the superintendent with a useful estimate of the effect on test scores of changing class size, holding constant the fraction of English learners. Such an estimate can be provided, however, using the method of multiple regression.

6.2 The Multiple Regression Model

The **multiple regression model** extends the single variable regression model of Chapters 4 and 5 to include additional variables as regressors. This model permits estimating the effect on Y_i of changing one variable (X_{1i}) while holding the other regressors (X_{2i}, X_{3i}, and so forth) constant. In the class size problem, the multiple regression model provides a way to isolate the effect on test scores (Y_i) of the student–teacher ratio (X_{1i}) while holding constant the percentage of students in the district who are English learners (X_{2i}).

The Population Regression Line

Suppose for the moment that there are only two independent variables, X_{1i} and X_{2i}. In the linear multiple regression model, the average relationship between these two independent variables and the dependent variable, Y, is given by the linear function

$$E(Y_i|X_{1i} = x_1, X_{2i} = x_2) = \beta_0 + \beta_1 x_1 + \beta_2 x_2, \qquad (6.2)$$

where $E(Y_i|X_{1i} = x_1, X_{2i} = x_2)$ is the conditional expectation of Y_i given that $X_{1i} = x_1$ and $X_{2i} = x_2$. That is, if the student–teacher ratio in the ith district (X_{1i}) equals some value x_1 and the percentage of English learners in the ith district (X_{2i}) equals x_2, then the expected value of Y_i given the student–teacher ratio and the percentage of English learners is given by Equation (6.2).

Equation (6.2) is the **population regression line** or **population regression function** in the multiple regression model. The coefficient β_0 is the **intercept**, the coefficient β_1 is the **slope coefficient of X_{1i}** or, more simply, the **coefficient on X_{1i}**, and the coefficient β_2 is the **slope coefficient of X_{2i}** or, more simply, the **coefficient on X_{2i}**. One or more of the independent variables in the multiple regression model are sometimes referred to as **control variables**.

The interpretation of the coefficient β_1 in Equation (6.2) is different than it was when X_{1i} was the only regressor: In Equation (6.2), β_1 is the effect on Y of a unit change in X_1, **holding X_2 constant** or **controlling for X_2**.

This interpretation of β_1 follows from the definition that the expected effect on Y of a change in X_1, ΔX_1, holding X_2 constant, is the difference between the expected value of Y when the independent variables take on the values $X_1 + \Delta X_1$ and X_2 and the expected value of Y when the independent variables take on the values X_1 and X_2. Accordingly, write the population regression function in Equation (6.2) as $Y = \beta_0 + \beta_1 X_1 + \beta_2 X_2$, and imagine changing X_1 by the amount ΔX_1 while not changing X_2, that is, while holding X_2 constant. Because X_1 has changed, Y will change by some amount, say ΔY. After this change, the new value of Y, $Y + \Delta Y$, is

$$Y + \Delta Y = \beta_0 + \beta_1(X_1 + \Delta X_1) + \beta_2 X_2. \tag{6.3}$$

An equation for ΔY in terms of ΔX_1 is obtained by subtracting the equation $Y = \beta_0 + \beta_1 X_1 + \beta_2 X_2$ from Equation (6.3), yielding $\Delta Y = \beta_1 \Delta X_1$. That is,

$$\beta_1 = \frac{\Delta Y}{\Delta X_1}, \text{holding } X_2 \text{ constant.} \tag{6.4}$$

The coefficient β_1 is the effect on Y (the expected change in Y) of a unit change in X_1, holding X_2 fixed. Another phrase used to describe β_1 is the **partial effect** on Y of X_1, holding X_2 fixed.

The interpretation of the intercept in the multiple regression model, β_0, is similar to the interpretation of the intercept in the single-regressor model: It is the expected value of Y_i when X_{1i} and X_{2i} are zero. Simply put, the intercept β_0 determines how far up the Y axis the population regression line starts.

The Population Multiple Regression Model

The population regression line in Equation (6.2) is the relationship between Y and X_1 and X_2 that holds on average in the population. Just as in the case of regression with a single regressor, however, this relationship does not hold exactly because many other factors influence the dependent variable. In addition to the student–teacher ratio and the fraction of students still learning English, for example, test scores are influenced by school characteristics, other student characteristics, and luck. Thus the population regression function in Equation (6.2) needs to be augmented to incorporate these additional factors.

Just as in the case of regression with a single regressor, the factors that determine Y_i in addition to X_{1i} and X_{2i} are incorporated into Equation (6.2) as an "error" term u_i. This error term is the deviation of a particular observation (test scores in the ith district in our example) from the average population relationship. Accordingly, we have

$$Y_i = \beta_0 + \beta_1 X_{1i} + \beta_2 X_{2i} + u_i, i = 1, \ldots, n, \tag{6.5}$$

where the subscript i indicates the ith of the n observations (districts) in the sample.

Equation (6.5) is the **population multiple regression model** when there are two regressors, X_{1i} and X_{2i}.

In regression with binary regressors it can be useful to treat β_0 as the coefficient on a regressor that always equals 1; think of β_0 as the coefficient on X_{0i}, where $X_{0i} = 1$ for $i = 1, \ldots, n$. Accordingly, the population multiple regression model in Equation (6.5) can alternatively be written as

$$Y_i = \beta_0 X_{0i} + \beta_1 X_{1i} + \beta_2 X_{2i} + u_i, \text{where } X_{0i} = 1, i = 1, \ldots, n. \tag{6.6}$$

The variable X_{0i} is sometimes called the **constant regressor** because it takes on the same value—the value 1—for all observations. Similarly, the intercept, β_0, is sometimes called the **constant term** in the regression.

The two ways of writing the population regression model, Equations (6.5) and (6.6), are equivalent.

The discussion so far has focused on the case of a single additional variable, X_2. In practice, however, there might be multiple factors omitted from the single-regressor model. For example, ignoring the students' economic background might result in omitted variable bias, just as ignoring the fraction of English learners did. This reasoning leads us to consider a model with three regressors or, more generally, a model that includes k regressors. The multiple regression model with k regressors, $X_{1i}, X_{2i}, \ldots, X_{ki}$, is summarized as Key Concept 6.2.

The definitions of homoskedasticity and heteroskedasticity in the multiple regression model are extensions of their definitions in the single-regressor model. The error term u_i in the multiple regression model is **homoskedastic** if the variance of the conditional distribution of u_i given $X_{1i}, \ldots, X_{ki}$, $\text{var}(u_i | X_{1i}, \ldots, X_{ki})$, is constant for $i = 1, \ldots, n$ and thus does not depend on the values of $X_{1i}, \ldots, X_{ki}$. Otherwise, the error term is **heteroskedastic**.

The multiple regression model holds out the promise of providing just what the superintendent wants to know: the effect of changing the student–teacher ratio, holding constant other factors that are beyond her control. These factors include not just the percentage of English learners, but other measurable factors that might affect test performance, including the economic background of the students. To be

KEY CONCEPT

THE MULTIPLE REGRESSION MODEL

6.2

The multiple regression model is

$$Y_i = \beta_0 + \beta_1 X_{1i} + \beta_2 X_{2i} + \cdots + \beta_k X_{ki} + u_i, i = 1, \ldots, n \qquad (6.7)$$

where

- Y_i is i^{th} observation on the dependent variable; $X_{1i}, X_{2i}, \ldots, X_{ki}$ are the ith observations on each of the k regressors; and u_i is the error term.

- The population regression line is the relationship that holds between Y and the X's on average in the population:

$$E(Y \mid X_{1i} = x_1, X_{2i} = x_2, \ldots, X_{ki} = x_k)$$
$$= \beta_0 + \beta_1 x_1 + \beta_2 x_2 + \cdots + \beta_k x_k.$$

- β_1 is the slope coefficient on X_1, β_2 is the coefficient on X_2, and so on. The coefficient β_1 is the expected change in Y_i resulting from changing X_{1i} by one unit, holding constant $X_{2i}, \ldots, X_{ki}$. The coefficients on the other X's are interpreted similarly.

- The intercept β_0 is the expected value of Y when all the X's equal 0. The intercept can be thought of as the coefficient on a regressor, X_{0i}, that equals 1 for all i.

of practical help to the superintendent, however, we need to provide her with estimates of the unknown population coefficients $\beta_0, \ldots, \beta_k$ of the population regression model calculated using a sample of data. Fortunately, these coefficients can be estimated using ordinary least squares.

6.3   The OLS Estimator in Multiple Regression

This section describes how the coefficients of the multiple regression model can be estimated using OLS.

The OLS Estimator

Section 4.2 shows how to estimate the intercept and slope coefficients in the single-regressor model by applying OLS to a sample of observations of Y and X. The key idea is that these coefficients can be estimated by minimizing the sum of squared prediction mistakes, that is, by choosing the estimators b_0 and b_1 so as to minimize $\sum_{i=1}^{n}(Y_i - b_0 - b_1X_i)^2$. The estimators that do so are the OLS estimators, $\hat{\beta}_0$ and $\hat{\beta}_1$.

The method of OLS also can be used to estimate the coefficients $\beta_0, \beta_1, \ldots,$ β_k in the multiple regression model. Let $b_0, b_1, \ldots, b_k$ be estimators of $\beta_0, \beta_1, \ldots,$ β_k. The predicted value of Y_i, calculated using these estimators, is $b_0 + b_1X_{1i} + \cdots + b_kX_{ki}$, and the mistake in predicting Y_i is $Y_i - (b_0 + b_1X_{1i} + \cdots + b_kX_{ki}) = Y_i - b_0 - b_1X_{1i} - \cdots - b_kX_{ki}$. The sum of these squared prediction mistakes over all n observations thus is

$$\sum_{i=1}^{n} (Y_i - b_0 - b_1X_{1i} - \cdots - b_kX_{ki})^2. \tag{6.8}$$

The sum of the squared mistakes for the linear regression model in expression (6.8) is the extension of the sum of the squared mistakes given in Equation (4.6) for the linear regression model with a single regressor.

The estimators of the coefficients $\beta_0, \beta_1, \ldots, \beta_k$ that minimize the sum of squared mistakes in expression (6.8) are called the **ordinary least squares (OLS) estimators** of $\beta_0, \beta_1, \ldots, \beta_k$. The OLS estimators are denoted $\hat{\beta}_0, \hat{\beta}_1, \ldots, \hat{\beta}_k$.

The terminology of OLS in the linear multiple regression model is the same as in the linear regression model with a single regressor. The **OLS regression line** is the straight line constructed using the OLS estimators: $\hat{\beta}_0 + \hat{\beta}_1X_1 + \cdots + \hat{\beta}_kX_k$. The **predicted value** of Y_i given $X_{1i}, \ldots, X_{ki}$, based on the OLS regression line, is $\hat{Y}_i = \hat{\beta}_0 + \hat{\beta}_1X_{1i} + \cdots + \hat{\beta}_kX_{ki}$. The **OLS residual** for the ith observation is the difference between Y_i and its OLS predicted value, that is, the OLS residual is $\hat{u}_i = Y_i - \hat{Y}_i$.

The OLS estimators could be computed by trial and error, repeatedly trying different values of $b_0, \ldots, b_k$ until you are satisfied that you have minimized the total sum of squares in expression (6.8). It is far easier, however, to use explicit formulas for the OLS estimators that are derived using calculus. The formulas for the OLS estimators in the multiple regression model are similar to those in Key Concept 4.2 for the single-regressor model. These formulas are incorporated into modern statistical software. In the multiple regression model, the formulas for general k are best expressed and discussed using matrix notation, so their presentation is omitted. The formulas for $k = 2$ are given in Appendix 6.3.

KEY CONCEPT 6.3	THE OLS ESTIMATORS, PREDICTED VALUES, AND RESIDUALS IN THE MULTIPLE REGRESSION MODEL

The OLS estimators $\hat{\beta}_0, \hat{\beta}_1, \ldots, \hat{\beta}_k$ are the values of $b_0, b_1, \ldots, b_k$ that minimize the sum of squared prediction mistakes $\sum_{i=1}^{n} (Y_i - b_0 - b_1 X_{1i} - \cdots - b_k X_{ki})^2$. The OLS predicted values $\hat{Y}_i$ and residuals $\hat{u}_i$ are

$$\hat{Y}_i = \hat{\beta}_0 + \hat{\beta}_1 X_{1i} + \cdots + \hat{\beta}_k X_{ki}, i = 1, \ldots, n, \text{ and} \tag{6.9}$$

$$\hat{u}_i = Y_i - \hat{Y}_i, i = 1, \ldots, n. \tag{6.10}$$

The OLS estimators $\hat{\beta}_0, \hat{\beta}_1, \ldots, \hat{\beta}_k$ and residual $\hat{u}_i$ are computed from a sample of n observations of $(X_{1i}, \ldots, X_{ki}, Y_i), i = 1, \ldots, n$. These are estimators of the unknown true population coefficients $\beta_0, \beta_1, \ldots, \beta_k$ and error term, u_i.

The definitions and terminology of OLS in multiple regression are summarized in Key Concept 6.3.

Application to Test Scores and the Student–Teacher Ratio

In Section 4.2, we used OLS to estimate the intercept and slope coefficient of the regression relating test scores (*TestScore*) to the student–teacher ratio (*STR*), using our 420 observations for California school districts; the estimated OLS regression line, reported in Equation (4.11), is

$$\widehat{TestScore} = 698.9 - 2.28 \times STR. \tag{6.11}$$

Our concern has been that this relationship is misleading because the student–teacher ratio might be picking up the effect of having many English learners in districts with large classes. That is, it is possible that the OLS estimator is subject to omitted variable bias.

We are now in a position to address this concern by using OLS to estimate a multiple regression in which the dependent variable is the test score (Y_i) and there are two regressors: the student–teacher ratio (X_{1i}) and the percentage of English learners in the school district (X_{2i}) for our 420 districts ($i = 1, \ldots, 420$). The estimated OLS regression line for this multiple regression is

$$\widehat{TestScore} = 686.0 - 1.10 \times STR - 0.65 \times PctEL, \tag{6.12}$$

where *PctEL* is the percentage of students in the district who are English learners. The OLS estimate of the intercept ($\hat{\beta}_0$) is 686.0, the OLS estimate of the coefficient on the student–teacher ratio ($\hat{\beta}_1$) is -1.10, and the OLS estimate of the coefficient on the percentage English learners ($\hat{\beta}_2$) is -0.65.

The estimated effect on test scores of a change in the student–teacher ratio in the multiple regression is approximately half as large as when the student–teacher ratio is the only regressor: in the single-regressor equation [Equation (6.11)], a unit decrease in the *STR* is estimated to increase test scores by 2.28 points, but in the multiple regression equation [Equation (6.12)], it is estimated to increase test scores by only 1.10 points. This difference occurs because the coefficient on *STR* in the multiple regression is the effect of a change in *STR,* holding constant (or controlling for) *PctEL,* whereas in the single-regressor regression, *PctEL* is not held constant.

These two estimates can be reconciled by concluding that there is omitted variable bias in the estimate in the single-regressor model in Equation (6.11). In Section 6.1, we saw that districts with a high percentage of English learners tend to have not only low test scores but also a high student–teacher ratio. If the fraction of English learners is omitted from the regression, reducing the student–teacher ratio is estimated to have a larger effect on test scores, but this estimate reflects *both* the effect of a change in the student–teacher ratio *and* the omitted effect of having fewer English learners in the district.

We have reached the same conclusion that there is omitted variable bias in the relationship between test scores and the student–teacher ratio by two different paths: the tabular approach of dividing the data into groups (Section 6.1) and the multiple regression approach [Equation (6.12)]. Of these two methods, multiple regression has two important advantages. First, it provides a quantitative estimate of the effect of a unit decrease in the student–teacher ratio, which is what the superintendent needs to make her decision. Second, it readily extends to more than two regressors, so that multiple regression can be used to control for measurable factors other than just the percentage of English learners.

The rest of this chapter is devoted to understanding and to using OLS in the multiple regression model. Much of what you learned about the OLS estimator with a single regressor carries over to multiple regression with few or no modifications, so we will focus on that which is new with multiple regression. We begin by discussing measures of fit for the multiple regression model.

6.4   Measures of Fit in Multiple Regression

Three commonly used summary statistics in multiple regression are the standard error of the regression, the regression R^2, and the adjusted R^2 (also known as $\bar{R}^2$). All three statistics measure how well the OLS estimate of the multiple regression line describes, or "fits," the data.

The Standard Error of the Regression (SER)

The standard error of the regression (SER) estimates the standard deviation of the error term u_i. Thus, the SER is a measure of the spread of the distribution of Y around the regression line. In multiple regression, the SER is

$$SER = s_{\hat{u}}, \text{ where } s_{\hat{u}}^2 = \frac{1}{n-k-1}\sum_{i=1}^{n}\hat{u}_i^2 = \frac{SSR}{n-k-1}, \qquad (6.13)$$

where the SSR is the sum of squared residuals, $SSR = \sum_{i=1}^{n}\hat{u}_i^2$.

The only difference between the definition in Equation (6.13) and the definition of the SER in Section 4.3 for the single-regressor model is that here the divisor is $n - k - 1$ rather than $n - 2$. In Section 4.3, the divisor $n - 2$ (rather than n) adjusts for the downward bias introduced by estimating two coefficients (the slope and intercept of the regression line). Here, the divisor $n - k - 1$ adjusts for the downward bias introduced by estimating $k + 1$ coefficients (the k slope coefficients plus the intercept). As in Section 4.3, using $n - k - 1$ rather than n is called a degrees-of-freedom adjustment. If there is a single regressor, then $k = 1$, so the formula in Section 4.3 is the same as in Equation (6.13). When n is large, the effect of the degrees-of-freedom adjustment is negligible.

The R^2

The regression **R^2** is the fraction of the sample variance of Y_i explained by (or predicted by) the regressors. Equivalently, the R^2 is 1 minus the fraction of the variance of Y_i *not* explained by the regressors.

The mathematical definition of the R^2 is the same as for regression with a single regressor:

$$R^2 = \frac{ESS}{TSS} = 1 - \frac{SSR}{TSS}, \qquad (6.14)$$

where the explained sum of squares is $ESS = \sum_{i=1}^{n}(\hat{Y}_i - \bar{Y})^2$ and the total sum of squares is $TSS = \sum_{i=1}^{n}(Y_i - \bar{Y})^2$.

In multiple regression, the R^2 increases whenever a regressor is added, unless the estimated coefficient on the added regressor is exactly zero. To see this, think about starting with one regressor and then adding a second. When you use OLS to estimate the model with both regressors, OLS finds the values of the coefficients that minimize the sum of squared residuals. If OLS happens to choose the coefficient on the new regressor to be exactly zero, then the SSR will be the same whether or not the second variable is included in the regression. But if OLS chooses any value other than zero, then it must be that this value reduced the SSR relative to the regression that excludes this regressor. In practice it is extremely unusual for an estimated coefficient to be exactly zero, so in general the SSR will decrease when a new regressor is added. But this means that the R^2 generally increases (and never decreases) when a new regressor is added.

The "Adjusted R^2"

Because the R^2 increases when a new variable is added, an increase in the R^2 does not mean that adding a variable actually improves the fit of the model. In this sense, the R^2 gives an inflated estimate of how well the regression fits the data. One way to correct for this is to deflate or reduce the R^2 by some factor, and this is what the adjusted R^2, or $\overline{R}^2$, does.

The **adjusted R^2**, or $\overline{R}^2$, is a modified version of the R^2 that does not necessarily increase when a new regressor is added. The $\overline{R}^2$ is

$$\overline{R}^2 = 1 - \frac{n-1}{n-k-1}\frac{SSR}{TSS} = 1 - \frac{s_{\hat{u}}^2}{s_Y^2}. \tag{6.15}$$

The difference between this formula and the second definition of the R^2 in Equation (6.14) is that the ratio of the sum of squared residuals to the total sum of squares is multiplied by the factor $(n-1)/(n-k-1)$. As the second expression in Equation (6.15) shows, this means that the adjusted R^2 is 1 minus the ratio of the sample variance of the OLS residuals [with the degrees-of-freedom correction in Equation (6.13)] to the sample variance of Y.

There are three useful things to know about the $\overline{R}^2$. First, $(n-1)/(n-k-1)$ is always greater than 1, so $\overline{R}^2$ is always less than R^2.

Second, adding a regressor has two opposite effects on the $\overline{R}^2$. On the one hand, the SSR falls, which increases the $\overline{R}^2$. On the other hand, the factor $(n-1)/(n-k-1)$ increases. Whether the $\overline{R}^2$ increases or decreases depends on which of these two effects is stronger.

Third, the $\overline{R}^2$ can be negative. This happens when the regressors, taken together, reduce the sum of squared residuals by such a small amount that this reduction fails to offset the factor $(n-1)/(n-k-1)$.

Application to Test Scores

Equation (6.12) reports the estimated regression line for the multiple regression relating test scores (*TestScore*) to the student–teacher ratio (*STR*) and the percentage of English learners (*PctEL*). The R^2 for this regression line is $R^2 = 0.426$, the adjusted R^2 is $\overline{R}^2 = 0.424$, and the standard error of the regression is *SER* = 14.5.

Comparing these measures of fit with those for the regression in which *PctEL* is excluded [Equation (6.11)] shows that including *PctEL* in the regression increased the R^2 from 0.051 to 0.426. When the only regressor is *STR*, only a small fraction of the variation in *TestScore* is explained, however, when *PctEL* is added to the regression, more than two-fifths (42.6%) of the variation in test scores is explained. In this sense, including the percentage of English learners substantially improves the fit of the regression. Because *n* is large and only two regressors appear in Equation (6.12), the difference between R^2 and adjusted R^2 is very small ($R^2 = 0.426$ versus $\overline{R}^2 = 0.424$).

The *SER* for the regression excluding *PctEL* is 18.6; this value falls to 14.5 when *PctEL* is included as a second regressor. The units of the *SER* are points on the standardized test. The reduction in the *SER* tells us that predictions about standardized test scores are substantially more precise if they are made using the regression with both *STR* and *PctEL* than if they are made using the regression with only *STR* as a regressor.

Using the R^2 and adjusted R^2.   The $\overline{R}^2$ is useful because it quantifies the extent to which the regressors account for, or explain, the variation in the dependent variable. Nevertheless, heavy reliance on the $\overline{R}^2$ (or R^2) can be a trap. In applications, "maximize the $\overline{R}^2$" is rarely the answer to any economically or statistically meaningful question. Instead, the decision about whether to include a variable in a multiple regression should be based on whether including that variable allows you better to estimate the causal effect of interest. We return to the issue of how to decide which variables to include—and which to exclude—in Chapter 7. First, however, we need to develop methods for quantifying the sampling uncertainty of the OLS estimator. The starting point for doing so is extending the least squares assumptions of Chapter 4 to the case of multiple regressors.

6.5   The Least Squares Assumptions in Multiple Regression

There are four least squares assumptions in the multiple regression model. The first three are those of Section 4.3 for the single regressor model

(Key Concept 4.3), extended to allow for multiple regressors, and these are discussed only briefly. The fourth assumption is new and is discussed in more detail.

Assumption #1: The Conditional Distribution of u_i Given $X_{1i}, X_{2i}, \ldots, X_{ki}$ Has a Mean of Zero

The first assumption is that the conditional distribution of u_i given $X_{1i}, \ldots, X_{ki}$ has a mean of zero. This assumption extends the first least squares assumption with a single regressor to multiple regressors. This assumption means that sometimes Y_i is above the population regression line and sometimes Y_i is below the population regression line, but on average over the population Y_i falls on the population regression line. Therefore, for any value of the regressors, the expected value of u_i is zero. As is the case for regression with a single regressor, this is the key assumption that makes the OLS estimators unbiased. We return to omitted variable bias in multiple regression in Section 7.5.

Assumption #2: $(X_{1i}, X_{2i}, \ldots, X_{ki}, Y_i), i = 1, \ldots, n$ Are i.i.d.

The second assumption is that $(X_{1i}, \ldots, X_{ki}, Y_i), i = 1, \ldots, n$ are independently and identically distributed (i.i.d.) random variables. This assumption holds automatically if the data are collected by simple random sampling. The comments on this assumption appearing in Section 4.3 for a single regressor also apply to multiple regressors.

Assumption #3: Large Outliers Are Unlikely

The third least squares assumption is that large outliers—that is, observations with values far outside the usual range of the data—are unlikely. This assumption serves as a reminder that, as in single-regressor case, the OLS estimator of the coefficients in the multiple regression model can be sensitive to large outliers.

The assumption that large outliers are unlikely is made mathematically precise by assuming that $X_{1i}, \ldots, X_{ki}$ and Y_i have nonzero finite fourth moments: $0 < E(X_{1i}^4) < \infty, \ldots, 0 < E(X_{ki}^4) < \infty$ and $0 < E(Y_i^4) < \infty$. Another way to state this assumption is that the dependent variable and regressors have finite kurtosis. This assumption is used to derive the properties of OLS regression statistics in large samples.

Assumption #4: No Perfect Multicollinearity

The fourth assumption is new to the multiple regression model. It rules out an inconvenient situation, called perfect multicollinearity, in which it is impossible to

THE LEAST SQUARES ASSUMPTIONS IN THE MULTIPLE REGRESSION MODEL

6.4

$$Y_i = \beta_0 + \beta_1 X_{1i} + \beta_2 X_{2i} + \ldots + \beta_k X_{ki} + u_i, i = 1, \ldots, n, \text{ where}$$

1. u_i has conditional mean zero given $X_{1i}, X_{2i}, \ldots, X_{ki}$; that is,

$$E(u_i | X_{1i}, X_{2i}, \ldots, X_{ki}) = 0.$$

2. $(X_{1i}, X_{2i}, \ldots, X_{ki}, Y_i), i = 1, \ldots, n$ are independently and identically distributed (i.i.d.) draws from their joint distribution.

3. Large outliers are unlikely: $X_{1i}, \ldots, X_{ki}$ and Y_i have nonzero finite fourth moments.

4. There is no perfect multicollinearity.

compute the OLS estimator. The regressors are said to be **perfectly multicollinear** (or to exhibit **perfect multicollinearity**) if one of the regressors is a perfect linear function of the other regressors. The fourth least squares assumption is that the regressors are not perfectly multicollinear.

Why does perfect multicollinearity make it impossible to compute the OLS estimator? Suppose you want to estimate the coefficient on *STR* in a regression of *TestScore*$_i$ on *STR*$_i$ and *PctEL*$_i$, except that you make a typographical error and accidentally type in *STR*$_i$ a second time instead of *PctEL*$_i$; that is, you regress *TestScore*$_i$ on *STR*$_i$ and *STR*$_i$. This is a case of perfect multicollinearity because one of the regressors (the first occurrence of *STR*) is a perfect linear function of another regressor (the second occurrence of *STR*). Depending on how your software package handles perfect multicollinearity, if you try to estimate this regression the software will do one of three things: (1) It will drop one of the occurrences of *STR*; (2) it will refuse to calculate the OLS estimates and give an error message; or (3) it will crash the computer. The mathematical reason for this failure is that perfect multicollinearity produces division by zero in the OLS formulas.

At an intuitive level, perfect multicollinearity is a problem because you are asking the regression to answer an illogical question. In multiple regression, the coefficient on one of the regressors is the effect of a change in that regressor, holding the other regressors constant. In the hypothetical regression of *TestScore* on *STR* and *STR*, the coefficient on the first occurrence of *STR* is the effect on test scores of a change in *STR*, holding constant *STR*. This makes no sense, and OLS cannot estimate this nonsensical partial effect.

The solution to perfect multicollinearity in this hypothetical regression is simply to correct the typo and to replace one of the occurrences of *STR* with the variable you originally wanted to include. This example is typical: When perfect multicollinearity occurs, it often reflects a logical mistake in choosing the regressors or some previously unrecognized feature of the data set. In general, the solution to perfect multicollinearity is to modify the regressors to eliminate the problem.

Additional examples of perfect multicollinearity are given in Section 6.7, which also defines and discusses imperfect multicollinearity.

The least squares assumptions for the multiple regression model are summarized in Key Concept 6.4.

6.6   The Distribution of the OLS Estimators in Multiple Regression

Because the data differ from one sample to the next, different samples produce different values of the OLS estimators. This variation across possible samples gives rise to the uncertainty associated with the OLS estimators of the population regression coefficients, $\beta_0, \beta_1, \ldots, \beta_k$. Just as in the case of regression with a single regressor, this variation is summarized in the sampling distribution of the OLS estimators.

Recall from Section 4.4 that, under the least squares assumptions, the OLS estimators ($\hat{\beta}_0$ and $\hat{\beta}_1$) are unbiased and consistent estimators of the unknown coefficients (β_0 and β_1) in the linear regression model with a single regressor. In addition, in large samples, the sampling distribution of $\hat{\beta}_0$ and $\hat{\beta}_1$ is well approximated by a bivariate normal distribution.

These results carry over to multiple regression analysis. That is, under the least squares assumptions of Key Concept 6.4, the OLS estimators $\hat{\beta}_0, \hat{\beta}_1, \ldots, \hat{\beta}_k$ are unbiased and consistent estimators of $\beta_0, \beta_1, \ldots, \beta_k$ in the linear multiple regression model. In large samples, the joint sampling distribution of $\hat{\beta}_0, \hat{\beta}_1, \ldots, \hat{\beta}_k$ is well approximated by a multivariate normal distribution, which is the extension of the bivariate normal distribution to the general case of two or more jointly normal random variables (Section 2.4).

Although the algebra is more complicated when there are multiple regressors, the central limit theorem applies to the OLS estimators in the multiple regression model for the same reason that it applies to $\overline{Y}$ and to the OLS estimators when there is a single regressor: The OLS estimators $\hat{\beta}_0, \hat{\beta}_1, \ldots, \hat{\beta}_k$ are averages of the randomly sampled data, and if the sample size is sufficiently large the sampling distribution of those averages becomes normal. Because the multivariate normal

KEY CONCEPT

6.5

LARGE SAMPLE DISTRIBUTION OF $\hat{\beta}_0, \hat{\beta}_1, \ldots, \hat{\beta}_k$

If the least squares assumptions (Key Concept 6.4) hold, then in large samples the OLS estimators $\hat{\beta}_0, \hat{\beta}_1, \ldots, \hat{\beta}_k$ are jointly normally distributed and each $\hat{\beta}_j$ is distributed $N(\beta_j, \sigma^2_{\hat{\beta}_j}), j = 0, \ldots, k$.

distribution is best handled mathematically using matrix algebra, the expressions for the joint distribution of the OLS estimators are omitted.

Key Concept 6.5 summarizes the result that, in large samples, the distribution of the OLS estimators in multiple regression is approximately jointly normal. In general, the OLS estimators are correlated; this correlation arises from the correlation between the regressors. The joint sampling distribution of the OLS estimators is discussed in more detail for the case that there are two regressors and homoskedastic errors in Appendix 6.2.

6.7 Multicollinearity

As discussed in Section 6.5, perfect multicollinearity arises when one of the regressors is a perfect linear combination of the other regressors. This section provides some examples of perfect multicollinearity and discusses how perfect multicollinearity can arise, and can be avoided, in regressions with multiple binary regressors. Imperfect multicollinearity arises when one of the regressors is very highly correlated—but not perfectly correlated—with the other regressors. Unlike perfect multicollinearity, imperfect multicollinearity does not prevent estimation of the regression, nor does it imply a logical problem with the choice of regressors. However, it does mean that one or more regression coefficients could be estimated imprecisely.

Examples of Perfect Multicollinearity

We continue the discussion of perfect multicollinearity from Section 6.5 by examining three additional hypothetical regressions. In each, a third regressor is added to the regression of $TestScore_i$ on STR_i and $PctEL_i$ in Equation (6.12).

Example #1: Fraction of English learners.   Let $FracEL_i$ be the fraction of English learners in the ith district, which varies between 0 and 1. If the variable $FracEL_i$ were included as a third regressor in addition to STR_i and $PctEL_i$, the regressors would be perfectly multicollinear. The reason is that $PctEL$ is the *percentage* of English learners, so that $PctEL_i = 100 \times FracEL_i$ for every district. Thus one of the regressors ($PctEL_i$) can be written as a perfect linear function of another regressor ($FracEL_i$).

Because of this perfect multicollinearity, it is impossible to compute the OLS estimates of the regression of $TestScore_i$ on STR_i, $PctEL_i$, and $FracEL_i$. At an intuitive level, OLS fails because you are asking, What is the effect of a unit change in the *percentage* of English learners, holding constant the *fraction* of English learners? Because the percentage of English learners and the fraction of English learners move together in a perfect linear relationship, this question makes no sense and OLS cannot answer it.

Example #2: "Not very small" classes.   Let NVS_i be a binary variable that equals 1 if the student–teacher ratio in the ith district is "not very small," specifically, NVS_i equals 1 if $STR_i \geq 12$ and equals 0 otherwise. This regression also exhibits perfect multicollinearity, but for a more subtle reason than the regression in the previous example. There are in fact no districts in our data set with $STR_i <$ 12; as you can see in the scatterplot in Figure 4.2, the smallest value of STR is 14. Thus, $NVS_i = 1$ for all observations. Now recall that the linear regression model with an intercept can equivalently be thought of as including a regressor, X_{0i}, that equals 1 for all i, as is shown in Equation (6.6). Thus we can write $NVS_i = 1 \times X_{0i}$ for all the observations in our data set; that is, NVS_i can be written as a perfect linear combination of the regressors; specifically, it equals X_{0i}.

This illustrates two important points about perfect multicollinearity. First, when the regression includes an intercept, then one of the regressors that can be implicated in perfect multicollinearity is the constant regressor X_{0i}. Second, perfect multicollinearity is a statement about the data set you have on hand. While it is possible to imagine a school district with fewer than 12 students per teacher, there are no such districts in our data set so we cannot analyze them in our regression.

Example #3: Percentage of English speakers.   Let $PctES_i$ be the percentage of "English speakers" in the ith district, defined to be the percentage of students who are not English learners. Again the regressors will be perfectly multicollinear. Like the previous example, the perfect linear relationship among the regressors involves the constant regressor X_{0i}: For every district, $PctES_i = 100 \times X_{0i} - PctEL_i$.

This example illustrates another point: perfect multicollinearity is a feature of the entire set of regressors. If either the intercept (i.e., the regressor X_{0i}) or $PctEL_i$ were excluded from this regression, the regressors would not be perfectly multicollinear.

The dummy variable trap.   Another possible source of perfect multicollinearity arises when multiple binary, or dummy, variables are used as regressors. For example, suppose you have partitioned the school districts into three categories: rural, suburban, and urban. Each district falls into one (and only one) category. Let these binary variables be $Rural_i$, which equals 1 for a rural district and equals 0 otherwise; $Suburban_i$, and $Urban_i$. If you include all three binary variables in the regression along with a constant, the regressors will be perfect multicollinearity: Because each district belongs to one and only one category, $Rural_i + Suburban_i + Urban_i = 1 = X_{0i}$, where X_{0i} denotes the constant regressor introduced in Equation (6.6). Thus, to estimate the regression, you must exclude one of these four variables, either one of the binary indicators or the constant term. By convention, the constant term is retained, in which case one of the binary indicators is excluded. For example, if $Rural_i$ were excluded, then the coefficient on $Suburban_i$ would be the average difference between test scores in suburban and rural districts, holding constant the other variables in the regression.

In general, if there are G binary variables, if each observation falls into one and only one category, if there is an intercept in the regression, and if all G binary variables are included as regressors, then the regression will fail because of perfect multicollinearity. This situation is called the **dummy variable trap**. The usual way to avoid the dummy variable trap is to exclude one of the binary variables from the multiple regression, so only $G - 1$ of the G binary variables are included as regressors. In this case, the coefficients on the included binary variables represent the incremental effect of being in that category, relative to the base case of the omitted category, holding constant the other regressors. Alternatively, all G binary regressors can be included if the intercept is omitted from the regression.

Solutions to perfect multicollinearity.   Perfect multicollinearity typically arises when a mistake has been made in specifying the regression. Sometimes the mistake is easy to spot (as in the first example) but sometimes it is not (as in the second example). In one way or another your software will let you know if you make such a mistake because it cannot compute the OLS estimator if you have.

When your software lets you know that you have perfect multicollinearity, it is important that you modify your regression to eliminate it. Some software is unreliable when there is perfect multicollinearity, and at a minimum you will be ceding control over your choice of regressors to your computer if your regressors are perfectly multicollinear.

Imperfect Multicollinearity

Despite its similar name, imperfect multicollinearity is conceptually quite different than perfect multicollinearity. **Imperfect multicollinearity** means that two or more of the regressors are highly correlated, in the sense that there is a linear function of the regressors that is highly correlated with another regressor. Imperfect multicollinearity does not pose any problems for the theory of the OLS estimators; indeed, a purpose of OLS is to sort out the independent influences of the various regressors when these regressors are potentially correlated.

If the regressors are imperfectly multicollinear, then the coefficients on at least one individual regressor will be imprecisely estimated. For example, consider the regression of *TestScore* on *STR* and *PctEL*. Suppose we were to add a third regressor, the percentage the district's residents who are first-generation immigrants. First-generation immigrants often speak English as a second language, so the variables *PctEL* and percentage immigrants will be highly correlated: Districts with many recent immigrants will tend to have many students who are still learning English. Because these two variables are highly correlated, it would be difficult to use these data to estimate the partial effect on test scores of an increase in *PctEL*, holding constant the percentage immigrants. In other words, the data set provides little information about what happens to test scores when the percentage of English learners is low but the fraction of immigrants is high, or vice versa. If the least squares assumptions hold, then the OLS estimator of the coefficient on *PctEL* in this regression will be unbiased; however, it will have a larger variance than if the regressors *PctEL* and percentage immigrants were uncorrelated.

The effect of imperfect multicollinearity on the variance of the OLS estimators can be seen mathematically by inspecting Equation (6.17) in Appendix 6.2, which is the variance of $\hat{\beta}_1$ in a multiple regression with two regressors (X_1 and X_2) for the special case of a homoskedastic error. In this case, the variance of $\hat{\beta}_1$ is inversely proportional to $1 - \rho^2_{X_1,X_2}$, where ρ_{X_1,X_2} is the correlation between X_1 and X_2. The larger is the correlation between the two regressors, the closer is this term to zero and the larger is the variance of $\hat{\beta}_1$. More generally, when multiple regressors are imperfectly multicollinear, then the coefficients on one or more of these regressors will be imprecisely estimated—that is, they will have a large sampling variance.

Perfect multicollinearity is a problem that often signals the presence of a logical error. In contrast, imperfect multicollinearity is not necessarily an error, but rather just a feature of OLS, your data, and the question you are trying to answer. If the variables in your regression are the ones you meant to include—the ones you chose to address the potential for omitted variable bias—then imperfect multicollinearity implies that it will be difficult to estimate precisely one or more of the partial effects using the data at hand.

6.8 Conclusion

Regression with a single regressor is vulnerable to omitted variable bias: If an omitted variable is a determinant of the dependent variable and is correlated with the regressor, then the OLS estimator of the slope coefficient will be biased and will reflect both the effect of the regressor and the effect of the omitted variable. Multiple regression makes it possible to mitigate omitted variable bias by including the omitted variable in the regression. The coefficient on a regressor, X_1, in multiple regression is the partial effect of a change in X_1, holding constant the other included regressors. In the test score example, including the percentage of English learners as a regressor made it possible to estimate the effect on test scores of a change in the student–teacher ratio, holding constant the percentage of English learners. Doing so reduced by half the estimated effect on test scores of a change in the student-teacher ratio.

The statistical theory of multiple regression builds on the statistical theory of regression with a single regressor. The least squares assumptions for multiple regression are extensions of the three least squares assumptions for regression with a single regressor, plus a fourth assumption ruling out perfect multicollinearity. Because the regression coefficients are estimated using a single sample, the OLS estimators have a joint sampling distribution and, therefore, have sampling uncertainty. This sampling uncertainty must be quantified as part of an empirical study, and the ways to do so in the multiple regression model are the topic of the next chapter.

Summary

1. Omitted variable bias occurs when an omitted variable (1) is correlated with an included regressor and (2) is a determinant of Y.
2. The multiple regression model is a linear regression model that includes multiple regressors, $X_1, X_2, \ldots, X_k$. Associated with each regressor is a regression coefficient, $\beta_1, \beta_2, \ldots, \beta_k$. The coefficient β_1 is the expected change in Y associated with a one-unit change in X_1, holding the other regressors constant. The other regression coefficients have an analogous interpretation.
3. The coefficients in multiple regression can be estimated by OLS. When the four least squares assumptions in Key Concept 6.4 are satisfied, the OLS estimators are unbiased, consistent, and normally distributed in large samples.
4. Perfect multicollinearity, which occurs when one regressor is an exact linear function of the other regressors, usually arises from a mistake in choosing which

regressors to include in a multiple regression. Solving perfect multicollinearity requires changing the set of regressors.

5. The standard error of the regression, the R^2, and the $\overline{R}^2$ are measures of fit for the multiple regression model.

Key Terms

omitted variable bias (185)
multiple regression model (191)
population regression line (191)
population regression function (191)
intercept (191)
slope coefficient of X_{1i} (191)
coefficient on X_{1i} (191)
slope coefficient of X_{2i} (191)
coefficient on X_{2i} (191)
control variable (191)
holding X_2 constant (192)
controlling for X_2 (192)
partial effect (192)

population multiple regression
   model (193)
constant regressor constant term (193)
homoskedastic (193)
heteroskedastic (193)
OLS estimators of $\beta_0, \beta_1, \ldots, \beta_k$ (195)
OLS regression line (195)
predicted value (195)
OLS residual (195)
R^2 and adjusted R^2 ($\overline{R}^2$) (198, 199)
perfect multicollinearity or to exhibit
   perfect multicollinearity (202)
dummy variable trap (206)
imperfect multicollinearity (207)

Review the Concepts

6.1 A researcher is interested in the effect on test scores of computer usage. Using school district data like that used in this chapter, she regresses district average test scores on the number of computers per student. Will $\hat{\beta}_1$ be an unbiased estimator of the effect on test scores of increasing the number of computers per student? Why or why not? If you think $\hat{\beta}_1$ is biased, is it biased up or down? Why?

6.2 A multiple regression includes two regressors: $Y_i = \beta_0 + \beta_1 X_{1i} + \beta_2 X_{2i} + u_i$. What is the expected change in Y if X_1 increases by 3 units and X_2 is unchanged? What is the expected change in Y if X_2 decreases by 5 units and X_1 is unchanged? What is the expected change in Y if X_1 increases by 3 units and X_2 decreases by 5 units?

6.3 Explain why two perfectly multicollinear regressors cannot be included in a linear multiple regression. Give two examples of a pair of perfectly multicollinear regressors.

6.4 Explain why it is difficult to estimate precisely the partial effect of X_1, holding X_2 constant, if X_1 and X_2 are highly correlated.

Exercises

The first four exercises refer to the table of estimated regressions on page 213, computed using data for 1998 from the CPS. The data set consists of information on 4000 full-time full-year workers. The highest educational achievement for each worker was either a high school diploma or a bachelor's degree. The worker's ages ranged from 25 to 34 years. The data set also contained information on the region of the country where the person lived, marital status, and number of children. For the purposes of these exercises let

AHE = average hourly earnings (in 1998 dollars)
$College$ = binary variable (1 if college, 0 if high school)
$Female$ = binary variable (1 if female, 0 if male)
Age = age (in years)
$Ntheast$ = binary variable (1 if Region = Northeast, 0 otherwise)
$Midwest$ = binary variable (1 if Region = Midwest, 0 otherwise)
$South$ = binary variable (1 if Region = South, 0 otherwise)
$West$ = binary variable (1 if Region = West, 0 otherwise)

6.1 Compute $\overline{R}^2$ for each of the regressions.

6.2 Using the regression results in column (1):

a. Do workers with college degrees earn more, on average, than workers with only high school degrees? How much more?

b. Do men earn more than women on average? How much more?

6.3 Using the regression results in column (2):

a. Is age an important determinant of earnings? Explain.

b. Sally is 29-year-old female college graduate. Betsy is a 34-year-old female college graduate. Predict Sally's and Betsy's earnings.

6.4 Using the regression results in column (3):

a. Do there appear to be important regional differences?

b. Why is the regressor *West* omitted from the regression? What would happen if it was included?

Results of Regressions of Average Hourly Earnings on Gender and Education Binary Variables and Other Characteristics Using 1998 Data from the Current Population Survey

Dependent variable: average hourly earnings (AHE).

Regressor	(1)	(2)	(3)
College (X_1)	5.46	5.48	5.44
Female (X_2)	−2.64	−2.62	−2.62
Age (X_3)		0.29	0.29
Northeast (X_4)			0.69
Midwest (X_5)			0.60
South (X_6)			−0.27
Intercept	12.69	4.40	3.75
Summary Statistics			
SER	6.27	6.22	6.21
R^2	0.176	0.190	0.194
$\overline{R}^2$			
n	4000	4000	4000

   c. Juanita is a 28-year-old female college graduate from the South. Jennifer is a 28-year-old female college graduate from the Midwest. Calculate the expected difference in earnings between Juanita and Jennifer.

6.5 Data were collected from a random sample of 220 home sales from a community in 2003. Let *Price* denote the selling price (in $1000), *BDR* denote the number of bedrooms, *Bath* denote the number of bathrooms, *Hsize* denote the size of the house (in square feet), *Lsize* denote the lot size (in square feet), *Age* denote the age of the house (in years), and *Poor* denote a binary variable that is equal to 1 if the condition of the house is reported as "poor." An estimated regression yields

$$\widehat{Price} = 119.2 + 0.485BDR + 23.4Bath + 0.156Hsize + 0.002Lsize$$
$$+ 0.090Age - 48.8Poor, \ \overline{R}^2 = 0.72, \ SER = 41.5.$$

a. Suppose that a homeowner converts part of an existing family room in her house into a new bathroom. What is the expected increase in the value of the house?

b. Suppose that a homeowner adds a new bathroom to her house, which increases the size of the house by 100 square feet. What is the expected increase in the value of the house?

c. What is the loss in value if a homeowner lets his house run down so that its condition becomes "poor"?

d. Compute the R^2 for the regression.

6.6 A researcher plans to study the causal effect of police on crime using data from a random sample of U.S. counties. He plans to regress the county's crime rate on the (per capita) size of the county's police force.

a. Explain why this regression is likely to suffer from omitted variable bias. Which variables would you add to the regression to control for important omitted variables?

b. Use your answer to (a) and the expression for omitted variable bias given in Equation (6.1) to determine whether the regression will likely over- or underestimate the effect of police on the crime rate. (That is, do you think that $\hat{\beta}_1 > \beta_1$ or $\hat{\beta}_1 < \beta_1$?)

6.7 Critique each of the following proposed research plans. Your critique should explain any problems with the proposed research and describe how the research plan might be improved. Include a discussion of any additional data that need to be collected and the appropriate statistical techniques for analyzing the data.

a. A researcher is interested in determining whether a large aerospace firm is guilty of gender bias in setting wages. To determine potential bias, the researcher collects salary and gender information for all of the firm's engineers. The researcher then plans to conduct a "difference in means" test to determine whether the average salary for women are significantly less than the average salary for men.

b. A researcher is interested in determining whether time spent in prison has a permanent effect on a person's wage rate. He collects data on a random sample of people who have been out of prison for at least fifteen years. He collects similar data on a random sample of people who have never served time in prison. The data set includes information on each person's current wage, education, age, ethnicity, gender, tenure (time in current job), occupation, and union status, as well as whether the person was ever incarcerated. The researcher plans to estimate the effect of incarceration on wages by regressing wages on an indicator variable for incarceration, including in the regression the other potential determinants of wages (education, tenure, union status, and so on).

6.8 A recent study found that the death rate for people who sleep six to seven hours per night is lower than the death rate for people who sleep eight or more hours, and higher than the death rate for people who sleep five or fewer hours. The 1.1 million observations used for this study came from a random survey of Americans aged 30 to 102. Each survey respondent was tracked for four years. The death rate for people sleeping seven hours was calculated as the ratio of the number of deaths over the span of the study among people sleeping seven hours to the total number of survey respondents who slept seven hours. This calculation was then repeated for people sleeping six hours, and so on. Based on this summary, would you recommend that Americans who sleep nine hours per night consider reducing their sleep to six or seven hours if they want to prolong their lives? Why or why not? Explain.

6.9 (Y_i, X_{1i}, X_{2i}) satisfy the assumptions in Key Concept 6.4. You are interested in β_1, the causal effect of X_1 on Y. Suppose that X_1 and X_2 are uncorrelated. You estimate β_1 by regressing Y onto X_1 (so that X_2 is not included in the regression). Does this estimator suffer from omitted variable bias? Explain.

6.10 (Y_i, X_{1i}, X_{2i}) satisfy the assumptions in Key Concept 6.4; in addition, $var(u_i | X_{1i}, X_{2i}) = 4$ and $var(X_{1i}) = 6$. A random sample of size $n = 400$ is drawn from the population.

    a. Assume that X_1 and X_2 are uncorrelated. Compute the variance of $\hat{\beta}_1$. [*Hint:* Look at Equation (6.17) in the Appendix 6.2.)

    b. Assume that $cor(X_1, X_2) = 0.5$. Compute the variance of $\hat{\beta}_1$.

    c. Comment on the following statements: "When X_1 and X_2 are correlated, the variance of $\hat{\beta}_1$ is larger than it would be if X_1 and X_2 were uncorrelated. Thus, if you are interested in β_1, it is best to leave X_2 out of the regression if it is correlated with X_1."

6.11 (Requires calculus) Consider the regression model

$$Y_i = \beta_1 X_{1i} + \beta_2 X_{2i} + u_i$$

for $i = 1, \ldots, n$. (Notice that there is no constant term in the regression.) Following analysis like that used in Appendix 4.2:

a. Specify the least squares function that is minimized by OLS.

b. Compute the partial derivatives of the objection function with respect to b_1 and b_2.

c. Suppose $\sum_{i=1}^{n} X_{1i} X_{2i} = 0$. Show that $\hat{\beta}_1 = \sum_{i=1}^{n} X_{1i} Y_i / \sum_{i=1}^{n} X_{1i}^2$.

d. Suppose $\sum_{i=1}^{n} X_{1i} X_{2i} \neq 0$. Derive an expression for $\hat{\beta}_1$ as a function of the data $(Y_i, X_{1i}, X_{2i}), i = 1, \ldots, n$.

e. Suppose that the model includes an intercept:
$Y_i = \beta_0 + \beta_1 X_{1i} + \beta_2 X_{2i} + u_i$. Show that the least squares estimators satisfy $\hat{\beta}_0 = \overline{Y} - \hat{\beta}_1 \overline{X}_1 - \hat{\beta}_2 \overline{X}_2$.

Empirical Exercises

E6.1 Using the data set **TeachingRatings** described in Empirical Exercises 4.2, carry out the following exercises.

a. Run a regression of *Course_Eval* on *Beauty*. What is the estimated slope?

b. Run a regression of *Course_Eval* on *Beauty*, including some additional variables to control for the type of course and professor characteristics. In particular, include as additional regressors *Intro, OneCredit, Female, Minority,* and *NNEnglish*. What is the estimated effect of *Beauty* on *Course_Eval*? Does the regression in (a) suffer from important omitted variable bias?

c. Professor Smith is a black male with average beauty and is a native English speaker. He teaches a three-credit upper-division course. Predict Professor Smith's course evaluation.

E6.2 Using the data set **CollegeDistance** described in Empirical Exercise 4.3, carry out the following exercises.

a. Run a regression of years of completed education (*ED*) on distance to the nearest college (*Dist*). What is the estimated slope?

b. Run a regression of *ED* on *Dist*, but include some additional regressors to control for characteristics of the student, the student's family, and the local labor market. In particular, include as additional regressors *Bytest, Female, Black, Hispanic, Incomehi, Ownhome, DadColl, Cue80,* and *Stwmfg80*. What is the estimated effect of *Dist* on *ED*?

c. Is the estimated effect of *Dist* on *ED* in the regression in (b) substantively different from the regression in (a)? Based on this, does the regression in (a) seem to suffer from important omitted variable bias?

d. Compare the fit of the regression in (a) and (b) using the regression standard errors, R^2 and $\overline{R}^2$. Why are the R^2 and $\overline{R}^2$ so similar in regression (b)?

e. The value of the coefficient on *DadColl* is positive. What does this coefficient measure?

f. Explain why *Cue80* and *Swmfg80* appear in the regression. Are the signs of their estimated coefficients (+ or −) what you would have believed? Interpret the magnitudes of these coefficients.

g. Bob is a black male. His high school was 20 miles from the nearest college. His base-year composite test score (*Bytest*) was 58. His family income in 1980 was $26,000, and his family owned a home. His mother attended college, but his father did not. The unemployment rate in his county was 7.5%, and the state average manufacturing hourly wage was $9.75. Predict Bob's years of completed schooling using the regression in (b).

h. Jim has the same characteristics as Bob except that his high school was 40 miles from the nearest college. Predict Jim's years of completed schooling using the regression in (b).

E6.3 Using the data set **Growth** described in Empirical Exercise 4.4, but excluding the data for Malta, carry out the following exercises.

a. Construct a table that shows the sample mean, standard deviation, and minimum and maximum values for the series *Growth, TradeShare, YearsSchool, Oil, Rev_Coups, Assassinations, RGDP60*. Include the appropriate units for all entries.

b. Run a regression of *Growth* on *TradeShare, YearsSchool, Rev_Coups, Assassinations* and *RGDP60*. What is the value of the coefficient on *Rev_Coups*? Interpret the value of this coefficient. Is it large or small in a real-world sense?

c. Use the regression to predict the average annual growth rate for a country that has average values for all regressors.

d. Repeat (c) but now assume that the country's value for *TradeShare* is one standard deviation above the mean.

e. Why is *Oil* omitted from the regression? What would happen if it were included?

6.1 Derivation of Equation (6.1)

This appendix presents a derivation of the formula for omitted variable bias in Equation (6.1). Equation (4.30) in Appendix 4.3 states that

$$\hat{\beta}_1 = \beta_1 + \frac{\frac{1}{n}\sum_{i=1}^{n}(X_i - \overline{X})u_i}{\frac{1}{n}\sum_{i=1}^{n}(X_i - \overline{X})^2}. \qquad (6.16)$$

Under the last two assumptions in Key Concept 4.3, $\frac{1}{n}\sum_{i=1}^{n}(X_i - \overline{X})^2 \xrightarrow{p} \sigma_X^2$ and $\frac{1}{n}\sum_{i=1}^{n}(X_i - \overline{X})u_i \xrightarrow{p} \mathrm{cov}(u_i, X_i) = \rho_{Xu}\sigma_u\sigma_X$. Substitution of these limits into Equation (6.16) yields Equation (6.1).

6.2 Distribution of the OLS Estimators When There Are Two Regressors and Homoskedastic Errors

Although the general formula for the variance of the OLS estimators in multiple regression is complicated, if there are two regressors ($k = 2$) and the errors are homoskedastic, then the formula simplifies enough to provide some insights into the distribution of the OLS estimators.

Because the errors are homoskedastic, the conditional variance of u_i can be written as $\mathrm{var}(u_i | X_{1i}, X_{2i}) = \sigma_u^2$. When there are two regressors, X_{1i} and X_{2i}, and the error term is homoskedastic, in large samples the sampling distribution of $\hat{\beta}_1$ is $N(\beta_1, \sigma_{\hat{\beta}_1}^2)$, where the variance of this distribution, $\sigma_{\hat{\beta}_1}^2$, is

$$\sigma_{\hat{\beta}_1}^2 = \frac{1}{n}\left[\frac{1}{1 - \rho_{X_1, X_2}^2}\right]\frac{\sigma_u^2}{\sigma_{X_1}^2}, \qquad (6.17)$$

where ρ_{X_1, X_2} is the population correlation between the two regressors X_1 and X_2 and $\sigma_{X_1}^2$ is the population variance of X_1.

The variance $\sigma_{\hat{\beta}_1}^2$ of the sampling distribution of $\hat{\beta}_1$ depends on the squared correlation between the regressors. If X_1 and X_2 are highly correlated, either positively or negatively, then $\rho^2_{X_1,X_2}$ is close to 1, and thus the term $1 - \rho^2_{X_1,X_2}$ in the denominator of Equation (6.17) is small and the variance of $\hat{\beta}_1$ is larger than it would be if ρ_{X_1,X_2} were close to 0.

Another feature of the joint normal large-sample distribution of the OLS estimators is that $\hat{\beta}_1$ and $\hat{\beta}_2$ are in general correlated. When the errors are homoskedastic, the correlation between the OLS estimators $\hat{\beta}_1$ and $\hat{\beta}_2$ is the negative of the correlation between the two regressors:

$$\text{corr}(\hat{\beta}_1,\hat{\beta}_2) = -\rho_{X_1,X_2}. \tag{6.18}$$

APPENDIX
6.3 The OLS Estimator With Two Regressors

When there are $k = 2$ regressors [see Equation (6.5)], there is a relatively simple formula for the OLS estimator. Specifically, the OLS estimator for the coefficient β_1 on the regressor X_1 can be computed in two steps. In the first step, regress Y on X_2 (including an intercept), and denote the residuals from this regression as $Y^\perp$. Similarly, regress X_1 on X_2 (including an intercept), and denote the residuals from this regression by $X_1^\perp$. In the second step, regress $Y^\perp$ on $X_1^\perp$, excluding an intercept. The OLS coefficient in this second step is,

$$\hat{\beta}_1 = \frac{\displaystyle\sum_{i=1}^n X_{1,i}^\perp Y_i^\perp}{\displaystyle\sum_{i=1}^n (X_{1,i}^\perp)^2} \tag{6.19}$$

The estimator in Equation (6.19) is the OLS estimator of the coefficient on X_1 in the multiple regression of Y on X_1 and X_2, including an intercept. (This second-step regression does not, however, report the correct standard error for $\hat{\beta}_1$.)

The OLS estimator of $\hat{\beta}_2$ is obtained analogously by switching X_1 and X_2 in the algorithm of the previous paragraph. The OLS estimator of β_0 is then given by $\hat{\beta}_0 = \bar{Y} - \hat{\beta}_1\bar{X}_1 - \hat{\beta}_2\bar{X}_2$.

Equation (6.19) has the following interpretation: because the residual $X_1^\perp$ is uncorrelated with X_2 in the sample, the OLS estimator of β_1 in the multiple regression including X_1 and X_2 is obtained using the part of X_1 that is uncorrelated with X_2 in the sample.

CHAPTER 7

Hypothesis Tests and Confidence Intervals in Multiple Regression

As discussed in Chapter 6, multiple regression analysis provides a way to mitigate the problem of omitted variable bias by including additional regressors, thereby controlling for the effects of those additional regressors. The coefficients of the multiple regression model can be estimated by OLS. Like all estimators, the OLS estimator has sampling uncertainty because its value differs from one sample to the next.

This chapter presents methods for quantifying the sampling uncertainty of the OLS estimator through the use of standard errors, statistical hypothesis tests, and confidence intervals. One new possibility that arises in multiple regression is a hypothesis that simultaneously involves two or more regression coefficients. The general approach to testing such "joint" hypotheses involves a new test statistic, the *F*-statistic.

Section 7.1 extends the methods for statistical inference in regression with a single regressor to multiple regression. Sections 7.2 and 7.3 show how to test hypotheses that involve two or more regression coefficients. Section 7.4 extends the notion of confidence intervals for a single coefficient to confidence sets for multiple coefficients. Deciding which variables to include in a regression is an important practical issue, so Section 7.5 discusses ways to approach this problem. In Section 7.6, we apply multiple regression analysis to obtain improved estimates of the effect on test scores of a reduction in the student–teacher ratio using the California test score data set.

7.1   Hypothesis Tests and Confidence Intervals for a Single Coefficient

This section describes how to compute the standard error, how to test hypotheses, and how to construct confidence intervals for a single coefficient in a multiple regression equation.

Standard Errors for the OLS Estimators

Recall that, in the case of a single regressor, it was possible to estimate the variance of the OLS estimator by substituting sample averages for expectations, which led to the estimator $\hat{\sigma}^2_{\hat{\beta}_1}$ given in Equation (5.4). Under the least squares assumptions, the law of large numbers implies that these sample averages converge to their population counterparts, so for example $\hat{\sigma}^2_{\hat{\beta}_1} / \sigma^2_{\hat{\beta}_1} \xrightarrow{p} 1$. The square root of $\hat{\sigma}^2_{\hat{\beta}_1}$ is the standard error of $\hat{\beta}_1$, $SE(\hat{\beta}_1)$, an estimator of the standard deviation of the sampling distribution of $\hat{\beta}_1$.

All this extends directly to multiple regression. The OLS estimator $\hat{\beta}_j$ of the jth regression coefficient has a standard deviation, and this standard deviation is estimated by its standard error, $SE(\hat{\beta}_j)$. The formula for the standard error is most easily stated using matrices. The important point is that, as far as standard errors are concerned, there is nothing conceptually different between the single- or multiple-regressor cases. The key ideas—the large-sample normality of the estimators and the ability to estimate consistently the standard deviation of their sampling distribution—are the same whether one has one, two, or 12 regressors.

Hypothesis Tests for a Single Coefficient

Suppose that you want to test the hypothesis that a change in the student–teacher ratio has no effect on test scores, holding constant the percentage of English learners in the district. This corresponds to hypothesizing that the true coefficient β_1 on the student–teacher ratio is zero in the population regression of test scores on STR and $PctEL$. More generally, we might want to test the hypothesis that the true coefficient β_j on the jth regressor takes on some specific value, $\beta_{j,0}$. The null value $\beta_{j,0}$ comes either from economic theory or, as in the student–teacher ratio example, from the decision-making context of the application. If the alternative hypothesis is two-sided, then the two hypotheses can be written mathematically as

$$H_0: \beta_j = \beta_{j,0} \text{ vs. } H_1: \beta_j \neq \beta_{j,0} \quad \text{(two-sided alternative)}. \qquad (7.1)$$

TESTING THE HYPOTHESIS $\beta_j = \beta_{j,0}$ AGAINST THE ALTERNATIVE $\beta_j \neq \beta_{j,0}$

1. Compute the standard error of $\hat{\beta}_j$, $SE(\hat{\beta}_j)$.

2. Compute the t-statistic,

$$t = \frac{\hat{\beta}_j - \beta_{j,0}}{SE(\hat{\beta}_j)}.$$ (7.2)

3. Compute the p-value,

$$p\text{-value} = 2\Phi(-|t^{act}|),$$ (7.3)

where t^{act} is the value of the t-statistic actually computed. Reject the hypothesis at the 5% significance level if the p-value is less than 0.05 or, equivalently, if $|t^{act}| > 1.96$.

The standard error and (typically) the t-statistic and p-value testing $\beta_j = 0$ are computed automatically by regression software.

For example, if the first regressor is *STR*, then the null hypothesis that changing the student–teacher ratio has no effect on class size corresponds to the null hypothesis that $\beta_1 = 0$ (so $\beta_{1,0} = 0$). Our task is to test the null hypothesis H_0 against the alternative H_1 using a sample of data.

Key Concept 5.2 gives a procedure for testing this null hypothesis when there is a single regressor. The first step in this procedure is to calculate the standard error of the coefficient. The second step is to calculate the t-statistic using the general formula in Key Concept 5.1. The third step is to compute the p-value of the test using the cumulative normal distribution in Appendix Table 1 or, alternatively, to compare the t-statistic to the critical value corresponding to the desired significance level of the test. The theoretical underpinning of this procedure is that the OLS estimator has a large-sample normal distribution which, under the null hypothesis, has as its mean the hypothesized true value, and that the variance of this distribution can be estimated consistently.

This underpinning is present in multiple regression as well. As stated in Key Concept 6.5, the sampling distribution of $\hat{\beta}_j$ is approximately normal. Under the null hypothesis the mean of this distribution is $\beta_{j,0}$. The variance of this distribution can be estimated consistently. Therefore we can simply follow the same procedure as in the single-regressor case to test the null hypothesis in Equation (7.1).

The procedure for testing a hypothesis on a single coefficient in multiple regression is summarized as Key Concept 7.1. The t-statistic actually computed is

---

CONFIDENCE INTERVALS FOR A SINGLE
COEFFICIENT IN MULTIPLE REGRESSION

KEY CONCEPT

7.2

A 95% two-sided confidence interval for the coefficient β_j is an interval that contains the true value of β_j with a 95% probability; that is, it contains the true value of β_j in 95% of all possible randomly drawn samples. Equivalently, it is the set of values of β_j that cannot be rejected by a 5% two-sided hypothesis test. When the sample size is large, the 95% confidence interval is

$$95\% \text{ confidence interval for } \beta_j = [\hat{\beta}_j - 1.96SE(\hat{\beta}_j), \hat{\beta}_j + 1.96SE(\hat{\beta}_j)]. \quad (7.4)$$

A 90% confidence interval is obtained by replacing 1.96 in Equation (7.4) with 1.645.

---

denoted t^{act} in this Key Concept. However, it is customary to denote this simply as t, and we adopt this simplified notation for the rest of the book.

Confidence Intervals for a Single Coefficient

The method for constructing a confidence interval in the multiple regression model is also the same as in the single-regressor model. This method is summarized as Key Concept 7.2.

The method for conducting a hypothesis test in Key Concept 7.1 and the method for constructing a confidence interval in Key Concept 7.2 rely on the large-sample normal approximation to the distribution of the OLS estimator $\hat{\beta}_j$. Accordingly, it should be kept in mind that these methods for quantifying the sampling uncertainty are only guaranteed to work in large samples.

Application to Test Scores and the Student–Teacher Ratio

Can we reject the null hypothesis that a change in the student–teacher ratio has no effect on test scores, once we control for the percentage of English learners in the district? What is a 95% confidence interval for the effect on test scores of a change in the student–teacher ratio, controlling for the percentage of English learners? We are now able to find out. The regression of test scores against *STR* and *PctEL,* estimated by OLS, was given in Equation (6.12) and is restated here with standard errors in parentheses below the coefficients:

$$\widehat{TestScore} = 686.0 - 1.10 \times STR - 0.650 \times PctEL. \qquad (7.5)$$
$$\quad\ (8.7)\ \ (0.43) \qquad\qquad (0.031)$$

To test the hypothesis that the true coefficient on STR is 0, we first need to compute the t-statistic in Equation (7.2). Because the null hypothesis says that the true value of this coefficient is zero, the t-statistic is $t = (-1.10 - 0)/0.43 = -2.54$. The associated p-value is $2\Phi(-2.54) = 1.1\%$; that is, the smallest significance level at which we can reject the null hypothesis is 1.1%. Because the p-value is less than 5%, the null hypothesis can be rejected at the 5% significance level (but not quite at the 1% significance level).

A 95% confidence interval for the population coefficient on STR is $-1.10 \pm 1.96 \times 0.43 = (-1.95, -0.26)$; that is, we can be 95% confident that the true value of the coefficient is between -1.95 and -0.26. Interpreted in the context of the superintendent's interest in decreasing the student–teacher ratio by 2, the 95% confidence interval for the effect on test scores of this reduction is $(-1.95 \times 2, -0.26 \times 2) = (-3.90, -0.52)$.

Adding expenditures per pupil to the equation   Your analysis of the multiple regression in Equation (7.5) has persuaded the superintendent that, based on the evidence so far, reducing class size will help test scores in her district. Now, however, she moves on to a more nuanced question. If she is to hire more teachers, she can pay for those teachers either through cuts elsewhere in the budget (no new computers, reduced maintenance, and so on), or by asking for an increase in her budget, which taxpayers do not favor. What, she asks, is the effect on test scores of reducing the student–teacher ratio, holding expenditures per pupil (and the percentage of English learners) constant?

This question can be addressed by estimating a regression of test scores on the student–teacher ratio, total spending per pupil, and the percentage of English learners. The OLS regression line is

$$\widehat{TestScore} = 649.6 - 0.29 \times STR + 3.87 \times Expn - 0.656 \times PctEL, \quad (7.6)$$
$$\quad\ (15.5)\ \ (0.48) \qquad\quad (1.59) \qquad\qquad (0.032)$$

where $Expn$ is total annual expenditures per pupil in the district in thousands of dollars.

The result is striking. Holding expenditures per pupil and the percentage of English learners constant, changing the student–teacher ratio is estimated to have a very small effect on test scores: The estimated coefficient on STR is -1.10 in Equation (7.5) but, after adding $Expn$ as a regressor in Equation (7.6), it is only -0.29. Moreover, the t-statistic for testing that the true value of the coefficient is zero is now $t = (-0.29 - 0)/0.48 = -0.60$, so the hypothesis that the population value of this coefficient is indeed zero cannot be rejected even at the 10% significance level ($|-0.60| < 1.645$). Thus Equation (7.6) provides no evidence that hiring more teachers improves test scores if overall expenditures per pupil are held constant.

One interpretation of the regression in Equation (7.6) is that, in these California data, school administrators allocate their budgets efficiently. Suppose, counterfactually, that the coefficient on STR in Equation (7.6) were negative and large. If so, school districts could raise their test scores simply by decreasing funding for other purposes (textbooks, technology, sports, and so on) and transferring those funds to hire more teachers, thereby reducing class sizes while holding expenditures constant. However, the small and statistically insignificant coefficient on STR in Equation (7.6) indicates that this transfer would have little effect on test scores. Put differently, districts are already allocating their funds efficiently.

Note that the standard error on STR increased when $Expn$ was added, from 0.43 in Equation (7.5) to 0.48 in Equation (7.6). This illustrates the general point, introduced in Section 6.7 in the context of imperfect multicollinearity, that correlation between regressors (the correlation between STR and $Expn$ is -0.62) can make the OLS estimators less precise.

What about our angry taxpayer? He asserts that the population values of *both* the coefficient on the student–teacher ratio (β_1) *and* the coefficient on spending per pupil (β_2) are zero, that is, he hypothesizes that both $\beta_1 = 0$ and $\beta_2 = 0$. Although it might seem that we can reject this hypothesis because the t-statistic testing $\beta_2 = 0$ in Equation (7.6) is $t = 3.87/1.59 = 2.43$, this reasoning is flawed. The taxpayer's hypothesis is a joint hypothesis, and to test it we need a new tool, the F-statistic.

7.2   Tests of Joint Hypotheses

This section describes how to formulate joint hypotheses on multiple regression coefficients and how to test them using an F-statistic.

Testing Hypotheses on Two or More Coefficients

Joint null hypotheses.   Consider the regression in Equation (7.6) of the test score against the student–teacher ratio, expenditures per pupil, and the percentage of English learners. Our angry taxpayer hypothesizes that neither the student–teacher ratio nor expenditures per pupil have an effect on test scores, once we control for the percentage of English learners. Because STR is the first regressor in Equation (7.6) and $Expn$ is the second, we can write this hypothesis mathematically as

$$H_0\colon \beta_1 = 0 \text{ and } \beta_2 = 0 \text{ vs. } H_1\colon \beta_1 \neq 0 \text{ and/or } \beta_2 \neq 0. \qquad (7.7)$$

The hypothesis that *both* the coefficient on the student–teacher ratio (β_1) *and* the coefficient on expenditures per pupil (β_2) are zero is an example of a joint hypothesis on the coefficients in the multiple regression model. In this case, the null hypothesis restricts the value of two of the coefficients, so as a matter of terminology we can say that the null hypothesis in Equation (7.7) imposes two **restrictions** on the multiple regression model: $\beta_1 = 0$ *and* $\beta_2 = 0$.

In general, a **joint hypothesis** is a hypothesis that imposes two or more restrictions on the regression coefficients. We consider joint null and alternative hypotheses of the form

$$\begin{aligned} &H_0\colon \beta_j = \beta_{j,0}, \beta_m = \beta_{m,0}, \ldots, \text{ for a total of } q \text{ restrictions, vs.} \\ &H_1\colon \text{one or more of the } q \text{ restrictions under } H_0 \text{ does not hold,} \end{aligned} \qquad (7.8)$$

where $\beta_j, \beta_m, \ldots,$ refer to different regression coefficients, and $\beta_{j,0}, \beta_{m,0}, \ldots,$ refer to the values of these coefficients under the null hypothesis. The null hypothesis in Equation (7.7) is an example of Equation (7.8). Another example is that, in a regression with $k = 6$ regressors, the null hypothesis is that the coefficients on the $2^{nd}, 4^{th},$ and 5th regressors are zero; that is, $\beta_2 = 0, \beta_4 = 0,$ and $\beta_5 = 0,$ so that there are $q = 3$ restrictions. In general, under the null hypothesis H_0 there are q such restrictions.

If any one (or more than one) of the equalities under the null hypothesis H_0 in Equation (7.8) is false, then the joint null hypothesis itself is false. Thus, the alternative hypothesis is that at least one of the equalities in the null hypothesis H_0 does not hold.

Why can't I just test the individual coefficients one at a time? Although it seems it should be possible to test a joint hypothesis by using the usual t-statistics to test the restrictions one at a time, the following calculation shows that this approach is unreliable. Specifically, suppose that you are interested in testing the joint null hypothesis in Equation (7.6) that $\beta_1 = 0$ and $\beta_2 = 0$. Let t_1 be the t-statistic for testing the null hypothesis that $\beta_1 = 0$, and let t_2 be the t-statistic for testing the null hypothesis that $\beta_2 = 0$. What happens when you use the "one at a time" testing procedure: Reject the joint null hypothesis if either t_1 or t_2 exceeds 1.96 in absolute value?

Because this question involves the two random variables t_1 and t_2, answering it requires characterizing the joint sampling distribution of t_1 and t_2. As mentioned in Section 6.6, in large samples $\hat{\beta}_1$ and $\hat{\beta}_2$ have a joint normal distribution, so under the joint null hypothesis the t-statistics t_1 and t_2 have a bivariate normal distribution, where each t-statistic has mean equal to 0 and variance equal to 1.

First consider the special case in which the t-statistics are uncorrelated and thus are independent. What is the size of the "one at a time" testing procedure; that is, what is the probability that you will reject the null hypothesis when it is true? More than 5%! In this special case we can calculate the rejection probability of this method exactly. The null is *not* rejected only if both $|t_1| \leq 1.96$ and $|t_2| \leq 1.96$. Because the t-statistics are independent, $\Pr(|t_1| \leq 1.96 \text{ and } |t_2| \leq 1.96)$ $= \Pr(|t_1| \leq 1.96) \times \Pr(|t_2| \leq 1.96) = 0.95^2 = 0.9025 = 90.25\%$. So the probability of rejecting the null hypothesis when it is true is $1 - 0.95^2 = 9.75\%$. This "one at a time" method rejects the null too often because it gives you too many chances: If you fail to reject using the first t-statistic, you get to try again using the second.

If the regressors are correlated, the situation is even more complicated. The size of the "one at a time" procedure depends on the value of the correlation between the regressors. Because the "one at a time" testing approach has the wrong size—that is, its rejection rate under the null hypothesis does not equal the desired significance level—a new approach is needed.

One approach is to modify the "one at a time" method so that it uses different critical values that ensure that its size equals its significance level. This method, called the Bonferroni method, is described in Appendix 7.1. The advantage of the Bonferroni method is that it applies very generally. Its disadvantage is that it can have low power; it frequently fails to reject the null hypothesis when in fact the alternative hypothesis is true.

Fortunately, there is another approach to testing joint hypotheses that is more powerful, especially when the regressors are highly correlated. That approach is based on the F-statistic.

The *F*-Statistic

The **F-statistic** is used to test joint hypothesis about regression coefficients. The formulas for the F-statistic are integrated into modern regression software. We first discuss the case of two restrictions, then turn to the general case of q restrictions.

The F-statistic with q = 2 restrictions.   When the joint null hypothesis has the two restrictions that $\beta_1 = 0$ and $\beta_2 = 0$, the F-statistic combines the two t-statistics t_1 and t_2 using the formula

$$F = \frac{1}{2}\left(\frac{t_1^2 + t_2^2 - 2\hat{\rho}_{t_1,t_2}t_1t_2}{1 - \hat{\rho}_{t_1,t_2}^2}\right), \tag{7.9}$$

where $\hat{\rho}_{t_1,t_2}$ is an estimator of the correlation between the two t-statistics.

To understand the F-statistic in Equation (7.9), first suppose that we know that the t-statistics are uncorrelated so we can drop the terms involving $\hat{\rho}_{t_1,t_2}$. If so, Equation (7.9) simplifies and $F = \frac{1}{2}(t_1^2 + t_2^2)$; that is, the F-statistic is the average of the squared t-statistics. Under the null hypothesis, t_1 and t_2 are independent standard normal random variables (because the t-statistics are uncorrelated by assumption), so under the null hypothesis F has an $F_{2,\infty}$ distribution (Section 2.4). Under the alternative hypothesis that either β_1 is nonzero or β_2 is nonzero (or both), then either t_1^2 or t_2^2 (or both) will be large, leading the test to reject the null hypothesis.

In general the t-statistics are correlated, and the formula for the F-statistic in Equation (7.9) adjusts for this correlation. This adjustment is made so that, under the null hypothesis, the F-statistic has an $F_{2,\infty}$ distribution in large samples whether or not the t-statistics are correlated.

The F-statistic with q restrictions. The formula for the heteroskedasticity-robust F-statistic testing the q restrictions of the joint null hypothesis in Equation (7.8) is a matrix extension of the formula for the heteroskedasticity-robust t-statistic. This formula is incorporated into regression software, making the F-statistic easy to compute in practice.

Under the null hypothesis, the F-statistic has a sampling distribution that, in large samples, is given by the $F_{q,\infty}$ distribution. That is, in large samples, under the null hypothesis

$$\text{the } F\text{-statistic is distributed } F_{q,\infty}. \tag{7.10}$$

Thus the critical values for the F-statistic can be obtained from the tables of the $F_{q,\infty}$ distribution in Appendix Table 4 for the appropriate value of q and the desired significance level.

Computing the heteroskedasticity-robust F-statistic in statistical software. If the F-statistic is computed using the general heteroskedasticity-robust formula, its large-n distribution under the null hypothesis is $F_{q,\infty}$ regardless of whether the errors are homoskedastic or heteroskedastic. As discussed in Section 5.4, for historical reasons most statistical software computes homoskedasticity-only standard errors by default. Consequently, in some software packages you must select a "robust" option so that the F-statistic is computed using heteroskedasticity-robust standard errors (and, more generally, a heteroskedasticity-robust estimate of the "covariance matrix"). The homoskedasticity-only version of the F-statistic is discussed at the end of this section.

Computing the p-value using the F-statistic.   The *p*-value of the *F*-statistic can be computed using the large-sample $F_{q,\infty}$ approximation to its distribution. Let F^{act} denote the value of the *F*-statistic actually computed. Because the *F*-statistic has a large-sample $F_{q,\infty}$ distribution under the null hypothesis, the *p*-value is

$$p\text{-value} = \Pr[F_{q,\infty} > F^{act}]. \tag{7.11}$$

The *p*-value in Equation (7.11) can be evaluated using a table of the $F_{q,\infty}$ distribution (or, alternatively, a table of the χ_q^2 distribution, because a χ_q^2-distributed random variable is *q* times an $F_{q,\infty}$-distributed random variable). Alternatively, the *p*-value can be evaluated using a computer, because formulas for the cumulative chi-squared and *F* distributions have been incorporated into most modern statistical software.

The "overall" regression F-statistic.   The "overall" regression *F*-statistic tests the joint hypothesis that *all* the slope coefficients are zero. That is, the null and alternative hypotheses are

$$H_0: \beta_1 = 0, \beta_2 = 0, \ldots, \beta_k = 0 \text{ vs. } H_1: \beta_j \neq 0, \text{ at least one } j, j = 1, \ldots, k. \tag{7.12}$$

Under this null hypothesis, none of the regressors explains any of the variation in Y_i, although the intercept (which under the null hypothesis is the mean of Y_i) can be nonzero. The null hypothesis in Equation (7.12) is a special case of the general null hypothesis in Equation (7.8), and the overall regression *F*-statistic is the *F*-statistic computed for the null hypothesis in Equation (7.12). In large samples, the overall regression *F*-statistic has an $F_{k,\infty}$ distribution when the null hypothesis is true.

The F-statistic when q = 1.   When *q* = 1, the *F*-statistic tests a single restriction. Then the joint null hypothesis reduces to the null hypothesis on a single regression coefficient, and the *F*-statistic is the square of the *t*-statistic.

Application to Test Scores and the Student–Teacher Ratio

We are now able to test the null hypothesis that the coefficients on *both* the student–teacher ratio *and* expenditures per pupil are zero, against the alternative that at least one coefficient is nonzero, controlling for the percentage of English learners in the district.

To test this hypothesis, we need to compute the heteroskedasticity-robust *F*-statistic of the test that $\beta_1 = 0$ and $\beta_2 = 0$ using the regression of *TestScore* on

STR, Expn, and *PctEL* reported in Equation (7.6). This *F*-statistic is 5.43. Under the null hypothesis, in large samples this statistic has an $F_{2,\infty}$ distribution. The 5% critical value of the $F_{2,\infty}$ distribution is 3.00 (Appendix Table 4), and the 1% critical value is 4.61. The value of the *F*-statistic computed from the data, 5.43, exceeds 4.61, so the null hypothesis is rejected at the 1% level. It is very unlikely that we would have drawn a sample that produced an *F*-statistic as large as 5.43 if the null hypothesis really were true (the *p*-value is 0.005). Based on the evidence in Equation (7.6) as summarized in this *F*-statistic, we can reject the taxpayer's hypothesis that *neither* the student–teacher ratio *nor* expenditures per pupil have an effect on test scores (holding constant the percentage of English learners).

The Homoskedasticity-Only *F*-Statistic

One way to restate the question addressed by the *F*-statistic is to ask whether relaxing the *q* restrictions that constitute the null hypothesis improves the fit of the regression by enough that this improvement is unlikely to be the result merely of random sampling variation if the null hypothesis is true. This restatement suggests that there is a link between the *F*-statistic and the regression R^2: A large *F*-statistic should, it seems, be associated with a substantial increase in the R^2. In fact, if the error u_i is homoskedastic, this intuition has an exact mathematical expression. That is, if the error term is homoskedastic, the *F*-statistic can be written in terms of the improvement in the fit of the regression as measured either by the sum of squared residuals or by the regression R^2. The resulting *F*-statistic is referred to as the homoskedasticity-only *F*-statistic, because it is valid only if the error term is homoskedastic. In contrast, the heteroskedasticity-robust *F*-statistic is valid whether the error term is homoskedastic or heteroskedastic. Despite this significant limitation of the homoskedasticity-only *F*-statistic, its simple formula sheds light on what the *F*-statistic is doing. In addition, the simple formula can be computed using standard regression output, such as might be reported in a table that includes regression R^2's but not *F*-statistics.

The homoskedasticity-only *F*-statistic is computed using a simple formula based on the sum of squared residuals from two regressions. In the first regression, called the **restricted regression**, the null hypothesis is forced to be true. When the null hypothesis is of the type in Equation (7.8), where all the hypothesized values are zero, the restricted regression is the regression in which those coefficients are set to zero, that is, the relevant regressors are excluded from the regression. In the second regression, called the **unrestricted regression**, the alternative hypothesis is allowed to be true. If the sum of squared residuals is sufficiently smaller in the unrestricted than the restricted regression, then the test rejects the null hypothesis.

The **homoskedasticity-only *F*-statistic** is given by the formula

$$F = \frac{(SSR_{restricted} - SSR_{unrestricted})/q}{SSR_{unrestricted}/(n - k_{unrestricted} - 1)}, \tag{7.13}$$

where $SSR_{restricted}$ is the sum of squared residuals from the restricted regression, $SSR_{unrestricted}$ is the sum of squared residuals from the unrestricted regression, q is the number of restrictions under the null hypothesis, and $k_{unrestricted}$ is the number of regressors in the unrestricted regression. An alternative equivalent formula for the homoskedasticity-only *F*-statistic is based on the R^2 of the two regressions:

$$F = \frac{(R^2_{unrestricted} - R^2_{restricted})/q}{(1 - R^2_{unrestricted})/(n - k_{unrestricted} - 1)}. \tag{7.14}$$

If the errors are homoskedastic, then the difference between the homoskedasticity-only *F*-statistic computed using Equation (7.13) or (7.14) and the heteroskedasticity-robust *F*-statistic vanishes as the sample size n increases. Thus, if the errors are homoskedastic, the sampling distribution of the rule-of-thumb *F*-statistic under the null hypothesis is, in large samples, $F_{q,\infty}$.

The formulas in Equations (7.13) and (7.14) are easy to compute and have an intuitive interpretation in terms of how well the unrestricted and restricted regressions fit the data. Unfortunately, they are valid only if the errors are homoskedastic. Because homoskedasticity is a special case that cannot be counted on in applications with economic data, or more generally with data sets typically found in the social sciences, in practice the homoskedasticity-only *F*-statistic is not a satisfactory substitute for the heteroskedasticity-robust *F*-statistic.

Using the homoskedasticity-only F-statistic when n is small. If the errors are homoskedastic and are i.i.d. normally distributed, then the homoskedasticity-only *F*-statistic defined in Equations (7.13) and (7.14) has an $F_{q,n-k_{unrestricted}-1}$ distribution under the null hypothesis. Critical values for this distribution, which depend on both q and $n - k_{unrestricted} - 1$, are given in Appendix Table 5. As discussed in Section 2.4, the $F_{q,n-k_{unrestricted}-1}$ distribution converges to the $F_{q,\infty}$ distribution as n increases; for large sample sizes, the differences between the two distributions are negligible. For small samples, however, the two sets of critical values differ.

Application to Test Scores and the Student–Teacher Ratio. To test the null hypothesis that the population coefficients on *STR* and *Expn* are 0, controlling for *PctEL*, we need to compute the *SSR* (or R^2) for the restricted and unrestricted regression. The unrestricted regression has the regressors *STR*, *Expn*, and *PctEL*, and is given in Equation (7.6); its R^2 is 0.4366; that is, $R^2_{unrestricted} = 0.4366$. The restricted regression imposes the joint null hypothesis that the true coefficients on *STR* and *Expn* are zero; that is, under the null hypothesis *STR* and *Expn* do not enter the population regression, although *PctEL* does (the null hypothesis does not restrict the coefficient on *PctEL*). The restricted regression, estimated by OLS, is

$$\widehat{TestScore} = 664.7 - 0.671 \times PctEL, R^2 = 0.4149. \qquad (7.15)$$
$$(1.0) \quad (0.032)$$

so $R^2_{restricted} = 0.4149$. The number of restrictions is $q = 2$, the number of observations is $n = 420$, and the number of regressors in the unrestricted regression is $k = 3$. The homoskedasticity-only F-statistic, computed using Equation (7.14), is

$$F = [(0.4366 - 0.4149)/2]/[(1 - 0.4366)/(420 - 3 - 1)] = 8.01.$$

Because 8.01 exceeds the 1% critical value of 4.61, the hypothesis is rejected at the 1% level using this rule-of-thumb approach.

This example illustrates the advantages and disadvantages of the homoskedasticity-only F-statistic. Its advantage is that it can be computed using a calculator. Its disadvantage is that the values of the homoskedasticity-only and heteroskedasticity-robust F-statistics can be very different: The heteroskedasticity-robust F-statistic testing this joint hypothesis is 5.43, quite different from the less reliable homoskedasticity-only rule-of-thumb value of 8.01.

7.3 Testing Single Restrictions Involving Multiple Coefficients

Sometimes economic theory suggests a single restriction that involves two or more regression coefficients. For example, theory might suggest a null hypothesis of the form $\beta_1 = \beta_2$; that is, the effects of the first and second regressor are the same. In this case, the task is to test this null hypothesis against the alternative that the two coefficients differ:

$$H_0: \beta_1 = \beta_2 \text{ vs. } H_1: \beta_1 \neq \beta_2. \qquad (7.16)$$

This null hypothesis has a single restriction, so $q = 1$, but that restriction involves multiple coefficients (β_1 and β_2). We need to modify the methods presented so far to test this hypothesis. There are two approaches; which one will be easiest depends on your software.

Approach #1: Test the restriction directly. Some statistical packages have a specialized command designed to test restrictions like Equation (7.16) and the result is an F-statistic that, because $q = 1$, has an $F_{1,\infty}$ distribution under the null hypothesis. (Recall from Section 2.4 that the square of a standard normal random variable has an $F_{1,\infty}$ distribution, so the 95% percentile of the $F_{1,\infty}$ distribution is $1.96^2 = 3.84$.)

Approach #2: Transform the regression. If your statistical package cannot test the restriction directly, the hypothesis in Equation (7.16) can be tested using a trick in which the original regression equation is rewritten to turn the restriction in Equation (7.16) into a restriction on a single regression coefficient. To be concrete, suppose there are only two regressors, X_{1i} and X_{2i} in the regression, so the population regression has the form

$$Y_i = \beta_0 + \beta_1 X_{1i} + \beta_2 X_{2i} + u_i. \tag{7.17}$$

Here is the trick: By subtracting and adding $\beta_2 X_{1i}$, we have that $\beta_1 X_{1i} + \beta_2 X_{2i} = \beta_1 X_{1i} - \beta_2 X_{1i} + \beta_2 X_{1i} + \beta_2 X_{2i} = (\beta_1 - \beta_2)X_{1i} + \beta_2(X_{1i} + X_{2i}) = \gamma_1 X_{1i} + \beta_2 W_i$, where $\gamma_1 = \beta_1 - \beta_2$ and $W_i = X_{1i} + X_{2i}$. Thus, the population regression in Equation (7.17) can be rewritten as

$$Y_i = \beta_0 + \gamma_1 X_{1i} + \beta_2 W_i + u_i. \tag{7.18}$$

Because the coefficient γ_1 in this equation is $\gamma_1 = \beta_1 - \beta_2$, under the null hypothesis in Equation (7.16), $\gamma_1 = 0$ while under the alternative, $\gamma_1 \neq 0$. Thus, by turning Equation (7.17) into Equation (7.18), we have turned a restriction on two regression coefficients into a restriction on a single regression coefficient.

Because the restriction now involves the single coefficient γ_1, the null hypothesis in Equation (7.16) can be tested using the t-statistic method of Section 7.1. In practice, this is done by first constructing the new regressor W_i as the sum of the two original regressors, then estimating the regression of Y_i on X_{1i} and W_i. A 95% confidence interval for the difference in the coefficients $\beta_1 - \beta_2$ can be calculated as $\hat{\gamma}_1 \pm 1.96 SE(\hat{\gamma}_1)$.

This method can be extended to other restrictions on regression equations using the same trick (see Exercise 7.9).

The two methods (Approaches #1 and #2) are equivalent, in the sense that the F-statistic from the first method equals the square of the t-statistic from the second method.

Extension to q > 1. In general it is possible to have q restrictions under the null hypothesis in which some or all of these restrictions involve multiple coefficients. The F-statistic of Section 7.2 extends to this type of joint hypothesis. The F-statistic can be computed by either of the two methods just discussed for $q = 1$. Precisely how best to do this in practice depends on the specific regression software being used.

7.4 Confidence Sets for Multiple Coefficients

This section explains how to construct a confidence set for two or more regression coefficients. The method is conceptually similar to the method in Section 7.1 for constructing a confidence set for a single coefficient using the t-statistic, except that the confidence set for multiple coefficients is based on the F-statistic.

A **95% confidence set** for two or more coefficients is a set that contains the true population values of these coefficients in 95% of randomly drawn samples. Thus, a confidence set is the generalization to two or more coefficients of a confidence interval for a single coefficient.

Recall that a 95% confidence interval is computed by finding the set of values of the coefficients that are not rejected using a t-statistic at the 5% significance level. This approach can be extended to the case of multiple coefficients. To make this concrete, suppose you are interested in constructing a confidence set for two coefficients, β_1 and β_2. Section 7.2 showed how to use the F-statistic to test a joint null hypothesis that $\beta_1 = \beta_{1,0}$ and $\beta_2 = \beta_{2,0}$. Suppose you were to test every possible value of $\beta_{1,0}$ and $\beta_{2,0}$ at the 5% level. For each pair of candidates $(\beta_{1,0}, \beta_{2,0})$, you construct the F-statistic and reject it if it exceeds the 5% critical value of 3.00. Because the test has a 5% significance level, the true population values of β_1 and β_2 will not be rejected in 95% of all samples. Thus, the set of values not rejected at the 5% level by this F-statistic constitutes a 95% confidence set for β_1 and β_2.

Although this method of trying all possible values of $\beta_{1,0}$ and $\beta_{2,0}$ works in theory, in practice it is much simpler to use an explicit formula for the confidence set. This formula for the confidence set for an arbitrary number of coefficients is based on the formula for the F-statistic. When there are two coefficients, the resulting confidence sets are ellipses.

As an illustration, Figure 7.1 shows a 95% confidence set (confidence ellipse) for the coefficients on the student–teacher ratio and expenditure per pupil, holding constant the percentage of English learners, based on the estimated regression in Equation (7.6). This ellipse does not include the point (0,0). This means that the null hypothesis that these two coefficients are both zero is rejected using the F-statistic at the 5% significance level, which we already knew from Section 7.2.

FIGURE 7.1   **95% Confidence Set for Coefficients on *STR* and *Expn* from Equation (7.6)**

The 95% confidence set for the coefficients on *STR* (β_1) and *Expn* (β_2) is an ellipse. The ellipse contains the pairs of values of β_1 and β_2 that cannot be rejected using the *F*-statistic at the 5% significance level.

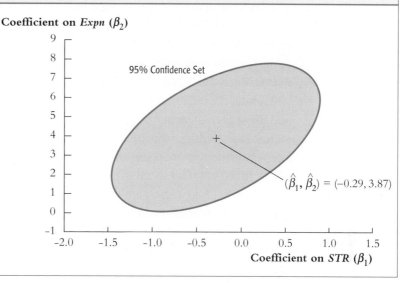

The confidence ellipse is a fat sausage with the long part of the sausage oriented in the lower-left/upper-right direction. The reason for this orientation is that the estimated correlation between $\hat{\beta}_1$ and $\hat{\beta}_2$ is positive, which in turn arises because the correlation between the regressors *STR* and *Expn* is negative (schools that spend more per pupil tend to have fewer students per teacher).

7.5   Model Specification for Multiple Regression

The job of determining which variables to include in multiple regression—that is, the problem of choosing a regression specification—can be quite challenging, and no single rule applies in all situations. But do not despair, because some useful guidelines are available. The starting point for choosing a regression specification is thinking through the possible sources of omitted variable bias. It is important to rely on your expert knowledge of the empirical problem and to focus on obtaining an unbiased estimate of the causal effect of interest; do not rely solely on purely statistical measures of fit such as the R^2 or $\overline{R}^2$.

Omitted Variable Bias in Multiple Regression

The OLS estimators of the coefficients in multiple regression will have omitted variable bias if an omitted determinant of Y_i is correlated with at least one of the regressors. For example, students from affluent families often have more learning opportunities than do their less affluent peers, which could lead to better test scores. Moreover, if the district is a wealthy one, then the schools will tend to have larger budgets and lower student–teacher ratios. If so, the affluence of the students and the student–teacher ratio would be negatively correlated, and the OLS estimate of the coefficient on the student–teacher ratio would pick up the effect of average district income, even after controlling for the percentage of English learners. In short, omitting the students' economic background could lead to omitted variable bias in the regression of test scores on the student–teacher ratio and the percentage of English learners.

The general conditions for omitted variable bias in multiple regression are similar to those for a single regressor: If an omitted variable is a determinant of Y_i and if it is correlated with at least one of the regressors, then the OLS estimators will have omitted variable bias. As was discussed in Section 6.6, the OLS estimators are correlated, so in general the OLS estimators of all the coefficients will be biased. The two conditions for omitted variable bias in multiple regression are summarized in Key Concept 7.3.

At a mathematical level, if the two conditions for omitted variable bias are satisfied, then at least one of the regressors is correlated with the error term. This means that the conditional expectation of u_i given $X_{1i}, \ldots, X_{ki}$ is nonzero, so that the first least squares assumption is violated. As a result, the omitted variable bias persists even if the sample size is large, that is, omitted variable bias implies that the OLS estimators are inconsistent.

Model Specification in Theory and in Practice

In theory, when data are available on the omitted variable, the solution to omitted variable bias is to include the omitted variable in the regression. In practice, however, deciding whether to include a particular variable can be difficult and requires judgment.

Our approach to the challenge of potential omitted variable bias is twofold. First, a core or base set of regressors should be chosen using a combination of expert judgment, economic theory, and knowledge of how the data were collected; the regression using this base set of regressors is sometimes referred to as a **base specification**. This base specification should contain the variables of primary interest and the control variables suggested by expert judgment and economic theory.

OMITTED VARIABLE BIAS IN MULTIPLE REGRESSION	KEY CONCEPT
	7.3

Omitted variable bias is the bias in the OLS estimator that arises when one or more included regressors are correlated with an omitted variable. For omitted variable bias to arise, two things must be true:

1. At least one of the included regressors must be correlated with the omitted variable.

2. The omitted variable must be a determinant of the dependent variable, Y.

Expert judgment and economic theory are rarely decisive, however, and often the variables suggested by economic theory are not the ones on which you have data. Therefore the next step is to develop a list of candidate **alternative specifications**, that is, alternative sets of regressors. If the estimates of the coefficients of interest are numerically similar across the alternative specifications, then this provides evidence that the estimates from your base specification are reliable. If, on the other hand, the estimates of the coefficients of interest change substantially across specifications, this often provides evidence that the original specification had omitted variable bias. We elaborate on this approach to model specification in Section 9.2 after studying some tools for specifying regressions.

Interpreting the R^2 and the Adjusted R^2 in Practice

An R^2 or an $\overline{R}^2$ near 1 means that the regressors are good at predicting the values of the dependent variable in the sample, and an R^2 or an $\overline{R}^2$ near 0 means they are not. This makes these statistics useful summaries of the predictive ability of the regression. However, it is easy to read more into them than they deserve.

There are four potential pitfalls to guard against when using the R^2 or $\overline{R}^2$:

1. *An increase in the R^2 or $\overline{R}^2$ does not necessarily mean that an added variable is statistically significant.* The R^2 increases whenever you add a regressor, whether or not it is statistically significant. The $\overline{R}^2$ does not always increase, but if it does this does not necessarily mean that the coefficient on that added regressor is statistically significant. To ascertain whether an added variable is statistically significant, you need to perform a hypothesis test using the t-statistic.

KEY CONCEPT

7.4

R^2 AND $\overline{R}^2$: WHAT THEY TELL YOU— AND WHAT THEY DON'T

The R^2 and $\overline{R}^2$ tell you whether the regressors are good at predicting, or "explaining," the values of the dependent variable in the sample of data on hand. If the R^2 (or $\overline{R}^2$) is nearly 1, then the regressors produce good predictions of the dependent variable in that sample, in the sense that the variance of the OLS residual is small compared to the variance of the dependent variable. If the R^2 (or $\overline{R}^2$) is nearly 0, the opposite is true.

The R^2 and $\overline{R}^2$ do NOT tell you whether:

1. An included variable is statistically significant;

2. The regressors are a true cause of the movements in the dependent variable;

3. There is omitted variable bias; or

4. You have chosen the most appropriate set of regressors.

2. *A high R^2 or $\overline{R}^2$ does not mean that the regressors are a true cause of the dependent variable.* Imagine regressing test scores against parking lot area per pupil. Parking lot area is correlated with the student–teacher ratio, with whether the school is in a suburb or a city, and possibly with district income— all things that are correlated with test scores. Thus the regression of test scores on parking lot area per pupil could have a high R^2 and $\overline{R}^2$, but the relationship is not causal (try telling the superintendent that the way to increase test scores is to increase parking space!).

3. *A high R^2 or $\overline{R}^2$ does not mean there is no omitted variable bias.* Recall the discussion of Section 6.1, which concerned omitted variable bias in the regression of test scores on the student–teacher ratio. The R^2 of the regression never came up because it played no logical role in this discussion. Omitted variable bias can occur in regressions with a low R^2, a moderate R^2, or a high R^2. Conversely, a low R^2 does not imply that there necessarily is omitted variable bias.

4. *A high R^2 or $\overline{R}^2$ does not necessarily mean you have the most appropriate set of regressors, nor does a low R^2 or $\overline{R}^2$ necessarily mean you have an inappropriate set of regressors.* The question of what constitutes the right set of regressors in multiple regression is difficult and we return to it throughout this textbook. Decisions about the regressors must weigh issues of omitted variable bias, data availability, data quality, and, most importantly, economic theory and the nature of the substantive questions being addressed. None of

these questions can be answered simply by having a high (or low) regression R^2 or $\overline{R}^2$.

These points are summarized in Key Concept 7.4.

7.6 Analysis of the Test Score Data Set

This section presents an analysis of the effect on test scores of the student–teacher ratio using the California data set. Our primary purpose is to provide an example in which multiple regression analysis is used to mitigate omitted variable bias. Our secondary purpose is to demonstrate how to use a table to summarize regression results.

Discussion of the base and alternative specifications.   This analysis focuses on estimating the effect on test scores of a change in the student–teacher ratio, holding constant student characteristics that the superintendent cannot control. Many factors potentially affect the average test score in a district. Some of the factors that could affect test scores are correlated with the student–teacher ratio, so omitting them from the regression will result in omitted variable bias. If data are available on these omitted variables, the solution to this problem is to include them as additional regressors in the multiple regression. When we do this, the coefficient on the student–teacher ratio is the effect of a change in the student–teacher ratio, holding constant these other factors.

Here we consider three variables that control for background characteristics of the students that could affect test scores. One of these control variables is the one we have used previously, the fraction of students who are still learning English. The two other variables are new and control for the economic background of the students. There is no perfect measure of economic background in the data set, so instead we use two imperfect indicators of low income in the district. The first new variable is the percentage of students who are eligible for receiving a subsidized or free lunch at school. Students are eligible for this program if their family income is less than a certain threshold (approximately 150% of the poverty line). The second new variable is the percentage of students in the district whose families qualify for a California income assistance program. Families are eligible for this income assistance program depending in part on their family income, but the threshold is lower (stricter) than the threshold for the subsidized lunch program. These two variables thus measure the fraction of economically disadvantaged children in the district; although they are related, they are not perfectly correlated (their correlation coefficient is 0.74). Although theory suggests that economic background could be an important omitted factor, theory and expert judgment do not really help us decide which of these two variables (percentage eligible for a subsidized lunch or percentage eligible for income assistance) is a better measure of background. For our base specification, we choose the percentage eligible for a subsidized lunch as the economic background variable, but we consider an alternative specification that includes the other variable as well.

Scatterplots of tests scores and these variables are presented in Figure 7.2. Each of these variables exhibits a negative correlation with test scores. The correlation between test scores and the percentage of English learners is -0.64; between test scores and the percentage eligible for a subsidized lunch is -0.87; and between test scores and the percentage qualifying for income assistance is -0.63.

What scale should we use for the regressors?   A practical question that arises in regression analysis is what scale you should use for the regressors. In Figure 7.2, the units of the variables are percent, so the maximum possible range of the data is 0 to 100. Alternatively, we could have defined these variables to be a *decimal fraction* rather than a percent; for example, *PctEL* could be replaced by the *fraction* of English learners, *FracEL* ($= PctEL/100$), which would range between 0 and 1 instead of between 0 and 100. More generally, in regression analysis some decision usually needs to be made about the scale of both the dependent and independent variables. How, then, should you choose the scale, or units, of the variables?

The general answer to the question of choosing the scale of the variables is to make the regression results easy to read and to interpret. In the test score application, the natural unit for the dependent variable is the score of the test itself. In the regression of *TestScore* on *STR* and *PctEL* reported in Equation (7.5), the coefficient on *PctEL* is -0.650. If instead the regressor had been *FracEL,* the regression would have had an identical R^2 and *SER*; however, the coefficient on *FracEL* would have been -65.0. In the specification with *PctEL,* the coefficient is the predicted change in test scores for a one-percentage-point increase in English learners, holding *STR* constant; in the specification with *FracEL,* the coefficient is the predicted change in test scores for an increase by 1 in the fraction of English learners—that is, for a 100-percentage-point-increase—holding *STR* constant. Although these two specifications are mathematically equivalent, for the purposes of interpretation the one with *PctEL* seems, to us, more natural.

Another consideration when deciding on a scale is to choose the units of the regressors so that the resulting regression coefficients are easy to read. For example, if a regressor is measured in dollars and has a coefficient of 0.00000356, it is easier to read if the regressor is converted to millions of dollars and the coefficient 3.56 is reported.

FIGURE 7.2   **Scatterplots of Test Scores vs. Three Student Characteristics**

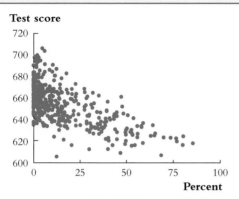

(a)   Percentage of English language learners

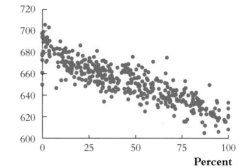

(b)   Percentage qualifying for reduced price lunch

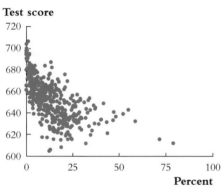

(c)   Percentage qualifying for income assistance

The scatterplots show a negative relationship between test scores and (a) the percentage of English learners (correlation = −0.64), (b) the percentage of students qualifying for a subsidized lunch (correlation = −0.87); and (c) the percentage qualifying for income assistance (correlation = −0.63).

Tabular presentation of result.   We are now faced with a communication problem. What is the best way to show the results from several multiple regressions that contain different subsets of the possible regressors? So far, we have presented regression results by writing out the estimated regression equations, as in Equation (7.6). This works well when there are only a few regressors and only a few equations, but with more regressors and equations this method of presentation can be confusing. A better way to communicate the results of several regressions is in a table.

Table 7.1 summarizes the results of regressions of the test score on various sets of regressors. Each column summarizes a separate regression. Each regression has

TABLE 7.1	Results of Regressions of Test Scores on the Student–Teacher Ratio and Student Characteristic Control Variables Using California Elementary School Districts				

Dependent variable: average test score in the district.

Regressor	(1)	(2)	(3)	(4)	(5)
Student–teacher ratio (X_1)	−2.28**	−1.10*	−1.00**	−1.31**	−1.01**
	(0.52)	(0.43)	(0.27)	(0.34)	(0.27)
Percent English learners (X_2)		−0.650**	−0.122**	−0.488**	−0.130**
		(0.031)	(0.033)	(0.030)	(0.036)
Percent eligible for subsidized lunch (X_3)			−0.547**		−0.529**
			(0.024)		(0.038)
Percent on public income assistance (X_4)				−0.790**	0.048
				(0.068)	(0.059)
Intercept	698.9**	686.0**	700.2**	698.0**	700.4**
	(10.4)	(8.7)	(5.6)	(6.9)	(5.5)
Summary Statistics					
SER	18.58	14.46	9.08	11.65	9.08
$\overline{R}^2$	0.049	0.424	0.773	0.626	0.773
n	420	420	420	420	420

These regressions were estimated using the data on K-8 school districts in California, described in Appendix 4.1. Standard errors are given in parentheses under coefficients. The individual coefficient is statistically significant at the *5% level or **1% significance level using a two-sided test.

the same dependent variable, test score. The entries in the first five rows are the estimated regression coefficients, with their standard errors below them in parentheses. The asterisks indicate whether the *t*-statistics, testing the hypothesis that the relevant coefficient is zero, is significant at the 5% level (one asterisk) or the 1% level (two asterisks). The final three rows contain summary statistics for the regression (the standard error of the regression, *SER*, and the adjusted R^2, $\overline{R}^2$) and the sample size (which is the same for all of the regressions, 420 observations).

All the information that we have presented so far in equation format appears as a column of this table. For example, consider the regression of the test score against the student–teacher ratio, with no control variables. In equation form, this regression is

$$\widehat{TestScore} = 698.9 - 2.28 \times STR, \ \overline{R}^2 = 0.049, SER = 18.58, n = 420. \tag{7.19}$$
$$(10.4) \quad (0.52)$$

All this information appears in column (1) of Table 7.1. The estimated coefficient on the student–teacher ratio (−2.28) appears in the first row of numerical entries, and its standard error (0.52) appears in parentheses just below the estimated coefficient. The intercept (698.9) and its standard error (10.4) are given in the row labeled "Intercept." (Sometimes you will see this row labeled "constant" because, as discussed in Section 6.2, the intercept can be viewed as the coefficient on a regressor that is always equal to 1.) Similarly, the $\overline{R}^2$ (0.049), the *SER* (18.58), and the sample size n (420) appear in the final rows. The blank entries in the rows of the other regressors indicate that those regressors are not included in this regression.

Although the table does not report *t*-statistics, these can be computed from the information provided; for example, the *t*-statistic testing the hypothesis that the coefficient on the student–teacher ratio in column (1) is zero is −2.28/0.52 = −4.38. This hypothesis is rejected at the 1% level, which is indicated by the double asterisk next to the estimated coefficient in the table.

Regressions that include the control variables measuring student characteristics are reported in columns (2)−(5). Column (2), which reports the regression of test scores on the student–teacher ratio and on the percentage of English learners, was previously stated as Equation (7.5).

Column (3) presents the base specification, in which the regressors are the student–teacher ratio and two control variables, the percentage of English learners and the percentage of students eligible for a free lunch.

Columns (4) and (5) present alternative specifications that examine the effect of changes in the way the economic background of the students is measured. In column (4), the percentage of students on income assistance is included as a regressor, and in column (5) both of the economic background variables are included.

Discussion of empirical results. These results suggest three conclusions:

1. Controlling for these student characteristics cuts the effect of the student–teacher ratio on test scores approximately in half. This estimated effect is not very sensitive to which specific control variables are included in the regression. In all cases the coefficient on the student–teacher ratio remains statistically significant at the 5% level. In the four specifications with control variables, regressions (2)−(5), reducing the student–teacher ratio by one student per teacher is estimated to increase average test scores by approximately one point, holding constant student characteristics.

2. The student characteristic variables are very useful predictors of test scores. The student–teacher ratio alone explains only a small fraction of the variation in test scores: The $\overline{R}^2$ in column (1) is 0.049. The $\overline{R}^2$ jumps, however, when the student characteristic variables are added. For example, the $\overline{R}^2$ in the base

specification, regression (3), is 0.773. The signs of the coefficients on the student demographic variables are consistent with the patterns seen in Figure 7.2: Districts with many English learners and districts with many poor children have lower test scores.

3. The control variables are not always individually statistically significant: In specification (5), the hypothesis that the coefficient on the percentage qualifying for income assistance is zero is not rejected at the 5% level (the *t*-statistic is −0.82). Because adding this control variable to the base specification (3) has a negligible effect on the estimated coefficient for the student-teacher ratio and its standard error, and because the coefficient on this control variable is not significant in specification (5), this additional control variable is redundant, at least for the purposes of this analysis.

7.7   Conclusion

Chapter 6 began with a concern: In the regression of test scores against the student–teacher ratio, omitted student characteristics that influence test scores might be correlated with the student–teacher ratio in the district, and if so the student–teacher ratio in the district would pick up the effect on test scores of these omitted student characteristics. Thus, the OLS estimator would have omitted variable bias. To mitigate this potential omitted varible bias, we augmented the regression by including variables that control for various student characteristics (the percentage of English learners and two measures of student economic background). Doing so cuts the estimated effect of a unit change in the student–teacher ratio in half, although it remains possible to reject the null hypothesis that the population effect on test scores, holding these control variables constant, is zero at the 5% significance level. Because they eliminate omitted variable bias arising from these student characteristics, these multiple regression estimates, hypothesis tests, and confidence intervals are much more useful for advising the superintendent than the single-regressor estimates of Chapters 4 and 5.

The analysis in this and the preceding chapter has presumed that the population regression function is linear in the regressors—that is, that the conditional expectation of Y_i given the regressors is a straight line. There is, however, no particular reason to think this is so. In fact, the effect of reducing the student–teacher ratio might be quite different in districts with large classes than in districts that already have small classes. If so, the population regression line is not linear in the X's but rather is a nonlinear function of the X's. To extend our analysis to regression functions that are nonlinear in the X's, however, we need the tools developed in the next chapter.

Summary

1. Hypothesis tests and confidence intervals for a single regression coefficient are carried out using essentially the same procedures that were used in the one-variable linear regression model of Chapter 5. For example, a 95% confidence interval for β_1 is given by $\hat{\beta}_1 \pm 1.96SE(\hat{\beta}_1)$.

2. Hypotheses involving more than one restriction on the coefficients are called joint hypotheses. Joint hypotheses can be tested using an F-statistic.

3. Regression specification proceeds by first determining a base specification chosen to address concern about omitted variable bias. The base specification can be modified by including additional regressors that address other potential sources of omitted variable bias. Simply choosing the specification with the highest R^2 can lead to regression models that do not estimate the causal effect of interest.

Key Terms

restrictions (224)

joint hypothesis (224)

F-statistic (225)

restricted regression (228)

unrestricted regression (228)

homoskedasticity-only F-statistic (229)

95% confidence set (232)

base specification (234)

alternative specifications (235)

Bonferroni test (249)

Review the Concepts

7.1 Explain how you would test the null hypothesis that $\beta_1 = 0$ in the multiple regression model, $Y_i = \beta_0 + \beta_1 X_{1i} + \beta_2 X_{2i} + u_i$. Explain how you would test the null hypothesis that $\beta_2 = 0$. Explain how you would test the joint hypothesis that $\beta_1 = 0$ *and* $\beta_2 = 0$. Why isn't the result of the joint test implied by the results of the first two tests?

7.2 Provide an example of a regression that arguably would have a high value of R^2 but would produce biased and inconsistent estimators of the regression coefficient(s). Explain why the R^2 is likely to be high. Explain why the OLS estimators would be biased and inconsistent.

Exercises

The first six exercises refer to the table of estimated regressions on page 245, computed using data for 1998 from the CPS. The data set consists of information on 4000 full-time full-year workers. The highest educational achievement for each worker was either a high school diploma or a bachelor's degree. The worker's ages ranged from 25 to 34 years. The data set also contained information on the region of the country where the person lived, marital status, and number of children. For the purposes of these exercises let

AHE = average hourly earnings (in 1998 dollars)
$College$ = binary variable (1 if college, 0 if high school)
$Female$ = binary variable (1 if female, 0 if male)
Age = age (in years)
$Ntheast$ = binary variable (1 if Region = Northeast, 0 otherwise)
$Midwest$ = binary variable (1 if Region = Midwest, 0 otherwise)
$South$ = binary variable (1 if Region = South, 0 otherwise)
$West$ = binary variable (1 if Region = West, 0 otherwise)

7.1   Add "*" (5%) and "**" (1%) to the table to indicate the statistical significance of the coefficients.

7.2   Using the regression results in column (1):

    a. Is the college–high school earnings difference estimated from this regression statistically significant at the 5% level? Construct a 95% confidence interval of the difference.

    b. Is the male–female earnings difference estimated from this regression statistically significant at the 5% level? Construct a 95% confidence interval for the difference.

7.3   Using the regression results in column (2):

    a. Is age an important determinant of earnings? Use an appropriate statistical test and/or confidence interval to explain your answer.

    b. Sally is a 29-year-old female college graduate. Betsy is a 34-year-old female college graduate. Construct a 95% confidence interval for the expected difference between their earnings.

7.4   Using the regression results in column (3):

    a. Do there appear to be important regional differences? Use an appropriate hypothesis test to explain your answer.

Results of Regressions of Average Hourly Earnings on Gender and Education Binary Variables and Other Characteristics Using 1998 Data from the Current Population Survey

Dependent variable: average hourly earnings (AHE).

Regressor	(1)	(2)	(3)
College (X_1)	5.46	5.48	5.44
	(0.21)	(0.21)	(0.21)
Female (X_2)	−2.64	−2.62	−2.62
	(0.20)	(0.20)	(0.20)
Age (X_3)		0.29	0.29
		(0.04)	(0.04)
Northeast (X_4)			0.69
			(0.30)
Midwest (X_5)			0.60
			(0.28)
South (X_6)			−0.27
			(0.26)
Intercept	12.69	4.40	3.75
	(0.14)	(1.05)	(1.06)
Summary Statistics and Joint Tests			
F-statistic for regional effects = 0			6.10
SER	6.27	6.22	6.21
R^2	0.176	0.190	0.194
n	4000	4000	4000

b. Juanita is a 28-year-old female college graduate from the South. Molly is a 28-year-old female college graduate from the West. Jennifer is a 28-year-old female college graduate from the Midwest.

  i. Construct a 95% confidence interval for the difference in expected earnings between Juanita and Molly.

  ii. Explain how you would construct a 95% confidence interval for the difference in expected earnings between Juanita and Jennifer. (*Hint:* What would happen if you included *West* and excluded *Midwest* from the regression?)

7.5 The regression shown in column (2) was estimated again, this time using data from 1992 (4000 observations selected at random from the March 1993 CPS, converted into 1998 dollars using the consumer price index). The results are

$$\widehat{AHE} = 0.77 + 5.29College - 2.59Female + 0.40Age, SER = 5.85, \overline{R}^2 = 0.21.$$
$$\quad (0.98)\ (0.20) \qquad\qquad (0.18) \qquad\qquad (0.03)$$

Comparing this regression to the regression for 1998 shown in column (2), was there a statistically significant change in the coefficient on *College*?

7.6 Evaluate the following statement: "In all of the regressions, the coefficient on *Female* is negative, large, and statistically significant. This provides strong statistical evidence of gender discrimination in the U.S. labor market."

7.7 Question 6.5 reported the following regression (where standard errors have been added):

$$\widehat{Price} = 119.2 + 0.485BDR + 23.4Bath + 0.156Hsize + 0.002Lsize$$
$$\qquad (23.9)\quad (2.61) \qquad\quad (8.94) \qquad (0.011) \qquad\quad (0.00048)$$

$$+\ 0.090Age - 48.8Poor,\ \overline{R}^2 = 0.72,\ SER = 41.5$$
$$\quad (0.311) \qquad (10.5)$$

a. Is the coefficient on *BDR* statistically significantly different from zero?

b. Typically five-bedroom houses sell for much more than two-bedroom houses. Is this consistent with your answer to (a) and with the regression more generally?

c. A homeowner purchases 2000 square feet from an adjacent lot. Construct a 99% confident interval for the change in the value of her house.

d. Lot size is measured in square feet. Do you think that another scale might be more appropriate? Why or why not?

e. The *F*-statistic for omitting *BDR* and *Age* from the regression is $F = 0.08$. Are the coefficients on *BDR* and *Age* statistically different from zero at the 10% level?

7.8 Referring to Table 7.1 in the text:

a. Construct the R^2 for each of the regressions.

b. Construct the homoskedasticity-only *F*-statistic for testing $\beta_3 = \beta_4 = 0$ in the regression shown in column (5). Is the statistic significant at the 5% level?

c. Test $\beta_3 = \beta_4 = 0$ in the regression shown in column (5) using the Bonferroni test discussed in Appendix 7.1.

d. Construct a 99% confidence interval for β_1 for the regression in column 5.

7.9 Consider the regression model $Y_i = \beta_0 + \beta_1 X_{1i} + \beta_2 X_{2i} + u_i$. Use "Approach #2" from Section 7.3 to transform the regression so that you can use a t-statistic to test

   a. $\beta_1 = \beta_2$;

   b. $\beta_1 + a\beta_2 = 0$, where a is a constant;

   c. $\beta_1 + \beta_2 = 1$. (*Hint:* You must redefine the dependent variable in the regression.)

7.10 Equations (7.13) and (7.14) show two formulas for the homoskedasticity-only F-statistic. Show that the two formulas are equivalent.

Empirical Exercises

E7.1 Use the data set **CPS04** described in Empirical Exercise 4.1 to answer the following questions.

   a. Run a regression of average hourly earnings (*AHE*) on age (*Age*). What is the estimated intercept? What is the estimated slope?

   b. Run a regression of *AHE* on *Age*, gender (*Female*), and education (*Bachelor*). What is the estimated effect of *Age* on earnings? Construct a 95% confidence interval for the coefficient on *Age* in the regression.

   c. Are the results from the regression in (b) substantively different from the results in (a) regarding the effects of *Age* and *AHE*? Does the regression in (a) seem to suffer from omitted variable bias?

   d. Bob is a 26-year-old male worker with a high school diploma. Predict Bob's earnings using the estimated regression in (b). Alexis is a 30-year-old female worker with a college degree. Predict Alexis's earnings using the regression.

   e. Compare the fit of the regression in (a) and (b) using the regression standard errors, R^2 and $\bar{R}^2$. Why are the R^2 and $\bar{R}^2$ so similar in regression (b)?

   f. Are gender and education determinants of earnings? Test the null hypothesis that *Female* can be deleted from the regression. Test the null hypothesis that *Bachelor* can be deleted from the regression. Test the null hypothesis that both *Female* and *Bachelor* can be deleted from the regression.

g. A regression will suffer from omitted variable bias when two conditions hold. What are these two conditions? Do these conditions seem to hold here?

E7.2 Using the data set **TeachingRatings** described in Empirical Exercise 4.2, carry out the following exercises.

    a. Run a regression of *Course_Eval* on *Beauty*. Construct a 95% confidence interval for the effect of *Beauty* on *Course_Eval*.

    b. Consider the various control variables in the data set. Which do you think should be included in the regression? Using a table like Table 7.1, examine the robustness of the confidence interval that you constructed in (a). What is a reasonable 95% confidence interval for the effect of *Beauty* on *Course_Eval*?

E7.3 Use the data set **CollegeDistance** described in Empirical Exercise 4.3 to answer the following questions.

    a. An education advocacy group argues that, on average, a person's educational attainment would increase by approximately 0.15 year if distance to the nearest college is decreased by 20 miles. Run a regression of years of completed education (*ED*) on distance to the nearest college (*Dist*). Is the advocacy groups' claim consistent with the estimated regression? Explain.

    b. Other factors also affect how much college a person completes. Does controlling for these other factors change the estimated effect of distance on college years completed? To answer this question, construct a table like Table 7.1. Include a simple specification [constructed in (a)], a base specification (that includes a set of important control variables), and several modifications of the base specification. Discuss how the estimated effect of *Dist* on *ED* changes across the specifications.

    c. It has been argued that, controlling for other factors, blacks and Hispanics complete more college than whites. Is this result consistent with the regressions that you constructed in part (b)?

E7.4 Using the data set **Growth** described in Empirical Exercise 4.4, but excluding the data for Malta, carry out the following exercises.

    a. Run a regression of *Growth* on *TradeShare, YearsSchool, Rev_Coups, Assassinations* and *RGDP60*. Construct a 95% confidence interval for the coefficient on *TradeShare*. Is the coefficient statistically significant at the 5% level?

b. Test whether, taken as a group, *YearsSchool, Rev_Coups, Assassina-tions,* and *RGDP60* can be omitted from the regression. What is the *p*-value of the *F*-statistic?

APPENDIX
7.1 | The Bonferroni Test of a Joint Hypotheses

The method of Section 7.2 is the preferred way to test joint hypotheses in multiple regres-sion. However, if the author of a study presents regression results but did not test a joint restriction in which you are interested, and you do not have the original data, then you will not be able to compute the *F*-statistic of Section 7.2. This appendix describes a way to test joint hypotheses that can be used when you only have a table of regression results. This method is an application of a very general testing approach based on Bonferroni's inequality.

The Bonferroni test is a test of a joint hypotheses based on the *t*-statistics for the indi-vidual hypotheses; that is, the Bonferroni test is the one-at-a-time *t*-statistic test of Section 7.2 done properly. The **Bonferroni test** of the joint null hypothesis $\beta_1 = \beta_{1,0}$ and $\beta_2 = \beta_{2,0}$ based on the critical value $c > 0$ uses the following rule:

$$\text{Accept if } |t_1| \le c \text{ and if } |t_2| \le c; \text{ otherwise, reject}$$
(7.20)
$$\text{(Bonferroni one-at-a-time } t\text{-statistic test)},$$

where t_1 and t_2 are the *t*-statistics that test the restrictions on β_1 and β_2, respectully.

The trick is to choose the critical value *c* in such a way that the probability that the one-at-a-time test rejects when the null hypothesis is true is no more than the desired signifi-cance level, say 5%. This is done by using Bonferroni's inequality to choose the critical value *c* to allow both for the fact that two restrictions are being tested and for any possible cor-relation between t_1 and t_2.

Bonferroni's Inequality

Bonferroni's inequality is a basic result of probability theory. Let *A* and *B* be events. Let $A \cap B$ be the event "both *A* and *B*" (the intersection of *A* and *B*), and let $A \cup B$ be the event "*A* or *B* or both" (the union of *A* and *B*). Then $\Pr(A \cup B) = \Pr(A) + \Pr(B) - \Pr(A \cap B)$. Because $\Pr(A \cap B) \ge 0$, it follows that $\Pr(A \cup B) \le \Pr(A) + \Pr(B)$. This inequality in turn implies that $1 - \Pr(A \cup B) \ge 1 - [\Pr(A) + \Pr(B)]$. Let A^c and B^c be the complements of

A and B, that is, the events "not A" and "not B." Because the complement of $A \cup B$ is $A^c \cap B^c$, $1 - \Pr(A \cup B) = \Pr(A^c \cap B^c)$, which yields Bonferroni's inequality, $\Pr(A^c \cap B^c) \geq 1 - [\Pr(A) + \Pr(B)]$.

Now let A be the event that $|t_1| > c$ and B be the event that $|t_2| > c$. Then the inequality $\Pr(A \cup B) \leq \Pr(A) + \Pr(B)$ yields

$$\Pr(|t_1| > c \text{ or } |t_2| > c \text{ or both}) \leq \Pr(|t_1| > c) + \Pr(|t_2| > c). \tag{7.21}$$

Bonferroni Tests

Because the event "$|t_1| > c$ or $|t_2| > c$ or both" is the rejection region of the one-at-a-time test, Equation (7.21) provides a way to choose the critical value c so that the "one at a time" t-statistic has the desired significance level in large samples. Under the null hypothesis in large samples, $\Pr(|t_1| > c) = \Pr(|t_2| > c) = \Pr(|Z| > c)$. Thus Equation (7.21) implies that, in large samples, the probability that the one-at-a-time test rejects under the null is

$$\Pr_{H_0}(\text{one-at-a-time test rejects}) \leq 2\Pr(|Z| > c). \tag{7.22}$$

The inequality in Equation (7.22) provides a way to choose critical value c so that the probability of the rejection under the null hypothesis equals the desired significance level. The Bonferroni approach can be extended to more than two coefficients; if there are q restrictions under the null, the factor of 2 on the right-hand side in Equation (7.22) is replaced by q.

Table 7.3 presents critical values c for the one-at-a-time Bonferroni test for various significance levels and $q = 2, 3$, and 4. For example, suppose the desired significance level is 5% and $q = 2$. According to Table 7.3, the critical value c is 2.241. This critical value is the 1.25% percentile of the standard normal distribution, so $\Pr(|Z| > 2.241) = 2.5\%$. Thus Equation (7.22) tells us that, in large samples, the one-at-a-time test in Equation (7.20) will reject at most 5% of the time under the null hypothesis.

The critical values in Table 7.3 are larger than the critical values for testing a single restriction. For example, with $q = 2$, the one-at-a-time test rejects if at least one t-statistic exceeds 2.241 in absolute value. This critical value is greater than 1.96 because it properly corrects for the fact that, by looking at two t-statistics, you get a second chance to reject the joint null hypothesis, as discussed in Section 7.2.

If the individual t-statistics are based on heteroskedasticity-robust standard errors, then the Bonferroni test is valid whether or not there is heteroskedasticity, but if the t-statistics are based on homoskedasticity-only standard errors, the Bonferroni test is valid only under homoskedasticity.

TABLE 7.3	Bonferroni Critical Values c for the One-at-a-time t-Statistic Test of a Joint Hypothesis		
	Significance Level		
Number of Restrictions (q)	10%	5%	1%
2	1.960	2.241	2.807
3	2.128	2.394	2.935
4	2.241	2.498	3.023

Application to Test Scores

The t-statistics testing the joint null hypothesis that the true coefficients on test scores and expenditures per pupil in Equation (7.6) are, respectively, $t_1 = -0.60$ and $t_2 = 2.43$. Although $|t_1| < 2.241$, because $|t_2| > 2.241$, we can reject the joint null hypothesis at the 5% significance level using the Bonferroni test. However, both t_1 and t_2 are less than 2.807 in absolute value, so we cannot reject the joint null hypothesis at the 1% significance level using the Bonferroni test. In contrast, using the F-statistic in Section 7.2, we were able to reject this hypothesis at the 1% significance level.

CHAPTER 8

Nonlinear Regression Functions

In Chapters 4–7, the population regression function was assumed to be linear. In other words, the slope of the population regression function was constant, so that the effect on Y of a unit change in X does not itself depend on the value of X. But what if the effect on Y of a change in X does depend on the value of one or more of the independent variables? If so, the population regression function is nonlinear.

This chapter develops two groups of methods for detecting and modeling nonlinear population regression functions. The methods in the first group are useful when the effect on Y of a change in one independent variable, X_1, depends on the value of X_1 itself. For example, reducing class sizes by one student per teacher might have a greater effect if class sizes are already manageably small than if they are so large that the teacher can do little more than keep the class under control. If so, the test score (Y) is a nonlinear function of the student–teacher ratio (X_1), where this function is steeper when X_1 is small. An example of a nonlinear regression function with this feature is shown in Figure 8.1. Whereas the linear population regression function in Figure 8.1a has a constant slope, the nonlinear population regression function in Figure 8.1b has a steeper slope when X_1 is small than when it is large. This first group of methods is presented in Section 8.2.

The methods in the second group are useful when the effect on Y of a change in X_1 depends on the value of another independent variable, say X_2. For example, students still learning English might especially benefit from having more one-on-one attention; if so, the effect on test scores of reducing the student–teacher ratio will be greater in districts with many students still learning English than in districts with few English learners. In this example, the effect on

FIGURE 8.1   **Population Regression Functions with Different Slopes**

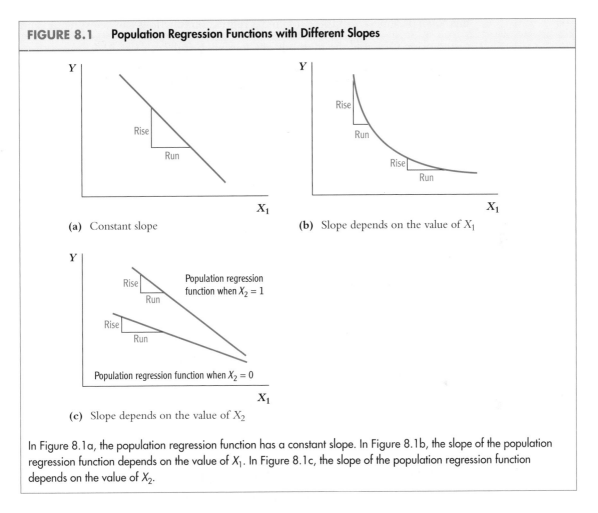

(a) Constant slope

(b) Slope depends on the value of X_1

(c) Slope depends on the value of X_2

In Figure 8.1a, the population regression function has a constant slope. In Figure 8.1b, the slope of the population regression function depends on the value of X_1. In Figure 8.1c, the slope of the population regression function depends on the value of X_2.

test scores (Y) of a reduction in the student–teacher ratio (X_1) depends on the percentage of English learners in the district (X_2). As shown in Figure 8.1c, the slope of this type of population regression function depends on the value of X_2. This second group of methods is presented in Section 8.3.

     In the models of Sections 8.2 and 8.3, the population regression function is a nonlinear function of the independent variables, that is, the conditional expectation $E(Y_i | X_{1i}, \ldots, X_{ki})$ is a nonlinear function of one or more of the X's. Although they are nonlinear in the X's, these models are linear functions of the unknown coefficients (or parameters) of the population regression model and thus are versions of the multiple regression model of Chapters 6 and 7. Therefore, the unknown parameters of these nonlinear regression functions can be estimated and tested using OLS and the methods of Chapters 6 and 7.

Sections 8.1 and 8.2 introduce nonlinear regression functions in the context of regression with a single independent variable, and Section 8.3 extends this to two independent variables. To keep things simple, additional control variables are omitted in the empirical examples of Sections 8.1–8.3. In practice, however, it is important to analyze nonlinear regression functions in models that control for omitted variable bias by including control variables as well. In Section 8.5, we combine nonlinear regression functions and additional control variables when we take a close look at possible nonlinearities in the relationship between test scores and the student–teacher ratio, holding student characteristics constant. In some applications, the regression function is a nonlinear function of the X's *and* of the parameters. If so, the parameters cannot be estimated by OLS, but they can be estimated using nonlinear least squares. Appendix 8.1 provides examples of such functions and describes the nonlinear least squares estimator.

8.1 A General Strategy for Modeling Nonlinear Regression Functions

This section lays out a general strategy for modeling nonlinear population regression functions. In this strategy, the nonlinear models are extensions of the multiple regression model and therefore can be estimated and tested using the tools of Chapters 6 and 7. First, however, we return to the California test score data and consider the relationship between test scores and district income.

Test Scores and District Income

In Chapter 7, we found that the economic background of the students is an important factor in explaining performance on standardized tests. That analysis used two economic background variables (the percentage of students qualifying for a subsidized lunch and the percentage of district families qualifying for income

FIGURE 8.2   Scatterplot of Test Score vs. District Income with a Linear OLS Regression Function

There is a positive correlation between test scores and district income (correlation = 0.71), but the linear OLS regression line does not adequately describe the relationship between these variables.

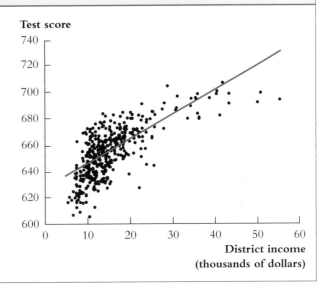

assistance) to measure the fraction of students in the district coming from poor families. A different, broader measure of economic background is the average annual per capita income in the school district ("district income"). The California data set includes district income measured in thousands of 1998 dollars. The sample contains a wide range of income levels: For the 420 districts in our sample, the median district income is 13.7 (that is, $13,700 per person), and it ranges from 5.3 ($5300 per person) to 55.3 ($55,300 per person).

Figure 8.2 shows a scatterplot of fifth-grade test scores against district income for the California data set, along with the OLS regression line relating these two variables. Test scores and average income are strongly positively correlated, with a correlation coefficient of 0.71; students from affluent districts do better on the tests than students from poor districts. But this scatterplot has a peculiarity: Most of the points are below the OLS line when income is very low (under $10,000) or very high (over $40,000), but are above the line when income is between $15,000 and $30,000. There seems to be some curvature in the relationship between test scores and income that is not captured by the linear regression.

In short, it seems that the relationship between district income and test scores is not a straight line. Rather, it is nonlinear. A nonlinear function is a function with a slope that is not constant: The function $f(X)$ is linear if the slope of $f(X)$ is the same for all values of X, but if the slope depends on the value of X, then $f(X)$ is nonlinear.

If a straight line is not an adequate description of the relationship between district income and test scores, what is? Imagine drawing a curve that fits the points in Figure 8.2. This curve would be steep for low values of district income, then would flatten out as district income gets higher. One way to approximate such a curve mathematically is to model the relationship as a quadratic function. That is, we could model test scores as a function of income *and* the square of income.

A quadratic population regression model relating test scores and income is written mathematically as

$$TestScore_i = \beta_0 + \beta_1 Income_i + \beta_2 Income_i^2 + u_i, \qquad (8.1)$$

where β_0, β_1, and β_2 are coefficients, $Income_i$ is the income in the ith district, $Income_i^2$, is the square of income in the ith district, and u_i is an error term that, as usual, represents all the other factors that determine test scores. Equation (8.1) is called the **quadratic regression model** because the population regression function, $E(TestScore_i | Income_i) = \beta_0 + \beta_1 Income_i + \beta_2 Income_i^2$, is a quadratic function of the independent variable, *Income.*

If you knew the population coefficients β_0, β_1, and β_2 in Equation (8.1), you could predict the test score of a district based on its average income. But these population coefficients are unknown and therefore must be estimated using a sample of data.

At first, it might seem difficult to find the coefficients of the quadratic function that best fits the data in Figure 8.2. If you compare Equation (8.1) with the multiple regression model in Key Concept 6.2, however, you will see that Equation (8.1) is in fact a version of the multiple regression model with two regressors: The first regressor is *Income,* and the second regressor is *Income²*. Thus, after defining the regressors as *Income* and *Income²*, the nonlinear model in Equation (8.1) is simply a multiple regression model with two regressors!

Because the quadratic regression model is a variant of multiple regression, its unknown population coefficients can be estimated and tested using the OLS methods described in Chapters 6 and 7. Estimating the coefficients of Equation (8.1) using OLS for the 420 observations in Figure 8.2 yields

$$\widehat{TestScore} = 607.3 + 3.85 Income - 0.0423 Income^2, \overline{R}^2 = 0.554, \qquad (8.2)$$
$$(2.9) \quad (0.27) \qquad\qquad (0.0048)$$

where (as usual) standard errors of the estimated coefficients are given in parentheses. The estimated regression function (8.2) is plotted in Figure 8.3,

---

FIGURE 8.3   **Scatterplot of Test Score vs. District Income with Linear and Quadratic Regression Functions**

The quadratic OLS regression function fits the data better than the linear OLS regression function.

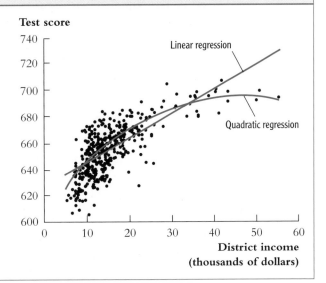

---

superimposed over the scatterplot of the data. The quadratic function captures the curvature in the scatterplot: It is steep for low values of district income but flattens out when district income is high. In short, the quadratic regression function seems to fit the data better than the linear one.

We can go one step beyond this visual comparison and formally test the hypothesis that the relationship between income and test scores is linear, against the alternative that it is nonlinear. If the relationship is linear, then the regression function is correctly specified as Equation (8.1), except that the regressor *Income*^{2} is absent; that is, if the relationship is linear, then Equation (8.1) holds with $\beta_2 = 0$. Thus, we can test the null hypothesis that the population regression function is linear against the alternative that it is quadratic by testing the null hypothesis that $\beta_2 = 0$ against the alternative that $\beta_2 \neq 0$.

Because Equation (8.1) is just a variant of the multiple regression model, the null hypothesis that $\beta_2 = 0$ can be tested by constructing the t-statistic for this hypothesis. This t-statistic is $t = (\hat{\beta}_2 - 0)/SE(\hat{\beta}_2)$, which from Equation (8.2) is $t = -0.0423/0.0048 = -8.81$. In absolute value, this exceeds the 5% critical value of this test (which is 1.96). Indeed the p-value for the t-statistic is less than 0.01%, so we can reject the hypothesis that $\beta_2 = 0$ at all conventional significance levels. Thus this formal hypothesis test supports our informal inspection of Figures 8.2 and 8.3: The quadratic model fits the data better than the linear model.

The Effect on Y of a Change in X in Nonlinear Specifications

Put aside the test score example for a moment and consider a general problem. You want to know how the dependent variable Y is expected to change when the independent variable X_1 changes by the amount ΔX_1, holding constant other independent variables $X_2, \ldots, X_k$. When the population regression function is linear, this effect is easy to calculate: As shown in Equation (6.4), the expected change in Y is $\Delta Y = \beta_1 \Delta X_1$, where β_1 is the population regression coefficient multiplying X_1. When the regression function is nonlinear, however, the expected change in Y is more complicated to calculate because it can depend on the values of the independent variables.

A general formula for a nonlinear population regression function.[1]   The nonlinear population regression models considered in this chapter are of the form

$$Y_i = f(X_{1i}, X_{2i}, \ldots, X_{ki}) + u_i, i = 1, \ldots, n, \tag{8.3}$$

where $f(X_{1i}, X_{2i}, \ldots, X_{ki})$ is the population **nonlinear regression function**, a possibly nonlinear function of the independent variables $X_{1i}, X_{2i}, \ldots, X_{ki}$, and u_i is the error term. For example, in the quadratic regression model in Equation (8.1), only one independent variable is present, so X_1 is *Income* and the population regression function is $f(Income_i) = \beta_0 + \beta_1 Income_i + \beta_2 Income_i^2$.

Because the population regression function is the conditional expectation of Y_i given $X_{1i}, X_{2i}, \ldots, X_{ki}$, in Equation (8.3) we allow for the possibility that this conditional expectation is a nonlinear function of $X_{1i}, X_{2i}, \ldots, X_{ki}$, that is, $E(Y_i | X_{1i}, X_{2i}, \ldots, X_{ki}) = f(X_{1i}, X_{2i}, \ldots, X_{ki})$, where f can be a nonlinear function. If the population regression function is linear, then $f(X_{1i}, X_{2i}, \ldots, X_{ki}) = \beta_0 + \beta_1 X_{1i} + \beta_2 X_{2i} + \cdots + \beta_k X_{ki}$, and Equation (8.3) becomes the linear regression model in Key Concept 6.2. However, Equation (8.3) allows for nonlinear regression functions as well.

The effect on Y of a change in X_1.   As discussed in Section 6.2, the effect on Y of a change in $X_1, \Delta X_1$, holding $X_2, \ldots, X_k$ constant, is the difference in the

---

[1]The term "nonlinear regression" applies to two conceptually different families of models. In the first family, the population regression function is a nonlinear function of the X's but is a linear function of the unknown parameters (the β's). In the second family, the population regression function is a nonlinear function of the unknown parameters and may or may not be a nonlinear function of the X's. The models in the body of this chapter are all in the first family. Appendix 8.1 takes up models from the second family.

THE EXPECTED EFFECT ON Y OF A CHANGE IN X_1 IN THE NONLINEAR REGRESSION MODEL (8.3)	KEY CONCEPT **8.1**

The expected change in Y, ΔY, associated with the change in X_1, ΔX_1, holding X_2, $\ldots$, X_k constant, is the difference between the value of the population regression function before and after changing X_1, holding $X_2, \ldots, X_k$ constant. That is, the expected change in Y is the difference:

$$\Delta Y = f(X_1 + \Delta X_1, X_2, \ldots, X_k) - f(X_1, X_2, \ldots, X_k). \qquad (8.4)$$

The estimator of this unknown population difference is the difference between the predicted values for these two cases. Let $\hat{f}(X_1, X_2, \ldots, X_k)$ be the predicted value of Y based on the estimator $\hat{f}$ of the population regression function. Then the predicted change in Y is

$$\Delta \hat{Y} = \hat{f}(X_1 + \Delta X_1, X_2, \ldots, X_k) - \hat{f}(X_1, X_2, \ldots, X_k). \qquad (8.5)$$

---

expected value of Y when the independent variables take on the values $X_1 + \Delta X_1$, $X_2, \ldots, X_k$ and the expected value of Y when the independent variables take on the values $X_1, X_2, \ldots, X_k$. The difference between these two expected values, say ΔY, is what happens to Y on average in the population when X_1 changes by an amount ΔX_1, holding constant the other variables $X_2, \ldots, X_k$. In the nonlinear regression model of Equation (8.3), this effect on Y is $\Delta Y = f(X_1 + \Delta X_1, X_2, \ldots, X_k) - f(X_1, X_2, \ldots, X_k)$.

Because the regression function f is unknown, the population effect on Y of a change in X_1 is also unknown. To estimate the population effect, first estimate the population regression function. At a general level, denote this estimated function by $\hat{f}$; an example of such an estimated function is the estimated quadratic regression function in Equation (8.2). The estimated effect on Y (denoted $\Delta \hat{Y}$) of the change in X_1 is the difference between the predicted value of Y when the independent variables take on the values $X_1 + \Delta X_1, X_2, \ldots, X_k$ and the predicted value of Y when they take on the values $X_1, X_2, \ldots, X_k$.

The method for calculating the expected effect on Y of a change in X_1 is summarized in Key Concept 8.1.

Application to test scores and income. What is the predicted change in test scores associated with a change in district income of $1000, based on the estimated quadratic regression function in Equation (8.2)? Because that regression function is quadratic, this effect depends on the initial district income. We therefore consider two cases: an increase in district income from 10 to 11 (i.e., from $10,000 per capita to $11,000) and an increase in district income from 40 to 41.

To compute $\Delta \hat{Y}$ associated with the change in income from 10 to 11, we can apply the general formula in Equation (8.5) to the quadratic regression model. Doing so yields

$$\Delta \hat{Y} = (\hat{\beta}_0 + \hat{\beta}_1 \times 11 + \hat{\beta}_2 \times 11^2) - (\hat{\beta}_0 + \hat{\beta}_1 \times 10 + \hat{\beta}_2 \times 10^2), \qquad (8.6)$$

where $\hat{\beta}_0, \hat{\beta}_1$, and $\hat{\beta}_2$ are the OLS estimators.

The term in the first set of parentheses in Equation (8.6) is the predicted value of Y when *Income* $= 11$, and the term in the second set of parentheses is the predicted value of Y when *Income* $= 10$. These predicted values are calculated using the OLS estimates of the coefficients in Equation (8.2). Accordingly, when *Income* $= 10$, the predicted value of test scores is $607.3 + 3.85 \times 10 - 0.0423 \times 10^2 = 641.57$. When *Income* $= 11$, the predicted value is $607.3 + 3.85 \times 11 - 0.0423 \times 11^2 = 644.53$. The difference in these two predicted values is $\Delta \hat{Y} = 644.53 - 641.57 = 2.96$ points, that is, the predicted difference in test scores between a district with average income of $11,000 and one with average income of $10,000 is 2.96 points.

In the second case, when income changes from $40,000 to $41,000, the difference in the predicted values in Equation (8.6) is $\Delta \hat{Y} = (607.3 + 3.85 \times 41 - 0.0423 \times 41^2) - (607.3 + 3.85 \times 40 - 0.0423 \times 40^2) = 694.04 - 693.62 = 0.42$ points. Thus, a change of income of $1000 is associated with a larger change in predicted test scores if the initial income is $10,000 than if it is $40,000 (the predicted changes are 2.96 points versus 0.42 point). Said differently, the slope of the estimated quadratic regression function in Figure 8.3 is steeper at low values of income (like $10,000) than at the higher values of income (like $40,000).

Standard errors of estimated effects.   The estimator of the effect on Y of changing X_1 depends on the estimator of the population regression function, $\hat{f}$, which varies from one sample to the next. Therefore the estimated effect contains sampling error. One way to quantify the sampling uncertainty associated with the estimated effect is to compute a confidence interval for the true population effect. To do so, we need to compute the standard error of $\Delta \hat{Y}$ in Equation (8.5).

It is easy to compute a standard error for $\Delta \hat{Y}$ when the regression function is linear. The estimated effect of a change in X_1 is $\hat{\beta}_1 \Delta X_1$, so a 95% confidence interval for the estimated change is $\hat{\beta}_1 \Delta X_1 \pm 1.96 SE(\hat{\beta}_1) \Delta X_1$.

In the nonlinear regression models of this chapter, the standard error of $\Delta \hat{Y}$ can be computed using the tools introduced in Section 7.3 for testing a single restriction involving multiple coefficients. To illustrate this method, consider the estimated change in test scores associated with a change in income from 10 to 11 in Equation (8.6), which is $\Delta\hat{Y} = \hat{\beta}_1 \times (11 - 10) + \hat{\beta}_2 \times (11^2 - 10^2) = \hat{\beta}_1 + 21\hat{\beta}_2$. The standard error of the predicted change therefore is

$$SE(\Delta\hat{Y}) = SE(\hat{\beta}_1 + 21\hat{\beta}_2). \qquad (8.7)$$

Thus, if we can compute the standard error of $\hat{\beta}_1 + 21\hat{\beta}_2$, then we have computed the standard error of $\Delta\hat{Y}$. There are two methods for doing this using standard regression software, which correspond to the two approaches in Section 7.3 for testing a single restriction on multiple coefficients.

The first method is to use "approach #1" of Section 7.3, which is to compute the F-statistic testing the hypothesis that $\beta_1 + 21\beta_2 = 0$. The standard error of $\Delta\hat{Y}$ is then given by[2]

$$SE(\Delta\hat{Y}) = \frac{|\Delta\hat{Y}|}{\sqrt{F}}. \qquad (8.8)$$

When applied to the quadratic regression in Equation (8.2), the F-statistic testing the hypothesis that $\beta_1 + 21\beta_2 = 0$ is $F = 299.94$. Because $\Delta\hat{Y} = 2.96$, applying Equation (8.8) gives $SE(\Delta\hat{Y}) = 2.96/\sqrt{299.94} = 0.17$. Thus a 95% confidence interval for the change in the expected value of Y is $2.96 \pm 1.96 \times 0.17$ or $(2.63, 3.29)$.

The second method is to use "approach #2" of Section 7.3, which entails transforming the regressors so that, in the transformed regression, one of the coefficients is $\beta_1 + 21\beta_2$. Doing this transformation is left as an exercise (Exercise 8.9).

A comment on interpreting coefficients in nonlinear specifications. In the multiple regression model of Chapters 6 and 7, the regression coefficients had a natural interpretation. For example, β_1 is the expected change in Y associated with a change in X_1, holding the other regressors constant. But, as we have seen, this is not generally the case in a nonlinear model. That is, it is not very helpful to think of β_1 in Equation (8.1) as being the effect of changing the district's income, holding the square of the district's income constant. This means that in nonlinear models, the regression function is best interpreted by graphing it and by calculating the predicted effect on Y of changing one or more of the independent variables.

---

[2]Equation (8.8) is derived by noting that the F-statistic is the square of the t-statistic testing this hypothesis, that is, $F = t^2 = [(\hat{\beta}_1 + 21\hat{\beta}_2)/SE(\hat{\beta}_1 + 21\hat{\beta}_2)]^2 = [\Delta\hat{Y}/SE(\Delta\hat{Y})]^2$, and solving for $SE(\Delta\hat{Y})$.

A General Approach to Modeling Nonlinearities Using Multiple Regression

The general approach to modeling nonlinear regression functions taken in this chapter has five elements:

1. *Identify a possible nonlinear relationship.* The best thing to do is to use economic theory and what you know about the application to suggest a possible nonlinear relationship. Before you even look at the data, ask yourself whether the slope of the regression function relating Y and X might reasonably depend on the value of X or on another independent variable. Why might such nonlinear dependence exist? What nonlinear shapes does this suggest? For example, thinking about classroom dynamics with 11-year-olds suggests that cutting class size from 18 students to 17 could have a greater effect than cutting it from 30 to 29.

2. *Specify a nonlinear function and estimate its parameters by OLS.* Sections 8.2 and 8.3 contain various nonlinear regression functions that can be estimated by OLS. After working through these sections you will understand the characteristics of each of these functions.

3. *Determine whether the nonlinear model improves upon a linear model.* Just because you think a regression function is nonlinear does not mean it really is! You must determine empirically whether your nonlinear model is appropriate. Most of the time you can use t-statistics and F-statistics to test the null hypothesis that the population regression function is linear against the alternative that it is nonlinear.

4. *Plot the estimated nonlinear regression function.* Does the estimated regression function describe the data well? Looking at Figures 8.2 and 8.3 suggested that the quadratic model fit the data better than the linear model.

5. *Estimate the effect on Y of a change in X.* The final step is to use the estimated regression to calculate the effect on Y of a change in one or more regressors X using the method in Key Concept 8.1.

8.2   Nonlinear Functions of a Single Independent Variable

This section provides two methods for modeling a nonlinear regression function. To keep things simple, we develop these methods for a nonlinear regression function that involves only one independent variable, X. As we see in Section 8.5, however, these models can be modified to include multiple independent variables.

The first method discussed in this section is polynomial regression, an extension of the quadratic regression used in the last section to model the relationship between test scores and income. The second method uses logarithms of X and/or Y. Although these methods are presented separately, they can be used in combination.

Polynomials

One way to specify a nonlinear regression function is to use a polynomial in X. In general, let r denote the highest power of X that is included in the regression. The **polynomial regression model** of degree r is

$$Y_i = \beta_0 + \beta_1 X_i + \beta_2 X_i^2 + \cdots + \beta_r X_i^r + u_i. \tag{8.9}$$

When $r = 2$, Equation (8.9) is the quadratic regression model discussed in Section 8.1. When $r = 3$, so that the highest power of X included is X^3, Equation (8.9) is called the **cubic regression model.**

The polynomial regression model is similar to the multiple regression model of Chapter 6, except that in Chapter 6 the regressors were distinct independent variables, whereas here the regressors are powers of the same dependent variable, X, that is, the regressors are X, X^2, X^3, and so on. Thus the techniques for estimation and inference developed for multiple regression can be applied here. In particular, the unknown coefficients $\beta_0, \beta_1, \ldots, \beta_r$ in Equation (8.9) can be estimated by OLS regression of Y_i against $X_i, X_i^2, \ldots, X_i^r$.

Testing the null hypothesis that the population regression function is linear.   If the population regression function is linear, then the quadratic and higher-order terms do not enter the population regression function. Accordingly, the null hypothesis (H_0) that the regression is linear and the alternative (H_1) that it is a polynomial of degree r correspond to

$$H_0: \beta_2 = 0, \beta_3 = 0, \ldots, \beta_r = 0 \text{ vs. } H_1: \text{at least one } \beta_j \neq 0, j = 2, \ldots, r. \tag{8.10}$$

The null hypothesis that the population regression function is linear can be tested against the alternative that it is a polynomial of degree r by testing H_0 against H_1 in Equation (8.10). Because H_0 is a joint null hypothesis with $q = r - 1$ restrictions on the coefficients of the population polynomial regression model, it can be tested using the F-statistic as described in Section 7.2.

Which degree polynomial should I use?   That is, how many powers of X should be included in a polynomial regression? The answer balances a tradeoff between flexibility and statistical precision. Increasing the degree r introduces more flexibility into the regression function and allows it to match more shapes; a polynomial of degree r can have up to $r - 1$ bends (that is, inflection points) in its graph. But increasing r means adding more regressors, which can reduce the precision of the estimated coefficients.

Thus the answer to the question of how many terms to include is that you should include enough to model the nonlinear regression function adequately, but no more. Unfortunately, this answer is not very useful in practice!

A practical way to determine the degree of the polynomial is to ask whether the coefficients in Equation (8.9) associated with largest values of r are zero. If so, then these terms can be dropped from the regression. This procedure, which is called sequential hypothesis testing because individual hypotheses are tested sequentially, is summarized in the following steps:

1. Pick a maximum value of r and estimate the polynomial regression for that r.

2. Use the t-statistic to test the hypothesis that the coefficient on X^r [β_r in Equation (8.9)] is zero. If you reject this hypothesis, then X^r belongs in the regression, so use the polynomial of degree r.

3. If you do not reject $\beta_r = 0$ in step 2, eliminate X^r from the regression and estimate a polynomial regression of degree $r - 1$. Test whether the coefficient on X^{r-1} is zero. If you reject, use the polynomial of degree $r - 1$.

4. If you do not reject $\beta_{r-1} = 0$ in step 3, continue this procedure until the coefficient on the highest power in your polynomial is statistically significant.

This recipe has one missing ingredient: the initial degree r of the polynomial. In many applications involving economic data, the nonlinear functions are smooth, that is, they do not have sharp jumps or "spikes." If so, then it is appropriate to choose a small maximum order for the polynomial, such as 2, 3, or 4—that is, begin with $r = 2$ or 3 or 4 in step 1.

Application to district income and test scores.   The estimated cubic regression function relating district income to test scores is

$$\widehat{TestScore} = 600.1 + 5.02 Income - 0.096 Income^2 + 0.00069 Income^3,$$
$$\phantom{\widehat{TestScore} =} (5.1) \ (0.71) (0.029) (0.00035)$$

$$\overline{R}^2 = 0.555.$$

(8.11)

The t-statistic on $Income^3$ is 1.97, so the null hypothesis that the regression function is a quadratic is rejected against the alternative that it is a cubic at the 5%

level. Moreover, the F-statistic testing the joint null hypothesis that the coefficients on $Income^2$ and $Income^3$ are both zero is 37.7, with a p-value less than 0.01%, so the null hypothesis that the regression function is linear is rejected against the alternative that it is either a quadratic or a cubic.

Interpretation of coefficients in polynomial regression models. The coefficients in polynomial regressions do not have a simple interpretation. The best way to interpret polynomial regressions is to plot the estimated regression function and to calculate the estimated effect on Y associated with a change in X for one or more values of X.

Logarithms

Another way to specify a nonlinear regression function is to use the natural logarithm of Y and/or X. Logarithms convert changes in variables into percentage changes, and many relationships are naturally expressed in terms of percentages. Here are some examples:

- The box in Chapter 3, "The Gender Gap in Earnings of College Graduates in the United States," examined the wage gap between male and female college graduates. In that discussion, the wage gap was measured in terms of dollars. However, it is easier to compare wage gaps across professions and over time when they are expressed in percentage terms.

- In Section 8.1, we found that district income and test scores were nonlinearly related. Would this relationship be linear using percentage changes? That is, might it be that a change in district income of 1%—rather than $1000—is associated with a change in test scores that is approximately constant for different values of income?

- In the economic analysis of consumer demand, it is often assumed that a 1% increase in price leads to a certain *percentage* decrease in the quantity demanded. The percentage decrease in demand resulting from a 1% increase in price is called the price **elasticity**.

Regression specifications that use natural logarithms allow regression models to estimate percentage relationships such as these. Before introducing those specifications, we review the exponential and natural logarithm functions.

The exponential function and the natural logarithm. The exponential function and its inverse, the natural logarithm, play an important role in modeling nonlinear regression functions. The **exponential function** of x is e^x (that is, e raised to the power x), where e is the constant $2.71828\ldots$; the exponential function is

---

FIGURE 8.4   **The Logarithm Function, Y = ln(X)**

The logarithmic function $Y = \ln(X)$ is steeper for small than for large values of X, is only defined for $X > 0$, and has slope $1/X$.

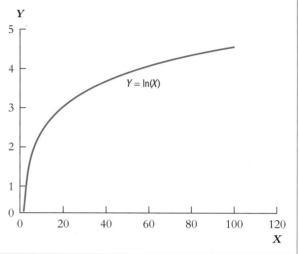

---

also written as $\exp(x)$. The **natural logarithm** is the inverse of the exponential function; that is, the natural logarithm is the function for which $x = \ln(e^x)$ or, equivalently, $x = \ln[\exp(x)]$. The base of the natural logarithm is e. Although there are logarithms in other bases, such as base 10, in this book we consider only logarithms in base e, that is, the natural logarithm, so when we use the term "logarithm" we always mean "natural logarithm."

The logarithm function, $y = \ln(x)$, is graphed in Figure 8.4. Note that the logarithm function is defined only for positive values of x. The logarithm function has a slope that is steep at first, then flattens out (although the function continues to increase). The slope of the logarithm function $\ln(x)$ is $1/x$.

The logarithm function has the following useful properties:

$$\ln(1/x) = -\ln(x); \tag{8.12}$$

$$\ln(ax) = \ln(a) + \ln(x); \tag{8.13}$$

$$\ln(x/a) = \ln(x) - \ln(a); \text{ and} \tag{8.14}$$

$$\ln(x^a) = a\ln(x). \tag{8.15}$$

Logarithms and percentages.   The link between the logarithm and percentages relies on a key fact: When Δx is small, the difference between the logarithm of $x + \Delta x$ and the logarithm of x is approximately $\frac{\Delta x}{x}$, the percentage change in x divided by 100. That is,

$$\ln(x + \Delta x) - \ln(x) \cong \frac{\Delta x}{x} \quad \left(\text{when } \frac{\Delta x}{x} \text{ is small}\right), \tag{8.16}$$

where "$\cong$" means "approximately equal to." The derivation of this approximation relies on calculus, but it is readily demonstrated by trying out some values of x and Δx. For example, when $x = 100$ and $\Delta x = 1$, then $\Delta x/x = 1/100 = 0.01$ (or 1%), while $\ln(x + \Delta x) - \ln(x) = \ln(101) - \ln(100) = 0.00995$ (or 0.995%). Thus $\Delta x/x$ (which is 0.01) is very close to $\ln(x + \Delta x) - \ln(x)$ (which is 0.00995). When $\Delta x = 5, \Delta x/x = 5/100 = 0.05$, while $\ln(x + \Delta x) - \ln(x) = \ln(105) - \ln(100) = 0.04879$.

The three logarithmic regression models.   There are three different cases in which logarithms might be used: when X is transformed by taking its logarithm but Y is not; when Y is transformed to its logarithm but X is not; and when both Y and X are transformed to their logarithms. The interpretation of the regression coefficients is different in each case. We discuss these three cases in turn.

Case I: X is in logarithms, Y is not.   In this case, the regression model is

$$Y_i = \beta_0 + \beta_1 \ln(X_i) + u_i, i = 1, \ldots, n. \tag{8.17}$$

Because Y is not in logarithms but X is, this is sometimes referred to as a **linear-log model**.

In the linear-log model, a 1% change in X is associated with a change in Y of $0.01\beta_1$. To see this, consider the difference between the population regression function at values of X that differ by ΔX: This is $[\beta_0 + \beta_1 \ln(X + \Delta X)] - [\beta_0 + \beta_1 \ln(X)]$ $= \beta_1[\ln(X + \Delta X) - \ln(X)] \cong \beta_1(\Delta X/X)$ where the final step uses the approximation in Equation (8.16). If X changes by 1%, then $\Delta X/X = 0.01$; thus, in this model a 1% change in X is associated with a change of Y of $0.01\beta_1$.

The only difference between the regression model in Equation (8.17) and the regression model of Chapter 4 with a single regressor is that the right-hand variable is now the logarithm of X rather than X itself. To estimate the coefficients β_0 and β_1 in Equation (8.17), first compute a new variable, $\ln(X)$; this is readily done using a spreadsheet or statistical software. Then β_0 and β_1 can be estimated by the OLS regression of Y_i on $\ln(X_i)$, hypotheses about β_1 can be tested using the t-statistic, and a 95% confidence interval for β_1 can be constructed as $\hat{\beta}_1 \pm 1.96SE(\hat{\beta}_1)$.

As an example, return to the relationship between district income and test scores. Instead of the quadratic specification, we could use the linear-log specification in Equation (8.17). Estimating this regression by OLS yields

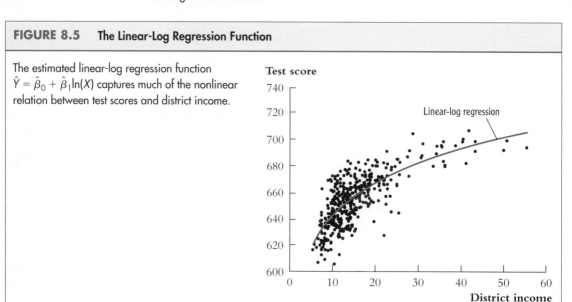

FIGURE 8.5 **The Linear-Log Regression Function**

The estimated linear-log regression function $\hat{Y} = \hat{\beta}_0 + \hat{\beta}_1 \ln(X)$ captures much of the nonlinear relation between test scores and district income.

$$\widehat{TestScore} = 557.8 + 36.42\ln(Income), \ \overline{R}^2 = 0.561. \qquad (8.18)$$
$$(3.8) \quad (1.40)$$

According to Equation (8.18), a 1% increase in income is associated with an increase in test scores of $0.01 \times 36.42 = 0.36$ points.

To estimate the effect on Y of a change in X in its original units of thousands of dollars (not in logarithms), we can use the method in Key Concept 8.1. For example, what is the predicted difference in test scores for districts with average incomes of \$10,000 versus \$11,000? The estimated value of ΔY is the difference between the predicted values: $\Delta\hat{Y} = [557.8 + 36.42\ln(11)] - [557.8 + 36.42\ln(10)] = 36.42 \times [\ln(11) - \ln(10)] = 3.47$. Similarly, the predicted difference between a district with average income of \$40,000 and a district with average income of \$41,000 is $36.42 \times [\ln(41) - \ln(40)] = 0.90$. Thus, like the quadratic specification, this regression predicts that a \$1000 increase in income has a larger effect on test scores in poor districts than it does in affluent districts.

The estimated linear-log regression function in Equation (8.18) is plotted in Figure 8.5. Because the regressor in Equation (8.18) is the natural logarithm of income rather than income, the estimated regression function is not a straight line. Like the quadratic regression function in Figure 8.3, it is initially steep but then flattens out for higher levels of income.

Case II: Y is in logarithms, X is not. In this case, the regression model is

$$\ln(Y_i) = \beta_0 + \beta_1 X_i + u_i. \tag{8.19}$$

Because Y is in logarithms but X is not, this is referred to as a **log-linear model**.

In the log-linear model, a one-unit change in X ($\Delta X = 1$) is associated with a $100 \times \beta_1\%$ change in Y. To see this, compare the expected values of $\ln(Y)$ for values of X that differ by ΔX. The expected value of $\ln(Y)$ given X is $\ln(Y) = \beta_0 + \beta_1 X$. When X is $X + \Delta X$, the expected value is given by $\ln(Y + \Delta Y) = \beta_0 + \beta_1(X + \Delta X)$. Thus the difference between these expected values is $\ln(Y + \Delta Y) - \ln(Y) = [\beta_0 + \beta_1(X + \Delta X)] - [\beta_0 + \beta_1 X] = \beta_1 \Delta X$. From the approximation in Equation (8.16), however, if $\beta_1 \Delta X$ is small, then $\ln(Y + \Delta Y) - \ln(Y) \cong \Delta Y / Y$. Thus, $\Delta Y / Y \cong \beta_1 \Delta X$. If $\Delta X = 1$, so that X changes by one unit, then $\Delta Y / Y$ changes by β_1. Translated into percentages, a unit change in X is associated with a $100 \times \beta_1\%$ change in Y.

As an illustration, we return to the empirical example of Section 3.7, the relationship between age and earnings of college graduates. Many employment contracts specify that, for each additional year of service, a worker gets a certain percentage increase in his or her wage. This percentage relationship suggests estimating the log-linear specification in Equation (8.19) so that each additional year of age (X) is, on average in the population, associated with some constant percentage increase in earnings (Y). By first computing the new dependent variable, $\ln(Earnings_i)$, the unknown coefficients β_0 and β_1 can be estimated by the OLS regression of $\ln(Earnings_i)$ against Age_i. When estimated using the 12,777 observations on college graduates in the 2005 Current Population Survey (the data are described in Appendix 3.1), this relationship is

$$\widehat{\ln(Earnings)} = 2.655 + 0.0086 Age, \overline{R}^2 = 0.030. \tag{8.20}$$
$$(0.019) \quad (0.0005)$$

According to this regression, earnings are predicted to increase by 0.86% $[(100 \times 0.0086)\%]$ for each additional year of age.

Case III: Both X and Y are in logarithms. In this case, the regression model is

$$\ln(Y_i) = \beta_0 + \beta_1 \ln(X_i) + u_i. \tag{8.21}$$

Because both Y and X are specified in logarithms, this is referred to as a **log-log model**.

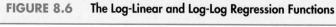

FIGURE 8.6 **The Log-Linear and Log-Log Regression Functions**

In the log-linear regression function, ln(Y) is a linear function of X. In the log-log regression function, ln(Y) is a linear function of ln(X).

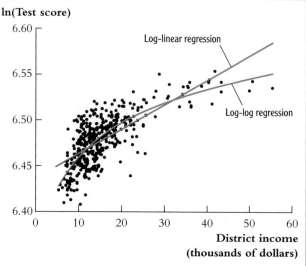

In the log-log model, a 1% change in X is associated with a $\beta_1\%$ change in Y. Thus, in this specification β_1 is the elasticity of Y with respect to X. To see this, again apply Key Concept 8.1; thus $\ln(Y + \Delta Y) - \ln(Y) = [\beta_0 + \beta_1\ln(X + \Delta X)] - [\beta_0 + \beta_1\ln(X)] = \beta_1[\ln(X + \Delta X) - \ln(X)]$. Application of the approximation in Equation (8.16) to both sides of this equation yields

$$\frac{\Delta Y}{Y} \cong \beta_1\frac{\Delta X}{X} \text{ or}$$

$$\beta_1 = \frac{\Delta Y/Y}{\Delta X/X} = \frac{100 \times (\Delta Y/Y)}{100 \times (\Delta X/X)} = \frac{\text{percentage change in } Y}{\text{percentage change in } X}. \tag{8.22}$$

Thus, in the log-log specification β_1 is the ratio of the percentage change in Y associated with the percentage change in X. If the percentage change in X is 1% (that is, if $\Delta X = 0.01X$), then β_1 is the percentage change in Y associated with a 1% change in X. That is, β_1 is the elasticity of Y with respect to X.

As an illustration, return to the relationship between income and test scores. When this relationship is specified in this form, the unknown coefficients are estimated by a regression of the logarithm of test scores against the logarithm of income. The resulting estimated equation is

$$\widehat{\ln(TestScore)} = 6.336 + 0.0554\ln(Income), \overline{R}^2 = 0.557. \tag{8.23}$$
$$(0.006) \quad (0.0021)$$

LOGARITHMS IN REGRESSION: THREE CASES

Logarithms can be used to transform the dependent variable Y, an independent variable X, or both (but they must be positive). The following table summarizes these three cases and the interpretation of the regression coefficient β_1. In each case, β_1 can be estimated by applying OLS after taking the logarithm of the dependent and/or independent variable.

Case	Regression Specification	Interpretation of β_1
I	$Y_i = \beta_0 + \beta_1 \ln(X_i) + u_i$	A 1% change in X is associated with a change in Y of $0.01\beta_1$.
II	$\ln(Y_i) = \beta_0 + \beta_1 X_i + u_i$	A change in X by 1 unit ($\Delta X = 1$) is associated with a $100\beta_1\%$ change in Y.
III	$\ln(Y_i) = \beta_0 + \beta_1 \ln(X_i) + u_i$	A 1% change in X is associated with a $\beta_1\%$ change in Y, so β_1 is the elasticity of Y with respect to X.

According to this estimated regression function, a 1% increase in income is estimated to correspond to a 0.0554% increase in test scores.

The estimated log-log regression function in Equation (8.23) is plotted in Figure 8.6. Because Y is in logarithms, the vertical axis in Figure 8.6 is the logarithm of the test score, and the scatterplot is the logarithm of test scores versus district income. For comparison purposes, Figure 8.6 also shows the estimated regression function for a log-linear specification, which is

$$\widehat{\ln(TestScore)} = 6.439 + 0.00284 Income, \ \overline{R}^2 = 0.497. \qquad (8.24)$$
$$(0.003) \quad (0.00018)$$

Because the vertical axis is in logarithms, the regression function in Equation (8.24) is the straight line in Figure 8.6.

As you can see in Figure 8.6, the log-log specification fits slightly better than the log-linear specification. This is consistent with the higher $\overline{R}^2$ for the log-log regression (0.557) than for the log-linear regression (0.497). Even so, the log-log specification does not fit the data especially well: At the lower values of income, most of the observations fall below the log-log curve, while in the middle income range most of the observations fall above the estimated regression function.

The three logarithmic regression models are summarized in Key Concept 8.2.

A difficulty with comparing logarithmic specifications. Which of the log regression models best fits the data? As we saw in the discussion of Equations (8.23) and (8.24), the $\overline{R}^2$ can be used to compare the log-linear and log-log models; as it happened, the log-log model had the higher $\overline{R}^2$. Similarly, the $\overline{R}^2$ can be used to compare the linear-log regression in Equation (8.18) and the linear regression of Y against X. In the test score and income regression, the linear-log regression has an $\overline{R}^2$ of 0.561 while the linear regression has an $\overline{R}^2$ of 0.508, so the linear-log model fits the data better.

How can we compare the linear-log model and the log-log model? Unfortunately, the $\overline{R}^2$ *cannot* be used to compare these two regressions because their dependent variables are different [one is Y_i, the other is $\ln(Y_i)$]. Recall that the $\overline{R}^2$ measures the fraction of the variance of the dependent variable explained by the regressors. Because the dependent variables in the log-log and linear-log models are different, it does not make sense to compare their $\overline{R}^2$'s.

Because of this problem, the best thing to do in a particular application is to decide, using economic theory and either your or other experts' knowledge of the problem, whether it makes sense to specify Y in logarithms. For example, labor economists typically model earnings using logarithms because wage comparisons, contract wage increases, and so forth are often most naturally discussed in percentage terms. In modeling test scores, it seems (to us, anyway) natural to discuss test results in terms of points on the test rather than percentage increases in the test scores, so we focus on models in which the dependent variable is the test score rather than its logarithm.

Computing predicted values of Y when Y is in logarithms. [3] If the dependent variable Y has been transformed by taking logarithms, the estimated regression can be used to compute directly the predicted value of $\ln(Y)$. However, it is a bit trickier to compute the predicted value of Y itself.

To see this, consider the log-linear regression model in Equation (8.19), and rewrite it so that it is specified in terms of Y rather than $\ln(Y)$. To do so, take the exponential function of both sides of the Equation (8.19); the result is

$$Y_i = \exp(\beta_0 + \beta_1 X_i + u_i) = e^{\beta_0 + \beta_1 X_i} e^{u_i}. \tag{8.25}$$

If u_i is distributed independently of X_i, then the expected value of Y_i given X_i is $E(Y_i|X_i) = E(e^{\beta_0 + \beta_1 X_i} e^{u_i}|X_i) = e^{\beta_0 + \beta_1 X_i} E(e^{u_i})$. The problem is that even if $E(u_i) = 0$, $E(e^{u_i}) \neq 1$. Thus, the appropriate predicted value of Y_i is not simply obtained

---

[3]This material is more advanced and can be skipped without loss of continuity.

by taking the exponential function of $\hat{\beta}_0 + \hat{\beta}_1 X_i$, that is, by setting $\hat{Y}_i = e^{\hat{\beta}_0 + \hat{\beta}_1 X_i}$. This predicted value is biased because of the missing factor $E(e^{u_i})$.

One solution to this problem is to estimate the factor $E(e^{u_i})$ and to use this estimate when computing the predicted value of Y, but this gets complicated and we do not pursue it further.

Another solution, which is the approach used in this book, is to compute predicted values of the logarithm of Y but not to transform them to their original units. In practice, this is often acceptable because when the dependent variable is specified as a logarithm, it is often most natural just to use the logarithmic specification (and the associated percentage interpretations) throughout the analysis.

Polynomial and Logarithmic Models of Test Scores and District Income

In practice, economic theory or expert judgment might suggest a functional form to use, but in the end the true form of the population regression function is unknown. In practice, fitting a nonlinear function therefore entails deciding which method or combination of methods works best. As an illustration, we compare logarithmic and polynomial models of the relationship between district income and test scores.

Polynomial specifications.   We considered two polynomial specifications specified using powers of *Income,* quadratic [Equation (8.2)] and cubic [Equation (8.11)]. Because the coefficient on *Income*^{3} in Equation (8.11) was significant at the 5% level, the cubic specification provided an improvement over the quadratic, so we select the cubic model as the preferred polynomial specification.

Logarithmic specifications.   The logarithmic specification in Equation (8.18) seemed to provide a good fit to these data, but we did not test this formally. One way to do so is to augment it with higher powers of the logarithm of income. If these additional terms are not statistically different from zero, then we can conclude that the specification in Equation (8.18) is adequate in the sense that it cannot be rejected against a polynomial function of the logarithm. Accordingly, the estimated cubic regression (specified in powers of the logarithm of income) is

$$\widehat{TestScore} = 486.1 + 113.4\ln(Income) - 26.9[\ln(Income)]^2$$
$$\quad\;(79.4)\quad\;(87.9)\qquad\qquad(31.7)$$
$$+\; 3.06[\ln(Income)]^3,\, \overline{R}^2 = 0.560.$$
$$\quad(3.74)$$

$$(8.26)$$

The *t*-statistic on the coefficient on the cubic term is 0.818, so the null hypothesis that the true coefficient is zero is not rejected at the 10% level. The *F*-statistic testing the joint hypothesis that the true coefficients on the quadratic and cubic term are both zero is 0.44, with a *p*-value of 0.64, so this joint null hypothesis is not rejected at the 10% level. Thus the cubic logarithmic model in Equation (8.26) does not provide a statistically significant improvement over the model in Equation (8.18), which is linear in the logarithm of income.

Comparing the cubic and linear-log specifications. Figure 8.7 plots the estimated regression functions from the cubic specification in Equation (8.11) and the linear-log specification in Equation (8.18). The two estimated regression functions are quite similar. One statistical tool for comparing these specifications is the $\bar{R}^2$. The $\bar{R}^2$ of the logarithmic regression is 0.561 and for the cubic regression it is 0.555. Because the logarithmic specification has a slight edge in terms of the $\bar{R}^2$, and because this specification does not need higher-order polynomials in the logarithm of income to fit these data, we adopt the logarithmic specification in Equation (8.18).

FIGURE 8.7 **The Linear-Log and Cubic Regression Functions**

The estimated cubic regression function [Equation (8.11)] and the estimated linear-log regression function [Equation (8.18)] are nearly identical in this sample.

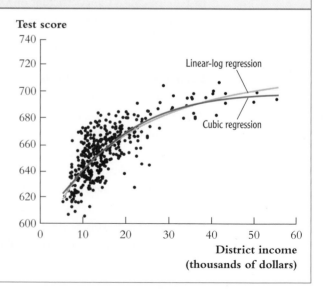

8.3   Interactions Between Independent Variables

In the introduction to this chapter we wondered whether reducing the student–teacher ratio might have a bigger effect on test scores in districts where many students are still learning English than in those with few still learning English. This could arise, for example, if students who are still learning English benefit differentially from one-on-one or small-group instruction. If so, the presence of many English learners in a district would interact with the student–teacher ratio in such a way that the effect on test scores of a change in the student–teacher ratio would depend on the fraction of English learners.

This section explains how to incorporate such interactions between two independent variables into the multiple regression model. The possible interaction between the student–teacher ratio and the fraction of English learners is an example of the more general situation in which the effect on Y of a change in one independent variable depends on the value of another independent variable. We consider three cases: when both independent variables are binary, when one is binary and the other is continuous, and when both are continuous.

Interactions Between Two Binary Variables

Consider the population regression of log earnings [Y_i, where $Y_i = \ln(Earnings_i)$] against two binary variables, the individual's gender (D_{1i}, which $= 1$ if the ith person is female) and whether he or she has a college degree (D_{2i}, where $D_{2i} = 1$ if the ith person graduated from college). The population linear regression of Y_i on these two binary variables is

$$Y_i = \beta_0 + \beta_1 D_{1i} + \beta_2 D_{2i} + u_i. \tag{8.27}$$

In this regression model, β_1 is the effect on log earnings of being female, holding schooling constant, and β_2 is the effect of having a college degree, holding gender constant.

The specification in Equation (8.27) has an important limitation: The effect of having a college degree in this specification, holding constant gender, is the same for men and women. There is, however, no reason that this must be so. Phrased mathematically, the effect of D_{2i} on Y_i, holding D_{1i} constant, could depend on the value of D_{1i}. In other words, there could be an interaction between gender and having a college degree so that the value in the job market of a degree is different for men and women.

Although the specification in Equation (8.27) does not allow for this interaction between gender and acquiring a college degree, it is easy to modify the specification so that it does by introducing another regressor, the product of the two binary variables, $D_{1i} \times D_{2i}$. The resulting regression is

$$Y_i = \beta_0 + \beta_1 D_{1i} + \beta_2 D_{2i} + \beta_3 (D_{1i} \times D_{2i}) + u_i. \tag{8.28}$$

The new regressor, the product $D_{1i} \times D_{2i}$, is called an **interaction term** or an **interacted regressor,** and the population regression model in Equation (8.28) is called a binary variable **interaction regression model**.

The interaction term in Equation (8.28) allows the population effect on log earnings (Y_i) of having a college degree (changing D_{2i} from $D_{2i} = 0$ to $D_{2i} = 1$) to depend on gender (D_{1i}). To show this mathematically, calculate the population effect of a change in D_{2i} using the general method laid out in Key Concept 8.1. The first step is to compute the conditional expectation of Y_i for $D_{2i} = 0$, given a value of D_{1i}; this is $E(Y_i | D_{1i} = d_1, D_{2i} = 0) = \beta_0 + \beta_1 \times d_1 + \beta_2 \times 0 + \beta_3 \times (d_1 \times 0) = \beta_0 + \beta_1 d_1$. The next step is to compute the conditional expectation of Y_i after the change—that is, for $D_{2i} = 1$, given the same value of D_{1i}; this is $E(Y_i | D_{1i} = d_1, D_{2i} = 1) = \beta_0 + \beta_1 \times d_1 + \beta_2 \times 1 + \beta_3 \times (d_1 \times 1) = \beta_0 + \beta_1 d_1 + \beta_2 + \beta_3 d_1$. The effect of this change is the difference of expected values [that is, the difference in Equation (8.4)], which is

$$E(Y_i | D_{1i} = d_1, D_{2i} = 1) - E(Y_i | D_{1i} = d_1, D_{2i} = 0) = \beta_2 + \beta_3 d_1. \tag{8.29}$$

Thus, in the binary variable interaction specification in Equation (8.28), the effect of acquiring a college degree (a unit change in D_{2i}) depends on the person's gender [the value of D_{1i}, which is d_1 in Equation (8.29)]. If the person is male ($d_1 = 0$), the effect of acquiring a college degree is β_2, but if the person is female ($d_1 = 1$), the effect is $\beta_2 + \beta_3$. The coefficient β_3 on the interaction term is the difference in the effect of acquiring a college degree for women versus men.

Although this example was phrased using log earnings, gender, and acquiring a college degree, the point is a general one. The binary variable interaction regression allows the effect of changing one of the binary independent variables to depend on the value of the other binary variable.

The method we used here to interpret the coefficients was, in effect, to work through each possible combination of the binary variables. This method, which applies to all regressions with binary variables, is summarized in Key Concept 8.3.

A METHOD FOR INTERPRETING COEFFICIENTS IN REGRESSIONS WITH BINARY VARIABLES

First compute the expected values of Y for each possible case described by the set of binary variables. Next compare these expected values. Each coefficient can then be expressed either as an expected value or as the difference between two or more expected values.

Application to the student–teacher ratio and the percentage of English learners.   Let $HiSTR_i$ be a binary variable that equals 1 if the student–teacher ratio is 20 or more and equals 0 otherwise, and let $HiEL_i$ be a binary variable that equals 1 if the percentage of English learners is 10% or more and equals 0 otherwise. The interacted regression of test scores against $HiSTR_i$ and $HiEL_i$ is

$$\widehat{TestScore} = 664.1 - 18.2HiEL - 1.9HiSTR - 3.5(HiSTR \times HiEL),$$
$$\qquad\qquad (1.4)\quad (2.3)\qquad (1.9)\qquad\quad (3.1) \qquad\qquad\qquad\qquad\qquad (8.30)$$
$$\overline{R}^2 = 0.290.$$

The predicted effect of moving from a district with a low student–teacher ratio to one with a high student–teacher ratio, holding constant whether the percentage of English learners is high or low, is given by Equation (8.29), with estimated coefficients replacing the population coefficients. According to the estimates in Equation (8.30), this effect thus is $-1.9 - 3.5HiEL$. That is, if the fraction of English learners is low ($HiEL = 0$), then the effect on test scores of moving from $HiSTR = 0$ to $HiSTR = 1$ is for test scores to decline by 1.9 points. If the fraction of English learners is high, test scores are estimated to decline by $1.9 + 3.5 = 5.4$ points.

The estimated regression in Equation (8.30) also can be used to estimate the mean test scores for each of the four possible combinations of the binary variables. This is done using the procedure in Key Concept 8.3. Accordingly, the sample average test score for districts with low student–teacher ratios ($HiSTR_i = 0$) and low fractions of English learners ($HiEL_i = 0$) is 664.1. For districts with $HiSTR_i = 1$ (high student–teacher ratios) and $HiEL_i = 0$ (low fractions of English learners), the sample average is 662.2 ($= 664.1 - 1.9$). When $HiSTR_i = 0$ and $HiEL_i = 1$, the sample average is 645.9 ($= 664.1 - 18.2$), and when $HiSTR_i = 1$ and $HiEL_i = 1$, the sample average is 640.5 ($= 664.1 - 18.2 - 1.9 - 3.5$).

FIGURE 8.8 **Regression Functions Using Binary and Continuous Variables**

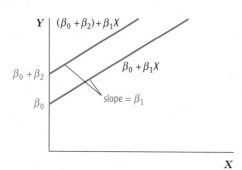

(a) Different intercepts, same slope

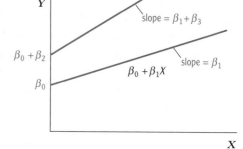

(b) Different intercepts, different slopes

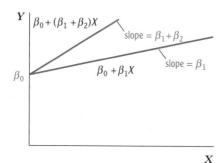

(c) Same intercept, different slopes

Interactions of binary variables and continuous variables can produce three different population regression functions: (a) $\beta_0 + \beta_1 X + \beta_2 D$ allows for different intercepts but has the same slope; (b) $\beta_0 + \beta_1 X + \beta_2 D + \beta_3 (X \times D)$ allows for different intercepts and different slopes; and (c) $\beta_0 + \beta_1 X + \beta_2 (X \times D)$ has the same intercept but allows for different slopes.

Interactions Between a Continuous and a Binary Variable

Next consider the population regression of log earnings [$Y_i = \ln(Earnings_i)$] against one continuous variable, the individual's years of work experience (X_i) and one binary variable, whether the worker has a college degree (D_i, where $D_i = 1$ if the ith person is a college graduate). As shown in Figure 8.8, the population regression line relating Y and the continuous variable X can depend on the binary variable D in three different ways.

In Figure 8.8a, the two regression lines differ only in their intercept. The corresponding population regression model is

$$Y_i = \beta_0 + \beta_1 X_i + \beta_2 D_i + u_i. \tag{8.31}$$

This is the familiar multiple regression model with a population regression function that is linear in X_i and D_i. When $D_i = 0$, the population regression function is $\beta_0 + \beta_1 X_i$, so the intercept is β_0 and the slope is β_1. When $D_i = 1$, the population regression function is $\beta_0 + \beta_1 X_i + \beta_2$, so the slope remains β_1 but the intercept is $\beta_0 + \beta_2$. Thus β_2 is the difference between the intercepts of the two regression lines, as shown in Figure 8.8a. Stated in terms of the earnings example, β_1 is the effect on log earnings of an additional year of work experience, holding college degree status constant, and β_2 is the effect of a college degree on log earnings, holding years of experience constant. In this specification, the effect of an additional year of work experience is the same for college graduates and nongraduates, that is, the two lines in Figure 8.8a have the same slope.

In Figure 8.8b, the two lines have different slopes and intercepts. The different slopes permit the effect of an additional year of work to differ for college graduates and nongraduates. To allow for different slopes, add an interaction term to Equation (8.31):

$$Y_i = \beta_0 + \beta_1 X_i + \beta_2 D_i + \beta_3 (X_i \times D_i) + u_i, \tag{8.32}$$

where $X_i \times D_i$ is a new variable, the product of X_i and D_i. To interpret the coefficients of this regression, apply the procedure in Key Concept 8.3. Doing so shows that, if $D_i = 0$, the population regression function is $\beta_0 + \beta_1 X_i$, whereas if $D_i = 1$, the population regression function is $(\beta_0 + \beta_2) + (\beta_1 + \beta_3) X_i$. Thus, this specification allows for two different population regression functions relating Y_i and X_i, depending on the value of D_i, as is shown in Figure 8.8b. The difference between the two intercepts is β_2, and the difference between the two slopes is β_3. In the earnings example, β_1 is the effect of an additional year of work experience for nongraduates ($D_i = 0$) and $\beta_1 + \beta_3$ is this effect for graduates, so β_3 is the *difference* in the effect of an additional year of work experience for college graduates versus nongraduates.

A third possibility, shown in Figure 8.8c, is that the two lines have different slopes but the same intercept. The interacted regression model for this case is

$$Y_i = \beta_0 + \beta_1 X_i + \beta_2 (X_i \times D_i) + u_i. \tag{8.33}$$

The coefficients of this specification also can be interpreted using Key Concept 8.3. In terms of the earnings example, this specification allows for different effects of experience on log earnings between college graduates and nongraduates, but requires that expected log earnings be the same for both groups when they have no prior experience. Said differently, this specification corresponds to the population mean entry-level wage being the same for college graduates and

INTERACTIONS BETWEEN BINARY AND CONTINUOUS VARIABLES

Through the use of the interaction term $X_i \times D_i$, the population regression line relating Y_i and the continuous variable X_i can have a slope that depends on the binary variable D_i. There are three possibilities:

1. Different intercept, same slope (Figure 8.8a):
$$Y_i = \beta_0 + \beta_1 X_i + \beta_2 D_i + u_i;$$

2. Different intercept and slope (Figure 8.8b):
$$Y_i = \beta_0 + \beta_1 X_i + \beta_2 D_i + \beta_3(X_i \times D_i) + u_i;$$

3. Same intercept, different slope (Figure 8.8c):
$$Y_i = \beta_0 + \beta_1 X_i + \beta_2(X_i \times D_i) + u_i.$$

nongraduates. This does not make much sense in this application, and in practice this specification is used less frequently than Equation (8.32), which allows for different intercepts and slopes.

All three specifications, Equations (8.31), (8.32), and (8.33), are versions of the multiple regression model of Chapter 6 and, once the new variable $X_i \times D_i$ is created, the coefficients of all three can be estimated by OLS.

The three regression models with a binary and a continuous independent variable are summarized in Key Concept 8.4.

Application to the student–teacher ratio and the percentage of English learners. Does the effect on test scores of cutting the student–teacher ratio depend on whether the percentage of students still learning English is high or low? One way to answer this question is to use a specification that allows for two different regression lines, depending on whether there are a high or low percentage of English learners. This is achieved using the different intercept/different slope specification:

$$\widehat{TestScore} = 682.2 - 0.97STR + 5.6HiEL - 1.28(STR \times HiEL),$$
$$\quad\quad\quad (11.9)\quad (0.59)\quad\quad (19.5)\quad\quad (0.97)$$
$$\overline{R}^2 = 0.305,$$

(8.34)

where the binary variable $HiEL_i$ equals 1 if the percentage of students still learning English in the district is greater than 10% and equals 0 otherwise.

For districts with a low fraction of English learners ($HiEL_i = 0$), the estimated regression line is $682.2 - 0.97STR_i$. For districts with a high fraction of English learners ($HiEL_i = 1$), the estimated regression line is $682.2 + 5.6 - 0.97STR_i - 1.28STR_i = 687.8 - 2.25STR_i$. According to these estimates, reducing the student–teacher ratio by 1 is predicted to increase test scores by 0.97 point in districts with low fractions of English learners but by 2.25 points in districts with high fractions of English learners. The difference between these two effects, 1.28 points, is the coefficient on the interaction term in Equation (8.34).

The OLS regression in Equation (8.34) can be used to test several hypotheses about the population regression line. First, the hypothesis that the two lines are in fact the same can be tested by computing the F-statistic testing the joint hypothesis that the coefficient on $HiEL_i$ and the coefficient on the interaction term $STR_i \times HiEL_i$ are both zero. This F-statistic is 89.9, which is significant at the 1% level.

Second, the hypothesis that two lines have the same slope can be tested by testing whether the coefficient on the interaction term is zero. The t-statistic, $-1.28/0.97 = -1.32$, is less than 1.645 in absolute value, so the null hypothesis that the two lines have the same slope cannot be rejected using a two-sided test at the 10% significance level.

Third, the hypothesis that the lines have the same intercept can be tested by testing whether the population coefficient on $HiEL$ is zero. The t-statistic is $t = 5.6/19.5 = 0.29$, so the hypothesis that the lines have the same intercept cannot be rejected at the 5% level.

These three tests produce seemingly contradictory results: The joint test using the F-statistic rejects the joint hypothesis that the slope and the intercept are the same, but the tests of the individual hypotheses using the t-statistic fail to reject it. The reason for this is that the regressors, $HiEL$ and $STR \times HiEL,$ are highly correlated. This results in large standard errors on the individual coefficients. Even though it is impossible to tell which of the coefficients is nonzero, there is strong evidence against the hypothesis that *both* are zero.

Finally, the hypothesis that the student–teacher ratio does not enter this specification can be tested by computing the F-statistic for the joint hypothesis that the coefficients on STR and on the interaction term are both zero. This F-statistic is 5.64, which has a p-value of 0.004. Thus, the coefficients on the student–teacher ratio are statistically significant at the 1% significance level.

The Return to Education and the Gender Gap

In addition to its intellectual pleasures, education has economic rewards. As the boxes in Chapters 3 and 5 show, workers with more education tend to earn more than their counterparts with less education. The analysis in those boxes was incomplete, however, for at least three reasons. First, it failed to control for other determinants of earnings that might be correlated with educational achievement, so the OLS estimator of the coefficient on education could have omitted variable bias. Second, the functional form used in Chapter 5—a simple linear relation—implies that earnings change by a constant dollar

(continued)

TABLE 8.1 The Return to Education and the Gender Gap: Regression Results for the United States in 2004

Regressor:	Dependent variable: logarithm of *Hourly Earnings.*			
	(1)	(2)	(3)	(4)
Years of education	0.0914** (0.0008)	0.0934** (0.0008)	0.0861** (0.0011)	0.0899** (0.0011)
Female		−0.237** (0.004)	−0.484** (0.023)	−0.521** (0.022)
Female × *Years of education*			0.0180** (0.0016)	0.0207** (0.0016)
Potential experience				0.0232** (0.0008)
Potential experience^2				−0.000368** (0.000018)
Midwest				−0.058** (0.006)
South				−0.078** (0.006)
West				−0.030** (0.006)
Intercept	1.545** (0.011)	1.621** (0.011)	1.721** (0.015)	1.415** (0.018)
$\overline{R}^2$	0.174	0.220	0.221	0.242

The data are from the March 2005 Current Population Survey (see Appendix 3.1). The sample size is $n = 57,863$ observations for each regression. *Female* is an indicator variable that equals 1 for women and 0 for men. *Midwest, South,* and *West* are indicator variables denoting the region of the United States in which the worker lives: For example, *Midwest* equals 1 if the worker lives in the Midwest and equals 0 otherwise (the omitted region is *Northeast*). Standard errors are reported in parentheses below the estimated coefficients. Individual coefficients are statistically significant at the *5% or **1% significance level.

amount for each additional year of education, whereas one might suspect that the dollar change in earnings is actually larger at higher levels of education. Third, the box in Chapter 5 ignores the gender differences in earnings highlighted in the box in Chapter 3.

All of these limitations can be addressed by a multiple regression analysis that includes those determinants of earnings which, if omitted, could cause omitted variable bias, and that uses a nonlinear functional form relating education and earnings. Table 8.1 summarizes regressions estimated using data on full-time workers, ages 30 through 64, from the Current Population Survey (the CPS data are described in Appendix 3.1). The dependent variable is the logarithm of hourly earnings, so another year of education is associated with a constant percentage increase (not dollar increase) in earnings.

Table 8.1 has four salient results. First, the omission of gender in regression (1) does not result in substantial omitted variable bias: Even though gender enters regression (2) significantly and with a large coefficient, gender and years of education are uncorrelated, that is, on average men and women have nearly the same levels of education. Second, the returns to education are economically and statistically significantly different for men and women: In regression (3), the t-statistic testing the hypothesis that they are the same is 11.25 ($= 0.0180/0.0016$). Third, regression (4) controls for the region of the country in which the individual lives, thereby addressing potential omitted variable bias that might arise if years of education differ systematically by region. Controlling for region makes a small difference to the estimated coefficients on the education terms, relative to those reported in regression (3). Fourth, regression (4) controls for the potential experience of the worker, as measured by years since completion of schooling. The estimated coefficients imply a declining marginal value for each year of potential experience.

The estimated economic return on education in regression (4) is 8.99% for each year of education for men, and 11.06% ($= 0.0899 + 0.0207$, in percent) for women. Because the regression functions for men and women have different slopes, the gender gap depends on the years of education. For 12 years of education, the gender gap is estimated to be 27.3% ($= 0.0207 \times 12 - 0.521$, in percent); for 16 years of education, the gender gap is less in percentage terms, 19.0%.

These estimates of the return to education and the gender gap still have limitations, including the possibility of other omitted variables, notably the native ability of the worker, and potential problems associated with the way variables are measured in the CPS. Nevertheless, the estimates in Table 8.1 are consistent with those obtained by economists who carefully address these limitations. A recent survey by the econometrician David Card (1999) of dozens of empirical studies concludes that labor economists' best estimates of the return to education generally fall between 8% and 11%, and that the return depends on the quality of the education. If you are interested in learning more about the economic return to education, see Card (1999).

Interactions Between Two Continuous Variables

Now suppose that both independent variables (X_{1i} and X_{2i}) are continuous. An example is when Y_i is log earnings of the ith worker, X_{1i} is his or her years of work experience, and X_{2i} is the number of years he or she went to school. If the population regression function is linear, the effect on wages of an additional year of experience does not depend on the number of years of education or, equivalently, the effect of an additional year of education does not depend on the number of years of work experience. In reality, however, there might be an interaction between these two variables so that the effect on wages of an additional year of experience depends on the number of years of education. This interaction can be modeled by augmenting the linear regression model with an interaction term that is the product of X_{1i} and X_{2i}:

$$Y_i = \beta_0 + \beta_1 X_{1i} + \beta_2 X_{2i} + \beta_3 (X_{1i} \times X_{2i}) + u_i. \tag{8.35}$$

The interaction term allows the effect of a unit change in X_1 to depend on X_2. To see this, apply the general method for computing effects in nonlinear regression models in Key Concept 8.1. The difference in Equation (8.4), computed for the interacted regression function in Equation (8.35), is $\Delta Y = (\beta_1 + \beta_3 X_2)\Delta X_1$ [Exercise 8.10(a)]. Thus, the effect on Y of a change in X_1, holding X_2 constant, is

$$\frac{\Delta Y}{\Delta X_1} = \beta_1 + \beta_3 X_2, \tag{8.36}$$

which depends on X_2. For example, in the earnings example, if β_3 is positive, then the effect on log earnings of an additional year of experience is greater, by the amount β_3, for each additional year of education the worker has.

A similar calculation shows that the effect on Y of a change ΔX_2 in X_2, holding X_1 constant, is $\frac{\Delta Y}{\Delta X_2} = (\beta_2 + \beta_3 X_1)$.

Putting these two effects together shows that the coefficient β_3 on the interaction term is the effect of a unit increase in X_1 and X_2, above and beyond the sum of the effects of a unit increase in X_1 alone and a unit increase in X_2 alone. That is, if X_1 changes by ΔX_1 and X_2 changes by ΔX_2, then the expected change in Y is $\Delta Y = (\beta_1 + \beta_3 X_2)\Delta X_1 + (\beta_2 + \beta_3 X_1)\Delta X_2 + \beta_3 \Delta X_1 \Delta X_2$ [Exercise 8.10(c)]. The first term is the effect from changing X_1 holding X_2 constant; the second term is the effect from changing X_2 holding X_1 constant; and the final term, $\beta_3 \Delta X_1 \Delta X_2$, is the extra effect from changing both X_1 and X_2.

Interactions between two variables are summarized as Key Concept 8.5.

When interactions are combined with logarithmic transformations, they can be used to estimate price elasticities when the price elasticity depends on the

INTERACTIONS IN MULTIPLE REGRESSION

The interaction term between the two independent variables X_1 and X_2 is their product $X_1 \times X_2$. Including this interaction term allows the effect on Y of a change in X_1 to depend on the value of X_2 and, conversely, allows the effect of a change in X_2 to depend on the value of X_1.

The coefficient on $X_1 \times X_2$ is the effect of a unit increase in X_1 *and* X_2, above and beyond the sum of the individual effects of a unit increase in X_1 alone and a unit increase in X_2 alone. This is true whether X_1 and/or X_2 are continuous or binary.

characteristics of the good (see the box "The Demand for Economic Journals" for an example).

Application to the student–teacher ratio and the percentage of English learners. The previous examples considered interactions between the student–teacher ratio and a binary variable indicating whether the percentage of English learners is large or small. A different way to study this interaction is to examine the interaction between the student–teacher ratio and the continuous variable, the percentage of English learners ($PctEL$). The estimated interaction regression is

$$\widehat{TestScore} = 686.3 - 1.12STR - 0.67PctEL + 0.0012(STR \times PctEL),$$
$$\qquad\qquad (11.8) \quad (0.59) \qquad (0.37) \qquad\qquad (0.019)$$
$$\bar{R}^2 = 0.422. \tag{8.37}$$

When the percentage of English learners is at the median ($PctEL = 8.85$), the slope of the line relating test scores and the student–teacher ratio is estimated to be $-1.11 (= -1.12 + 0.0012 \times 8.85)$. When the percentage of English learners is at the 75th percentile ($PctEL = 23.0$), this line is estimated to be flatter, with a slope of $-1.09 (= -1.12 + 0.0012 \times 23.0)$. That is, for a district with 8.85% English learners, the estimated effect of a unit reduction in the student–teacher ratio is to increase test scores by 1.11 points, but for a district with 23.0% English learners, reducing the student–teacher ratio by one unit is predicted to increase test scores by only 1.09 points. The difference between these estimated effects is not statistically significant, however: The t-statistic testing whether the coefficient on the interaction term is zero is $t = 0.0012/0.019 = 0.06$, which is not significant at the 10% level.

The Demand for Economics Journals

Professional economists follow the most recent research in their areas of specialization. Most research in economics first appears in economics journals, so economists–or their libraries–subscribe to economics journals.

How elastic is the demand by libraries for economics journals? To find out, we analyzed the relationship between the number of subscriptions to a journal at U.S. libraries (Y_i) and its library subscrip-

tion price using data for the year 2000 for 180 economics journals. Because the product of a journal is not the paper on which it is printed but rather the ideas it contains, its price is logically measured not in dollars per year or dollars per page but instead in dollars per idea. Although we cannot measure "ideas" directly, a good indirect measure is the number of times that articles in a journal are *continued*

FIGURE 8.9   Library Subscriptions and Prices of Economics Journals

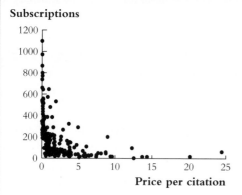

(a) Subscriptions and Price per citation

(b) ln(Subscriptions) and ln(Price per citation)

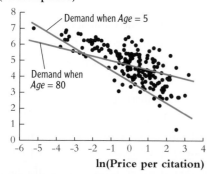

(c) ln(Subscriptions) and ln(Price per citation)

There is a nonlinear inverse relation between the number of U.S. library subscriptions (quantity) and the library price per citation (price), as shown in Figure 8.9a for 180 economics journals in 2000. But as seen in Figure 8.9b, the relation between log quantity and log price appears to be approximately linear. Figure 8.9c shows that demand is more elastic for young journals (*Age* = 5) than for old journals (*Age* = 80).

subsequently cited by other researchers. Accordingly, we measure price as the "price per citation" in the journal. The price range is enormous, from $\frac{1}{2}¢$ per citation (the *American Economic Review*) to 20¢ per citation or more. Some journals are expensive per citation because they have few citations, others because their library subscription price per year is very high: In 2006, a library subscription to the *Journal of Econometrics* cost more than $2700, almost 9 times the price of a library subscription to the *American Economic Review*!

Because we are interested in estimating elasticities, we use a log-log specification (Key Concept 8.2). The scatterplots in Figure 8.9a and 8.9b provide empirical support for this transformation. Because

continued

TABLE 8.2   Estimates of the Demand for Economic Journals

Dependent variable: logarithm of subscriptions at U.S. libraries in the Year 2000; 180 observations.

Regressor	(1)	(2)	(3)	(4)
ln(*Price per citation*)	−0.533** (0.034)	−0.408** (0.044)	−0.961** (0.160)	−0.899** (0.145)
[ln(*Price per citation*)]^2			0.017 (0.025)	
[ln(*Price per citation*)]^3			0.0037 (0.0055)	
ln(*Age*)		0.424** (0.119)	0.373** (0.118)	0.374** (0.118)
ln(*Age*) × ln(*Price per citation*)			0.156** (0.052)	0.141** (0.040)
ln(*Characters* ÷ 1,000,000)		0.206* (0.098)	0.235* (0.098)	0.229* (0.096)
Intercept	4.77** (0.055)	3.21** (0.38)	3.41** (0.38)	3.43** (0.38)
F-Statistics and Summary Statistics				
F-statistic testing coefficients on quadratic and cubic terms (*p*-value)			0.25 (0.779)	
SER	0.750	0.705	0.691	0.688
$\overline{R}^2$	0.555	0.607	0.622	0.626

The *F*-statistic tests the hypothesis that the coefficients on [ln(*Price per citation*)]^2 and [ln(*Price per citation*)]^3 are both zero. Standard errors are given in parentheses under coefficients, and *p*-values are given in parentheses under *F*-statistics. Individual coefficients are statistically significant at the *5% level or **1% level.

some of the oldest and most prestigious journals are the cheapest per citation, a regression of log quantity against log price could have omitted variable bias. Our regressions therefore include two control variables, the logarithm of age and the logarithm of the number of characters per year in the journal.

The regression results are summarized in Table 8.2. Those results yield the following conclusions (see if you can find the basis for these conclusions in the table!):

1. Demand is less elastic for older than for newer journals.

2. The evidence supports a linear, rather than a cubic, function of log price.

3. Demand is greater for journals with more characters, holding price and age constant.

So what is the elasticity of demand for economics journals? It depends on the age of the journal.

Demand curves for an 80-year-old journal and a 5-year-old upstart are superimposed on the scatterplot in Figure 8.9c; the older journal's demand elasticity is −0.28 (SE = 0.06), while the younger journal's is −0.67 (SE = 0.08).

This demand is very inelastic: Demand is very insensitive to price, especially for older journals. For libraries, having the most recent research on hand is a necessity, not a luxury. By way of comparison, experts estimate the demand elasticity for cigarettes to be in the range of −0.3 to −0.5. Economics journals are, it seems, as addictive as cigarettes—but a lot better for your health![1]

---

[1]These data were graciously provided by Professor Theodore Bergstrom of the Department of Economics at the University of California, Santa Barbara. If you are interested in learning more about the economics of economics journals, see Bergstrom (2001).

To keep the discussion focused on nonlinear models, the specifications in Sections 8.1–8.3 exclude additional control variables such as the students' economic background. Consequently, these results arguably are subject to omitted variable bias. To draw substantive conclusions about the effect on test scores of reducing the student–teacher ratio, these nonlinear specifications must be augmented with control variables, and it is to such an exercise that we now turn.

8.4   Nonlinear Effects on Test Scores of the Student–Teacher Ratio

This section addresses three specific questions about test scores and the student–teacher ratio. First, after controlling for differences in economic characteristics of different districts, does the effect on test scores of reducing the student–teacher ratio depend on the fraction of English learners? Second, does this effect depend on the value of the student–teacher ratio? Third, and most important, after taking economic factors and nonlinearities into account, what is the estimated effect on test scores of reducing the student–teacher ratio by two students per teacher, as our superintendent from Chapter 4 proposes to do?

We answer these questions by considering nonlinear regression specifications of the type discussed in Sections 8.2 and 8.3, extended to include two measures of the economic background of the students: the percentage of students eligible for a subsidized lunch and the logarithm of average district income. The logarithm of income is used because the empirical analysis of Section 8.2 suggests that this specification captures the nonlinear relationship between test scores and income. As in Section 7.6, we do not include expenditures per pupil as a regressor and in so doing we are considering the effect of decreasing the student–teacher ratio, allowing expenditures per pupil to increase (that is, we are not holding expenditures per pupil constant).

Discussion of Regression Results

The OLS regression results are summarized in Table 8.3. The columns labeled (1) through (7) each report separate regressions. The entries in the table are the coefficients, standard errors, certain F-statistics and their p-values, and summary statistics, as indicated by the description in each row.

The first column of regression results, labeled regression (1) in the table, is regression (3) in Table 7.1 repeated here for convenience. This regression does not control for income, so the first thing we do is check whether the results change substantially when log income is included as an additional economic control variable. The results are given in regression (2) in Table 8.3. The log of income is statistically significant at the 1% level and the coefficient on the student–teacher ratio becomes somewhat closer to zero, falling from -1.00 to -0.73, although it remains statistically significant at the 1% level. The change in the coefficient on STR is large enough between regressions (1) and (2) to warrant including the logarithm of income in the remaining regressions as a deterrent to omitted variable bias.

Regression (3) in Table 8.3 is the interacted regression in Equation (8.34) with the binary variable for a high or low percentage of English learners, but with no economic control variables. When the economic control variables (percentage eligible for subsidized lunch and log income) are added [regression (4) in the table], the coefficients change, but in neither case is the coefficient on the interaction term significant at the 5% level. Based on the evidence in regression (4), the hypothesis that the effect of STR is the same for districts with low and high percentages of English learners cannot be rejected at the 5% level (the t-statistic is $t = -0.58/0.50 = -1.16$).

Regression (5) examines whether the effect of changing the student–teacher ratio depends on the value of the student–teacher ratio by including a cubic specification in STR in addition to the other control variables in regression (4) [the interaction term, $HiEL \times STR$, was dropped because it was not significant in

TABLE 8.3 Nonlinear Regression Models of Test Scores

Dependent variable: average test score in district; 420 observations.

Regressor	(1)	(2)	(3)	(4)	(5)	(6)	(7)
Student–teacher ratio (STR)	−1.00** (0.27)	−0.73** (0.26)	−0.97 (0.59)	−0.53 (0.34)	64.33** (24.86)	83.70** (28.50)	65.29** (25.26)
STR^2					−3.42** (1.25)	−4.38** (1.44)	−3.47** (1.27)
STR^3					0.059** (0.021)	0.075** (0.024)	0.060** (0.021)
% English learners	−0.122** (0.033)	−0.176** (0.034)					−0.166** (0.034)
% English learners ≥ 10%? (Binary, $HiEL$)			5.64 (19.51)	5.50 (9.80)	−5.47** (1.03)	816.1* (327.7)	
$HiEL \times STR$			−1.28 (0.97)	−0.58 (0.50)		−123.3* (50.2)	
$HiEL \times STR^2$						6.12* (2.54)	
$HiEL \times STR^3$						−0.101* (0.043)	
% Eligible for subsidized lunch	−0.547** (0.024)	−0.398** (0.033)		−0.411** (0.029)	−0.420** (0.029)	−0.418** (0.029)	−0.402** (0.033)
Average district income (logarithm)		11.57** (1.81)		12.12** (1.80)	11.75** (1.78)	11.80** (1.78)	11.51** (1.81)
Intercept	700.2** (5.6)	658.6** (8.6)	682.2** (11.9)	653.6** (9.9)	252.0 (163.6)	122.3 (185.5)	244.8 (165.7)

F-Statistics and p-Values on Joint Hypotheses

(a) All STR variables and interactions = 0			5.64 (0.004)	5.92 (0.003)	6.31 (< 0.001)	4.96 (< 0.001)	5.91 (0.001)
(b) STR^2, $STR^3 = 0$					6.17 (< 0.001)	5.81 (0.003)	5.96 (0.003)
(c) $HiEL \times STR$, $HiEL \times STR^2$, $HiEL \times STR^3 = 0$						2.69 (0.046)	
SER	9.08	8.64	15.88	8.63	8.56	8.55	8.57
$\overline{R}^2$	0.773	0.794	0.305	0.795	0.798	0.799	0.798

These regressions were estimated using the data on K-8 school districts in California, described in Appendix 4.1. Standard errors are given in parentheses under coefficients, and p-values are given in parentheses under F-statistics. Individual coefficients are statistically significant at the *5% or **1% significance level.

regression (4) at the 10% level]. The estimates in regression (5) are consistent with the student–teacher ratio having a nonlinear effect. The null hypothesis that the relationship is linear is rejected at the 1% significance level against the alternative that it is cubic (the F-statistic testing the hypothesis that the true coefficients on STR^2 and STR^3 are zero is 6.17, with a p-value of <0.001).

Regression (6) further examines whether the effect of the student–teacher ratio depends not just on the value of the student–teacher ratio but also on the fraction of English learners. By including interactions between $HiEL$ and STR, STR^2, and STR^3, we can check whether the (possibly cubic) population regressions functions relating test scores and STR are different for low and high percentages of English learners. To do so, we test the restriction that the coefficients on the three interaction terms are zero. The resulting F-statistic is 2.69, which has a p-value of 0.046 and thus is significant at the 5% but not the 1% significance level. This provides some evidence that the regression functions are different for districts with high and low percentages of English learners; however, comparing regressions (6) and (4) makes it clear that these differences are associated with the quadratic and cubic terms.

Regression (7) is a modification of regression (5), in which the continuous variable $PctEL$ is used instead of the binary variable $HiEL$ to control for the percentage of English learners in the district. The coefficients on the other regressors do not change substantially when this modification is made, indicating that the results in regression (5) are not sensitive to what measure of the percentage of English learners is actually used in the regression.

In all the specifications, the hypothesis that the student–teacher ratio does not enter the regressions is rejected at the 1% level.

The nonlinear specifications in Table 8.3 are most easily interpreted graphically. Figure 8.10 graphs the estimated regression functions relating test scores and the student–teacher ratio for the linear specification (2) and the cubic specifications (5) and (7), along with a scatterplot of the data.[4] These estimated regression functions show the predicted value of test scores as a function of the student–teacher ratio, holding fixed other values of the independent variables in the regression. The estimated regression functions are all close to each other, although the cubic regressions flatten out for large values of the student–teacher ratio.

---

[4]For each curve, the predicted value was computed by setting each independent variable, other than STR, to its sample average value and computing the predicted value by multiplying these fixed values of the independent variables by the respective estimated coefficients from Table 8.3. This was done for various values of STR, and the graph of the resulting adjusted predicted values is the estimated regression line relating test scores and the STR, holding the other variables constant at their sample averages.

FIGURE 8.10 Three Regression Functions Relating Test Scores and Student–Teacher Ratio

The cubic regressions from columns (5) and (7) of Table 8.3 are nearly identical. They indicate a small amount of nonlinearity in the relation between test scores and student–teacher ratio.

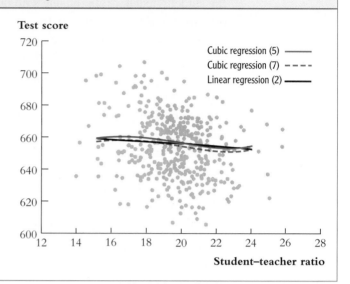

Regression (6) indicates a statistically significant difference in the cubic regression functions relating test scores and STR, depending on whether the percentage of English learners in the district is large or small. Figure 8.11 graphs these two estimated regression functions so that we can see whether this difference, in addition to being statistically significant, is of practical importance. As Figure 8.11 shows, for student–teacher ratios between 17 and 23—a range that includes 88% of the observations—the two functions are separated by approximately ten points but otherwise are very similar; that is, for STR between 17 and 23, districts with a lower percentage of English learners do better, holding constant the student–teacher ratio, but the effect of a change in the student–teacher ratio is essentially the same for the two groups. The two regression functions are different for student–teacher ratios below 16.5, but we must be careful not to read more into this than is justified. The districts with $STR < 16.5$ constitute only 6% of the observations, so the differences between the nonlinear regression functions are reflecting differences in these very few districts with very low student–teacher ratios. Thus, based on Figure 8.11, we conclude that the effect on test scores of a change in the student–teacher ratio does not depend on the percentage of English learners for the range of student–teacher ratios for which we have the most data.

FIGURE 8.11   **Regression Functions for Districts with High and Low Percentages of English Learners**

Districts with low percentages of English learners ($HiEL = 0$) are shown by gray dots and districts with $HiEL = 1$ are shown by colored dots. The cubic regression function for $HiEL = 1$ from regression (6) in Table 8.3 is approximately 10 points below the cubic regression function for $HiEL = 0$ for $17 \leq STR \leq 23$, but otherwise the two functions have similar shapes and slopes in this range. The slopes of the regression functions differ most for very large and small values of STR, for which there are few observations.

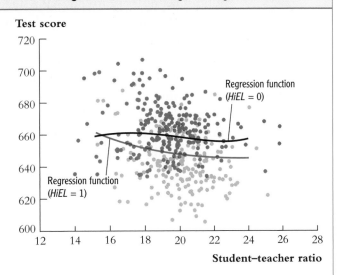

Summary of Findings

These results let us answer the three questions raised at the start of this section.

First, after controlling for economic background, whether there are many or few English learners in the district does not have a substantial influence on the effect on test scores of a change in the student–teacher ratio. In the linear specifications, there is no statistically significant evidence of such a difference. The cubic specification in regression (6) provides statistically significant evidence (at the 5% level) that the regression functions are different for districts with high and low percentages of English learners; as shown in Figure 8.11, however, the estimated regression functions have similar slopes in the range of student–teacher ratios containing most of our data.

Second, after controlling for economic background, there is evidence of a nonlinear effect on test scores of the student–teacher ratio. This effect is statistically significant at the 1% level (the coefficients on STR^2 and STR^3 are always significant at the 1% level).

Third, we now can return to the superintendent's problem that opened Chapter 4. She wants to know the effect on test scores of reducing the student–teacher ratio by two students per teacher. In the linear specification (2), this effect does not depend on the student–teacher ratio itself, and the estimated effect of this reduction is to improve test scores by 1.46 ($= -0.73 \times -2$) points. In the nonlinear specifications, this effect depends on the value of the student–teacher ratio. If her district currently has a student–teacher ratio of 20, and she is considering cutting it to 18, then based on regression (5) the estimated effect of this reduction is to improve test scores by 3.00 points, while based on regression (7) this estimate is 2.93. If her district currently has a student–teacher ratio of 22, and she is considering cutting it to 20, then based on regression (5) the estimated effect of this reduction is to improve test scores by 1.93 points, while based on regression (7) this estimate is 1.90. The estimates from the nonlinear specifications suggest that cutting the student–teacher ratio has a somewhat greater effect if this ratio is already small.

8.5   Conclusion

This chapter presented several ways to model nonlinear regression functions. Because these models are variants of the multiple regression model, the unknown coefficients can be estimated by OLS, and hypotheses about their values can be tested using t- and F-statistics as described in Chapter 7. In these models, the expected effect on Y of a change in one of the independent variables, X_1, holding the other independent variables $X_2, \ldots, X_k$ constant, in general depends on the values of $X_1, X_2, \ldots, X_k$.

There are many different models in this chapter, and you could not be blamed for being a bit bewildered about which to use in a given application. How should you analyze possible nonlinearities in practice? Section 8.1 laid out a general approach for such an analysis, but this approach requires you to make decisions and exercise judgment along the way. It would be convenient if there were a single recipe you could follow that would always work in every application, but in practice data analysis is rarely that simple.

The single most important step in specifying nonlinear regression functions is to "use your head." Before you look at the data, can you think of a reason, based on economic theory or expert judgment, why the slope of the population regression function might depend on the value of that, or another, independent variable? If so, what sort of dependence might you expect? And, most importantly, which nonlinearities (if any) could have major implications for the substantive issues addressed by your study? Answering these questions carefully will focus your analysis. In the test score application, for example, such reasoning led us to investigate whether hiring more teachers might have a greater effect in districts with a large percentage of students still learning English, perhaps because those students would differentially benefit from more personal attention. By making the question precise, we were able to find a precise answer: After controlling for the economic background of the students, we found no statistically significant evidence of such an interaction.

Summary

1. In a nonlinear regression, the slope of the population regression function depends on the value of one or more of the independent variables.
2. The effect on Y of a change in the independent variable(s) can be computed by evaluating the regression function at two values of the independent variable(s). The procedure is summarized in Key Concept 8.1.
3. A polynomial regression includes powers of X as regressors. A quadratic regression includes X and X^2, and a cubic regression includes X, X^2, and X^3.
4. Small changes in logarithms can be interpreted as proportional or percentage changes in a variable. Regressions involving logarithms are used to estimate proportional changes and elasticities.
5. The product of two variables is called an interaction term. When interaction terms are included as regressors, they allow the regression slope of one variable to depend on the value of another variable.

Key Terms

quadratic regression model (256)
nonlinear regression function (258)
polynomial regression model (263)
cubic regression model (263)
elasticity (265)
exponential function (265)
natural logarithm (266)
linear-log model (267)

log-linear model (269)
log-log model (269)
interaction term (276)
interacted regressor (276)
interaction regression model (276)
nonlinear least squares (307)
nonlinear least squares estimators (308)

Review the Concepts

8.1 Sketch a regression function that is increasing (has a positive slope) and is steep for small values of X but less steep for large values of X. Explain how you would specify a nonlinear regression to model this shape. Can you think of an economic relationship with a shape like this?

8.2 A "Cobb-Douglas" production function relates production (Q) to factors of production, capital (K), labor (L), and raw materials (M), and an error term u using the equation $Q = \lambda K^{\beta_1} L^{\beta_2} M^{\beta_3} e^u$, where λ, β_1, β_2, and β_3 are production parameters. Suppose you have data on production and the factors of production from a random sample of firms with the same Cobb-Douglas production function. How would you use regression analysis to estimate the production parameters?

8.3 A standard "money demand" function used by macroeconomists has the form $\ln(m) = \beta_0 + \beta_1 \ln(GDP) + \beta_2 R$, where m is the quantity of (real) money, GDP is the value of (real) gross domestic product, and R is the value of the nominal interest rate measured in percent per year. Suppose that $\beta_1 = 1.0$ and $\beta_2 = -0.02$. What will happen to the value of m if GDP increases by 2%? What will happen to m if the interest rate increases from 4% to 5%?

8.4 You have estimated a linear regression model relating Y to X. Your professor says, "I think that the relationship between Y and X is nonlinear." Explain how you would test the adequacy of your linear regression.

8.5 Suppose that in problem 8.2 you thought that the value of β_2 was not constant, but rather increased when K increased. How could you use an interaction term to capture this effect?

Exercises

8.1 Sales in a company are $196 million in 2001 and increase to $198 million in 2002.

    a. Compute the percentage increase in sales using the usual formula $100 \times \frac{Sales_{2002} - Sales_{2001}}{Sales_{2001}}$. Compare this value to the approximation $100 \times [\ln(Sales_{2002}) - \ln(Sales_{2001})]$.

    b. Repeat (a) assuming $Sales_{2002} = 205$; $Sales_{2002} = 250$; $Sales_{2002} = 500$.

    c. How good is the approximation when the change is small? Does the quality of the approximation deteriorate as the percentage change increases?

8.2 Suppose that a researcher collects data on houses that have sold in a particular neighborhood over the past year and obtains the regression results in the table shown below.

    a. Using the results in column (1), what is the expected change in price of building a 500-square-foot addition to a house? Construct a 95% confidence interval for the percentage change in price.

Regression Results for Exercise 8.2					
Dependent variable: ln(*Price*)					
Regressor	**(1)**	**(2)**	**(3)**	**(4)**	**(5)**
Size	0.00042 (0.000038)				
ln(*Size*)		0.69 (0.054)	0.68 (0.087)	0.57 (2.03)	0.69 (0.055)
ln(*Size*)^2				0.0078 (0.14)	
Bedrooms			0.0036 (0.037)		
Pool	0.082 (0.032)	0.071 (0.034)	0.071 (0.034)	0.071 (0.036)	0.071 (0.035)
View	0.037 (0.029)	0.027 (0.028)	0.026 (0.026)	0.027 (0.029)	0.027 (0.030)
Pool × *View*					0.0022 (0.10)
Condition	0.13 (0.045)	0.12 (0.035)	0.12 (0.035)	0.12 (0.036)	0.12 (0.035)
Intercept	10.97 (0.069)	6.60 (0.39)	6.63 (0.53)	7.02 (7.50)	6.60 (0.40)
Summary Statistics					
SER	0.102	0.098	0.099	0.099	0.099
$\overline{R}^2$	0.72	0.74	0.73	0.73	0.73

Variable definitions: Price 5 sale price ($); Size 5 house size (in square feet); Bedrooms 5 number of bedrooms; Pool 5 binary variable (1 if house has a swimming pool, 0 otherwise); View 5 binary variable (1 if house has a nice view, 0 otherwise); Condition 5 binary variable (1 if realtor reports house is in excellent condition, 0 otherwise).

b. Comparing columns (1) and (2), is it better to use *Size* or ln(*Size*) to explain house prices?

c. Using column (2), what is the estimated effect of pool on price? (Make sure you get the units right.) Construct a 95% confidence interval for this effect.

d. The regression in column (3) adds the number of bedrooms to the regression. How large is the estimated effect of an additional bedroom? Is the effect statistically significant? Why do you think the estimated effect is so small? (*Hint:* Which other variables are being held constant?)

e. Is the quadratic term $\ln(Size)^2$ important?

f. Use the regression in column (5) to compute the expected change in price when a pool is added to a house without a view. Repeat the exercise for a house with a view. Is there a large difference? Is the difference statistically significant?

8.3 After reading this chapter's analysis of test scores and class size, an educator comments, "In my experience, student performance depends on class size, but not in the way your regressions say. Rather, students do well when class size is less than 20 students and do very poorly when class size is greater than 25. There are no gains from reducing class size below 20 students, the relationship is constant in the intermediate region between 20 and 25 students, and there is no loss to increasing class size when it is already greater than 25." The educator is describing a "threshold effect" in which performance is constant for class sizes less than 20, then jumps and is constant for class sizes between 20 and 25, and then jumps again for class sizes greater than 25. To model these threshold effects, define the binary variables

$$STRsmall = 1 \text{ if } STR < 20, \text{ and } STRsmall = 0 \text{ otherwise;}$$

$$STRmoderate = 1 \text{ if } 20 \leq STR \leq 25, \text{ and } STRmoderate = 0 \text{ otherwise; and}$$

$$STRlarge = 1 \text{ if } STR > 25, \text{ and } STRmoderate = 0 \text{ otherwise.}$$

a. Consider the regression $TestScore_i = \beta_0 + \beta_1 STRsmall_i + \beta_2 STRlarge_i + u_i$. Sketch the regression function relating $TestScore$ to STR for hypothetical values of the regression coefficients that are consistent with the educator's statement.

b. A researcher tries to estimate the regression $TestScore_i = \beta_0 + \beta_1 STRsmall_i + \beta_2 STRmoderate_i + \beta_3 STRlarge_i + u_i$ and finds that her computer crashes. Why?

8.4 Read the box "The Returns to Education and the Gender Gap" in Section 8.3.

a. Consider a man with 16 years of education, and 2 years of experience, who is from a western state. Use the results from column (4) of Table 8.1 and the method in Key Concept 8.1 to estimate the expected change in the logarithm of average hourly earnings (AHE) associated with an additional year of experience.

b. Repeat (a) assuming 10 years of experience.

   c. Explain why the answers to (a) and (b) are different.

   d. Is the difference in the answers to (a) and (b) statistically significant at the 5% level? Explain.

   e. Would your answers to (a)–(d) change if the person was a woman? From the South? Explain.

   f. How would you change the regression if you suspected that the effect of experience on earnings was different for men than for women?

8.5 Read the box "The Demand for Economics Journals" in Section 8.3.

   a. The box reaches three conclusions. Looking at the results in the table, what is the basis for each of these conclusions?

   b. Using the results in regression (4), the box reports that the elasticity of demand for an 80-year-old journal is -0.28.

     i. How was this value determined from the estimated regression?

     ii. The box reports that the standard error for the estimated elasticity is 0.06. How would you calculate this standard error? (*Hint:* See the discussion "Standard errors of estimated effects" below Key Concept 8.1.)

   c. Suppose that the variable *Characters* had been divided by 1,000 instead of 1,000,000. How would the results in column (4) change?

8.6 Refer to Table 8.3.

   a. A researcher suspects that the effect of *%Eligible for subsidized lunch* has a nonlinear effect on test scores. In particular, he conjectures that increases in this variable from 10% to 20% have little effect on test scores, but that changes from 50% to 60% have a much larger effect.

     i. Describe a nonlinear specification that can be used to model this form of nonlinearity.

     ii. How would you test whether the researcher's conjecture was better than the linear specification in column (7) of Table 8.3?

   b. A researcher suspects that the effect of income on test scores is different in districts with small classes than in districts with large classes.

     i. Describe a nonlinear specification that can be used to model this form of nonlinearity.

     ii. How would you test whether the researcher's conjecture was better than the linear specification in column (7) of Table 8.3?

8.7 This problem is inspired by a study of the "gender gap" in earnings in top corporate jobs [Bertrand and Hallock (2001)]. The study compares total compensation among top executives in a large set of U.S. public corporations in the 1990s. (Each year these publicly traded corporations must report total compensation levels for their top five executives.)

a. Let *Female* be an indicator variable that is equal to 1 for females and 0 for males. A regression of the logarithm of earnings onto *Female* yields

$$\widehat{\ln(Earnings)} = 6.48 - 0.44 Female, SER = 2.65.$$
$$\quad\quad\quad (0.01) \quad (0.05)$$

i. The estimated coefficient on *Female* is -0.44. Explain what this value means.

ii. The *SER* is 2.65. Explain what this value means.

iii. Does this regression suggest that female top executives earn less than top male executives? Explain.

iv. Does this regression suggest that there is gender discrimination? Explain.

b. Two new variables, the market value of the firm (a measure of firm size, in millions of dollars) and stock return (a measure of firm performance, in percentage points), are added to the regression:

$$\widehat{\ln(Earnings)} = 3.86 - 0.28 Female + 0.37 \ln(MarketValue) + 0.004 Return,$$
$$\quad\quad\quad (0.03) \quad (0.04) \quad\quad\quad (0.004) \quad\quad\quad\quad\quad (0.003)$$
$$n = 46,670, \overline{R}^2 = 0.345.$$

i. The coefficient on $\ln(MarketValue)$ is 0.37. Explain what this value means.

ii. The coefficient on *Female* is now -0.28. Explain why it has changed from the regression in (a).

c. Are large firms more likely to have female top executives than small firms? Explain.

8.8 X is a continuous variable that takes on values between 5 and 100. Z is a binary variable. Sketch the following regression functions (with values of X between 5 and 100 on the horizontal axis and values of $\hat{Y}$ on the vertical axis):

a. $\hat{Y} = 2.0 + 3.0 \times \ln(X)$.

b. $\hat{Y} = 2.0 - 3.0 \times \ln(X)$.

c. **i.** $\hat{Y} = 2.0 + 3.0 \times \ln(X) + 4.0Z$, with $Z = 1$.

 ii. Same as (i), but with $Z = 0$.

d. **i.** $\hat{Y} = 2.0 + 3.0 \times \ln(X) + 4.0Z - 1.0 \times Z \times \ln(X)$, with $Z = 1$.

 ii. Same as (i), but with $Z = 0$.

e. $\hat{Y} = 1.0 + 125.0X - 0.01X^2$.

8.9 Explain how you would use "Approach #2" of Section 7.3 to calculate the confidence interval discussed below Equation (8.8). [*Hint:* This requires estimating a new regression using a different definition of the regressors and the dependent variable. See Exercise (7.9).]

8.10 Consider the regression model $Y_i = \beta_0 + \beta_1 X_{1i} + \beta_2 X_{2i} + \beta_3(X_{1i} \times X_{2i}) + u_i$. Use Key Concept 8.1 to show:

a. $\frac{\Delta Y}{\Delta X_1} = \beta_1 + \beta_3 X_2$ (effect of change in X_1 holding X_2 constant).

b. $\frac{\Delta Y}{\Delta X_2} = \beta_2 + \beta_3 X_1$ (effect of change in X_2 holding X_1 constant).

c. If X_1 changes by ΔX_1 and X_2 changes by ΔX_2, then $\Delta Y = (\beta_1 + \beta_3 X_2)\Delta X_1 + (\beta_2 + \beta_3 X_1)\Delta X_2 + \beta_3 \Delta X_1 \Delta X_2$.

Empirical Exercises

E8.1 Use the data set **CPS04** described in Empirical Exercise 4.1 to answer the following questions.

a. Run a regression of average hourly earnings (*AHE*) on age (*Age*), gender (*Female*), and education (*Bachelor*). If *Age* increases from 25 to 26, how are earnings expected to change? If *Age* increases from 33 to 34, how are earnings expected to change?

b. Run a regression of the logarithm average hourly earnings, ln(*AHE*), on *Age*, *Female*, and *Bachelor*. If *Age* increases from 25 to 26, how are earnings expected to change? If *Age* increases from 33 to 34, how are earnings expected to change?

c. Run a regression of the logarithm average hourly earnings, ln(*AHE*), on ln(*Age*), *Female*, and *Bachelor*. If *Age* increases from 25 to 26, how are earnings expected to change? If *Age* increases from 33 to 34, how are earnings expected to change?

d. Run a regression of the logarithm average hourly earnings, ln(*AHE*), on *Age*, *Age²*, *Female*, and *Bachelor*. If *Age* increases from 25 to 26, how are earnings expected to change? If *Age* increases from 33 to 34, how are earnings expected to change?

e. Do you prefer the regression in (c) to the regression in (b)? Explain.

f. Do you prefer the regression in (d) to the regression in (b)? Explain.

g. Do you prefer the regression in (d) to the regression in (c)? Explain.

h. Plot the regression relation between *Age* and ln(*AHE*) from (b), (c), and (d) for males with a high school diploma. Describe the similarities and differences between the estimated regression functions. Would your answer change if you plotted the regression function for females with college degrees?

i. Run a regression of ln(*AHE*), on *Age*, *Age²*, *Female*, *Bachelor*, and the interaction term *Female* × *Bachelor*. What does the coefficient on the interaction term measure? Alexis is a 30-year-old female with a bachelor's degree. What does the regression predict for her value of ln(*AHE*)? Jane is a 30-year-old female with a high school degree. What does the regression predict for her value of ln(*AHE*)? What is the predicted difference between Alexis's and Jane's earnings? Bob is a 30-year-old male with a bachelor's degree. What does the regression predict for his value of ln(*AHE*)? Jim is a 30-year-old male with a high school degree. What does the regression predict for his value of ln(*AHE*)? What is the predicted difference between Bob's and Jim's earnings?

j. Is the effect of *Age* on earnings different for males than for females? Specify and estimate a regression that you can use to answer this question.

k. Is the effect of *Age* on earnings different for high school graduates than college graduates? Specify and estimate a regression that you can use to answer this question.

l. After running all of these regressions (and any others that you want to run), summarize the effect of age on earnings for young workers.

E8.2 Using the data set **TeachingRatings** described in Empirical Exercise 4.2, carry out the following exercises.

a. Estimate a regression of *Course_Eval* on *Beauty, Intro, OneCredit, Female, Minority,* and *NNEnglish.*

b. Add *Age* and *Age*^{2} to the regression. Is there evidence that *Age* has a nonlinear effect on *Course_Eval*? Is there evidence that *Age* has any effect on *Course_Eval*?

c. Modify the regression in (a) so that the effect of *Beauty* on *Course_Eval* is different for men and women. Is the male–female difference in the effect of *Beauty* statistically significant?

d. Professor Smith is a man. He has cosmetic surgery that increases his beauty index from one standard deviation below the average to one standard deviation above the average. What is his value of *Beauty* before the surgery? After the surgery? Using the regression in (c), construct a 95% confidence for the increase in his course evaluation.

e. Repeat (d) for Professor Jones, who is a woman.

E8.3 Use the data set **CollegeDistance** described in Empirical Exercise 4.3 to answer the following questions.

a. Run a regression of *ED* on *Dist, Female, Bytest, Tuition, Black, Hispanic, Incomehi, Ownhome, DadColl, MomColl, Cue80,* and *Stwmfg80.* If *Dist* increases from 2 to 3 (that is, from 20 to 30 miles), how are years of education expected to change? If *Dist* increases from 6 to 7 (that is, from 60 to 70 miles), how are years of education expected to change?

b. Run a regression of ln(*ED*) on *Dist, Female, Bytest, Tuition, Black, Hispanic, Incomehi, Ownhome, DadColl, MomColl, Cue80,* and *Stwmfg80.* If *Dist* increases from 2 to 3 (from 20 to 30 miles), how are years of education expected to change? If *Dist* increases from 6 to 7 (from 60 to 70 miles), how are years of education expected to change?

c. Run a regression of *ED* on *Dist, Dist*^{2}, *Female, Bytest, Tuition, Black, Hispanic, Incomehi, Ownhome, DadColl, MomColl, Cue80,* and *Stwmfg80.* If *Dist* increases from 2 to 3 (from 20 to 30 miles), how are years of education expected to change? If *Dist* increases from 6 to 7 (from 60 to 70 miles), how are years of education expected to change?

d. Do you prefer the regression in (c) to the regression in (a)? Explain.

e. Consider a Hispanic female with *Tuition* = \$950, *Bytest* = 58, *Incomehi* = 0, *Ownhome* = 0, *DadColl* = 1, *MomColl* = 1, *Cue80* = 7.1, and *Stwmfg* = \$10.06.

    i. Plot the regression relation between *Dist* and *ED* from (a) and (c) for *Dist* in the range of 0 to 10 (from 0 to 100 miles). Describe the similarities and differences between the estimated regression functions. Would your answer change if you plotted the regression function for a white male with the same characteristics?

    ii. How does the regression function (c) behave for *Dist* > 10? How many observation are there with *Dist* > 10?

  f. Add the interaction term *DadColl* × *MomColl* to the regression in (c). What does the coefficient on the interaction term measure?

  g. Mary, Jane, Alexis, and Bonnie have the same values of *Dist, Bytest, Tuition, Female, Black, Hispanic, Fincome, Ownhome, Cue80* and *Stwmfg80*. Neither of Mary's parents attended college. Jane's father attended college, but her mother did not. Alexis's mother attended college, but her father did not. Both of Bonnie's parents attended college. Using the regressions from (f):

    i. What does the regression predict for the difference between Jane's and Mary's years of education?

    ii. What does the regression predict for the difference between Alexis's and Mary's years of education?

    iii. What does the regression predict for the difference between Bonnie's and Mary's years of education?

  h. Is there any evidence that the effect of *Dist* on *ED* depends on the family's income?

  i. After running all of these regressions (and any others that you want to run), summarize the effect of *Dist* on years of education.

E8.4 Using the data set **Growth** described in Empirical Exercise 4.4, excluding the data for Malta, run the following five regressions: *Growth* on (1) *TradeShare* and *YearsSchool*; (2) *TradeShare* and ln(*YearsSchool*); (3) *TradeShare*, ln(*YearsSchool*), *Rev_Coups, Assassinations* and ln(*RGDP60*); (4) *TradeShare*, ln(*YearsSchool*), *Rev_Coups, Assassinations,* ln(*RGDP60*), and *TradeShare* × ln(*YearsSchool*); and (5) *TradeShare*, *TradeShare*^{2}, *TradeShare*^{3}, ln(*YearsSchool*), *Rev_Coups, Assassinations,* and ln(*RGDP60*).

  a. Construct a scatterplot of *Growth* on *YearsSchool*. Does the relationship look linear or nonlinear? Explain. Use the plot to explain why regression (2) fits better than regression (1).

b. In 1960, a country contemplates an education policy that will increase average years of schooling from 4 years to 6 years. Use regression (1) to predict the increase in *Growth*. Use regression (2) to predict the increase in *Growth*.

c. Test whether the coefficients on *Assassinations* and *Rev_Coups* are equal to zero using regression (3).

d. Using regression (4), is there evidence that the effect of *TradeShare* on *Growth* depends on the level of education in the country?

e. Using regression (5) is there evidence of a nonlinear relationship between *TradeShare* and *Growth*?

f. In 1960, a country contemplates a trade policy that will increase the average value of *TradeShare* from 0.5 to 1. Use regression (3) to predict the increase in *Growth*. Use regression (5) to predict the increase in *Growth*.

APPENDIX	Regression Functions That
8.1	Are Nonlinear in the Parameters

The nonlinear regression functions considered in Sections 8.2 and 8.3 are nonlinear functions of the X's but are linear functions of the unknown parameters. Because they are linear in the unknown parameters, those parameters can be estimated by OLS after defining new regressors that are nonlinear transformations of the original X's. This family of nonlinear regression functions is both rich and convenient to use. In some applications, however, economic reasoning leads to regression functions that are not linear in the parameters. Although such regression functions cannot be estimated by OLS, they can be estimated using an extension of OLS called nonlinear least squares.

Functions That Are Nonlinear in the Parameters

We begin with two examples of functions that are nonlinear in the parameters. We then provide a general formulation.

Logistic curve. Suppose you are studying the market penetration of a technology—for example the adoption of database management software in different industries. The dependent variable is the fraction of firms in the industry that have adopted the software, a single independent variable X describes an industry characteristic, and you have data on n industries. The dependent variable is between 0 (no adopters) and 1 (100% adoption). Because a linear regression model could produce predicted values less than 0 or greater than 1, it makes sense to use instead a function that produces predicted values between 0 and 1.

The logistic function smoothly increases from a minimum of 0 to a maximum of 1. The logistic regression model with a single X is

$$Y_i = \frac{1}{1 + e^{-(\beta_0 + \beta_1 X_i)}} + u_i. \tag{8.38}$$

The logistic function with a single X is graphed in Figure 8.12a. As can be seen in the graph, the logistic function has an elongated "S" shape. For small values of X, the value of the function is nearly 0 and the slope is flat; the curve is steeper for moderate values of X; and for large values of X, the function approaches 1 and the slope is flat again.

Negative exponential growth.   The functions used in Section 8.2 to model the relation between test scores and income have some deficiencies. For example, the polynomial models can produce a negative slope for some values of income, which is implausible. The logarithmic specification has a positive slope for all values of income; however, as income gets very large, the predicted values increase without bound, so for some incomes the predicted value for a district will exceed the maximum possible score on the test.

The negative exponential growth model provides a nonlinear specification that has a positive slope for all values of income, has a slope that is greatest at low values of income and decreases as income rises, and has an upper bound (that is, an asymptote as income increases to infinity). The negative exponential growth regression model is

$$Y_i = \beta_0[1 - e^{-\beta_1(X_i - \beta_2)}] + u_i. \tag{8.39}$$

The negative exponential growth function is graphed in Figure 8.12b. The slope is steep for low values of X, but as X increases it reaches an asymptote of β_0.

General functions that are nonlinear in the parameters.   The logistic and negative exponential growth regression models are special cases of the general nonlinear regression model

$$Y_i = f(X_{1i}, \ldots, X_{ki}; \beta_0, \ldots, \beta_m) + u_i, \tag{8.40}$$

in which there are k independent variables and $m + 1$ parameters, $\beta_0, \ldots, \beta_m$. In the models of Sections 8.2 and 8.3, the X's entered this function nonlinearly, but the parameters entered linearly. In the examples of this appendix, the parameters enter nonlinearly as well.

FIGURE 8.12   Two Functions That Are Nonlinear in their Parameters

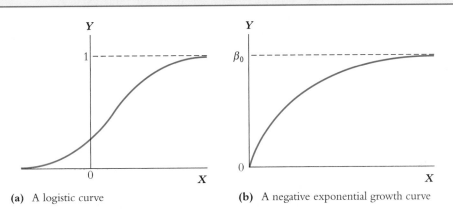

(a) A logistic curve   **(b)** A negative exponential growth curve

Part (a) plots the logistic function of Equation (8.38), which has predicted values that lie between 0 and 1. Part (b) plots the negative exponential growth function of Equation (8.39), which has a slope that is always positive and decreases as X increases, and an asymptote at β_0 as X tends to infinity.

If the parameters are known, then predicted effects may be computed using the method described in Section 8.1. In applications, however, the parameters are unknown and must be estimated from the data. Parameters that enter nonlinearly cannot be estimated by OLS, but they can be estimated by nonlinear least squares.

Nonlinear Least Squares Estimation

Nonlinear least squares is a general method for estimating the unknown parameters of a regression function when those parameters enter the population regression function non-linearly.

Recall the discussion in Section 5.3 of the OLS estimator of the coefficients of the linear multiple regression model. The OLS estimator minimizes the sum of squared prediction mistakes in Equation (5.8), $\sum_{i=1}^{n}[Y_i - (b_0 + b_1 X_{1i} + \cdots + b_k X_{ki})]^2$. In principle, the OLS estimator can be computed by checking many trial values of $b_0, \ldots, b_k$ and settling on the values that minimize the sum of squared mistakes.

This same approach can be used to estimate the parameters of the general nonlinear regression model in Equation (8.40). Because the regression model is nonlinear in the coefficients, this method is called **nonlinear least squares**. For a set of trial parameter values b_0, $b_1, \ldots, b_m$ construct the sum of squared prediction mistakes:

$$\sum_{i=1}^{n}[Y_i - f(X_{1i}, \ldots, X_{ki}, b_1, \ldots, b_m)]^2. \tag{8.41}$$

The **nonlinear least squares estimators** of $\beta_0, \beta_1, \ldots, \beta_m$ are the values of $b_0, b_1, \ldots, b_m$ that minimize the sum of squared prediction mistakes in Equation (8.41).

In linear regression, a relatively simple formula expresses the OLS estimator as a function of the data. Unfortunately, no such general formula exists for nonlinear least squares, so the nonlinear least squares estimator must be found numerically using a computer. Regression software incorporates algorithms for solving the nonlinear least squares minimization problem, which simplifies the task of computing the nonlinear least squares estimator in practice.

Under general conditions on the function f and the X's, the nonlinear least squares estimator shares two key properties with the OLS estimator in the linear regression model: It is consistent and it is normally distributed in large samples. In regression software that supports nonlinear least squares estimation, the output typically reports standard errors for the estimated parameters. As a consequence, inference concerning the parameters can proceed as usual; in particular, t-statistics can be constructed using the general approach in Key Concept 5.1, and a 95% confidence interval can be constructed as the estimated coefficient, plus or minus 1.96 standard errors. Just as in linear regression, the error term in the nonlinear regression model can be heteroskedastic, so heteroskedasticity-robust standard errors should be used.

Application to the Test Score–Income Relation

A negative exponential growth model, fit to district income (X) and test scores (Y), has the desirable features of a slope that is always positive [if β_1 in Equation (8.39) is positive] and an asymptote of β_0 as income increases to infinity. The result of estimating β_0, β_1, and β_2 in Equation (8.39) using the California test score data yields $\hat{\beta}_0 = 703.2$ (heteroskedasticity-robust standard error $= 4.44$), $\hat{\beta}_1 = 0.0552$ ($SE = 0.0068$), and $\hat{\beta}_2 = -34.0$ ($SE = 4.48$). Thus the estimated nonlinear regression function (with standard errors reported below the parameter estimates) is

$$\widehat{TestScore} = 703.2[1 - e^{-0.0552(Income + 34.0)}]. \tag{8.42}$$
$$\quad\quad\quad (4.44) \quad\quad (0.0068) \quad (4.48)$$

This estimated regression function is plotted in Figure 8.13, along with the logarithmic regression function and a scatterplot of the data. The two specifications are, in this case, quite similar. One difference is that the negative exponential growth curve flattens out at the highest levels of income, consistent with having an asymptote.

FIGURE 8.13 **The Negative Exponential Growth and Linear-Log Regression Functions**

The negative exponential growth regression function [Equation (8.42)] and the linear-log regression function [Equation 8.18)] both capture the nonlinear relation between test scores and district income. One difference between the two functions is that the negative exponential growth model has an asymptote as *Income* increases to infinity, but the linear-log regression function does not.

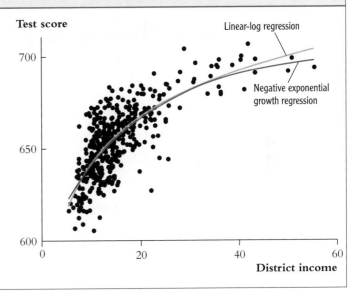

CHAPTER 9 | Assessing Studies Based on Multiple Regression

The preceding five chapters explain how to use multiple regression to analyze the relationship among variables in a data set. In this chapter, we step back and ask, What makes a study that uses multiple regression reliable or unreliable? We focus on statistical studies that have the objective of estimating the causal effect of a change in some independent variable, such as class size, on a dependent variable, such as test scores. For such studies, when will multiple regression provide a useful estimate of the causal effect and, just as importantly, when will it fail to do so?

To answer this question, this chapter presents a framework for assessing statistical studies in general, whether or not they use regression analysis. This framework relies on the concepts of internal and external validity. A study is internally valid if its statistical inferences about causal effects are valid for the population and setting studied; it is externally valid if its inferences can be generalized to other populations and settings. In Sections 9.1 and 9.2, we discuss internal and external validity, list a variety of possible threats to internal and external validity, and discuss how to identify those threats in practice. The discussion in Sections 9.1 and 9.2 focuses on the estimation of causal effects from observational data. Section 9.3 discusses a different use of regression models—forecasting—and provides an introduction to the threats to the validity of forecasts made using regression models.

As an illustration of the framework of internal and external validity, in Section 9.4 we assess the internal and external validity of the study of the effect on test scores of cutting the student–teacher ratio presented in Chapters 4–8.

INTERNAL AND EXTERNAL VALIDITY	KEY CONCEPT
A statistical analysis is **internally valid** if the statistical inferences about causal effects are valid for the population being studied. The analysis is **externally valid** if its inferences and conclusions can be generalized from the population and setting studied to other populations and settings.	9.1

9.1 Internal and External Validity

The concepts of internal and external validity, defined in Key Concept 9.1, provide a framework for evaluating whether a statistical or econometric study is useful for answering a specific question of interest.

Internal and external validity distinguish between the population and setting studied and the population and setting to which the results are generalized. The **population studied** is the population of entities—people, companies, school districts, and so forth—from which the sample was drawn. The population to which the results are generalized, or the **population of interest**, is the population of entities to which the causal inferences from the study are to be applied. For example, a high school (grades 9–12) principal might want to generalize our findings on class sizes and test scores in California elementary school districts (the population studied) to the population of high schools (the population of interest).

By "setting," we mean the institutional, legal, social, and economic environment. For example, it would be important to know whether the findings of a laboratory experiment assessing methods for growing organic tomatoes could be generalized to the field, that is, whether the organic methods that work in the setting of a laboratory also work in the setting of the real world. We provide other examples of differences in populations and settings later in this section.

Threats to Internal Validity

Internal validity has two components. First, the estimator of the causal effect should be unbiased and consistent. For example, if $\hat{\beta}_{STR}$ is the OLS estimator of the effect on test scores of a unit change in the student–teacher ratio in a certain regression, then $\hat{\beta}_{STR}$ should be an unbiased and consistent estimator of the true population causal effect of a change in the student–teacher ratio, β_{STR}.

Second, hypothesis tests should have the desired significance level (the actual rejection rate of the test under the null hypothesis should equal its desired significance level), and confidence intervals should have the desired confidence level. For example, if a confidence interval is constructed as $\hat{\beta}_{STR} \pm 1.96SE(\hat{\beta}_{STR})$, this confidence interval should contain the true population causal effect, β_{STR}, with probability 95% over repeated samples.

In regression analysis, causal effects are estimated using the estimated regression function and hypothesis tests are performed using the estimated regression coefficients and their standard errors. Accordingly, in a study based on OLS regression, the requirements for internal validity are that the OLS estimator is unbiased and consistent, and that standard errors are computed in a way that makes confidence intervals have the desired confidence level. There are various reasons this might not happen, and these reasons constitute threats to internal validity. These threats lead to failures of one or more of the least squares assumptions in Key Concept 6.4. For example, one threat that we have discussed at length is omitted variable bias; it leads to correlation between one or more regressors and the error term, which violates the first least squares assumption. If data on the omitted variable are available, then this threat can be avoided by including that variable as an additional regressor.

Section 9.2 provides a detailed discussion of the various threats to internal validity in multiple regression analysis and suggests how to mitigate them.

Threats to External Validity

Potential threats to external validity arise from differences between the population and setting studied and the population and setting of interest.

Differences in populations. Differences between the population studied and the population of interest can pose a threat to external validity. For example, laboratory studies of the toxic effects of chemicals typically use animal populations like mice (the population studied), but the results are used to write health and safety regulations for human populations (the population of interest). Whether mice and men differ sufficiently to threaten the external validity of such studies is a matter of debate.

More generally, the true causal effect might not be the same in the population studied and the population of interest. This could be because the population was chosen in way that makes it different from the population of interest, because of differences in characteristics of the populations, because of geographical differences, or because the study is out of date.

Differences in settings.   Even if the population being studied and the population of interest are identical, it might not be possible to generalize the study results if the **settings** differ. For example, a study of the effect on college binge drinking of an antidrinking advertising campaign might not generalize to another identical group of college students if the legal penalties for drinking at the two colleges differ. In this case, the legal setting in which the study was conducted differs from the legal setting to which its results are applied.

More generally, examples of differences in settings include differences in the institutional environment (public universities versus religious universities), differences in laws (differences in legal penalties), or differences in the physical environment (tailgate-party binge drinking in southern California versus Fairbanks, Alaska).

Application to test scores and the student–teacher ratio.   Chapters 7 and 8 reported statistically significant, but substantively small, estimated improvements in test scores resulting from reducing the student–teacher ratio. This analysis was based on test results for California school districts. Suppose for the moment that these results are internally valid. To what other populations and settings of interest could this finding be generalized?

The closer are the population and setting of the study to those of interest, the stronger is the case for external validity. For example, college students and college instruction are very different than elementary school students and instruction, so it is implausible that the effect of reducing class sizes estimated using the California elementary school district data would generalize to colleges. On the other hand, elementary school students, curriculum, and organization are broadly similar throughout the United States, so it is plausible that the California results might generalize to performance on standardized tests in other U.S. elementary school districts.

How to assess the external validity of a study.   External validity must be judged using specific knowledge of the populations and settings studied and those of interest. Important differences between the two will cast doubt on the external validity of the study.

Sometimes there are two or more studies on different but related populations. If so, the external validity of both studies can be checked by comparing their results. For example, in Section 9.4 we analyze test score and class size data for elementary school districts in Massachusetts and compare the Massachusetts and California results. In general, similar findings in two or more studies bolster claims to external validity, while differences in their findings that are not readily explained cast doubt on their external validity.[1]

How to design an externally valid study. Because threats to external validity stem from a lack of comparability of populations and settings, these threats are best minimized at the early stages of a study, before the data are collected. Study design is beyond the scope of this textbook, and the interested reader is referred to Shadish, Cook, and Campbell (2002).

9.2 Threats to Internal Validity of Multiple Regression Analysis

Studies based on regression analysis are internally valid if the estimated regression coefficients are unbiased and consistent, and if their standard errors yield confidence intervals with the desired confidence level. This section surveys five reasons why the OLS estimator of the multiple regression coefficients might be biased, even in large samples: omitted variables, misspecification of the functional form of the regression function, imprecise measurement of the independent variables ("errors in variables"), sample selection, and simultaneous causality. All five sources of bias arise because the regressor is correlated with the error term in the population regression, violating the first least squares assumption in Key Concept 6.4. For each, we discuss what can be done to reduce this bias. The section concludes with a discussion of circumstances that lead to inconsistent standard errors and what can be done about it.

Omitted Variable Bias

Recall that omitted variable bias arises when a variable that both determines Y and is correlated with one or more of the included regressors is omitted from the regression. This bias persists even in large samples, so that the OLS estimator is inconsistent. How best to minimize omitted variable bias depends on whether or not data are available for the potential omitted variable.

---

[1]A comparison of many related studies on the same topic is called a meta-analysis. The discussion in the box on the "Mozart effect" in Chapter 6 is based on a meta-analysis, for example. Performing a meta-analysis of many studies has its own challenges. How do you sort the good studies from the bad? How do you compare studies when the dependent variables differ? Should you put more weight on a large study than a small study? A discussion of meta-analysis and its challenges goes beyond the scope of this textbook. The interested reader is referred to Hedges and Olkin (1985) and Cooper and Hedges (1994).

Solutions to omitted variable bias when the omitted variable is observed.
If you have data on the omitted variable, then you can include this variable in a
multiple regression, thereby addressing the problem. However, adding a new variable has both costs and benefits. On the one hand, omitting the variable could
result in omitted variable bias. On the other hand, including the variable when it
does not belong (that is, when its population regression coefficient is zero) reduces
the precision of the estimators of the other regression coefficients. In other words,
the decision whether to include a variable involves a tradeoff between bias and
variance of the coefficients of interest. In practice, there are four steps that can
help you decide whether to include a variable or set of variables in a regression.

The first step is to identify the key coefficients of interest in your regression.
In the test score regressions, this is the coefficient on the student–teacher ratio,
because the question originally posed concerns the effect on test scores of reducing the student–teacher ratio.

The second step is to ask yourself: What are the most likely sources of important omitted variable bias in this regression? Answering this question requires
applying economic theory and expert knowledge, and should occur before you
actually run any regressions; because this is done before analyzing the data, this is
referred to as *a priori* ("before the fact") reasoning. In the test score example, this
step entails identifying those determinants of test scores that, if ignored, could bias
our estimator of the class size effect. The result of this step is a base regression
specification, the starting point for your empirical regression analysis, and a list of
additional "questionable" variables that might help to mitigate possible omitted
variable bias.

The third step is to augment your base specification with the additional questionable variables identified in the second step and to test the hypotheses that their
coefficients are zero. If the coefficients on the additional variables are statistically
significant, or if the estimated coefficients of interest change appreciably when the
additional variables are included, then they should remain in the specification and
you should modify your base specification. If not, then these variables can be
excluded from the regression.

The fourth step is to present an accurate summary of your results in tabular
form. This provides "full disclosure" to a potential skeptic, who can then draw his
or her own conclusions. Tables 7.1 and 8.3 are examples of this strategy. For example, in Table 8.3, we could have presented only the regression in column (7),
because that regression summarizes the relevant effects and nonlinearities in the
other regressions in that table. Presenting the other regressions, however, permits
the skeptical reader to draw his or her own conclusions.

These steps are summarized in Key Concept 9.2.

KEY CONCEPT	OMITTED VARIABLE BIAS: SHOULD I INCLUDE MORE VARIABLES IN MY REGRESSION?
9.2	

If you include another variable in your multiple regression, you will eliminate the possibility of omitted variable bias from excluding that variable but the variance of the estimator of the coefficients of interest can increase. Here are some guidelines to help you decide whether to include an additional variable:

1. Be specific about the coefficient or coefficients of interest.

2. Use *a priori* reasoning to identify the most important potential sources of omitted variable bias, leading to a base specification and some "questionable" variables.

3. Test whether additional questionable variables have nonzero coefficients.

4. Provide "full disclosure" representative tabulations of your results so that others can see the effect of including the questionable variables on the coefficient(s) of interest. Do your results change if you include a questionable variable?

Solutions to omitted variable bias when the omitted variable is not observed. Adding an omitted variable to a regression is not an option if you do not have data on that variable. Still, there are three other ways to solve omitted variable bias. Each of these three solutions circumvents omitted variable bias through the use of different types of data.

The first solution is to use data in which the same observational unit is observed at different points in time. For example, test score and related data might be collected for the same districts in 1995, then again in 2000. Data in this form are called panel data. Panel data make it possible to control for unobserved omitted variables as long as those omitted variables do not change over time.

The second solution is to use instrumental variables regression. This method relies on a new variable, called an instrumental variable, to isolate a part of the variation in X that is uncorrelated with the regression error.

The third solution is to use a study design in which the effect of interest (for example, the effect of reducing class size on student achievement) is studied using a randomized controlled experiment.

The regression methods studied in Chapters 4–8 can be extended to analyze panel data, to perform instrumental variables regression, and to analyze data from experiments. These extensions, however, go beyond the scope of this brief edition,

FUNCTIONAL FORM MISSPECIFICATION	KEY CONCEPT
	9.3

Functional form misspecification arises when the functional form of the estimated regression function differs from the functional form of the population regression function. If the functional form is misspecified, then the estimator of the partial effect of a change in one of the variables will, in general, be biased. Functional form misspecification often can be detected by plotting the data and the estimated regression function, and it can be corrected by using a different functional form.

and the interested reader is referred to Part III of the full edition of this book, Stock and Watson (2006).

Misspecification of the Functional Form of the Regression Function

If the true population regression function is nonlinear but the estimated regression is linear, then this **functional form misspecification** makes the OLS estimator biased. This bias is a type of omitted variable bias, in which the omitted variables are the terms that reflect the missing nonlinear aspects of the regression function. For example, if the population regression function is a quadratic polynomial, then a regression that omits the square of the independent variable would suffer from omitted variable bias. Bias arising from functional form misspecification is summerized in Key Concept 9.3.

Solutions to functional form misspecification. When the dependent variable is continuous (like test scores), this problem of potential nonlinearity can be solved using the methods of Chapter 8. If, however, the dependent variable is discrete or binary (for example, Y_i equals 1 if the ith person attended college and equals 0 otherwise), things are more complicated. Regression with a discrete dependent variable is discussed in Chapter 11 of the full edition of this book.

Errors-in-Variables

Suppose that in our regression of test scores against the student–teacher ratio we had inadvertently mixed up our data, so that we ended up regressing test scores for fifth graders on the student–teacher ratio for tenth graders in that district. Although the student–teacher ratio for elementary school students and tenth graders might be correlated, they are not the same, so this mix-up would lead to bias in the estimated coefficient. This is an example of **errors-in-variables bias** because its source is an error in the measurement of the independent variable. This bias persists even in very large samples, so that the OLS estimator is inconsistent if there is measurement error.

There are many possible sources of measurement error. If the data are collected through a survey, a respondent might give the wrong answer. For example, one question in the Current Population Survey involves last year's earnings. A respondent might not know his exact earnings, or he might misstate it for some other reason. If instead the data are obtained from computerized administrative records, there might have been typographical errors when the data were first entered.

To see that errors-in-variables results in correlation between the regressor and the error term, suppose there is a single regressor X_i (say, actual income) but that X_i is measured imprecisely by $\tilde{X}_i$ (the respondent's estimate of income). Because $\tilde{X}_i$, not X_i, is observed, the regression equation actually estimated is the one based on $\tilde{X}_i$. Written in terms of the imprecisely measured variable $\tilde{X}_i$, the population regression equation $Y_i = \beta_0 + \beta_1 X_i + u_i$ is

$$
\begin{aligned}
Y_i &= \beta_0 + \beta_1 \tilde{X}_i + [\beta_1(X_i - \tilde{X}_i) + u_i] \\
&= \beta_0 + \beta_1 \tilde{X}_i + v_i,
\end{aligned}
\tag{9.1}
$$

where $v_i = \beta_1(X_i - \tilde{X}_i) + u_i$. Thus, the population regression equation written in terms of $\tilde{X}_i$ has an error term that contains the difference between X_i and $\tilde{X}_i$. If this difference is correlated with the measured value $\tilde{X}_i$, then the regressor $\tilde{X}_i$ will be correlated with the error term and $\hat{\beta}_1$ will be biased and inconsistent.

The precise size and direction of the bias in $\hat{\beta}_1$ depend on the correlation between $\tilde{X}_i$ and $(X_i - \tilde{X}_i)$. This correlation depends, in turn, on the specific nature of the measurement error.

As an example, suppose that the survey respondent provides her best guess or recollection of the actual value of the independent variable X_i. A convenient way to represent this mathematically is to suppose that the measured value of X_i equals the actual, unmeasured value, plus a purely random component, w_i. Accordingly, the measured value of the variable, denoted by $\tilde{X}_i$, is $\tilde{X}_i = X_i + w_i$. Because the error is purely random, we might suppose that w_i has mean zero and variance σ_w^2 and is uncorrelated with X_i and the regression error u_i. Under this assumption, a bit of algebra[2] shows that $\hat{\beta}_1$ has the probability limit

---

[2]Under this measurement error assumption, $v_i = \beta_1(X_i - \tilde{X}_i) + u_i = -\beta_1 w_i + u_i$, $\text{cov}(X_i, u_i) = 0$, and $\text{cov}(\tilde{X}_1, w_i) = \text{cov}(X_i + w_i, w_i) = \sigma_w^2$, so $\text{cov}(\tilde{X}_i, v_i) = -\beta_1 \text{cov}(\tilde{X}_1, w_i) + \text{cov}(\tilde{X}_i, u_i) = -\beta_1 \sigma_w^2$. Thus, from Equation (6.1), $\hat{\beta}_1 \xrightarrow{p} \beta_1 - \beta_1 \sigma_w^2 / \sigma_{\tilde{X}}^2$. Now $\sigma_{\tilde{X}}^2 = \sigma_X^2 + \sigma_w^2$, so $\hat{\beta}_1 \xrightarrow{p} \beta_1 - \beta_1 \sigma_w^2 / (\sigma_X^2 + \sigma_w^2) = [\sigma_X^2 / (\sigma_X^2 + \sigma_w^2)]\beta_1$.

ERRORS-IN-VARIABLES BIAS	KEY CONCEPT
Errors-in-variables bias in the OLS estimator arises when an independent variable is measured imprecisely. This bias depends on the nature of the measurement error and persists even if the sample size is large. If the measured variable equals the actual value plus a mean-zero, independently distributed measurement error term, then the OLS estimator in a regression with a single right-hand variable is biased toward zero, and its probability limit is given in Equation (9.2).	9.4

$$\hat{\beta}_1 \xrightarrow{p} \frac{\sigma_X^2}{\sigma_X^2 + \sigma_w^2} \beta_1. \tag{9.2}$$

That is, if the measurement imprecision has the effect of simply adding a random element to the actual value of the independent variable, then $\hat{\beta}_1$ is inconsistent. Because the ratio $\frac{\sigma_X^2}{\sigma_X^2 + \sigma_w^2}$ is less than 1, $\hat{\beta}_1$ will be biased toward 0, even in large samples. In the extreme case that the measurement error is so large that essentially no information about X_i remains, the ratio of the variances in the final expression in Equation (9.2) is 0 and $\hat{\beta}_1$ converges in probability to 0. In the other extreme, when there is no measurement error, $\sigma_w^2 = 0$ so $\hat{\beta}_1 \xrightarrow{p} \beta_1$.

Although the result in Equation (9.2) is specific to this particular type of measurement error, it illustrates the more general proposition that if the independent variable is measured imprecisely then the OLS estimator is biased, even in large samples. Errors-in-variables bias is summarized in Key Concept 9.4.

Solutions to errors-in-variables bias.   The best way to solve the errors-in-variables problem is to get an accurate measure of X. If this is impossible, however, econometric methods can be used to mitigate errors-in-variables bias.

One such method is instrumental variables regression. It relies on having another variable (the "instrumental" variable) that is correlated with the actual value X_i but is uncorrelated with the measurement error. This method is described in Chapter 12 of the full edition of this book.

A second method is to develop a mathematical model of the measurement error and, if possible, to use the resulting formulas to adjust the estimates. For example, if a researcher believes that the measured variable is in fact the sum of the actual value and a random measurement error term, and if she knows or can estimate the ratio σ_w^2/σ_X^2, then she can use Equation (9.2) to compute an estimator of β_1 that corrects for the downward bias. Because this approach requires specialized knowledge about the nature of the measurement error, the details typically are specific to a given data set and its measurement problems and we shall not pursue this approach further in this textbook.

Sample Selection

Sample selection bias occurs when the availability of the data is influenced by a selection process that is related to the value of the dependent variable. This selection process can introduce correlation between the error term and the regressor, which leads to bias in the OLS estimator.

Sample selection that is unrelated to the value of the dependent variable does not introduce bias. For example, if data are collected from a population by simple random sampling, the sampling method (being drawn at random from the population) has nothing to do with the value of the dependent variable. Such sampling does not introduce bias.

Bias can be introduced when the method of sampling is related to the value of the dependent variable. An example of sample selection bias in polling was given in a box in Chapter 3. In that example, the sample selection method (randomly selected phone numbers of automobile owners) was related to the dependent variable (who the individual supported for president in 1936), because in 1936 car owners with phones were more likely to be Republicans.

An example of sample selection in economics arises in using a regression of wages on education to estimate the effect on wages of an additional year of education. Only individuals who have a job have wages, by definition. The factors (observable and unobservable) that determine whether someone has a job—education, experience, where one lives, ability, luck, and so forth—are similar to the factors that determine how much that person earns when employed. Thus, the fact that someone has a job suggests that, all else equal, the error term in the wage equation for that person is positive. Said differently, whether someone has a job is in part determined by the omitted variables in the error term in the wage regression. Thus, the simple fact that someone has a job, and thus appears in the data set, provides information that the error term in the regression is positive, at least on average, and could be correlated with the regressors. This too can lead to bias in the OLS estimator.

Sample selection bias is summarized in Key Concept 9.5. The box "Do Stock Mutual Funds Outperform the Market?" provides an example of sample selection bias in financial economics.

Solutions to selection bias.   The best solution to sample selection bias is to design the study and data set so that sample selection bias is avoided. For example, in the application to stock market mutual funds discussed in the box,

SAMPLE SELECTION BIAS	KEY CONCEPT
	9.5

Sample selection bias arises when a selection process influences the availability of data and that process is related to the dependent variable. Sample selection induces correlation between one or more regressors and the error term, leading to bias and inconsistency of the OLS estimator.

Do Stock Mutual Funds Outperform the Market?

Stock mutual funds are investment vehicles that hold a portfolio of stocks. By purchasing shares in a mutual fund, a small investor can hold a broadly diversified portfolio without the hassle and expense (transaction cost) of buying and selling shares in individual companies. Some mutual funds simply track the market (for example, by holding the stocks in the S&P 500), whereas others are actively managed by full-time professionals whose job is to make the fund earn a better return than the overall market—and competitors' funds. But do these actively managed funds achieve this goal? Do some mutual funds consistently beat other funds and the market?

One way to answer these questions is to compare future returns on mutual funds that had high returns over the past year to future returns on other funds and on the market as a whole. In making such comparisons, financial economists know that it is important to select the sample of mutual funds carefully. This task is not as straightforward as it seems, however. Some databases include historical data on funds currently available for purchase, but this approach means that the dogs—the most poorly performing funds—are omitted from the data set because they went out of business or were merged into other funds. For this reason, a study using data on historical performance of currently available funds is subject to sample selection bias: The sample is selected based on the value of the dependent variable, returns, because funds with the lowest returns are eliminated. The mean return of all funds (including the defunct) over a ten-year period will be less than the mean return of those funds still in existence at the end of those ten years, so a study of only the latter funds will overstate performance. Financial economists refer to this selection bias as "survivorship bias" because only the better funds survive to be in the data set.

When financial econometricians correct for survivorship bias by incorporating data on defunct funds, the results do not paint a flattering portrait of mutual fund managers. Corrected for survivorship bias, the econometric evidence indicates that actively managed stock mutual funds do not outperform the market on average, and past good performance does not predict future good performance. For further reading on mutual funds and survivorship bias, see Malkiel (2003, Chapter 11) and Carhart (1997).

researchers have addressed sample selection bias by tracking the returns on *all* mutual funds, including those that go out of business or merge. If it is not feasible to redesign a study to avoid sample selection bias, then in some cases it is possible to mitigate that bias by using specialized econometric methods. Those methods, however, are advanced and go beyond the scope of this book.

Simultaneous Causality

So far, we have assumed that causality runs from the regressors to the dependent variable (*X* causes *Y*). But what if causality also runs from the dependent variable to one or more regressors (*Y* causes *X*)? If so, causality runs "backward" as well as forward, that is, there is **simultaneous causality**. If there is simultaneous causality, an OLS regression picks up both effects so the OLS estimator is biased and inconsistent.

For example, our study of test scores focused on the effect on test scores of reducing the student–teacher ratio, so that causality is presumed to run from the student–teacher ratio to test scores. Suppose, however, that a government initiative subsidized hiring teachers in school districts with poor test scores. If so, causality would run in both directions: For the usual educational reasons low student–teacher ratios would arguably lead to high test scores, but because of the government program low test scores would lead to low student–teacher ratios.

Simultaneous causality leads to correlation between the regressor and the error term. In the test score example, suppose there is an omitted factor that leads to poor test scores; because of the government program, this factor that produces low scores in turn results in a low student–teacher ratio. Thus, a negative error term in the population regression of test scores on the student–teacher ratio reduces test scores, but because of the government program it also leads to a decrease in the student–teacher ratio. In other words, the student–teacher ratio is positively correlated with the error term in the population regression. This in turn leads to simultaneous causality bias and inconsistency of the OLS estimator.

This correlation between the error term and the regressor can be made precise mathematically by introducing an additional equation that describes the reverse causal link. For convenience, consider just the two variables *X* and *Y* and ignore other possible regressors. Accordingly, there are two equations, one in which *X* causes *Y*, and one in which *Y* causes *X*:

$$Y_i = \beta_0 + \beta_1 X_i + u_i \text{ and} \tag{9.3}$$

$$X_i = \gamma_0 + \gamma_1 Y_i + v_i. \tag{9.4}$$

	KEY CONCEPT
SIMULTANEOUS CAUSALITY BIAS	**9.6**

Simultaneous causality bias, also called simultaneous equations bias, arises in a regression of Y on X when, in addition to the causal link of interest from X to Y, there is a causal link from Y to X. This reverse causality makes X correlated with the error term in the population regression of interest.

Equation (9.3) is the familiar one in which β_1 is the effect on Y of a change in X, where u represents other factors. Equation (9.4) represents the reverse causal effect of Y on X. In the test score problem, Equation (9.3) represents the educational effect of class size on test scores, while Equation (9.4) represents the reverse causal effect of test scores on class size induced by the government program.

Simultaneous causality leads to correlation between X_i and the error term u_i in Equation (9.3). To see this, imagine that u_i is negative, which decreases Y_i. However, this lower value of Y_i affects the value of X_i through the second of these equations, and if γ_1 is positive, a low value of Y_i will lead to a low value of X_i. Thus, if γ_1 is positive, X_i and u_i will be positively correlated.[3]

Because this can be expressed mathematically using two simultaneous equations, the simultaneous causality bias is sometimes called **simultaneous equations bias**. Simultaneous causality bias is summarized in Key Concept 9.6.

Solutions to simultaneous causality bias.   There are two ways to mitigate simultaneous causality bias. One is to use instrumental variables regression, the topic of Chapter 12 of the full edition of this book. The second is to design and to implement a randomized controlled experiment in which the reverse causality channel is nullified, and such experiments are discussed in Chapter 13 of the full edition of this book.

Sources of Inconsistency of OLS Standard Errors

Inconsistent standard errors pose a different threat to internal validity. Even if the OLS estimator is consistent and the sample is large, inconsistent standard errors will produce hypothesis tests with size that differs from the desired significance

---

[3]To show this mathematically, note that Equation (9.4) implies that $\text{cov}(X_i, u_i) = \text{cov}(\gamma_0 + \gamma_1 Y_i + v_i, u_i)$ $= \gamma_1 \text{cov}(Y_i, u_i) + \text{cov}(v_i, u_i)$. Assuming that $\text{cov}(v_i, u_i) = 0$, by Equation (9.3) this in turn implies that $\text{cov}(X_i, u_i) = \gamma_1 \text{cov}(Y_i, u_i) = \gamma_1 \text{cov}(\beta_0 + \beta_1 X_i + u_i, u_i) = \gamma_1 \beta_1 \text{cov}(X_i, u_i) + \gamma_1 \sigma_u^2$. Solving for $\text{cov}(X_i, u_i)$ then yields the result $\text{cov}(X_i, u_i) = \gamma_1 \sigma_u^2/(1 - \gamma_1 \beta_1)$.

level and "95%" confidence intervals that fail to include the true value in 95% of repeated samples.

There are two main reasons for inconsistent standard errors: improperly handled heteroskedasticity and correlation of the error term across observations.

Heteroskedasticity. As discussed in Section 5.4, for historical reasons some regression software report homoskedasticity-only standard errors. If, however, the regression error is heteroskedastic, those standard errors are not a reliable basis for hypothesis tests and confidence intervals. The solution to this problem is to use heteroskedasticity-robust standard errors and to construct F-statistics using a heteroskedasticity-robust variance estimator. Heteroskedasticity-robust standard errors are provided as an option in modern software packages.

Correlation of the error term across observations. In some settings, the population regression error can be correlated across observations. This will not happen if the data are obtained by sampling at random from the population because the randomness of the sampling process ensures that the errors are independently distributed from one observation to the next. Sometimes, however, sampling is only partially random. The most common circumstance is when the data are repeated observations on the same entity over time, for example, the same school district for different years. If the omitted variables that constitute the regression error are persistent (like district demographics), then this induces "serial" correlation in the regression error over time. Serial correlation in the error term can arise in panel data (data on multiple districts for multiple years) and in time series data (data on a single district for multiple years).

Another situation in which the error term can be correlated across observations is when sampling is based on a geographical unit. If there are omitted variables that reflect geographic influences, these omitted variables could result in correlation of the regression errors for adjacent observations.

Correlation of the regression error across observations does not make the OLS estimator biased or inconsistent, but it does violate the second least squares assumption in Key Concept 6.4. The consequence is that the OLS standard errors—both homoskedasticity-only *and* heteroskedasticity-robust—are incorrect in the sense that they do not produce confidence intervals with the desired confidence level.

In many cases, this problem can be fixed by using an alternative formula for standard errors. These so-called heteroskedasticity- and autocorrelation-consistent (HAC) standard errors often are available as options in econometric software. HAC standard errors are not needed for the analysis of cross-sectional data, but they can be important for regressions using panel data or time series data.

THREATS TO THE INTERNAL VALIDITY OF A MULTIPLE REGRESSION STUDY	KEY CONCEPT 9.7

There are five primary threats to the internal validity of a multiple regression study:

1. Omitted variables

2. Functional form misspecification

3. Errors-in-variables (measurement error in the regressors)

4. Sample selection

5. Simultaneous causality

Each of these, if present, results in failure of the first least squares assumption, $E(u_i|X_{1i}, \ldots, X_{ki}) \neq 0$, which in turn means that the OLS estimator is biased and inconsistent.

Incorrect calculation of the standard errors also poses a threat to internal validity. Homoskedasticity-only standard errors are invalid if heteroskedasticity is present. If the variables are not independent across observations, as can arise in panel and time series data, then a further adjustment to the standard error formula is needed to obtain valid standard errors.

Applying this list of threats to a multiple regression study provides a systematic way to assess the internal validity of that study.

Key Concept 9.7 summarizes the threats to internal validity of a multiple regression study.

9.3   Internal and External Validity When the Regression Is Used for Forecasting

Up to now, the discussion of multiple regression analysis has focused on the estimation of causal effects. Regression models can be used for other purposes, however, including forecasting. When regression models are used for forecasting, concerns about external validity are very important, but concerns about unbiased estimation of causal effects are not.

Using Regression Models for Forecasting

Chapter 4 began by considering the problem of a school superintendent who wants to know how much test scores would increase if she reduced class sizes in her school district; that is, the superintendent wants to know the causal effect on test scores of a change in class size. Accordingly, Chapters 4–8 focused on using regression analysis to estimate causal effects using observational data.

Now consider a different problem. A parent moving to a metropolitan area plans to choose where to live based in part on the quality of the local schools. The parent would like to know how different school districts perform on standardized tests. Suppose, however, that test score data are not available (perhaps they are confidential) but data on class sizes are. In this situation, the parent must guess at how well the different districts perform on standardized tests based on a limited amount of information. That is, the parent's problem is to forecast average test scores in a given district based on information related to test scores—in particular, class size.

How can the parent make this forecast? Recall the regression of test scores on the student–teacher ratio (STR) from Chapter 4:

$$TestScore = 698.9 - 2.28 \times STR. \tag{9.5}$$

We concluded that this regression is not useful for the superintendent: The OLS estimator of the slope is biased because of omitted variables such as the composition of the student body and students' other learning opportunities outside school.

Nevertheless, Equation (9.5) could be useful to the parent trying to choose a home. To be sure, class size is not the only determinant of test performance, but from the parent's perspective what matters is whether it is a reliable predictor of test performance. The parent interested in forecasting test scores does not care whether the coefficient in Equation (9.5) estimates the causal effect on test scores of class size. Rather, the parent simply wants the regression to explain much of the variation in test scores across districts and to be stable—that is, to apply to the districts to which the parent is considering moving. Although omitted variable bias renders Equation (9.5) useless for answering the causal question, it still can be useful for forecasting purposes.

More generally, regression models can produce reliable forecasts, even if their coefficients have no causal interpretation. This recognition underlies much of the use of regression models for forecasting.

Assessing the Validity of Regression Models for Forecasting

Because the superintendent's problem and the parent's problem are conceptually very different, the requirements for the validity of the regression are different for their respective problems. To obtain credible estimates of causal effects, we must address the threats to internal validity summarized in Key Concept 9.7.

In contrast, if we are to obtain reliable forecasts, the estimated regression must have good explanatory power, its coefficients must be estimated precisely, and it must be stable in the sense that the regression estimated on one set of data can be reliably used to make forecasts using other data. When a regression model is used for forecasting, a paramount concern is that the model is externally valid, in the sense that it is stable and quantitatively applicable to the circumstance in which the forecast is made.

9.4   Example: Test Scores and Class Size

The framework of internal and external validity helps us to take a critical look at what we have learned—and what we have not—from our analysis of the California test score data.

External Validity

Whether the California analysis can be generalized—that is, whether it is externally valid—depends on the population and setting to which the generalization is made. Here, we consider whether the results can be generalized to performance on other standardized tests in other elementary public school districts in the United States.

Section 9.1 noted that having more than one study on the same topic provides an opportunity to assess the external validity of both studies by comparing their results. In the case of test scores and class size, other comparable data sets are, in fact, available. In this section, we examine a different data set, based on standardized test results for fourth graders in 220 public school districts in Massachusetts in 1998. Both the Massachusetts and California tests are broad measures of student knowledge and academic skills, although the details differ. Similarly, the organization of classroom instruction is broadly similar at the elementary school level in the two states (as it is in most U.S. elementary school districts), although aspects of elementary school funding and curriculum differ. Thus, finding similar results about the effect of the student–teacher ratio on test performance in the California and Massachusetts data would be evidence of external validity of the findings in California. Conversely, finding different results in the two states would raise questions about the internal or external validity of at least one of the studies.

TABLE 9.1	Summary Statistics for California and Massachusetts Test Score Data Sets			
	California		Massachusetts	
	Average	**Standard Deviation**	**Average**	**Standard Deviation**
Test scores	654.1	19.1	709.8	15.1
Student–teacher ratio	19.6	1.9	17.3	2.3
% English learners	15.8%	18.3%	1.1%	2.9%
% Receiving lunch subsidy	44.7%	27.1%	15.3%	15.1%
Average district income ($)	$15,317	$7226	$18,747	$5808
Number of observations	420		220	
Year	1999		1998	

Comparison of the California and Massachusetts data.   Like the California data, the Massachusetts data are at the school district level. The definitions of the variables in the Massachusetts data set are the same as those in the California data set, or nearly so. More information on the Massachusetts data set, including definitions of the variables, is given in Appendix 9.1.

Table 9.1 presents summary statistics for the California and Massachusetts samples. The average test score is higher in Massachusetts, but the test is different, so a direct comparison of scores is not appropriate. The average student–teacher ratio is higher in California (19.6 versus 17.3). Average district income is 20% higher in Massachusetts, but the standard deviation of income is greater in California, that is, there is a greater spread in average district incomes in California than in Massachusetts. The average percentage of students still learning English and the average percentage of students receiving subsidized lunches are both much higher in the California than in the Massachusetts districts.

Test scores and average district income.   To save space, we do not present scatterplots of all the Massachusetts data. Because it was a focus in Chapter 8, however, it is interesting to examine the relationship between test scores and average district income in Massachusetts. This scatterplot is presented in Figure 9.1. The general pattern of this scatterplot is similar to that in Figure 8.2 for the California data: The relationship between income and test scores appears to be steep for low values of income and flatter for high values. Evidently, the linear regression plotted in the figure misses this apparent nonlinearity. Cubic and logarithmic regression functions are also plotted in Figure 9.1. The cubic regression function has a

---

FIGURE 9.1   Test Scores vs. Income for Massachusetts Data

The estimated linear regression function does not capture the nonlinear relation between income and test scores in the Massachusetts data. The estimated linear-log and cubic regression functions are similar for district incomes between $13,000 and $30,000, the region containing most of the observations.

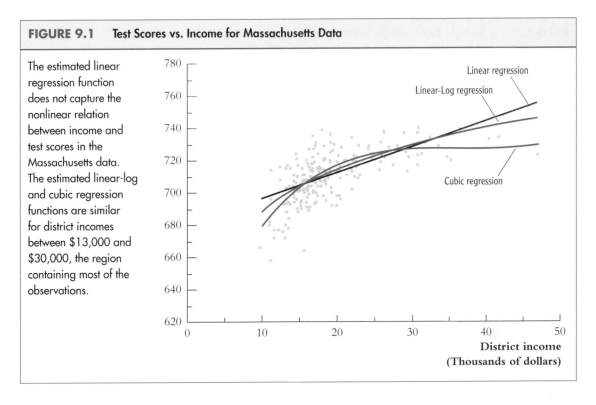

---

slightly higher $\overline{R}^2$ than the logarithmic specification (0.486 versus 0.455). Comparing Figures 8.7 and 9.1 shows that the general pattern of nonlinearity found in the California income and test score data is also present in the Massachusetts data. The precise functional forms that best describe this nonlinearity differ, however, with the cubic specification fitting best in Massachusetts but the linear-log specification fitting best in California.

Multiple regression results.   Regression results for the Massachusetts data are presented in Table 9.2. The first regression, reported in column (1) in the table, has only the student–teacher ratio as a regressor. The slope is negative (-1.72), and the hypothesis that the coefficient is zero can be rejected at the 1% significance level ($t = -1.72/0.50 = -3.44$).

The remaining columns report the results of including additional variables that control for student characteristics and of introducing nonlinearities into the estimated regression function. Controlling for the percentage of English learners, the percentage of students eligible for a free lunch, and average district income reduces the estimated coefficient on the student–teacher ratio by 60%, from -1.72 in regression (1) to -0.69 in regression (2) and -0.64 in regression (3).

TABLE 9.2 Multiple Regression Estimates
of the Student–Teacher Ratio and Test Scores: Data from Massachusetts

Dependent variable: average combined English, math,
and science test score in the school district, fourth grade; 220 observations.

Regressor	(1)	(2)	(3)	(4)	(5)	(6)
Student–teacher ratio (*STR*)	−1.72** (0.50)	−0.69* (0.27)	−0.64* (0.27)	12.4 (14.0)	−1.02** (0.37)	−0.67* (0.27)
STR^2				−0.680 (0.737)		
STR^3				0.011 (0.013)		
% English learners		−0.411 (0.306)	−0.437 (0.303)	−0.434 (0.300)		
% English learners > median? (Binary, *HiEL*)					−12.6 (9.8)	
$HiEL \times STR$					0.80 (0.56)	
% Eligible for free lunch		−0.521** (0.077)	−0.582** (0.097)	−0.587** (0.104)	−0.709** (0.091)	−0.653** (0.72)
District income (logarithm)		16.53** (3.15)				
District income			−3.07 (2.35)	−3.38 (2.49)	−3.87* (2.49)	−3.22 (2.31)
District income^2			0.164 (0.085)	0.174 (0.089)	0.184* (0.090)	0.165 (0.085)
District income^3			−0.0022* (0.0010)	−0.0023* (0.0010)	−0.0023* (0.0010)	−0.0022* (0.0010)
Intercept	739.6** (8.6)	682.4** (11.5)	744.0** (21.3)	665.5** (81.3)	759.9** (23.2)	747.4** (20.3)

(Table 9.2 continued)

Comparing the $\overline{R}^2$'s of regressions (2) and (3) indicates that the cubic specification (3) provides a better model of the relationship between test scores and income than does the logarithmic specification (2), even holding constant the student–teacher ratio. There is no statistically significant evidence of a nonlinear relationship between test scores and the student–teacher ratio: The *F*-statistic in regression (4) testing whether the population coefficients on STR^2 and STR^3 are zero has a *p*-value of 0.641. Similarly, there is no evidence that a reduction in the student–teacher ratio has a different effect in districts with many English learners

(Table 9.2 continued)
F-Statistics and p-Values Testing Exclusion of Groups of Variables

	(1)	(2)	(3)	(4)	(5)	(6)
All *STR* variables and interactions = 0				2.86 (0.038)	4.01 (0.020)	
$STR^2, STR^3 = 0$				0.45 (0.641)		
$Income^2, Income^3$			7.74 (<0.001)	7.75 (<0.001)	5.85 (0.003)	6.55 (0.002)
$HiEL, HiEL \times STR$					1.58 (0.208)	
SER	14.64	8.69	8.61	8.63	8.62	8.64
$\overline{R}^2$	0.063	0.670	0.676	0.675	0.675	0.674

These regressions were estimated using the data on Massachusetts elementary school districts described in Appendix 9.1. Standard errors are given in parentheses under the coefficients, and *p*-values are given in parentheses under the *F*-statistics. Individual coefficients are statistically significant at the *5% level or **1% level.

than with few [the *t*-statistic on $HiEL \times STR$ in regression (5) is 0.80/0.56 = 1.43]. Finally, regression (6) shows that the estimated coefficient on the student–teacher ratio does not change substantially when the percentage of English learners [which is insignificant in regression (3)] is excluded. In short, the results in regression (3) are not sensitive to the changes in functional form and specification considered in regressions (4)–(6) in Table 9.2. Therefore we adopt regression (3) as our base estimate of the effect in test scores of a change in the student–teacher ratio based on the Massachusetts data.

Comparison of Massachusetts and California results. For the California data, we found:

1. Adding variables that control for student background characteristics reduced the coefficient on the student–teacher ratio from −2.28 [Table 7.1, regression (1)] to −0.73 [Table 8.3, regression (2)], a reduction of 68%.

2. The hypothesis that the true coefficient on the student–teacher ratio is zero was rejected at the 1% significance level, even after adding variables that control for student background and district economic characteristics.

3. The effect of cutting the student–teacher ratio did not depend in an important way on the percentage of English learners in the district.

4. There is some evidence that the relationship between test scores and the student–teacher ratio is nonlinear.

Do we find the same things in Massachusetts? For findings (1), (2), and (3), the answer is yes. Including the additional control variables reduces the coefficient on the student–teacher ratio from −1.72 [Table 9.2, regression (1)] to −0.69 [Table 9.2, regression (2)], a reduction of 60%. The coefficients on the student–teacher ratio remain significant after adding the control variables. Those coefficients are only significant at the 5% level in the Massachusetts data, whereas they are significant at the 1% level in the California data. However, there are nearly twice as many observations in the California data, so it is not surprising that the California estimates are more precise. As in the California data, there is no statistically significant evidence in the Massachusetts data of an interaction between the student–teacher ratio and the binary variable indicating a large percentage of English learners in the district.

Finding (4), however, does not hold up in the Massachusetts data: The hypothesis that the relationship between the student–teacher ratio and test scores is linear cannot be rejected at the 5% significance level when tested against a cubic specification.

Because the two standardized tests are different, the coefficients themselves cannot be compared directly: One point on the Massachusetts test is not the same as one point on the California test. If, however, the test scores are put into the same units, then the estimated class size effects can be compared. One way to do this is to transform the test scores by standardizing them: Subtract the sample average and divide by the standard deviation so that they have a mean of 0 and a variance of 1. The slope coefficients in the regression with the transformed test score equal the slope coefficients in the original regression, divided by the standard deviation of the test. Thus the coefficient on the student–teacher ratio, divided by the standard deviation of test scores, can be compared across the two data sets.

This comparison is undertaken in Table 9.3. The first column reports the OLS estimates of the coefficient on the student–teacher ratio in a regression with the percentage of English learners, the percentage of students eligible for a free lunch, and the average district income included as control variables. The second column reports the standard deviation of the test scores across districts. The final two columns report the estimated effect on test scores of reducing the student–teacher ratio by two students per teacher (our superintendent's proposal), first in the units of the test, and second in standard deviation units. For the linear specification, the OLS coefficient estimate using California data is −0.73, so cutting the student–teacher ratio by two is estimated to increase district test scores by −0.73 × (−2) = 1.46 points. Because the standard deviation of test scores is 19.1 points, this corresponds to 1.46/19.1 = 0.076 standard deviations of the distribution of test scores across districts. The standard error of this estimate is 0.26 × 2/19.1 =

TABLE 9.3	**Student–Teacher Ratios and Test Scores: Comparing the Estimates from California and Massachusetts**				
			Estimated Effect of Two Fewer Students per Teacher, In Units of:		
	OLS Estimate $\hat{\beta}_{STR}$	**Standard Deviation of Test Scores Across Districts**	**Points on the Test**	**Standard Deviations**
California				
Linear: Table 8.3(2)	−0.73 (0.26)	19.1	1.46 (0.52)	0.076 (0.027)
Cubic: Table 8.3(7) *Reduce STR from 20 to 18*	—	19.1	2.93 (0.70)	0.153 (0.037)
Cubic: Table 8.3(7) *Reduce STR from 22 to 20*	—	19.1	1.90 (0.69)	0.099 (0.036)
Massachusetts				
Linear: Table 9.2(3)	−0.64 (0.27)	15.1	1.28 (0.54)	0.085 (0.036)

Standard errors are given in parentheses.

0.027. The estimated effects for the nonlinear models and their standard errors were computed using the method described in Section 8.1.

Based on the linear model using California data, a reduction of two students per teacher is estimated to increase test scores by 0.076 standard deviation unit, with a standard error of 0.027. The nonlinear models for California data suggest a somewhat larger effect, with the specific effect depending on the initial student–teacher ratio. Based on the Massachusetts data, this estimated effect is 0.085 standard deviation unit, with a standard error of 0.036.

These estimates are essentially the same. Cutting the student–teacher ratio is predicted to raise test scores, but the predicted improvement is small. In the California data, for example, the difference in test scores between the median district and a district at the 75th percentile is 12.2 test score points (Table 4.1), or 0.64 (= 12.2/19.1) standard deviations. The estimated effect from the linear model is just over one-tenth this size; in other words, according to this estimate, cutting the student teacher–ratio by two would move a district only one-tenth of the way from the median to the 75th percentile of the distribution of test scores across districts. Reducing the student–teacher ratio by two is a large change for a district, but the estimated benefits shown in Table 9.3, while nonzero, are small.

This analysis of Massachusetts data suggests that the California results are externally valid, at least when generalized to elementary school districts elsewhere in the United States.

Internal Validity

The similarity of the results for California and Massachusetts does not ensure their *internal* validity. Section 9.2 listed five possible threats to internal validity that could induce bias in the estimated effect on test scores on class size. We consider these threats in turn.

Omitted variables.   The multiple regressions reported in this and previous chapters control for a student characteristic (the percentage of English learners), a family economic characteristic (the percentage of students receiving a subsidized lunch), and a broader measure of the affluence of the district (average district income).

Possible omitted variables remain, such as other school and student characteristics, and their omission might cause omitted variables bias. For example, if the student–teacher ratio is correlated with teacher quality (perhaps because better teachers are attracted to schools with smaller student–teacher ratios), and if teacher quality affects test scores, then omission of teacher quality could bias the coefficient on the student–teacher ratio. Similarly, districts with a low student–teacher ratio might also offer many extracurricular learning opportunities. Also, districts with a low student–teacher ratio might attract families that are more committed to enhancing their children's learning at home. Such omitted factors could lead to omitted variable bias.

One way to eliminate omitted variable bias, at least in theory, is to conduct an experiment. For example, students could be randomly assigned to different size classes, and their subsequent performance on standardized tests could be compared. Such a study was in fact conducted in Tennessee, and the findings obtained using the Massachusetts and California observational data are closely consistent with the finding of the Tennessee class size experiment.

Functional form.   The analysis here and in Chapter 8 explored a variety of functional forms. We found that some of the possible nonlinearities investigated were not statistically significant, while those that were did not substantially alter the estimated effect of reducing the student–teacher ratio. Although further functional form analysis could be carried out, this suggests that the main findings of these studies are unlikely to be sensitive to using different nonlinear regression specifications.

Errors-in-variables.   The average student–teacher ratio in the district is a broad and potentially inaccurate measure of class size. For example, because students move in and out of districts, the student–teacher ratio might not accurately represent the actual class sizes experienced by the students taking the test, which in turn could lead to the estimated class size effect being biased toward zero. Another variable with potential measurement error is average district income. Those data were taken from the 1990 census, while the other data pertain to 1998 (Massachusetts) or 1999 (California). If the economic composition of the district changed substantially over the 1990s, this would be an imprecise measure of the actual average district income.

Selection.   The California and the Massachusetts data cover all the public elementary school districts in the state that satisfy minimum size restrictions, so there is no reason to believe that sample selection is a problem here.

Simultaneous causality.   Simultaneous causality would arise if the performance on standardized tests affected the student–teacher ratio. This could happen, for example, if there is a bureaucratic or political mechanism for increasing the funding of poorly performing schools or districts, which in turn resulted in hiring more teachers. In Massachusetts, no such mechanism for equalization of school financing was in place during the time of these tests. In California, a series of court cases led to some equalization of funding, but this redistribution of funds was not based on student achievement. Thus, in neither Massachusetts nor California does simultaneous causality appear to be a problem.

Heteroskedasticity and correlation of the error term across observations. All of the results reported here and in earlier chapters use heteroskedastic-robust standard errors, so heteroskedasticity does not threaten internal validity. Correlation of the error term across observations, however, could threaten the consistency of the standard errors because simple random sampling was not used (the sample consists of all elementary school districts in the state). Although there are alternative standard error formulas that could be applied to this situation, the details are complicated and specialized and we leave them to more advanced texts.

Discussion and Implications

The similarity between the Massachusetts and California results suggest that these studies are externally valid, in the sense that the main findings can be generalized to performance on standardized tests at other elementary school districts in the United States.

Some of the most important potential threats to internal validity have been addressed by controlling for student background, family economic background, and district affluence, and by checking for nonlinearities in the regression function. Still, some potential threats to internal validity remain. A leading candidate is omitted variable bias, perhaps arising because the control variables do not capture other characteristics of the school districts or extracurricular learning opportunities.

Based on both the California and the Massachusetts data, we are able to answer the superintendent's question from Section 4.1: After controlling for family economic background, student characteristics, and district affluence, and after modeling nonlinearities in the regression function, cutting the student–teacher ratio by two students per teacher is predicted to increase test scores by approximately 0.08 standard deviation of the distribution of test scores across districts. This effect is statistically significant, but it is quite small. This small estimated effect is in line with the results of the many studies that have investigated the effects on test scores of class size reductions.[4]

The superintendent can now use this estimate to help her decide whether to reduce class sizes. In making this decision, she will need to weigh the costs of the proposed reduction against the benefits. The costs include teacher salaries and expenses for additional classrooms. The benefits include improved academic performance, which we have measured by performance on standardized tests, but there are other potential benefits that we have not studied, including lower dropout rates and enhanced future earnings. The estimated effect of the proposal on standardized test performance is one important input into her calculation of costs and benefits.

9.5 Conclusion

The concepts of internal and external validity provide a framework for assessing what has been learned from an econometric study.

A study based on multiple regression is internally valid if the estimated coefficients are unbiased and consistent, and if standard errors are consistent. Threats to the internal validity of such a study include omitted variables, misspecification of functional form (nonlinearities), imprecise measurement of the independent

---

[4]If you are interested in learning more about the relationship between class size and test scores, see the reviews by Ehrenberg, Brewer, Gamoran, and Willms (2001a, 2001b).

variables (errors-in-variables), sample selection, and simultaneous causality. Each of these introduces correlation between the regressor and the error term, which in turn makes OLS estimators biased and inconsistent. If the errors are correlated across observations, as they can be with time series data, or if they are heteroskedastic but the standard errors are computed using the homoskedasticity-only formula, then internal validity is compromised because the standard errors will be inconsistent. These latter problems can be addressed by computing the standard errors properly.

A study using regression analysis, like any statistical study, is externally valid if its findings can be generalized beyond the population and setting studied. Sometimes it can help to compare two or more studies on the same topic. Whether or not there are two or more such studies, however, assessing external validity requires making judgments about the similarities of the population and setting studied and the population and setting to which the results are being generalized.

Summary

1. Statistical studies are evaluated by asking whether the analysis is internally and externally valid. A study is internally valid if the statistical inferences about causal effects are valid for the population being studied. A study is externally valid if its inferences and conclusions can be generalized from the population and setting studied to other populations and settings.

2. In regression estimation of causal effects, there are two types of threats to internal validity. First, OLS estimators will be inconsistent if the regressors and error terms are correlated. Second, confidence intervals and hypothesis tests are not valid when the standard errors are incorrect.

3. Regressors and error terms may be correlated when there are omitted variables, an incorrect functional form is used, one or more of the regressors is measured with error, the sample is chosen nonrandomly from the population, or there is simultaneous causality between the regressors and dependent variables.

4. Standard errors are incorrect when the errors are heteroskedastic and the computer software uses the homoskedasticity-only standard errors, or when the error term is correlated across different observations.

5. When regression models are used solely for forecasting, it is not necessary for the regression coefficients to be unbiased estimates of causal effects. It is critical, however, that the regression model be externally valid for the forecasting application at hand.

Key Terms

internal validity (311)
external validity (311)
population studied (311)
population of interest (311)
setting (313)

functional form misspecification (317)
errors-in-variable bias (318)
sample selection bias (320)
simultaneous causality (322)
simultaneous equations bias (323)

Review the Concepts

9.1 What is the difference between internal and external validity? Between the population studied and the population of interest?

9.2 Key Concept 9.2 describes the problem of variable selection in terms of a tradeoff between bias and variance. What is this tradeoff? Why could including an additional regressor decrease bias? Increase variance?

9.3 Economic variables are often measured with error. Does this mean that regression analysis is unreliable? Explain.

9.4 Suppose that a state offered voluntary standardized tests to all of its third graders, and these data were used in a study of class size on student performance. Explain how sample selection bias might invalidate the results.

9.5 A researcher estimates the effect on crime rates of spending on police by using city-level data. Explain how simultaneous causality might invalidate the results.

9.6 A researcher estimates a regression using two different software packages. The first uses the homoskedasticity-only formula for standard errors. The second uses the heteroskedasticity-robust formula. The standard errors are very different. Which should the researcher use? Why?

Exercises

9.1 Suppose that you have just read a careful statistical study of the effect of advertising on the demand for cigarettes. Using data from New York during the 1970s, it concluded that advertising on buses and subways was more effective than print advertising. Use the concept of external validity to determine if these results are likely to apply to Boston in the 1970s; Los Angeles in the 1970s; New York in 2006.

9.2 Consider the one-variable regression model: $Y_i = \beta_0 + \beta_1 X_i + u_i$, and suppose that it satisfies the assumption in Key Concept 4.3. Suppose that Y_i is measured with error, so that the data are $\tilde{Y}_i = Y_i + w_i$, where w_i is the measurement error which is i.i.d. and independent of Y_i and X_i. Consider the population regression $\tilde{Y}_i = \beta_0 + \beta_1 X_i + v_i$, where v_i is the regression error using the mismeasured dependent variable, $\tilde{Y}_i$.

  a. Show that $v_i = u_i + w_i$.

  b. Show that the regression $\tilde{Y}_i = \beta_0 + \beta_1 X_i + v_i$ satisfies the assumptions in Key Concept 4.3. (Assume that w_i is independent of Y_j and X_j for all values of i and j and has a finite fourth moment.)

  c. Are the OLS estimators consistent?

  d. Can confidence intervals be constructed in the usual way?

  e. Evaluate these statements: "Measurement error in the X's is a serious problem. Measurement error in Y is not."

9.3 Labor economists studying the determinants of women's earnings discovered a puzzling empirical result. Using randomly selected employed women, they regressed earnings on the women's number of children and a set of control variables (age, education, occupation, and so forth). They found that women with more children had higher wages, controlling for these other factors. Explain how sample selection might be the cause of this result. (*Hint:* Notice that the sample includes only women who are working.) (This empirical puzzle motivated James Heckman's research on sample selection that led to his 2000 Nobel Prize in economics.)

9.4 Using the regressions shown in column (2) of Table 8.3 and column (2) of Table 9.2, construct a table like Table 9.3 to compare the estimated effects of a 10% increase in district income on test scores in California and Massachusetts.

9.5 The demand for a commodity is given by $Q = \beta_0 + \beta_1 P + u$, where Q denotes quantity, P denotes price, and u denotes factors other than price that determine demand. Supply for the commodity is given by $Q = \gamma_0 + \gamma_1 P + v$, where v denotes factors other than price that determine supply. Suppose that u and v both have a mean of zero, have variances σ_u^2 and σ_v^2, and are mutually uncorrelated.

  a. Solve the two simultaneous equations to show how Q and P depend on u and v.

  b. Derive the means of P and Q.

    c. Derive the variance of P, the variance of Q, and the covariance between Q and P.

    d. A random sample of observations of (Q_i, P_i) is collected, and Q_i is regressed on P_i. (That is, Q_i is the regressand and P_i is the regressor.) Suppose that the sample is very large.

        i. Use your answers to (b) and (c) to derive values of the regression coefficients. [*Hint:* Use Equations (4.7) and (4.8).]

        ii. A researcher uses the slope of this regression as an estimate of the slope of the demand function (β_1). Is the estimated slope too large or too small? (*Hint:* Use the fact that demand curves slope down and supply curves slope up.)

9.6   Suppose $n = 100$ i.i.d. observations for (Y_i, X_i) yield the following regression results:

$$\hat{Y} = 32.1 + 66.8X, SER = 15.1, R^2 = 0.81.$$
$$(15.1) \quad (12.2)$$

Another researcher is interested in the same regression, but he makes an error when he enters the data into his regression program: He enters each observation twice, so he has 200 observations (with observation 1 entered twice, observation 2 entered twice, and so forth).

    a. Using these 200 observations, what results will be produced by his regression program? (*Hint:* Write the "incorrect" values of the sample means, variances and covariances of Y and X as functions of the "correct" values. Use these to determine the regression statistics.)

$$\hat{Y} = \underline{\quad} + \underline{\quad} X, SER = \underline{\quad}, R^2 = \underline{\quad}.$$
$$(\underline{\quad}) \quad (\underline{\quad})$$

    b. Which (if any) of the internal validity conditions are violated?

9.7   Are the following statements true or false? Explain your answer.

    a. "An ordinary least squares regression of Y onto X will be internally inconsistent if X is correlated with the error term."

    b. "Each of the five primary threats to internal validity implies that X is correlated with the error term."

9.8 Would the regression in Equation (9.5) be useful for predicting test scores in a school district in Massachusetts? Why or why not?

9.9 Consider the linear regression of *TestScore* on *Income* shown in Figure 8.2 and the nonlinear regression in Equation (8.18). Would either of these regressions provide a reliable estimate of the effect of income on test scores? Would either of these regressions provide a reliable method for forecasting test scores? Explain.

9.10 Read the box "The Returns to Education and the Gender Gap" in Section 8.3. Discuss the internal and external validity of the estimated effect of education on earnings.

9.11 Read the box "The Demand for Economics Journals" in Section 8.3. Discuss the internal and external validity of the estimated effect of price per citation on subscriptions.

Empirical Exercises

E9.1 Use the data set **CPS04** described in Empirical Exercise 4.1 to answer the following questions.

    a. Discuss the internal validity of the regressions that you used to answer Empirical Exercise 8.1(l). Include a discussion of possible omitted variable bias, misspecification of the functional form of the regression, errors-in-variables, sample selection, simultaneous causality, and inconsistency of the OLS standard errors.

    b. The data set **CPS92_04** described in Empirical Exercise 3.1 includes data from 2004 and 1992. Use these data to investigate the (temporal) external validity of the conclusions that you reached in Empirical Exercise 8.1(l). [*Note:* Remember to adjust for inflation as explained in Empirical Exercise 3.1(b).]

E9.2 A committee on improving undergraduate teaching at your college needs your help before reporting to the Dean. The committee seeks your advice, as an econometric expert, about whether your college should take physical appearance into account when hiring teaching faculty. (This is legal as long as doing so is blind to race, religion, age, and gender.) You do not have time to collect your own data, so you must base your recommendations on the analysis of the dataset **TeachingRatings** described in Empirical Exercise 4.2 that has served as the basis for several Empirical Exercises in Part II of the text. Based on your analysis of these data, what is your advice? Justify your advice based on a careful and complete assessment of the internal and external validity of the regressions that you carried out to answer the Empirical Exercises using these data in earlier chapters.

E9.3   Use the data set **CollegeDistance** described in Empirical Exercise 4.3 to answer the following questions.

    a. Discuss the internal validity of the regressions that you used to answer Empirical Exercise 8.3(i). Include a discussion of possible omitted variable bias, misspecification of the functional form of the regression, errors-in-variables, sample selection, simultaneous causality, and inconsistency of the OLS standard errors.

    b. The data set **CollegeDistance** excluded students from western states; data for these students are included in the data set **CollegeDistanceWest**. Use these data to investigate the (geographic) external validity of the conclusions that you reached in Empirical Exercise 8.3(i).

APPENDIX

9.1

The Massachusetts Elementary School Testing Data

The Massachusetts data are districtwide averages for public elementary school districts in 1998. The test score is taken from the Massachusetts Comprehensive Assessment System (MCAS) test administered to all fourth graders in Massachusetts public schools in the spring of 1998. The test is sponsored by the Massachusetts Department of Education and is mandatory for all public schools. The data analyzed here are the overall total score, which is the sum of the scores on the English, math, and science portions of the test.

    Data on the student–teacher ratio, the percentage of students receiving a subsidized lunch, and the percentage of students still learning English are averages for each elementary school district for the 1997–1998 school year, and were obtained from the Massachusetts Department of Education. Data on average district income were obtained from the 1990 U.S. Census.

| # Conducting a Regression Study Using Economic Data

Conducting an empirical analysis of economic data can be rewarding and informative. If you follow some basic guidelines, it is possible to use your time efficiently and to avoid some potentially frustrating pitfalls. This chapter provides suggestions for how to conduct a regression study using economic data and how to report the results of that study.

One reason that this book repeatedly uses the California test score data is to illustrate the steps involved in undertaking a serious empirical application: becoming familiar with the data, developing and estimating a base regression specification, thinking through potential omitted variables, modeling relevant nonlinearities, performing sensitivity analysis, assessing the internal and external validity of the findings, and reporting the results and their limitations. This chapter steps back from the details of the test score application and describes the main steps in conducting an empirical analysis and reporting the results.

It is important to approach an empirical analysis with an open mind. It is tempting to think that your goal should be a high adjusted R^2 or an estimated coefficient of interest that is economically large and statistically significant. But this is not the purpose of a thoughtful empirical analysis; instead, the purpose is to answer a specific question while using your best judgment and being honest about what the data do and do not tell you. The coefficient of interest might be large and well estimated; it might be small and well estimated; or it might just be imprecisely estimated because of limitations of the data or because the question being asked is a very difficult one. Reaching any one of these conclusions—whether it confirms your prior suspicions or not—is interesting and helps you better to understand the topic you are researching.

In our analysis of the California test score data, if our objective had been to find a large coefficient, we might have stopped at the regression of test scores against the student–teacher ratio and never included any control variables. But, upon reflection, it became clear that that estimate was subject to considerable omitted variable bias, which was addressed by including the control variables. By the end of the analysis, we had concluded that the class size effect, while statistically significant, is economically small—a conclusion confirmed using a different observational data set (the Massachusetts data). The distinction is subtle between trying to measure an effect as reliably as possible and trying to prove that the effect is important, but it can make the difference between a study that is credible and one that is not.

10.1 Choosing a Topic

The first step in conducting an empirical analysis is choosing the topic you want to study and, within that topic, the specific question or questions you will investigate. Although there is not a single best way to choose a topic, the following suggestions might be useful.

1. *Pick a topic that you find personally interesting, ideally one about which you already have some knowledge.* The topic might be related to your career interests, summer work you did, employment experience of a family member, or something of intellectual interest to you. Often, a specific policy problem, a personal decision, or a business issue raises questions that can be addressed by an empirical study.

2. *Make the question that will be the main focus of your study as specific as possible.* The question, should the government increase school spending to reduce class sizes? is an important one but is too vague for immediate empirical study. The question, does a reduction in class size make students better off? is an improvement because it relates to a specific causal effect—the effect of class size reductions on student welfare—but it still is too vague (what does "better off" mean?). But, upon further narrowing, the question, does a reduction

in class size result in an increase in test scores? can in principle be answered using empirical analysis. The more narrowly the question relates to a measurable causal effect, the easier it will be to answer.

3. *Check the related literature.* You might find published studies on topics closely related to yours. Do not let this discourage you! Instead, use previous work to give you ideas about data sources and about what questions have not yet been answered. Web tools are very useful for finding related literature, and your instructor can give you additional suggestions about what journals to look in.

4. *Choose a question that can be answered using the available data.* Data sources and types of data are discussed in the next section. Although the question you originally pose might not be answerable using available data, the data might support the analysis of a related and equally interesting question.

5. *Discuss your topic with a classmate or your instructor.* If you find your topic interesting, then the odds are that others will too, and an instructor or classmate might suggest an angle that you have not thought of.

The choice of a question for analysis is linked to finding suitable data with which to answer the question.

10.2 Collecting Data

Finding a Data Set

The first step toward finding a data set is being as specific as possible about what data would help you to answer the question you are investigating. To do so, it helps to be clear about how you might actually conduct your analysis. What unit of observation would be most useful (individuals? firms? local governmental data? cross-country data? etc.)? What should you use as the dependent variable? What is the main independent variable of interest? What control variables would you consider to be most important, so as to address the main concerns about omitted variable bias?

With your list of variables in hand, the next step is to look for a data set. Your college or university might have a data librarian in the economics or social science library. If so, he or she might be able to suggest some data sets. An additional advantage of going to your college data librarian is that some data sets are only available to subscribers, and your college or university might subscribe to such data sets.

In addition to your data librarian, investigation on the Web can lead to some good data sources. Links to some of the main public sources for economic data are available on this textbook's Web site (**www.aw-bc.com/stock_watson**). The data sources on this Web site include data in labor economics, law and economics, political economy, the economics of education, health economics, macroeconomics, and international economics.

With some creativity, the Web can be used to assemble interesting and new data sets. For example, one of our students collected data on the world top-100 times in the 100-meter dash each year since the early 1980s, along with control variables (such as wind speed and athlete age), and used regression methods to see if the usual annual improvement in these times was reduced when track and field authorities stepped up their enforcement of anti-doping rules (it was). All the data used in that analysis were downloaded from track and field Web sites. As a second example, Miles (2005) collected data from the Web sites of U.S. law enforcement agencies to see whether appearing on the TV show *America's Most Wanted* increased the chances of the subject being caught (it does; the researcher also collected data by watching the show).

In some cases, existing data sources might not suffice to answer the question you have in mind. Depending on your topic, you could consider conducting your own survey. However, this is not something you should embark on lightly. There are many pitfalls in survey design and survey administration, and conducting a survey can take a great deal of time. If you are contemplating conducting your own survey, you should consult a textbook on survey design.

Time Series Data and Panel Data

This book has focused on cross-sectional data. As discussed in Chapter 1, a cross-sectional data set consists of observations on n "entities" (individuals, firms, countries, etc.); typically these observations are recorded at a given point in time (for example, the same year).

Chapter 1 also described two other types of data sets, time series data and panel data. Time series data consist of observations on a single entity collected at T different points in time. For example, the price of a share of stock in a specific firm might be collected on the final day of each month for ten years, for a total of $T = 120$ observations. Panel data has both a time series and a cross-sectional dimension: in panel data, there are observations on n entities, where data for each entity is recorded over T time periods. For example, a data set consisting of the annual earnings of $n = 350$ individuals for each of $T = 8$ consecutive years would be a panel data set.

The techniques of regression analysis developed in this book for cross-sectional data can be applied to time series data and panel data; however, those methods require some extensions and modifications. It is beyond the scope of this brief edition to go into those extensions in detail. However, if you have mastered the material in this book, it is not a big step to learn the necessary modifications to handle panel data and time series data. If you are interested in learning more about such data sets, see Chapter 10 (panel data) or Chapters 14 and 15 (time series data) in the full edition of this book.

Preparing the Data for Regression Analysis

A practical problem is that the data you collect needs to be prepared in an electronic form suitable for regression software. Often data come in text (ASCII) form, in which case it can be convenient to read or to paste the data into a spreadsheet in which columns denote the variable and rows denote the observation. The spreadsheet can then be saved in a format (such as comma separated value) that can be read by your statistical software.

10.3   Conducting Your Regression Analysis

Students who have worked through the empirical exercises in this textbook will be familiar with the steps involved in conducting a regression analysis using a given data set. These steps involve familiarizing yourself with the data, estimating one or more base specifications, thinking through potential nonlinearities, conducting a sensitivity analysis by estimating alternative specifications, and assessing (and addressing when possible) potential threats to the internal validity of the study.

The starting point for your empirical analysis is getting acquainted with the data. Plot the data, using histograms and/or scatterplots. Are there big outliers, and if so are those observations accurately recorded or are they typographical or data manipulation errors? Typographical or computer errors should be corrected in your master data spreadsheet. Once you are confident that the data are free from such errors, you can turn to specific relations. Are the units of the data the ones you expected, and are they the ones you want to use? Do the relations you see in the scatterplots make sense? Do relationships look linear, or do they look nonlinear?

Once you are familiar with your data set, you can begin your regression analysis. This is the point at which all the preparatory work you have done thinking through your study begins to pay off. Because you have thought hard about your problem and the data, you should already have in mind a base specification, along with some possible alternative specifications. The process of determining a base specification and alternative specifications is discussed in Section 7.5, and the guidelines for whether to include a variable in a regression are given in Key Concept 9.2. Some of the alternative specifications might investigate possible nonlinearities, as illustrated in the analysis in Section 8.4 of the California test score data.

After you have some regression results, it is useful to go through the checklist of threats to internal validity in Key Concept 9.7. Are there arguably important threats to the internal validity of your study? If so, can you address them using multiple regression analysis of your data?

At this point, it is useful to share your findings with a classmate or instructor. The process of explaining what you have done and what you have found will help you think through any shortcomings of the analysis—your classmate or instructor can help with this too—and this in turn will point to additional specifications and additional sensitivity analysis to undertake. In this way, conducting an empirical analysis is a process that goes through multiple iterations.

10.4 Writing Up Your Results

Successful papers describing an empirical study often have five sections.

1. *Introduction.* The introduction succinctly states the problem you are interested in, briefly describes your data and the method of analysis, and summarizes your main conclusions.

2. *Discussion of Relevant Literature and Economic Theory.* This section describes closely related previous studies on your topic and summarizes any relevant economic theory. The length of this section depends on the scope of the paper; for a senior thesis, this section, especially the literature review, might be lengthy, but for a term paper this section might be short.

3. *Data Description.* This section provides the details of the data sources, any transformations you have done to the data (for example, changing the units of some variables), gives a table of summary statistics (means and standard deviations) of the variables, and provides scatterplots and/or other relevant plots of the data. If there are outliers other than those arising from corrected typographical or computer errors, this is the place to point them out.

4. *Empirical Results.* This section provides the main empirical results in the paper. Conventionally, regression results are presented in tabular form, with footnotes clearly explaining the entries; Tables 7.1, 8.2, 8.3, 9.1, and 9.2 can serve as templates. The initial table of results should present the main results; sensitivity analysis using alternative specifications can be presented in additional columns in that table or in subsequent tables. The text should provide

a careful discussion of the results, including assessments both of statistical significance and of economic significance, that is, the magnitude of the estimated relations in a real-world sense. Present "full disclosure" results: report results that you consider to be an honest and complete summary of what the data say concerning your question of interest, including results that raise doubts about or suggest limitations of your interpretation.

The empirical analyses of the test score data in Sections 7.6 and 8.4 provide examples of discussions of base and alternative specifications. This section of your paper should also contain a discussion of the potential threats to the validity of your analysis. Key Concept 9.7 provides a list of five potential threats to internal validity of regression studies using observational data. Some of those threats might not be relevant to your study, and this section should focus on the most salient threats. All empirical analyses have limitations, and it is important to provide a concise statement of what you consider to be the most substantial limitations of your analysis.

5. *Summary and Discussion*. This section summarizes your main empirical findings and discusses their implications for the original question of interest.

The guidelines in this chapter for conducting an empirical study are summarized in Key Concept 10.1.

GUIDELINES FOR CONDUCTING AN EMPIRICAL ECONOMIC STUDY

The following guidelines can help you be efficient when you undertake an empirical study.

1. Choose a topic that interests you personally.

2. Develop a few narrow questions and think through an empirical analysis that would answer them. For each question, what base specification would you use? What is the key regressor and what is the regression coefficient of interest? What might be important sources of omitted variable bias?

3. Learn about relevant data sets by consulting a data librarian or the Web (see **www.aw-bc.com/stock_watson**).

4. Narrow your question further. Will your candidate data set plausibly help you to estimate the parameter of interest?

5. Format the data so that they can be read into your statistical software.

6. Compute summary statistics, scatterplots, and other data diagnostics. Correct or discard outliers arising from data entry or computer errors.

7. Conduct your regression analysis:
   a. Estimate your base regression.
   b. Estimate alternative specifications that address potential nonlinearity and omitted variable bias.
   c. Assess the threats to the internal validity of your analysis using the list in Key Concept 9.7.
   d. Explain to a classmate or instructor what you have done, why you have done it, and what you have found.
   e. Repeat steps a–d until you are satisfied that you have addressed, as best you can, the main threats to the internal validity of your analysis.

8. Write up your results using the outline in Section 10.4. Discuss the statistical and economic (real-world) significance of your results, report "full disclosure" results, and discuss any remaining threats to internal and external validity.

Appendix

continued on next page

TABLE 1 The Cumulative Standard Normal Distribution Function, $\Phi(z) = \Pr(Z \le z)$

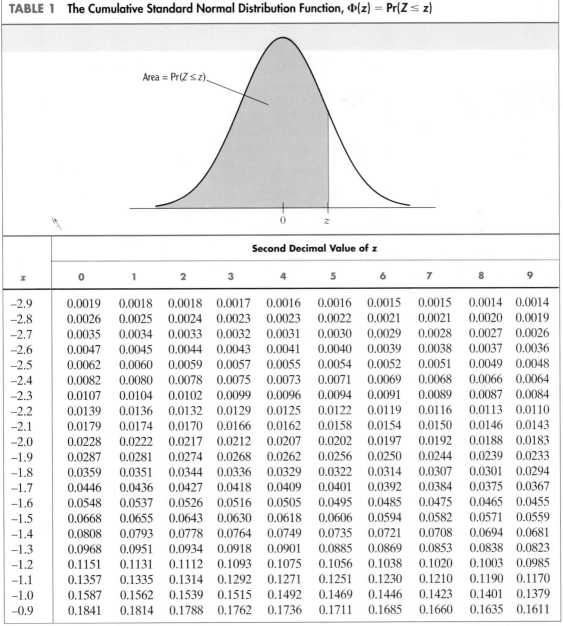

Area $= \Pr(Z \le z)$

	Second Decimal Value of z									
z	0	1	2	3	4	5	6	7	8	9
−2.9	0.0019	0.0018	0.0018	0.0017	0.0016	0.0016	0.0015	0.0015	0.0014	0.0014
−2.8	0.0026	0.0025	0.0024	0.0023	0.0023	0.0022	0.0021	0.0021	0.0020	0.0019
−2.7	0.0035	0.0034	0.0033	0.0032	0.0031	0.0030	0.0029	0.0028	0.0027	0.0026
−2.6	0.0047	0.0045	0.0044	0.0043	0.0041	0.0040	0.0039	0.0038	0.0037	0.0036
−2.5	0.0062	0.0060	0.0059	0.0057	0.0055	0.0054	0.0052	0.0051	0.0049	0.0048
−2.4	0.0082	0.0080	0.0078	0.0075	0.0073	0.0071	0.0069	0.0068	0.0066	0.0064
−2.3	0.0107	0.0104	0.0102	0.0099	0.0096	0.0094	0.0091	0.0089	0.0087	0.0084
−2.2	0.0139	0.0136	0.0132	0.0129	0.0125	0.0122	0.0119	0.0116	0.0113	0.0110
−2.1	0.0179	0.0174	0.0170	0.0166	0.0162	0.0158	0.0154	0.0150	0.0146	0.0143
−2.0	0.0228	0.0222	0.0217	0.0212	0.0207	0.0202	0.0197	0.0192	0.0188	0.0183
−1.9	0.0287	0.0281	0.0274	0.0268	0.0262	0.0256	0.0250	0.0244	0.0239	0.0233
−1.8	0.0359	0.0351	0.0344	0.0336	0.0329	0.0322	0.0314	0.0307	0.0301	0.0294
−1.7	0.0446	0.0436	0.0427	0.0418	0.0409	0.0401	0.0392	0.0384	0.0375	0.0367
−1.6	0.0548	0.0537	0.0526	0.0516	0.0505	0.0495	0.0485	0.0475	0.0465	0.0455
−1.5	0.0668	0.0655	0.0643	0.0630	0.0618	0.0606	0.0594	0.0582	0.0571	0.0559
−1.4	0.0808	0.0793	0.0778	0.0764	0.0749	0.0735	0.0721	0.0708	0.0694	0.0681
−1.3	0.0968	0.0951	0.0934	0.0918	0.0901	0.0885	0.0869	0.0853	0.0838	0.0823
−1.2	0.1151	0.1131	0.1112	0.1093	0.1075	0.1056	0.1038	0.1020	0.1003	0.0985
−1.1	0.1357	0.1335	0.1314	0.1292	0.1271	0.1251	0.1230	0.1210	0.1190	0.1170
−1.0	0.1587	0.1562	0.1539	0.1515	0.1492	0.1469	0.1446	0.1423	0.1401	0.1379
−0.9	0.1841	0.1814	0.1788	0.1762	0.1736	0.1711	0.1685	0.1660	0.1635	0.1611

TABLE 1 (continued)

z	\multicolumn{10}{c}{Second Decimal Value of z}
	0	1	2	3	4	5	6	7	8	9
−0.8	0.2119	0.2090	0.2061	0.2033	0.2005	0.1977	0.1949	0.1922	0.1894	0.1867
−0.7	0.2420	0.2389	0.2358	0.2327	0.2296	0.2266	0.2236	0.2206	0.2177	0.2148
−0.6	0.2743	0.2709	0.2676	0.2643	0.2611	0.2578	0.2546	0.2514	0.2483	0.2451
−0.5	0.3085	0.3050	0.3015	0.2981	0.2946	0.2912	0.2877	0.2843	0.2810	0.2776
−0.4	0.3446	0.3409	0.3372	0.3336	0.3300	0.3264	0.3228	0.3192	0.3156	0.3121
−0.3	0.3821	0.3783	0.3745	0.3707	0.3669	0.3632	0.3594	0.3557	0.3520	0.3483
−0.2	0.4207	0.4168	0.4129	0.4090	0.4052	0.4013	0.3974	0.3936	0.3897	0.3859
−0.1	0.4602	0.4562	0.4522	0.4483	0.4443	0.4404	0.4364	0.4325	0.4286	0.4247
−0.0	0.5000	0.4960	0.4920	0.4880	0.4840	0.4801	0.4761	0.4721	0.4681	0.4641
0.0	0.5000	0.5040	0.5080	0.5120	0.5160	0.5199	0.5239	0.5279	0.5319	0.5359
0.1	0.5398	0.5438	0.5478	0.5517	0.5557	0.5596	0.5636	0.5675	0.5714	0.5753
0.2	0.5793	0.5832	0.5871	0.5910	0.5948	0.5987	0.6026	0.6064	0.6103	0.6141
0.3	0.6179	0.6217	0.6255	0.6293	0.6331	0.6368	0.6406	0.6443	0.6480	0.6517
0.4	0.6554	0.6591	0.6628	0.6664	0.6700	0.6736	0.6772	0.6808	0.6844	0.6879
0.5	0.6915	0.6950	0.6985	0.7019	0.7054	0.7088	0.7123	0.7157	0.7190	0.7224
0.6	0.7257	0.7291	0.7324	0.7357	0.7389	0.7422	0.7454	0.7486	0.7517	0.7549
0.7	0.7580	0.7611	0.7642	0.7673	0.7704	0.7734	0.7764	0.7794	0.7823	0.7852
0.8	0.7881	0.7910	0.7939	0.7967	0.7995	0.8023	0.8051	0.8078	0.8106	0.8133
0.9	0.8159	0.8186	0.8212	0.8238	0.8264	0.8289	0.8315	0.8340	0.8365	0.8389
1.0	0.8413	0.8438	0.8461	0.8485	0.8508	0.8531	0.8554	0.8577	0.8599	0.8621
1.1	0.8643	0.8665	0.8686	0.8708	0.8729	0.8749	0.8770	0.8790	0.8810	0.8830
1.2	0.8849	0.8869	0.8888	0.8907	0.8925	0.8944	0.8962	0.8980	0.8997	0.9015
1.3	0.9032	0.9049	0.9066	0.9082	0.9099	0.9115	0.9131	0.9147	0.9162	0.9177
1.4	0.9192	0.9207	0.9222	0.9236	0.9251	0.9265	0.9279	0.9292	0.9306	0.9319
1.5	0.9332	0.9345	0.9357	0.9370	0.9382	0.9394	0.9406	0.9418	0.9429	0.9441
1.6	0.9452	0.9463	0.9474	0.9484	0.9495	0.9505	0.9515	0.9525	0.9535	0.9545
1.7	0.9554	0.9564	0.9573	0.9582	0.9591	0.9599	0.9608	0.9616	0.9625	0.9633
1.8	0.9641	0.9649	0.9656	0.9664	0.9671	0.9678	0.9686	0.9693	0.9699	0.9706
1.9	0.9713	0.9719	0.9726	0.9732	0.9738	0.9744	0.9750	0.9756	0.9761	0.9767
2.0	0.9772	0.9778	0.9783	0.9788	0.9793	0.9798	0.9803	0.9808	0.9812	0.9817
2.1	0.9821	0.9826	0.9830	0.9834	0.9838	0.9842	0.9846	0.9850	0.9854	0.9857
2.2	0.9861	0.9864	0.9868	0.9871	0.9875	0.9878	0.9881	0.9884	0.9887	0.9890
2.3	0.9893	0.9896	0.9898	0.9901	0.9904	0.9906	0.9909	0.9911	0.9913	0.9916
2.4	0.9918	0.9920	0.9922	0.9925	0.9927	0.9929	0.9931	0.9932	0.9934	0.9936
2.5	0.9938	0.9940	0.9941	0.9943	0.9945	0.9946	0.9948	0.9949	0.9951	0.9952
2.6	0.9953	0.9955	0.9956	0.9957	0.9959	0.9960	0.9961	0.9962	0.9963	0.9964
2.7	0.9965	0.9966	0.9967	0.9968	0.9969	0.9970	0.9971	0.9972	0.9973	0.9974
2.8	0.9974	0.9975	0.9976	0.9977	0.9977	0.9978	0.9979	0.9979	0.9980	0.9981
2.9	0.9981	0.9982	0.9982	0.9983	0.9984	0.9984	0.9985	0.9985	0.9986	0.9986

This table can be used to calculate $\Pr(Z \leq z)$ where Z is a standard normal variable. For example, when $z = 1.17$, this probability is 0.8790, which is the table entry for the row labeled 1.1 and the column labeled 7.

TABLE 2   Critical Values for Two-Sided and One-Sided Tests Using the Student *t* Distribution

Degrees of Freedom	Significance Level				
	20% (2-Sided) 10% (1-Sided)	10% (2-Sided) 5% (1-Sided)	5% (2-Sided) 2.5% (1-Sided)	2% (2-Sided) 1% (1-Sided)	1% (2-Sided) 0.5% (1-Sided)
1	3.08	6.31	12.71	31.82	63.66
2	1.89	2.92	4.30	6.96	9.92
3	1.64	2.35	3.18	4.54	5.84
4	1.53	2.13	2.78	3.75	4.60
5	1.48	2.02	2.57	3.36	4.03
6	1.44	1.94	2.45	3.14	3.71
7	1.41	1.89	2.36	3.00	3.50
8	1.40	1.86	2.31	2.90	3.36
9	1.38	1.83	2.26	2.82	3.25
10	1.37	1.81	2.23	2.76	3.17
11	1.36	1.80	2.20	2.72	3.11
12	1.36	1.78	2.18	2.68	3.05
13	1.35	1.77	2.16	2.65	3.01
14	1.35	1.76	2.14	2.62	2.98
15	1.34	1.75	2.13	2.60	2.95
16	1.34	1.75	2.12	2.58	2.92
17	1.33	1.74	2.11	2.57	2.90
18	1.33	1.73	2.10	2.55	2.88
19	1.33	1.73	2.09	2.54	2.86
20	1.33	1.72	2.09	2.53	2.85
21	1.32	1.72	2.08	2.52	2.83
22	1.32	1.72	2.07	2.51	2.82
23	1.32	1.71	2.07	2.50	2.81
24	1.32	1.71	2.06	2.49	2.80
25	1.32	1.71	2.06	2.49	2.79
26	1.32	1.71	2.06	2.48	2.78
27	1.31	1.70	2.05	2.47	2.77
28	1.31	1.70	2.05	2.47	2.76
29	1.31	1.70	2.05	2.46	2.76
30	1.31	1.70	2.04	2.46	2.75
60	1.30	1.67	2.00	2.39	2.66
90	1.29	1.66	1.99	2.37	2.63
120	1.29	1.66	1.98	2.36	2.62
∞	1.28	1.64	1.96	2.33	2.58

Values are shown for the critical values for two-sided ($\neq$) and one-sided ($>$) alternative hypotheses. The critical value for the one-sided ($<$) test is the negative of the one-sided ($>$) critical value shown in the table. For example, 2.13 is the critical value for a two-sided test with a significance level of 5% using the Student *t* distribution with 15 degrees of freedom.

TABLE 3   Critical Values for the χ^2 Distribution

Degrees of Freedom	Significance Level		
	10%	5%	1%
1	2.71	3.84	6.63
2	4.61	5.99	9.21
3	6.25	7.81	11.34
4	7.78	9.49	13.28
5	9.24	11.07	15.09
6	10.64	12.59	16.81
7	12.02	14.07	18.48
8	13.36	15.51	20.09
9	14.68	16.92	21.67
10	15.99	18.31	23.21
11	17.28	19.68	24.72
12	18.55	21.03	26.22
13	19.81	22.36	27.69
14	21.06	23.68	29.14
15	22.31	25.00	30.58
16	23.54	26.30	32.00
17	24.77	27.59	33.41
18	25.99	28.87	34.81
19	27.20	30.14	36.19
20	28.41	31.41	37.57
21	29.62	32.67	38.93
22	30.81	33.92	40.29
23	32.01	35.17	41.64
24	33.20	36.41	42.98
25	34.38	37.65	44.31
26	35.56	38.89	45.64
27	36.74	40.11	46.96
28	37.92	41.34	48.28
29	39.09	42.56	49.59
30	40.26	43.77	50.89

This table contains the 90th, 95th, and 99th percentiles of the χ^2 distribution. These serve as critical values for tests with significance levels of 10%, 5%, and 1%.

TABLE 4 Critical Values for the $F_{m,\infty}$ Distribution

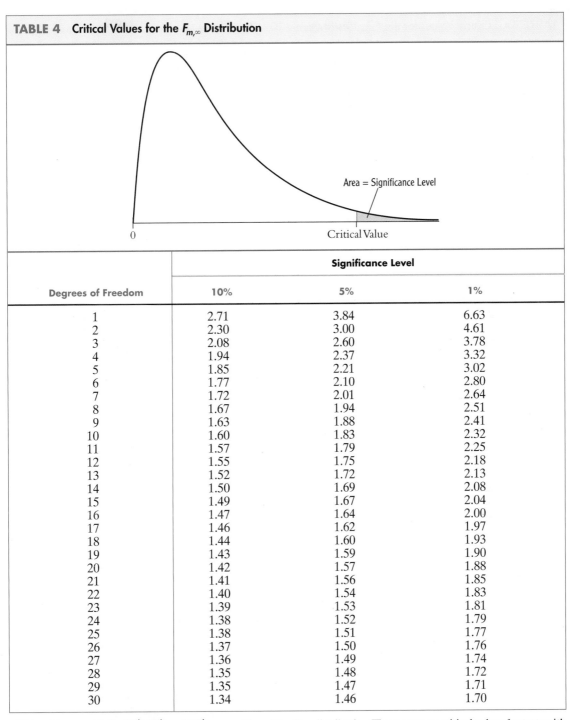

	Significance Level		
Degrees of Freedom	**10%**	**5%**	**1%**
1	2.71	3.84	6.63
2	2.30	3.00	4.61
3	2.08	2.60	3.78
4	1.94	2.37	3.32
5	1.85	2.21	3.02
6	1.77	2.10	2.80
7	1.72	2.01	2.64
8	1.67	1.94	2.51
9	1.63	1.88	2.41
10	1.60	1.83	2.32
11	1.57	1.79	2.25
12	1.55	1.75	2.18
13	1.52	1.72	2.13
14	1.50	1.69	2.08
15	1.49	1.67	2.04
16	1.47	1.64	2.00
17	1.46	1.62	1.97
18	1.44	1.60	1.93
19	1.43	1.59	1.90
20	1.42	1.57	1.88
21	1.41	1.56	1.85
22	1.40	1.54	1.83
23	1.39	1.53	1.81
24	1.38	1.52	1.79
25	1.38	1.51	1.77
26	1.37	1.50	1.76
27	1.36	1.49	1.74
28	1.35	1.48	1.72
29	1.35	1.47	1.71
30	1.34	1.46	1.70

This table contains the 90th, 95th, and 99th percentiles of the $F_{m,\infty}$ distribution. These serve as critical values for tests with significance levels of 10%, 5%, and 1%.

TABLE 5A   Critical Values for the F_{n_1, n_2} Distribution—10% Significance Level

Denominator Degrees of Freedom (n_2)	Numerator Degrees of Freedom (n_1)									
	1	2	3	4	5	6	7	8	9	10
1	39.86	49.50	53.59	55.83	57.24	58.20	58.90	59.44	59.86	60.20
2	8.53	9.00	9.16	9.24	9.29	9.33	9.35	9.37	9.38	9.39
3	5.54	5.46	5.39	5.34	5.31	5.28	5.27	5.25	5.24	5.23
4	4.54	4.32	4.19	4.11	4.05	4.01	3.98	3.95	3.94	3.92
5	4.06	3.78	3.62	3.52	3.45	3.40	3.37	3.34	3.32	3.30
6	3.78	3.46	3.29	3.18	3.11	3.05	3.01	2.98	2.96	2.94
7	3.59	3.26	3.07	2.96	2.88	2.83	2.78	2.75	2.72	2.70
8	3.46	3.11	2.92	2.81	2.73	2.67	2.62	2.59	2.56	2.54
9	3.36	3.01	2.81	2.69	2.61	2.55	2.51	2.47	2.44	2.42
10	3.29	2.92	2.73	2.61	2.52	2.46	2.41	2.38	2.35	2.32
11	3.23	2.86	2.66	2.54	2.45	2.39	2.34	2.30	2.27	2.25
12	3.18	2.81	2.61	2.48	2.39	2.33	2.28	2.24	2.21	2.19
13	3.14	2.76	2.56	2.43	2.35	2.28	2.23	2.20	2.16	2.14
14	3.10	2.73	2.52	2.39	2.31	2.24	2.19	2.15	2.12	2.10
15	3.07	2.70	2.49	2.36	2.27	2.21	2.16	2.12	2.09	2.06
16	3.05	2.67	2.46	2.33	2.24	2.18	2.13	2.09	2.06	2.03
17	3.03	2.64	2.44	2.31	2.22	2.15	2.10	2.06	2.03	2.00
18	3.01	2.62	2.42	2.29	2.20	2.13	2.08	2.04	2.00	1.98
19	2.99	2.61	2.40	2.27	2.18	2.11	2.06	2.02	1.98	1.96
20	2.97	2.59	2.38	2.25	2.16	2.09	2.04	2.00	1.96	1.94
21	2.96	2.57	2.36	2.23	2.14	2.08	2.02	1.98	1.95	1.92
22	2.95	2.56	2.35	2.22	2.13	2.06	2.01	1.97	1.93	1.90
23	2.94	2.55	2.34	2.21	2.11	2.05	1.99	1.95	1.92	1.89
24	2.93	2.54	2.33	2.19	2.10	2.04	1.98	1.94	1.91	1.88
25	2.92	2.53	2.32	2.18	2.09	2.02	1.97	1.93	1.89	1.87
26	2.91	2.52	2.31	2.17	2.08	2.01	1.96	1.92	1.88	1.86
27	2.90	2.51	2.30	2.17	2.07	2.00	1.95	1.91	1.87	1.85
28	2.89	2.50	2.29	2.16	2.06	2.00	1.94	1.90	1.87	1.84
29	2.89	2.50	2.28	2.15	2.06	1.99	1.93	1.89	1.86	1.83
30	2.88	2.49	2.28	2.14	2.05	1.98	1.93	1.88	1.85	1.82
60	2.79	2.39	2.18	2.04	1.95	1.87	1.82	1.77	1.74	1.71
90	2.76	2.36	2.15	2.01	1.91	1.84	1.78	1.74	1.70	1.67
120	2.75	2.35	2.13	1.99	1.90	1.82	1.77	1.72	1.68	1.65
∞	**2.71**	**2.30**	**2.08**	**1.94**	**1.85**	**1.77**	**1.72**	**1.67**	**1.63**	**1.60**

This table contains the 90th percentile of the F_{n_1, n_2} distribution, which serves as the critical values for a test with a 10% significance level.

TABLE 5B Critical Values for the F_{n_1, n_2} Distribution—5% Significance Level

Denominator Degrees of Freedom (n_2)	Numerator Degrees of Freedom (n_1)									
	1	2	3	4	5	6	7	8	9	10
1	161.40	199.50	215.70	224.60	230.20	234.00	236.80	238.90	240.50	241.90
2	18.51	19.00	19.16	19.25	19.30	19.33	19.35	19.37	19.39	19.40
3	10.13	9.55	9.28	9.12	9.01	8.94	8.89	8.85	8.81	8.79
4	7.71	6.94	6.59	6.39	6.26	6.16	6.09	6.04	6.00	5.96
5	6.61	5.79	5.41	5.19	5.05	4.95	4.88	4.82	4.77	4.74
6	5.99	5.14	4.76	4.53	4.39	4.28	4.21	4.15	4.10	4.06
7	5.59	4.74	4.35	4.12	3.97	3.87	3.79	3.73	3.68	3.64
8	5.32	4.46	4.07	3.84	3.69	3.58	3.50	3.44	3.39	3.35
9	5.12	4.26	3.86	3.63	3.48	3.37	3.29	3.23	3.18	3.14
10	4.96	4.10	3.71	3.48	3.33	3.22	3.14	3.07	3.02	2.98
11	4.84	3.98	3.59	3.36	3.20	3.09	3.01	2.95	2.90	2.85
12	4.75	3.89	3.49	3.26	3.11	3.00	2.91	2.85	2.80	2.75
13	4.67	3.81	3.41	3.18	3.03	2.92	2.83	2.77	2.71	2.67
14	4.60	3.74	3.34	3.11	2.96	2.85	2.76	2.70	2.65	2.60
15	4.54	3.68	3.29	3.06	2.90	2.79	2.71	2.64	2.59	2.54
16	4.49	3.63	3.24	3.01	2.85	2.74	2.66	2.59	2.54	2.49
17	4.45	3.59	3.20	2.96	2.81	2.70	2.61	2.55	2.49	2.45
18	4.41	3.55	3.16	2.93	2.77	2.66	2.58	2.51	2.46	2.41
19	4.38	3.52	3.13	2.90	2.74	2.63	2.54	2.48	2.42	2.38
20	4.35	3.49	3.10	2.87	2.71	2.60	2.51	2.45	2.39	2.35
21	4.32	3.47	3.07	2.84	2.68	2.57	2.49	2.42	2.37	2.32
22	4.30	3.44	3.05	2.82	2.66	2.55	2.46	2.40	2.34	2.30
23	4.28	3.42	3.03	2.80	2.64	2.53	2.44	2.37	2.32	2.27
24	4.26	3.40	3.01	2.78	2.62	2.51	2.42	2.36	2.30	2.25
25	4.24	3.39	2.99	2.76	2.60	2.49	2.40	2.34	2.28	2.24
26	4.23	3.37	2.98	2.74	2.59	2.47	2.39	2.32	2.27	2.22
27	4.21	3.35	2.96	2.73	2.57	2.46	2.37	2.31	2.25	2.20
28	4.20	3.34	2.95	2.71	2.56	2.45	2.36	2.29	2.24	2.19
29	4.18	3.33	2.93	2.70	2.55	2.43	2.35	2.28	2.22	2.18
30	4.17	3.32	2.92	2.69	2.53	2.42	2.33	2.27	2.21	2.16
60	4.00	3.15	2.76	2.53	2.37	2.25	2.17	2.10	2.04	1.99
90	3.95	3.10	2.71	2.47	2.32	2.20	2.11	2.04	1.99	1.94
120	3.92	3.07	2.68	2.45	2.29	2.18	2.09	2.02	1.96	1.91
∞	**3.84**	**3.00**	**2.60**	**2.37**	**2.21**	**2.10**	**2.01**	**1.94**	**1.88**	**1.83**

This table contains the 95th percentile of the distribution F_{n_1, n_2} which serves as the critical values for a test with a 5% significance level.

TABLE 5C   Critical Values for the F_{n_1/n_2} Distribution—1% Significance Level

Denominator Degrees of Freedom (n_2)	Numerator Degrees of Freedom (n_1)									
	1	2	3	4	5	6	7	8	9	10
1	4052.00	4999.00	5403.00	5624.00	5763.00	5859.00	5928.00	5981.00	6022.00	6055.00
2	98.50	99.00	99.17	99.25	99.30	99.33	99.36	99.37	99.39	99.40
3	34.12	30.82	29.46	28.71	28.24	27.91	27.67	27.49	27.35	27.23
4	21.20	18.00	16.69	15.98	15.52	15.21	14.98	14.80	14.66	14.55
5	16.26	13.27	12.06	11.39	10.97	10.67	10.46	10.29	10.16	10.05
6	13.75	10.92	9.78	9.15	8.75	8.47	8.26	8.10	7.98	7.87
7	12.25	9.55	8.45	7.85	7.46	7.19	6.99	6.84	6.72	6.62
8	11.26	8.65	7.59	7.01	6.63	6.37	6.18	6.03	5.91	5.81
9	10.56	8.02	6.99	6.42	6.06	5.80	5.61	5.47	5.35	5.26
10	10.04	7.56	6.55	5.99	5.64	5.39	5.20	5.06	4.94	4.85
11	9.65	7.21	6.22	5.67	5.32	5.07	4.89	4.74	4.63	4.54
12	9.33	6.93	5.95	5.41	5.06	4.82	4.64	4.50	4.39	4.30
13	9.07	6.70	5.74	5.21	4.86	4.62	4.44	4.30	4.19	4.10
14	8.86	6.51	5.56	5.04	4.69	4.46	4.28	4.14	4.03	3.94
15	8.68	6.36	5.42	4.89	4.56	4.32	4.14	4.00	3.89	3.80
16	8.53	6.23	5.29	4.77	4.44	4.20	4.03	3.89	3.78	3.69
17	8.40	6.11	5.18	4.67	4.34	4.10	3.93	3.79	3.68	3.59
18	8.29	6.01	5.09	4.58	4.25	4.01	3.84	3.71	3.60	3.51
19	8.18	5.93	5.01	4.50	4.17	3.94	3.77	3.63	3.52	3.43
20	8.10	5.85	4.94	4.43	4.10	3.87	3.70	3.56	3.46	3.37
21	8.02	5.78	4.87	4.37	4.04	3.81	3.64	3.51	3.40	3.31
22	7.95	5.72	4.82	4.31	3.99	3.76	3.59	3.45	3.35	3.26
23	7.88	5.66	4.76	4.26	3.94	3.71	3.54	3.41	3.30	3.21
24	7.82	5.61	4.72	4.22	3.90	3.67	3.50	3.36	3.26	3.17
25	7.77	5.57	4.68	4.18	3.85	3.63	3.46	3.32	3.22	3.13
26	7.72	5.53	4.64	4.14	3.82	3.59	3.42	3.29	3.18	3.09
27	7.68	5.49	4.60	4.11	3.78	3.56	3.39	3.26	3.15	3.06
28	7.64	5.45	4.57	4.07	3.75	3.53	3.36	3.23	3.12	3.03
29	7.60	5.42	4.54	4.04	3.73	3.50	3.33	3.20	3.09	3.00
30	7.56	5.39	4.51	4.02	3.70	3.47	3.30	3.17	3.07	2.98
60	7.08	4.98	4.13	3.65	3.34	3.12	2.95	2.82	2.72	2.63
90	6.93	4.85	4.01	3.53	3.23	3.01	2.84	2.72	2.61	2.52
120	6.85	4.79	3.95	3.48	3.17	2.96	2.79	2.66	2.56	2.47
∞	**6.63**	**4.61**	**3.78**	**3.32**	**3.02**	**2.80**	**2.64**	**2.51**	**2.41**	**2.32**

This table contains the 99th percentile of the F_{n_1, n_2} distribution, which serves as the critical values for a test with a 1% significance level.

References

Beck, Thorsten, Ross Levine, and Norman Loayza. 2000. "Finance and the Sources of Growth." *Journal of Financial Economics* 58: 261–300.

Bergstrom, Theodore A. 2001. "Free Labor for Costly Journals?" *Journal of Economic Perspectives* 15(4), Fall: 183–198.

Bertrand, Marianne, and Kevin Hallock. 2001. "The Gender Gap in Top Corporate Jobs." *Industrial and Labor Relations Review* 55(1): 3–21.

Card, David. 1999. "The Causal Effect of Education on Earnings." Chap. 30 in *The Handbook of Labor Economics,* edited by Orley C. Ashenfelter and David Card. Amsterdam: Elsevier.

Carhart, Mark M. 1997. "On Persistence in Mutual Fund Performance." *The Journal of Finance* 52(1): 57–82.

Cooper, Harris, and Larry. V. Hedges. 1994. *The Handbook of Research Synthesis.* New York: Russell Sage Foundation.

Ehrenberg, Ronald G., Dominic J. Brewer, Adam Gamoran, and J. Douglas Willms. 2001a. "Class Size and Student Achievement." *Psychological Science in the Public Interest* 2(1): 1–30.

Ehrenberg, Ronald G., Dominic J. Brewer, Adam Gamoran, and J. Douglas Willms. 2001b. "Does Class Size Matter?" *Scientific American* 285(5): 80–85.

Eicker, F. 1967. "Limit Theorems for Regressions with Unequal and Dependent Errors," *Proceedings of the Fifth Berkeley Symposium on Mathematical Statistics and Probability*, 1, 59–82. Berkeley: University of California Press.

Hamermesh, Daniel, and Amy Parker. 2005. "Beauty in the Classroom: Instructors' Pulchritude and Putative Pedagogical Productivity." *Economics of Education Review* 24(4): 369–376.

Hedges, Larry V., and Ingram Olkin. 1985. *Statistical Methods for Meta-analysis.* San Diego: Academic Press.

Hetland, Lois. 2000. "Listening to Music Enhances Spatial-Temporal Reasoning: Evidence for the 'Mozart Effect.'" *Journal of Aesthetic Education* 34(3-4): 179–238.

Huber, P. J. 1967. "The Behavior of Maximum Likelihood Estimates Under Nonstandard Conditions," *Proceedings of the Fifth Berkeley Symposium on Mathematical Statistics and Probability*, 1, 221–233. Berkeley: University of California Press.

Madrian, Brigette C., and Dennis F. Shea. 2001. "The Power of Suggestion: Inertia in 401(k) Participation and Savings Behavior." *Quarterly Journal of Economics* CXVI(4): 1149–1187.

Malkiel, Burton G. 2003. *A Random Walk Down Wall Street.* New York: W. W. Norton.

Miles, Thomas. 2005. "Estimating the Effect of *America's Most Wanted:* A Duration Analysis of Wanted Fugitives." *Journal of Law and Economics,* 281–306.

Rauscher, Frances, Gordon L. Shaw, and Katherine N. Ky. 1993. "Music and Spatial Task Performance." *Nature* 365(6447): 611.

Rouse, Cecilia. 1995. "Democratization or Diversion? The Effect of Community Colleges on Educational Attainment." *Journal of Business and Economic Statistics* 12(2): 217–224.

Shadish, William R., Thomas D. Cook, and Donald T. Campbell. 2002. *Experimental and Quasi-Experimental Designs for Generalized Causal Inference.* Boston: Houghton Mifflin.

Stock, James H., and Mark W. Watson. 2007. *Introduction to Econometrics,* 2nd ed. Boston: Addison Wesley.

Thaler, Richard, and Shlomo Benartzi. 2004. "Save More Tomorrow: Using Behavioral Economics to Increase Employee Savings." *Journal of Political Economy* 112(1), Part 2: S164–S187.

White, Halbert. 1980. "A Heteroskedasticity-Consistent Covariance Matrix Estimator and a Direct Test for Heteroskedasticity," *Econometrica,* 48, 827–838

Winner, Ellen, and Monica Cooper. 2000. "Mute Those Claims: No Evidence (Yet) for a Causal Link Between Arts Study and Academic Achievement." *Journal of Aesthetic Education* 34(3-4): 11–76.

Answers to the "Review the Concepts" Questions

Chapter 1

1.1 The experiment that you describe should have one or more treatment groups and a control group; for example, one "treatment" could be studying for four hours, and the control would be not studying (no treatment). Students would be randomly assigned to the treatment and control groups, and the causal effect of hours of study on midterm performance would be estimated by comparing the average midterm grades for each of the treatment groups to that of the control group. The largest impediment is to ensure that the students in the different treatment groups spend the correct number of hours studying. How can you make sure that the students in the control group do not study at all, since that might jeopardize their grade? How can you make sure that all students in the treatment group actually study for four hours?

1.2 This experiment needs the same ingredients as the experiment in the previous question: treatment and control groups, random assignment, and a procedure for analyzing the resulting experimental data. Here there are two treatment levels: not wearing a seatbelt (the control group) and wearing a seatbelt (the treated group). These treatments should be applied over a specified period of time, such as the next year. The effect of seat belt use on traffic fatalities could be estimated as the difference between fatality rates in the control and treatment group. One impediment to this study is ensuring that participants follow the treatment (do or do not wear a seat belt). More importantly, this study raises serious ethical concerns because it instructs participants to engage in known unsafe behavior (not wearing a seatbelt).

1.3 a. You will need to specify the treatment(s) and randomization method, as in Questions 1.1 and 1.2.

b. One such cross-sectional data set would consist of a number of different firms with the observations collected at the same point in time. For example, the data set might contain data on training levels and average labor productivity for 100 different firms during 2005. Chapter 4 intro-

duces linear regression as a way to estimate causal effects using cross-sectional data.

c. The time series data would consist of observations for a single firm collected at different points in time. For example, the data set might contain data on training levels and average labor productivity for the firm for each year between 1960 and 2005. Chapter 15 discusses how linear regression can be used to estimate causal effects using time series data.

d. Panel data would consist of observations from different firms, each observed at different points in time. For example, the data might consist of training levels and average labor productivity for 100 different firms, with data on each firm in 1985, 1995, and 2005. Chapter 10 discusses how linear regression can be used to estimate causal effects using panel data.

Chapter 2

2.1 These outcomes are random because they are not known with certainty until they actually occur. You do not know with certainty the gender of the next person you will meet, the time that it will take to commute to school, and so forth.

2.2 If X and Y are independent, then $\Pr(Y \leq y | X = x) = \Pr(Y \leq y)$ for all values of y and x. That is, independence means that the conditional and marginal distributions of Y are identical so that learning the value of X does not change the probability distribution of Y: Knowing the value of X says nothing about the probability that Y will take on different values.

2.3 Although there is no apparent causal link between rainfall and the number of children born, rainfall could tell you something about the number of children born. Knowing the amount of rainfall tells you something about the season, and births are seasonal. Thus, knowing rainfall tells you something about the month, which tell you something about the number of children born. Thus, rainfall and the number of children born are not independently distributed.

2.4 The average weight of four randomly selected students is unlikely to be exactly 145 lbs. Different groups of four students will have different sample average weights, sometimes greater than 145 lbs. and sometimes less. Because the four students were selected at random, their sample average weight is also random.

2.5 All of the distributions will have a normal shape and will be centered at 1, the mean of Y. However they will have different "spreads" because they have different variances. The variance of $\overline{Y}$ is $4/n$, so the variance shrinks as n gets larger. In your plots, the spread of the normal when $n = 2$ should be wider than when $n = 10$, which should be wider than when $n = 100$. As n gets very large, the variance approaches zero, and the normal distribution collapses around the mean of Y. That is, the distribution of $\overline{Y}$ becomes highly concentrated around μ_Y as n grows large (the probability that $\overline{Y}$ is close to μ_Y tends to 1), which is just what the law of large numbers says.

2.6 The normal approximation does not look good when $n = 5$, but looks good for $n = 25$ and $n = 100$. Thus $\Pr(\overline{Y} \le 0.1)$ is approximately equal to the value computed by the normal approximation when n is 25 or 100, but is not well approximated by the normal distribution when $n = 5$.

2.7 The probability distribution looks liked Figure 2.3b, but with more mass concentrated in the tails. Because the distribution is symmetric around $\mu_Y = 0$, $\Pr(Y > c) = \Pr(Y < -c)$ and, because this is substantial mass in the tails of the distribution, $\Pr(Y > c)$ remains significantly greater than zero even for large values of c.

Chapter 3

3.1 The population mean is the average in the population. The sample average $\overline{Y}$ is the average of a sample drawn from the population.

3.2 An estimator is a procedure for computing an educated guess of the value of a population parameter, such as the population mean. An estimate is the number that the estimator produces in a given sample. $\overline{Y}$ is an example of an estimator. It gives a procedure (add up all of the values of Y in the sample and divide by n) for computing an educated guess of the value of the population mean. If a sample of size $n = 4$ produces values of Y of 100, 104, 123, and 96, then the estimate computed using the estimator $\overline{Y}$ is 105.75.

3.3 In all cases the mean of $\overline{Y}$ is 10. The variance of $\overline{Y}$ is $var(Y)/n$, which yields $var(\overline{Y}) = 1.6$ when $n = 10$, $var(\overline{Y}) = 0.16$ when $n = 100$, and $var(\overline{Y}) = 0.016$ when $n = 1000$. Since $var(\overline{Y})$ converges to zero as n increases, then, with probability approaching 1, $\overline{Y}$ will

be close to 10 as n increases. This is what the law of large numbers says.

3.4 The central limit theorem plays a key role when hypotheses are tested using the sample mean. Since the sample mean is approximately normally distributed when the sample size is large, critical values for hypothesis tests and p-values for test statistics can be computed using the normal distribution. Normal critical values are also used in the construction of confidence intervals.

3.5 These are described in Section 3.2.

3.6 A confidence interval contains all values of the parameter (for example, the mean) that cannot be rejected when used as a null hypothesis. Thus, it summarizes the results from a very large number of hypothesis tests.

3.7 The treatment (or causal) effect is the difference between the mean outcomes of treatment and control groups when individuals in the *population* are randomly assigned to the two groups. The differences-in-mean estimator is the difference between the mean outcomes of treatment and control groups for a randomly selected *sample* of individuals in the population, who are then randomly assigned to the two groups.

3.8 The plot for (a) is upward sloping, and the points lie exactly on a line. The plot for (b) is downward sloping, and the points lie exactly on a line. The plot for (c) should show a positive relation, and the points should be close to, but not exactly on an upward-sloping line. The plot for (d) shows a generally negative relation between the variables, and the points are scattered around a downward-sloping line. The plot for (e) has no apparent linear relation between the variables.

Chapter 4

4.1 β_1 is the value of the slope in the population regression. This value is unknown. $\hat{\beta}_1$ (an estimator) gives a formula for estimating the unknown value of β_1 from a sample. Similarly, u_i is the value of the regression error for the ith observation; u_i is the difference between Y_i and the population regression line $\beta_0 + \beta_1 X_i$. Because the values of β_0 and β_1 are unknown, the value of u_i is unknown. In contrast, $\hat{u}_i$ is the difference between Y_i and $\hat{\beta}_0 + \hat{\beta}_1 X_i$; thus, $\hat{u}_i$ is an estimator of u_i. Finally, $E(Y|X) = \beta_0 + \beta_1 X$ is unknown because the values of β_0 and β_1 are unknown; an estimator for this is the OLS predicted value, $\hat{\beta}_0 + \hat{\beta}_1 X$.

4.2 There are many examples. Here is one for each assumption. If the value of X is assigned in a randomized controlled experiment, then (1) is satisfied. For the class size regression, if $X =$ class size is correlated with other factors that affect test scores, then u and X are correlated and (1) is violated. If entities (for example, workers or schools) are randomly selected from the population, then (2) is satisfied. For the class size regression, if only rural schools are included in the sample while the population of interest is all schools, then (2) is violated, If u is normally distributed, then (3) is satisfied. For the class size regression, if some test scores are misreported as 100,000 (out of a possible 1000), then large outliers are possible and (3) is violated.

4.3 The value of the R^2 indicates how dispersed the points are around the estimated regression line. When $R^2 = 0.9$, the scatter of points should lie very close to the regression line. When $R^2 = 0.5$, the points should be more dispersed about the line. The R^2 does not indicate whether the line has a positive or a negative slope.

Chapter 5

5.1. The p-value for a two-sided test of $H_0: \mu = 0$ using an i.i.d. set of observations $Y_i, i = 1, \ldots, n$ can be constructed in three steps: (1) compute the sample mean and the standard error $SE(\bar{Y})$; (2) compute the t-statistic for this sample $t^{act} = \bar{Y}^{act}/SE(\bar{Y})$; (3) using the standard normal table, compute the p-value $= \Pr(|Z| > |t^{act}|) = 2\Phi(-|t^{act}|)$. A similar three-step procedure is used to construct the p-value for a two-sided test of $H_0: \beta_1 = 0$: (1) compute the OLS estimate of the regression slope and the standard error $SE(\hat{\beta}_1)$; (2) compute the t-statistic for this sample $t^{act} = \hat{\beta}_1^{act}/SE(\hat{\beta}_1)$; (3) using the standard normal table, compute the p-value $= \Pr(|Z| > |t^{act}|) = 2\Phi(-|t^{act}|)$.

5.2. The wage gender gap for 1992 can be estimated using the regression in Equation (5.19) and the data summarized in the 1992 row of Table 3.1. The dependent variable is the hourly earnings of the ith person in the sample. The independent variable is a binary variable that equals 1 if the person is a male and equals 0 if the person is a female. The wage gender gap in the population is the population coefficient β_1 in the regression, which can be estimated using $\hat{\beta}_1$. The wage gender gap for the other years can be estimated in a similar fashion.

5.3 Homoskedasticity means that the variance of u is unrelated to the value of X. Heteroskedasticity means that the variance of u is related to the value of X. If the value of X is chosen using a randomized controlled experiment, then u is homoskedastic. In a regression of a worker's earnings (Y) on years of education (X), u would heteroskedastic if the variance of earnings is higher for college graduates than for non-college graduates. Figure 5.2 suggests that this is indeed the case.

Chapter 6

6.1 It is likely that $\hat{\beta}_1$ will be biased because of omitted variables. Schools in more affluent districts are likely to spend more on all educational inputs and thus would have smaller class sizes, more books in the library, and more computers. These other inputs may lead to higher average test scores. Thus, $\hat{\beta}_1$ will be biased upward because the number of computers per student is positively correlated with omitted variables that have a positive effect on average test scores.

6.2 If X_1 increases by 3 units and X_2 is unchanged, then Y is expected to change by $3\beta_1$ units. If X_2 decreases by 5 units and X_1 is unchanged, then Y is expected to change by $-5\beta_2$ units. If X_1 increases by 3 units and X_2 decreases by 5 units, then Y is expected to change by $3\beta_1 - 5\beta_2$ units.

6.3 The regression cannot determine the effect of a change in one of the regressors assuming no change in the other regressors, because if the value of one of the perfectly multicollinear regressors is held constant, then so is the value of the other. That is, there is no independent variation in one multicollinear regressor. Two examples of perfectly multicollinear regressors are (1) a person's weight measured in pounds and the same person's weight measured in kilograms, and (2) the fraction of students who are male and the constant term, when the data come from all-male schools.

6.4 If X_1 and X_2 are highly correlated, most of the variation in X_1 coincides with the variation in X_2. Thus there is little "variation in X_1, holding X_2 constant" that can be used to estimate the partial effect of X_1 on Y.

Chapter 7

7.1 The null hypothesis that $\beta_1 = 0$ can be tested using the t-statistic for β_1 as described in Key Concept 7.1. Similarly, the null hypothesis that $\beta_2 = 0$ can be tested using the t-statistic for β_2. The null hypothesis that $\beta_1 = 0$ and $\beta_2 = 0$ can be tested using the F-statistic from Section 7.2. The F-statistic is necessary to test a joint hypothesis because the test will be based on both $\hat{\beta}_1$ and $\hat{\beta}_2$, and this means that the testing procedure must use properties of their joint distribution.

7.2 Here is one example. Using data from several years of her econometrics class, a professor regresses students' scores on the final exam (Y) on their score from the midterm exam (X). This regression will have a high R^2, because people who do well on the midterm tend to do well on the final. However, this regression produces a biased estimate of the causal effect of midterm scores on the final. Students who do well on the midterm tend to be students who attend class regularly, study hard, and have an aptitude for the subject. The variables are correlated with the midterm score but are determinants of the final exam score, so omitting them leads to omitted variable bias.

Chapter 8

8.1 The regression function will look like the quadratic regression in Figure 8.3 or the logarithmic function in Figure 8.4. The first of these is specified as the regression of Y onto X and X^2, and the second as the regression of Y onto $\ln(X)$. There are many economic relations with this shape. For example, this shape might represent the decreasing marginal productivity of labor in a production function.

8.2 Taking logarithms of both sides of the equation yields $\ln(Q) = \beta_0 + \beta_1\ln(K) + \beta_2\ln(L) + \beta_3\ln(M) + u$, where $\beta_0 = \ln(\lambda)$. The production function parameters can be estimated by regressing the logarithm of production on the logarithms of capital, labor, and raw materials.

8.3 A 2% increase in GDP means that $\ln(GDP)$ increases by 0.02. The implied change in $\ln(m)$ is $1.0 \times 0.02 = 0.02$, which corresponds to a 2% increase in m. With R measured in percentage points, the increase in R is from 4.0 to 5.0 or 1.0 percentage point. This leads to a change of $\ln(m)$ of $-0.02 \times 1.0 = -0.02$, which corresponds to a 2% fall in m.

8.4 You want to compare the fit of your linear regression to the fit of a nonlinear regression. Your answer will depend on the nonlinear regression that you choose for the comparison. You might test your linear regression against a quadratic regression by adding X^2 to the linear regression. If the coefficient on X^2 is significantly different from zero, then you can reject the null hypothesis that the relationship is linear in favor of the alternative that it is quadratic.

8.5 Augmenting the equation in Question 8.2 with an interaction term yields. $\ln(Q) = \beta_0 + \beta_1\ln(K) + \beta_2\ln(L) + \beta_3\ln(M) + \beta_4[\ln(K) \times \ln(L)] + u$. The partial effect of $\ln(L)$ on $\ln(Q)$ is now $\beta_2 + \beta_4\ln(K)$.

Chapter 9

9.1 See Key Concept 9.1 and the paragraph that immediately follows the Key Concept box.

9.2 Including an additional variable that belongs in the regression will eliminate or reduce omitted variable bias. However, including an additional variable that does not belong in the regression will, in general, reduce the precision (increase the variance) of the estimator of the other coefficients.

9.3 It is important to distinguish between measurement error in Y and measurement error in X. If Y is measured with error, then the measurement error becomes part of the regression error term, u. If the assumptions of Key Concept 6.4 continue to hold, this will not affect the internal validity of OLS regression, although by making the variance of the regression error term larger, it increases the variance of the OLS estimator. If X is measured with error, however, this can result in correlation between the regressor and regression error, leading to inconsistency of the OLS estimator. As suggested by Equation (9.2), as this inconsistency becomes more severe, the larger is the measurement error [that is, the larger is σ_w^2 in Equation (9.2)].

9.4 Schools with higher-achieving students could be more likely to volunteer to take the test, so that the schools volunteering to take the test are not representative of the population of schools, and sample selection bias will result. For example, if all schools with a low student–teacher ratio take the test, but only the best-performing schools with a high student–teacher ratio do, the estimated class size effect will be biased.

9.5 Cities with high crime rates may decide that they need more police protection and spend more on police, but if police do their job then more police spending reduces crime. Thus, there are causal links from crime rates to police spending *and* from police spending to crime rates, leading to simultaneous causality bias.

9.6 If the regression has homoskedastic errors, then the homoskedastic and heteroskedastic standard errors generally are similar, because both are consistent. However, if the errors are heteroskedastic, then the homoskedastic standard errors are inconsistent, while the heteroskedastic standard errors are consistent. Thus, different values for the two standard errors constitutes evidence of heteroskedasticity, and this suggests that the heteroskedastic standard errors should be used.

Glossary

Acceptance region: The set of values of a test statistic for which the null hypothesis is accepted (is not rejected).

Adjusted R^2 ($\overline{R}^2$): A modified version of R^2 that does not necessarily increase when a new regressor is added to the regression.

Alternative hypothesis: The hypothesis that is assumed to be true if the null hypothesis is false. The alternative hypothesis is often denoted H_1.

Asymptotic distribution: The approximate sampling distribution of a random variable computed using a large sample. For example, the asymptotic distribution of the sample average is normal.

Asymptotic normal distribution: A normal distribution that approximates the sampling distribution of a statistic computed using a large sample.

Base specification: A baseline or benchmark regression specification that includes a set of regressors chosen using a combination of expert judgment, economic theory, and knowledge of how the data were collected.

Bernoulli distribution: The probability distribution of a Bernoulli random variable.

Bernoulli random variable: A random variable that takes on two values, 0 and 1.

Best linear unbiased estimator: An estimator that has the smallest variance of any estimator that is a linear function of the sample values Y and is unbiased. Under the Gauss-Markov conditions, the OLS estimator is the best linear unbiased estimator of the regression coefficients conditional on the values of the regressors.

Bias: The expected value of the difference between an estimator and the parameter that it is estimating. If $\hat{\mu}_Y$ is an estimator of μ_Y, then the bias of $\hat{\mu}_Y$ is $E(\hat{\mu}_Y) - \mu_Y$.

Binary variable: A variable that is either 0 or 1. A binary variable is used to indicate a binary outcome. For example, X is a binary (or indicator, or dummy) variable for a person's gender if $X = 1$ if the person is female and $X = 0$ if the person is male.

Bivariate normal distribution: A generalization of the normal distribution to describe the joint distribution of two random variables.

BLUE: See *best linear unbiased estimator*.

Causal effect: The expected effect of a given intervention or treatment as measured in an ideal randomized controlled experiment.

Central limit theorem: A result in mathematical statistics that says that, under general conditions, the sampling distribution of the standardized sample average is well approximated by a standard normal distribution when the sample size is large.

Chi-squared distribution: The distribution of the sum of m squared independent standard normal random variables. The parameter m is called the degrees of the freedom of the chi-squared distribution.

Coefficient of determination: See R^2.

Conditional distribution: The probability distribution of one random variable given that another random variable takes on a particular value.

Conditional expectation: The expected value of one random value given that another random variable takes on a particular value.

Conditional mean: The mean of a conditional distribution; see *conditional expectation*.

Conditional variance: The variance of a conditional distribution.

Confidence interval (or confidence set): An interval (or set) that contains the true value of a population parameter with a prespecified probability when computed over repeated samples.

Confidence level: The prespecified probability that a confidence interval (or set) contains the true value of the parameter.

Consistency: Means that an estimator is consistent. See *consistent estimator*.

Consistent estimator: An estimator that converges in probability to the parameter that it is estimating.

Constant regressor: The regressor associated with the regression intercept; this regressor is always equal to 1.

Constant term: The regression intercept.

Continuous random variable: A random variable that can take on a continuum of values.

Control group: The group that does not receive the treatment or intervention in an experiment.

Control variable: A regressor included to mitigate omitted variable bias; a regressor that controls for one of the factors that determine the dependent variable.

Convergence in distribution: When a sequence of distributions converges to a limit; a precise definition is given in Section 17.2.

Convergence in probability: When a sequence of random variables converges to a specific value; for example, when the sample average becomes close to the population mean as the sample size increases; see Key Concept 2.6 and Section 17.2.

Correlation: A unit-free measure of the extent to which two random variables move, or vary, together. The correlation (or correlation coefficient) between X and Y is $\sigma_{XY}/\sigma_X\sigma_Y$ and is denoted corr(X,Y).

Correlation coefficient: See *correlation*.

Covariance: A measure of the extent to which two random variables move together. The covariance between X and Y is the expected value $E[(X - \mu_X)(Y - \mu_Y)]$, and is denoted by cov($X,Y$) or by σ_{XY}.

Critical value: The value of a test statistic for which the test just rejects the null hypothesis at the given significance level.

Cross-sectional data: Data collected for different entities in a single time period.

Cubic regression model: A nonlinear regression function that includes X, X^2, and X^3 as regressors.

Cumulative distribution function (c.d.f.): See *cumulative probability distribution*.

Cumulative probability distribution: A function showing the probability that a random variable is less than or equal to a given number.

Dependent variable: The variable to be explained in a regression or other statistical model; the variable appearing on the left-hand side in a regression.

Discrete random variable: A random variable that takes on discrete values.

Dummy variable: See *binary variable*.

Dummy variable trap: A problem caused by including a full set of binary variables in a regression together with a constant regressor (intercept), leading to perfect multicollinearity.

Error term: The difference between Y and the population regression function, denoted by u in this textbook.

Errors-in-variables bias: The bias in an estimator of a regression coefficient that arises from measurement errors in the regressors.

Estimate: The numerical value of an estimator computed from data in a specific sample.

Estimator: A function of a sample of data to be drawn randomly from a population. An estimator is a procedure for using sample data to compute an educated guess of the value of a population parameter, such as the population mean.

Exact distribution: The exact probability distribution of a random variable.

Expected value: The long-run average value of a random variable over many repeated trials or occurrences. It is the probability-weighted average of all possible values that the random variable can take on. The expected value of Y is denoted $E(Y)$ and is also called the expectation of Y.

Experimental data: Data obtained from an experiment designed to evaluate a treatment or policy or to investigate a causal effect.

Explained sum of squares (*ESS*): The sum of squared deviations of the predicted values of Y_i, $\hat{Y}_i$, from their average; see Equation (4.14).

Explanatory variable: See *regressor*.

External validity: Inferences and conclusions from a statistical study are externally valid if they can be generalized from the population and the setting studied to other populations and settings.

***F*-statistic**: A statistic used to a test joint hypothesis concerning more than one of the regression coefficients.

$F_{m,n}$ distribution: The distribution of a ratio of independent random variables, where the numerator is a chi-squared random variable with m degrees of freedom, divided by m, and the denominator is a chi-squared random variable with n degrees of freedom divided by n.

$F_{m,\infty}$ distribution: The distribution of a random variable with a chi-squared distribution with m degrees of freedom, divided by m.

Fitted values: See *predicted values*.

Forecast error: The difference between the value of the variable that actually occurs and its forecasted value.

Functional form misspecification: When the form of the estimated regression function does not match the form of the population regression function; for example, when a linear specification is used but the true population regression function is quadratic.

Gauss-Markov theorem: Mathematical result stating that, under certain conditions, the OLS estimator is the best linear unbiased estimator of the regression coefficients conditional on the values of the regressors.

HAC standard errors: See *heteroskedasticity- and autocorrelation-consistent (HAC) standard errors*.

Heteroskedasticity: The situation in which the variance of the regression error term u_i, conditional on the regressors, is not constant.

Heteroskedasticity- and autocorrelation-consistent (HAC) standard errors: Standard errors for OLS estimators that are consistent whether or not the regression errors are heteroskedastic and autocorrelated.

Heteroskedasticity-robust standard error: Standard errors for the OLS estimator that are appropriate whether the error term is homoskedastic or heteroskedastic.

Heteroskedasticity-robust *t*-statistic: A *t*-statistic constructed using a heteroskedasticity-robust standard error.

Homoskedasticity: The variance of the error term u_i, conditional on the regressors, is constant.

Homoskedasticity-only *F* statistic: A form of the *F*-statistic that is valid only when the regression errors are homoskedastic.

Homoskedasticity-only standard errors: Standard errors for the OLS estimator that are appropriate only when the error term is homoskedastic.

Hypothesis test: A procedure for using sample evidence to help determine if a specific hypothesis about a population is true or false.

i.i.d.: Independently and indentically distributed.

Identically distributed: When two or more random variables have the same distribution.

Imperfect multicollinearity: The condition in which two or more regressors are highly correlated.

Independence: When knowing the value of one random variable provides no information about the value of another random variable. Two random variables are independent if their joint distribution is the product of their marginal distributions.

Indicator variable: See *binary variable*.

Instrumental variable: A variable that is correlated with an endogenous regressor (instrument relevance) and is uncorrelated with the regression error (instrument exogeneity).

Instrumental variables (IV) regression: A way to obtain a consistent estimator of the unknown coefficients of the population regression function when the regressor, X, is correlated with the error term, u.

Intercept: The value of β_0 in the linear regression model.

Internal validity: When inferences about causal effects in a statistical study are valid for the population being studied.

Joint hypothesis: A hypothesis consisting of two or more individual hypotheses, that is, involving more than one restriction on the parameters of a model.

Joint probability distribution: The probability distribution determining the probabilities of outcomes involving two or more random variables.

Kurtosis: A measure of how much mass is contained in the tails of a probability distribution.

Law of iterated expectations: A result in probability theory that says that the expected value of Y is the expected value of its conditional expectation given X, that is, $E(Y) = E[E(Y|X)]$.

Law of large numbers: According to this result from probability theory, under general conditions the sample average will be close to the population mean with very high probability when the sample size is large.

Least squares assumptions: The assumptions for the linear regression model listed in Key Concept 4.3 (single variable regression) and Key Concept 6.4 (multiple regression model).

Least squares estimator: An estimator formed by minimizing the sum of squared residuals.

Linear-log model: A nonlinear regression function in which the dependent variable is Y and the independent variable is $\ln(X)$.

Linear regression function: A regression function with a constant slope.

Log-linear model: A nonlinear regression function in which the dependent variable is $\ln(Y)$ and the independent variable is X.

Log-log model: A nonlinear regression function in which the dependent variable is $\ln(Y)$ and the independent variable is $\ln(X)$.

Logarithm: A mathematical function defined for a positive argument; its slope is always positive but tends to zero. The natural logarithm is the inverse of the exponential function, that is, $X = \ln(e^X)$.

Longitudinal data: See *panel data*.

Marginal probability distribution: Another name for the probability distribution of a random variable Y, which distinguishes the distribution of Y alone (the marginal distribution) from the joint distribution of Y and another random variable.

Mean: The expected value of a random variable. The mean of Y is denoted μ_Y.

Moments of a distribution: The expected value of a random variable raised to different powers. The rth moment of the random variable Y is $E(Y^r)$.

Multicollinearity: See *perfect multicollinearity* and *imperfect multicollinearity*.

Multiple regression model: An extension of the single variable regression model that allows Y to depend on k regressors.

Natural logarithm: See *logarithm*.

95% confidence set: A confidence set with a 95% confidence level; see *confidence interval*.

Nonlinear least squares: The analog of OLS that applies when the regression function is a nonlinear function of the unknown parameters.

Nonlinear least squares estimator: The estimator obtained by minimizing the sum of squared residuals when the regression function is nonlinear in the parameters.

Nonlinear regression function: A regression function with a slope that is not constant.

Normal distribution: A commonly used bell-shaped distribution of a continuous random variable.

Null hypothesis: The hypothesis being tested in a hypothesis test, often denoted by H_0.

Observation number: The unique identifier assigned to each entity in a data set.

Observational data: Data based on observing, or measuring, actual behavior outside an experimental setting.

OLS estimator. See *ordinary least squares estimator*.

OLS regression line: The regression line with population coefficients replaced by the OLS estimators.

OLS residual: The difference between Y_i and the OLS regression line, denoted by $\hat{u}_i$ in this textbook.

Omitted variables bias: The bias in an estimator that arises because a variable that is a determinant of Y and is correlated with a regressor has been omitted from the regression.

One-sided alternative hypothesis: The parameter of interest is on one side of the value given by the null hypothesis.

Ordinary least squares estimator: The estimator of the regression intercept and slope(s) that minimizes the sum of squared residuals.

Outlier: An exceptionally large or small value of a random variable.

p-value: The probability of drawing a statistic at least as adverse to the null hypothesis as the one actually computed, assuming the null hypothesis is correct. Also called the marginal significance probability, the p-value is the smallest significance level at which the null hypothesis can be rejected.

Panel data: Data for multiple entities where each entity is observed in two or more time periods.

Parameter: A constant that determines a characteristic of a probability distribution or population regression function.

Partial effect: The effect on Y of changing one of the regressors, holding the other regressors constant.

Perfect multicollinearity: Occurs when one of the regressors is an exact linear function of the other regressors.

Polynomial regression model: A nonlinear regression function that includes $X, X^2, \ldots$ and X^r as regressors, where r is an integer.

Population: The group of entities—such as people, companies, or school districts—being studied.

Population coefficients: See *population intercept and slope*.

Population intercept and slope: The true, or population, values of β_0 (the intercept) and β_1 (the slope) in a single variable regression. In a multiple regression, there are multiple slope coefficients $(\beta_1, \beta_2, \ldots, \beta_k)$, one for each regressor.

Population multiple regression model: The multiple regression model in Key Concept 6.2.

Population regression line: In a single variable regression, the population regression line is $\beta_0 + \beta_1 X_i$, and in a multiple regression it is $\beta_0 + \beta_1 X_{1i} + \beta_2 X_{2i} + \cdots + \beta_k X_{ki}$.

Power: The probability that a test correctly rejects the null hypothesis when the alternative is true.

Predicted value: The value of Y_i that is predicted by the OLS regression line, denoted by $\hat{Y}_i$ in this textbook.

Price elasticity: The percentage change in the quantity demanded resulting from a 1% increase in price.

Probability: The proportion of the time that an outcome (or event) will occur in the long run.

Probability density function (p.d.f.): For a continuous random variable, the area under the probability density function between any two points is the probability that the random variable falls between those two points.

Probability distribution: For a discrete random variable, a list of all values that a random variable can take on and the probability associated with each of these values.

Quadratic regression model: A nonlinear regression function that includes X and X^2 as regressors.

R^2: In a regression, the fraction of the sample variance of the dependent variable that is explained by the regressors.

$\overline{R}^2$: See *adjusted R^2*.

Randomized controlled experiment: An experiment in which participants are randomly assigned to a control group, which receives no treatment, or to a treatment group, which receives a treatment.

Regressand: See *dependent variable*.

Regression specification: A description of a regression that includes the set of regressors and any nonlinear transformation that has been applied.

Regressor: A variable appearing on the right-hand side of a regression; an independent variable in a regression.

Rejection region: The set of values of a test statistic for which the test rejects the null hypothesis.

Repeated cross-sectional data: A collection of cross-sectional data sets, where each cross-sectional data set corresponds to a different time period.

Restricted regression: A regression in which the coefficients are restricted to satisfy some condition. For example, when computing the homoskedasticity-only F-statistic, this is the regression with coefficients restricted to satisfy the null hypothesis.

Sample correlation: An estimator of the correlation between two random variables.

Sample covariance: An estimator of the covariance between two random variables.

Sample selection bias: The bias in an estimator of a regression coefficient that arises when a selection process influences the availability of data and that process is related to the dependent variable. This induces correlation between one or more regressors and the regression error.

Sample standard deviation: An estimator of the standard deviation of a random variable.

Sample variance: An estimator of the variance of a random variable.

Sampling distribution: The distribution of a statistic over all possible samples; the distribution arising from repeatedly evaluating the statistic using a series of randomly drawn samples from the same population.

Scatterplot: A plot of n observations on X_i and Y_i, in which each observation is represented by the point (X_i, Y_i).

Significance level: The prespecified rejection probability of a statistical hypothesis test when the null hypothesis is true.

Simple random sampling: When entities are chosen randomly from a population using a method that ensures that each entity is equally likely to be chosen.

Simultaneous causality bias: When, in addition to the causal link of interest from X to Y, there is a causal link from Y to X. Simultaneous causality makes X correlated with the error term in the population regression of interest.

Simultaneous equations bias: See *simultaneous causality bias*.

Size of a test: The probability that a test incorrectly rejects the null hypothesis when the null hypothesis is true.

Skewness: A measure of the aysmmetry of a probability distribution.

Standard deviation: The square root of the variance. The standard deviation of the random variable Y, denoted σ_Y, has the units of Y and is a measure of the spread of the distribution of Y around its mean.

Standard error of an estimator: An estimator of the standard deviation of the estimator.

Standard error of the regression (*SER*): An estimator of the standard deviation of the regression error u.

Standard normal distribution: The normal distribution with mean equal to 0 and variance equal to 1, denoted $N(0, 1)$.

Standardizing a random variable: An operation accomplished by subtracting the mean and dividing by the standard deviation, which produces a random variable with a mean of 0 and a standard deviation of 1. The standardized value of Y is $(Y - \mu_Y)/\sigma_Y$.

Statistically insignificant: The null hypothesis (typically, that a regression coefficient is zero) cannot be rejected at a given significance level.

Statistically significant: The null hypothesis (typically, that a regression coefficient is zero) is rejected at a given significance level.

Student t distribution: The Student t distribution with m degrees of freedom is the distribution of the ratio of a standard normal random variable, divided by the square root of an independently distributed chi-squared random variable with m degrees of freedom divided by m. As m gets large, the Student t distribution converges to the standard normal distribution.

Sum of squared residuals (SSR): The sum of the squared OLS residuals.

t-distribution: See *Student t distribution*.

t-ratio: See *t-statistic*.

t-statistic: A statistic used for hypothesis testing. See Key Concept 5.1.

Test for a difference in means: A procedure for testing whether two populations have the same mean.

Time series data: Data for the same entity for multiple time periods.

Total sum of squares (TSS): The sum of squared deviations of Y_i, from its average, $\overline{Y}$.

Treatment effect: The causal effect in an experiment or a quasi-experiment; see *causal effect*.

Treatment group: The group that receives the treatment or intervention in an experiment.

Two-sided alternative hypothesis: When, under the alternative hypothesis, the parameter of interest is not equal to the value given by the null hypothesis.

Type I error: In hypothesis testing, the error made when the null hypothesis is true but is rejected.

Type II error: In hypothesis testing, the error made when the null hypothesis is false but is not rejected.

Unbiased estimator: An estimator with a bias that is equal to zero.

Uncorrelated: Two random variables are uncorrelated if their correlation is zero.

Unrestricted regression: When computing the homoskedasticity-only F-statistic, this is the regression that applies under the alternative hypothesis, so the coefficients are not restricted to satisfy the null hypothesis.

Variance: The expected value of the squared difference between a random variable and its mean; the variance of Y is denoted σ_Y^2.

Weighted least squares (WLS): An alternative to OLS that can be used when the regression error is heteroskedastic and the form of the heteroskedasticity is known or can be estimated.

Index

Page numbers followed by italicized *f* and *t* refer to figures and tables, respectively.

Large-Sample Critical Values for the *t*-statistic from the Standard Normal Distibution

	Significance Level		
	10%	**5%**	**1%**
2-Sided Test (≠) Reject if $|t|$ is greater than	1.64	1.96	2.58
1-Sided Test (>) Reject if t is greater than	1.28	1.64	2.33
1-Sided Test (<) Reject if t is less than	−1.28	−1.64	−2.33